P9-EET-968

Information Systems Analysis

THEORY AND APPLICATIONS

M. J. Alexander

Auburn University

SCIENCE RESEARCH ASSOCIATES, INC.
Chicago, Palo Alto, Toronto
Henley-on-Thames, Sydney, Paris

A Subsidiary of IBM

Library of Congress Catalog Card Number: 73-89599

ISBN 0-574-19100-3

*The text of this book was composed in Electra by
Typographic Sales of St. Louis, Missouri, using the
VIP process. Heads are various sizes of Eurostile;
chapter numbers are Michel. Printing and binding were
done by the Kingsport Press of Kingsport, Tennessee.*

Sponsoring editor: Stephen Mitchell

Book design: Mike Rogondino

Technical art: Commart of Palo Alto, California

CONTENTS

PREFACE

The computer is no longer regarded with great awe and reverence by managers in the business world today. They have come to recognize that computers are not infallible brains but rather are sophisticated devices that can be harnessed to serve information needs and improve organizational efficiency. The business world now views the computer as a practical tool for overcoming information deficiencies and solving business-related problems.

The principal focus of data-processing courses offered by most colleges and universities has been, and is today, directed toward explaining computer operations and computer language instruction. As a result, many students are now graduating with a reasonably sound general knowledge of computer technology. Many of them can also write computer programs to solve mathematical problems. (Perhaps the principal reason for this pedagogical orientation is that educators are more familiar with this area and ample instructional materials are readily available.)

In contrast to the prevailing approach, the basic purpose of this book is to provide the student with a conceptual framework for applying computer technology to the functional areas of business. Instead of dwelling on the inner workings of the computer, this text emphasizes the manager's need to know how computers may be used within an organization. However, the text is not limited to the business-student audience: informed citizens, as well as future executives, need to appreciate the advantages, the limitations, the general characteristics, and the potential contributions to sound decision making that computerized information systems possess.

In order to accomplish this objective, the author believes that the student should have a thorough grounding in basic systems theory, a working knowledge of information systems analysis and design, and an exposure to the fundamental information systems present in most business firms. Although not required to assimilate the material contained in this book, a general knowledge of computer technology and/or a programming language will be helpful.

The text has been organized into three major sections. Part I (chapters 1 through 5) presents the basic concepts and terminology of systems theory and attempts to relate this theory to the operational and informational activities within the business firm. This section emphasizes the development of a system-oriented perspective of business operations and discusses the major information flows within the organization.

Part II of the book (chapters 6 through 9) deals with the information system development process. Beginning with background material development and an overview, the information system investigation and subsequent analysis are examined in detail. Information system design, the preparation of the system specification, and the implementation program are also discussed. A case study has been included that may be used to assist the presentation of the information system development process.

The final section of the book (chapters 10 through 16) presents selected information systems from the major functional areas (finance, personnel, inventory, production, and marketing) of the business firm. Each chapter begins with a brief system-oriented presentation of the functional area to present its general information requirements. Following this, selected information systems within the area are discussed to demonstrate specific computer applications. Special topics have been embedded in the applications portions of each chapter to present techniques and practices for handling certain information problems.

Probably any attempt to cover an area as broad as information systems in just one volume will be subject to the criticisms of superficiality and material omission. The author readily acknowledges the errors of omission as well as the errors of commission that are present in this book.

My sincerest thanks are due to the many executives who so freely give their time and contributed information about their operations. Without their gracious assistance the quality of realism would be lacking in the applications section. My thanks are also due to the many students who have suffered through the original drafts and revisions and provided helpful comments. And finally, my especial thanks to my wife, Helene, and my family for their patience and understanding during the long hours of separation.

m.j.a.
January, 1974

GENERAL SYSTEMS THEORY

For many centuries man has been attempting to gain a better understanding of the world in which he lives. He has long recognized that there is a certain amount of order in the universe, in the world, and in life itself. The principal task of scholars throughout the ages has been to organize their perceptions of the world and find the relations between various phenomena to understand the nature of the universe better. In the past several centuries this scholarly effort has been widened in scope and extended in depth through the widespread application of the scientific method.

In ancient times a few outstanding thinkers sought to organize their observations and thoughts into philosophical systems. Plato's *Republic* is an excellent example of the conceptual organizing process in which observations of human nature, politics, and management are blended to describe an idealized political system. Hebrew and Christian theology as revealed in the Bible presents the development of the relationship between God and man. All these early investigators noted relations among various things and set forth hypotheses about their nature.

In medieval times investigations of natural phenomena began to occur more frequently. Medieval scholars were able to be substantially more precise in the observation and fact-gathering phases of their studies since better measuring instruments had been developed. The result of their efforts was to generate a host of new questions about the nature of things, a fresh desire to determine relationships as accurately as possible, and a healthy skepticism toward older theories that could not be proved or demonstrated. For example, the investigations of Copernicus, Kepler, and other early astronomers revealed the presence of a precisely organized universe in which astronomical phenomena could be adequately explained and predicted with considerable accuracy. At this point the scientific method of inquiry had developed into a widely applicable tool for the development of knowledge.

New concepts about the nature of relations between natural processes also emerged. Dynamic life-associated processes became appropriate fields of investigation and produced new scientific insights. Harvey, through his investigation of blood circulation, demonstrated the fundamental notion of the hydraulic or flow concept in natural phenomena. His approach to the conceptualization of dynamic processes is evident today in the fields of hydraulics, electricity, and electronics.

During the medieval period of history the first recorded investigations into the nature of business relations also occurred. The development of double-entry bookkeeping by Paciolo (circa 1484) demonstrated the effectiveness of the systematic approach to recording business transactions and summarizing business activities. The debit-credit relation used to record financial data has become the ultimate base for the field of accounting. Today financial accounting is recognized as one of the major tools that provides managers with perceptive information about business activities.

Other investigators in more recent times have extended our knowledge of the ways basic natural processes function. Freud pointed out that human beings were able to store and recall stimuli and thus modify their responses to dynamic situations. Norbert Weiner further amplified our understanding of the nature of dynamic processes by introducing the feedback concept for maintaining stable transformation process conditions. These aspects of natural processes have been incorporated into our present-day computer and information technologies.

The efforts of these and countless other scholars appear on the surface to be simply diverse attempts to describe, understand, and predict activities, events, and processes. However, if we probe deeper we may discover a common unifying denominator in the efforts of all these intellectual pioneers: they were all investigating the ultimate nature of various systems. Their energies were dedicated to developing a systematic coherent description and explanation of the behavior of the "things" in a particular environment. In essence, most of these scholars were attempting to create systemic models that would agree with their observations and provide rational bases to predict future events.

Thus the systems approach to current problems that has recently become so widely publicized is not really a new thing at all. Scholars and scientists have been implicitly using it to study natural processes for centuries. They investigated particular natural phenomena; they observed and described the natural objects and their interrelations as accurately as possible; they postulated a basis for the occurrence of these natural events; and they verified the accuracy of their explanations by testing the system. The new twist is simply seeing all phenomena as manifestations of one or more systems that have organization, interrelations, boundaries, and an underlying purpose. If we assume that problems and phenomena are indications of a particular active system, we can immediately focus the entire investigatory procedure on exploring the nature of the system itself. The systems framework thus can provide a convenient conceptual reference point for preparing and conducting research studies by delineating boundaries, emphasizing relations, and determining the purpose of activity.

DEFINITION OF SYSTEMS

The word *systems* is widely used today in connection with many different phenomena in almost every conceivable field of activity. Much of the literature available today about systems, systems theory, and systems analysis begins with the tacit assumption that everyone understands what a system is. Perhaps the reason for this peculiar circumstance is the widespread use of the term. The word *systems* appears in so many places, in such widely varying settings, and with such frequency that asking for a definition seems almost impertinent. On the other hand, if we are to discuss this area further, we need a firm, precise definition.

The following list of definitions for the term *systems* presents a cross-section of many different viewpoints:

> "An assemblage or combination of things or parts forming a complex or unitary whole..."[1]

---

1. *The American College Dictionary,* ed. Jess Stein (New York: Random House), p. 1230.

"A set of objects with a given set of relationships between the objects and their attributes."[2]
"A set of objects together with the relationships between the objects and between their attributes."[3]
"The basic notion of a system is simply that it is a set of interrelated parts."[4]
"A system is a set of objects with relationships between the objects and between their attributes."[5]
"An array of components designed to accomplish a particular object according to plan."[6]
"A system is a device, procedure, or scheme which behaves according to some description, its function being to operate on information and/or energy and/or matter in a time reference to yield information and/or energy and/or matter."[7]
"A system is a network of related procedures developed according to an integrated scheme for performing a major activity of the business...."[8]
"A system is a complex of interrelated entities."[9]

Thus the following definition is presented as a composite general definition of the term *systems* that may be readily applied to many different systemic situations:

A system is a group of elements, either physical or non-physical in nature, that exhibit a set of interrelations among themselves and interact together toward one or more goals, objectives, or ends.

This definition may be dissected further. The word *elements* may refer to physical objects such as the component parts of

2. Stanford L. Optner, *Systems Analysis for Business and Industrial Problem Solving* (Englewood Cliffs, N. J.: Prentice-Hall, Inc., 1965), p. 26.
3. "The Definition of a System," *Yearbook for the Advancement of General Systems Theory* (1956), p. 74.
4. Seymour Tilles, "The Manager's Job—A Systems Approach," *Harvard Business Review,* January-February 1963, p. 74.
5. Arthur D. Hall, *A Methodology for Systems Engineering* (Princeton, N.J.: D. Van Nostrand Co., Inc., 1962), p.60.
6. Richard A. Johnson, Fremont E. Kast, and James E. Rosenzweig, *The Theory and Management of Systems* (New York: McGraw-Hill Book Company, 1967), p.113.
7. David O. Ellis and Fred J. Ludwig, *Systems Philosophy* (Englewood Cliffs, N. J.: Prentice-Hall, Inc., 1962), p.3.
8. Richard F. Neuschel, *Management by System* (New York: McGraw-Hill Book Company, Inc., 1960), p.10.
9. R. L. Ackoff, *Scientific Method: Optimizing Applied Research Decisions* (John Wiley & Sons: New York, 1962), p.121.

an automobile (pistons, crankshaft, fuel pump, transmission, and so forth). It may also refer to interrelated activities, such as the managerial activities of planning, organizing, directing, and controlling. Energy forms, such as electricity and heat, may also properly be considered as systemic elements. Ideas, concepts, or mathematical symbols may also be designated as elements as in philosophical systems and mathematical equations. Biological units such as plants, insects, and animals are the elements in various ecological systems. Finally, an element in a system may also be a lower-order system in itself, composed of any combination of the several elements.

The elements that comprise a particular system may be of several different types. Thus a missile system is composed of complex hardware (physical objects), missile fuel (potential energy), and astronauts (biological units)—all brought together by management (ideas) using mathematical formulas (symbols). As a matter of fact, the higher the systemic order, the greater is the probability that individual elements are systems themselves. Lower-order systems are more likely to contain only one type of element.

The specific relations that exist among a system's elements may also be examined in terms of the type of relation present. The spatial relation is characteristic of many static systems in which physical objects maintain a fixed relation in space among themselves—for example, the geographic relation between various communities in a physiographic region. Spatial relations may also be found in dynamic systems in which the physical objects move—for example, the solar system.

Another frequently encountered relation in many systems is based on time. Sidereal or clock time provides a means of differentiating the order of events within a system. We can distinguish a sequence of events in terms of time units that range from centuries to nanoseconds. In this sense time has an absolute quality. A second type of time relation may be called psychological time. In this case the time relation is influenced by personal perceptions that give rise to relative time observations—earlier, later; before, after. Time relations are present in all active systems; in certain systems—for example, network analysis—time is the principal relation.

An especially important relation found in nearly all dynamic systems is the one of cause and effect. The law of cause and effect may be called the greatest natural law. Only after mankind began to appreciate the fundamental relation expressed in this law was the development of the natural sciences and technology possible. In fact, we have come to understand most clearly the basic characters of natural processes by using the scientific method to study the cause and effect relations in natural phenomena.

On the whole, the law of cause and effect is most readily applied to irreversible processes that occur over a finite period of time. The cause appears at a point in time, exerts its influence, and the effect comes into existence at a later time. Application of the law of cause and effect to many complex dynamic systems that involve ongoing activities may be quite complicated since there is no discernable explicit beginning and/or end for each process. The study of dynamic systems under these circumstances may require that input/output relations be substituted for the cause and effect relations.

The law of conservation of matter and energy is the basis for a type of relation that may be termed the physical relation. Its nature may be seen in the transformation of matter from one form to another. The relation between the prior condition and the post condition is determined by the type of matter involved and the indestructability of matter under ordinary circumstances. For example, there is a physical or material relation between the coal fed into the fire and the resulting products of combustion.

The logical relation as expressed in the laws of logic is another very important one that exists in systems dealing largely with ideas and concepts. The syllogism, for example, expresses this type of relation. A computer program also is simply a series of independent instructions bound together with an inexorable pattern of applied logic. The link between each program step must, in order to operate successfully, be based on the application of logical relations.

Mathematical relations are perhaps a special form of logical relations. A mathematical statement of an equality or inequality specifies that a certain condition exists between the appropriate elements (variables). The relations that are postulated between the independent variables and the dependent ones are, of course, mathematical. Quite frequently the purpose of these mathematical relations is to depict or describe another peculiar relation that exists in the "real world." Some special types of mathematical relations are the additive (subtractive) ones, in which the sum of the individual elements is the total for the entire system, and the proportional (directly and inversely) relation, which specifies the interactive effect of two variables. A business-world example of the former would be the determination of the total cost of an economic good as the cost of each of the individual elements used in producing it; an example of the latter would be the use of substitutable goods in a production process in which there is a tradeoff rate between the two elements.

Symbiosis, the necessary relation of dissimilar organisms, is the basis for another type of relation. When two or more elements or subsystems require a *quid pro quo* relation to operate the system efficiently, there is a symbiotic relation among the elements. Examples of this type of relationship are the parasite-host relationship and the economic exchange (barter) system.

The third portion of the definition that merits discussion is the concept of purpose. Man-created systems are developed to perform some function: automobiles provide transportation; assembly lines produce goods; the public school system educates the young. The accomplishment of goals and objectives is the economic justification necessary for spending economic resources to create man-made systems.

The purpose or end of a natural system may be difficult to perceive. When a subsystem is a clearly defined integral part of a larger natural system, its purpose is usually to support the major system activities. Thus the purpose of the digestive system is to convert food into energy and the purpose of the family is to reproduce the species in a manner likely to maintain its existence.

Severe teleological difficulties do arise, however, when one seeks ultimate purposes for larger systems such as the earth, the universe, and life itself. For those of a religious persuasion, the concept of God as the Creator of all things offers a satisfactory solution to this problem. Perhaps others will be satisfied by equating system function and system purpose. The difficulty of "proving" the existence of purpose for all systems rests on what is considered to be ample evidence or "proof" and the level at which the purpose must be explained. Let us avoid any attempt to prove the existence of purpose in all systems and satisfy the present discussion by considering the function of a system to be synonymous with its purpose when its ultimate purpose is not otherwise apparent. Thus the purpose of the solar system would become "to maintain the present energy-matter equilibrium condition between the planets."

THE HIERARCHY OF SYSTEMS

The multiplicity of systems and the complexities of their relations presents a formidable obstacle to our conceptualizing reality from a systems viewpoint. The system of systems devised by Boulding that follows is a classification scheme dealing, primarily, with the intrinsic nature of systems themselves.[10]

1. The first level is that of static structure. It might be called the level of "frameworks." This is the geography and anatomy of the universe....The accurate description of these frameworks is the beginning of organized theoretical knowledge in almost any field, for without accuracy in this description of static relationships no accurate functional or dynamic theory is possible.

2. The next level of systematic analysis is that of the simple dynamic system with predetermined, necessary motions. This might be called the level of "clockworks." The solar system itself is of course the great clock of the universe from man's point of view, and the deliciously exact predictions of the astronomers are a testimony to the excellence of the clock which they study....The greater part of the theoretical structure of physics, chemistry, and even of economics falls into this category.

3. The next level is that of the control mechanism or cybernetic system, which might be nicknamed the level of the "thermostat." This differs from the simple stable equilibrium system mainly in the fact that the transmission and interpretation of information is an essential part of the system.... The homeostasis model, which is of such importance in physiology, is an example of a cybernetic mechanism, and such mechanisms exist through the whole empirical world of the biologist and the social scientist.

4. The fourth level is that of the "open system," or self-maintaining structure. This is the level at which life begins to

---

[10]Kenneth Boulding, "General Systems Theory: The Skeleton of Science," *Management Science,* April 1956, pp. 197–208.

differentiate itself from not-life: it might be called the level of the "cell."

⑤ The fifth level might be called the genetic-societal level; it is typified by the "plant," and it dominates the empirical world of the botanists.

⑥ As we move upward from the plant world towards the animal kingdom we gradually pass over into a new level, the "animal" level, characterized by increased mobility, teleological behavior, and self-awareness. Here we have the development of specialized information receptors (eyes, ears, etc.) leading to an enormous increase in intake of information: we also have a great development of nervous systems, leading ultimately to the brain, as an organizer of the information intake into a knowledge structure or "image." Increasingly as we ascend the scale of animal life, behavior is response not to a specific stimulus but to an "image" or knowledge structure or view of the environment as a whole....The difficulties in the prediction of the behavior of these systems arises largely because of this intervention of the image between the stimulus and the response.

⑦ The next level is the "human" level, that is, of the individual human being considered as a system. In addition to all, or nearly all, of the characteristics of animal systems man possesses self-consciousness, which is something different from mere awareness. His image, besides being much more complex that that even of the higher animals, has a self-reflective quality—he not only knows, but knows that he knows. This property is probably bound up with the phenomenon of language and symbolism. It is the capacity for speech—the ability to produce, absorb, and interpret "symbols", as opposed to mere signs like the warning cry of an animal—which most clearly marks man off from his humbler brethren.

⑧ Because of the vital importance for the individual man of symbolic images in behavior based on them it is not easy to separate clearly the level of the individual human organism from the next level, that of social organizations.... Nevertheless it is convenient for some purposes to distinguish the individual human as a system from the social systems which surround him, and in this sense social organizations may be said to constitute another level of organization.... At this level we must concern ourselves with the content and meaning of messages, the nature and dimensions of value systems, the transcription of images into historical record, the subtle symbolizations of art, music, and poetry, and the complex gamut of human emotion.

9. To complete the structure of systems we should add a final turret for transcendental systems, even if we may be accused at this point of having built Babel to the clouds. There are however the ultimates and absolutes and the inescapables and unknowables, and they also exhibit systematic structure and relationship. It will be a sad day for man when nobody is allowed to ask questions that do not have any answers.

The preceding classification system presents the general nature of the major types of systems according to their composition and the functional relations between their individual elements. The discussion suggests the idea that there are levels of systems—a hierarchical systems structure.

The development of an interlocking hierarchy of systems that encompasses the entire universe depends on the systemic nesting phenomenon that in turn is derived from the definition of the term *system.* Consider a given system—such as a man—as being composed of several elemental parts—the skeletal subsystem, the digestive subsystem, the central nervous system, and so forth. The principal subsystems of man are the elements of the system *man* and may be viewed as "subsystems within a system." The process of systems subdivision may quite readily be continued downward—as, for example, through the major parts of the digestive subsystem into the divisions of the small intestine, and even further.

Next consider the original system—a man—as an element in a larger system—the family. The original system has now become a part of a "supersystem." The process may be continued upward through the tribe or clan, the nation, to the whole human race.

We may postulate that each finite system is in fact only an element in a larger system—the supersystem—and is made up in turn of small systems or subsystems. In much of the real world we may distinguish well over a dozen distinct systemic levels that display this nesting phenomenon. All of reality becomes in effect a hierarchical system of systems.

The systemic nesting concept may be made clearer by

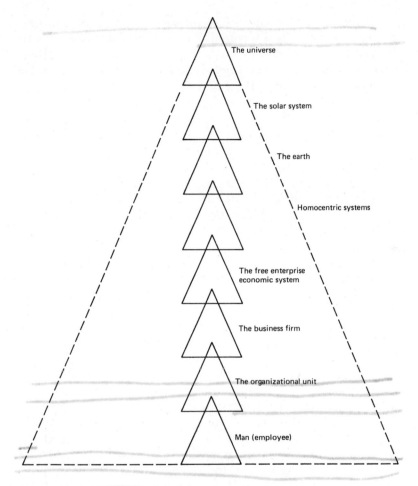

The universe

The solar system

The earth

Homocentric systems

The free enterprise economic system

The business firm

The organizational unit

Man (employee)

Fig. 1-1   A hierarchy of systems

considering an example of a nested systems hierarchy. One possible breakdown as it might apply to the business firm is shown in figure 1-1.

The first or primary systems level is designated as the universe and encompasses everything physical and non-physical of which we have any knowledge. The second level is the solar system, which includes the sun, the earth, and the other planets orbiting around the sun. The next lower systemic level is the earth itself; ecological or life-centered systems appear at the next lower level.

Homocentric systems are those in which man or mankind is one of the principal elements. Within homocentric systems the free enterprise economic system is one of the major subsystems. At the next lower level, business firms are one of the primary components of the free enterprise economic system.

The process of hierarchical systemic definition may be continued within the business firm. For example, the production system is one of the major functional systems in most businesses. Most production systems are composed of basic organizational units that produce the goods under the direction of a supervisor. The last hierarchical level we shall recognize in our systemic analysis is the individual within the organizational unit.

The foregoing systemic breakdown is an example of the hierarchical nesting relation that exists among systems of every description. Indeed, similar charts can be prepared for many other systems. It is scarcely any wonder that many scholars view systems theory as a unifying intellectual concept that binds all the separate areas within the range of man's intellect.

For all levels (except the universe) shown in figure 1-1 there are many different systems. Each one at any level could be defined as a unique individual system with finite boundaries that differentiate it from other systems at the same hierarchical level. The notion of boundaries is very important in systems theory, since it permits the systems analyst to differentiate between intra- and inter-systemic relations. In some cases there may even be no demarcation line between two systems as, for example, where the output of one system becomes the input to the next. In all cases, however, the boundaries between systems must be established to designate a starting point for systemic analysis. Only when the boundaries for a particular system have been clearly defined may the analysis of the system be focused directly on its elements and their interrelations.

The parameters of a system and its boundaries are related concepts that may easily be confused with each other. A system's parameters may be defined as the set of relations among the individual elements that establish the unique character of a given system. Consider, for example, a normal distribution of a population as a system (figure 1-2). The system parameters are the mean and the standard deviation. Once these two values are known, the basic characteristics of the population are established and the probability relations between an individual item and the entire population may be determined. A given population may

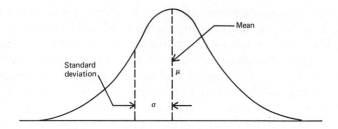

Fig. 1-2   Normal population distribution

be large or small, but as long as the parameters remain the same, the probability relations within the system will be the same.

We shall subsequently examine many systems that are very similar to each other. The fact that some of these have much the same parameters will enable us to build generalized systems models of particular systems. In this way we may examine their behavior and extrapolate their performance characteristics.

SYSTEMS THEORY AND MANAGEMENT THOUGHT

There are several different approaches that may be taken in studying the process of management. One widely used classification system divides the various approaches into different "schools" of management: the operational school, the empirical school, the human behavior school, the social system school, the decision theory school, and the mathematical school.[11] Each of these emphasizes different qualities of management and each of them has added new dimensions to our understanding of its nature.

The application of systems theory has heralded still another school of management thought. The special point of view this school stresses is the definition of the management process as a unique decision-making subsystem that integrates the functional subsystems of the business firm and establishes the relations between the firm and the business environment. The systems-school advocates view all the activities within the business enterprise as systems phenomena that are amenable to

11. H. Koontz and C. O'Donnell, *Principles of Management,* 5th ed. (New York: McGraw-Hill Book Company, 1972), pp. 34–42.

systemic classification and analysis. In effect, these individuals look at management through "systems colored" glasses.

The systems school of management thought has several unique characteristics that are not found in the other schools of management. Examining the special areas of management thought that will be affected by systems theory and analysis will both demonstrate how this school complements the others and show its potential areas of contribution to modern management theory.

First of all, systems theory is basically a unifying theory that seeks to identify relations and interdependencies among the elements of a system. One of the benefits of the application of systems theory to management thought may be to resolve some of the conflicts that presently beset it by stressing the harmonious, integrative aspects of the management functions. Systems of management are still evolving and there is still a tendency to view management activities as separate and unrelated. The value of a unified approach to management is undeniable, but more time and effort will be necessary before this objective can be reached.

Systems theory may also provide a means for training managers to develop a broad outlook. The complex nature of modern business has produced an almost insatiable demand for specialists of all types. The evidence seems to suggest that employees at the lower organizational levels are initially selected on the basis of the skills they possess or are expected to acquire shortly after employment. The result of emphasizing employee specialization during the hiring process is that there is a severe shortage in middle management of individuals who are generalists and are able to grasp the overall organizational interrelations. Top- and middle-level managers must be able to integrate and synthesize many concepts and ideas to make effective decisions.

The systems approach to the study of management may provide a partial solution to this managerial resource vacuum. Visualizing the business firm both as a subsystem within the free enterprise system and as a system composed of many smaller subsystems offers a means of relating the different business functions and can aid in conceptualizing business problems. The manager who uses a systems viewpoint recognizes that the daily crises in business operations are systemic dysfunctions that have one or more causes. The systems-oriented manager will be able to recognize the critical interrelations with other parts of the organization that could be affected by introducing a change into the system. In short, the systems vantage point will help provide the manager with the outlook of a generalist.

The systems approach to management thought will also help to emphasize the dynamic qualities of management. The vital, ongoing characteristics of the management process are very difficult to describe in adequate terms. The virtually constant activity of the business firm makes the use of static, experience-based decision-making techniques highly suspect. This shortcoming may be partially relieved by considering the management process to be a dynamic subsystem within another dynamic system, the business firm. In this way the changing, evolving nature of managerial decision-making may be more accurately presented and understood. This idea is currently being utilized in the construction of complex mathematical models of business games and in simulated studies of business operations.

For the practicing manager, a knowledge of systems theory and a comprehensive understanding of the operating characteristics for a particular production system furnishes an excellent basis for managing the system. Directing and controlling system behavior are, of course, very necessary activities for managers at all organizational levels, and, of course, require planning. Managerial planning must always be performed relative to the operation of a specific system or group of systems. Only if the characteristics of the operating system are known in considerable depth can the planning effort be sufficiently accurate to be of significant value. Similarly, effective process controls may be instituted only when the manager understands the production system well enough to know where the strategic control points are.

Research in the field of management, as in other fields, continues to yield a bountiful supply of information into relations among various managerial phenomena. The evaluation and utilization of research results is a most difficult problem for both managers and management scholars. However, if research efforts are examined to determine their contribution to our understanding of the systemic interrelations in business, a pragmatic evaluation of the results may be made. Good research investigations should not only increase the absolute quantity of knowledge but should amplify of our understanding of the system itself. Placing research findings in a systems context then becomes a very effective means of evaluating and integrating research information with the central body of knowledge about management.

Finally, the use of the systems approach is especially effective for instruction and communication. Casting organizational relations and management processes as systems phenomena is an efficient way to describe and communicate them. For example, depicting the traditional organizational hierarchy as a systems model (the organization chart) describes the superior-subordinate organizational relationships much more succinctly and forcefully than would a written description of a particular organization. Indeed, the use of charts (systems models) to increase the efficiency of the communication process has been known and practiced by good managers for many years.

The integration of systems theory and the practice of management offers tremendous opportunities for intellectual breakthroughs. Since all organizational units are, in reality, systems, the proper study for both present and future managers is the study of systems and their management. The following chapters will explore this wilderness.

SYSTEM MODELS

2

In the preceding chapter we noted that the real world could be viewed as many different systems that perform different functions and exhibit a broad spectrum of characteristics, yet are unified through the systems nesting concept. Perhaps the universal all-encompassing nature of systems has dulled man's ability to realize the full extent of systemic phenomena and to appreciate fully their all-inclusive nature. Only in the past few years have organized efforts been made to establish the systems reference framework; today the results of these efforts are becoming apparent in many different areas.

We have postulated the real world—the world of objects, things, events, and processes—to be a system of interconnected subsystems. The reality of the world is made recognizable to individuals through the perception of objects and their attributes.

The human nervous system transmits a tremendously large number of individual stimuli to the mind over a period of time. In spite of this vast quantity of raw data, the mind usually does not completely comprehend the identity of the object, event, or process. There are sound waves, for example, that cannot be heard and light waves that are not visible to the eye. Further, the mind is simply not able to use all of the raw stimulation data it receives. It simply ignores a substantial portion of the total stimuli as being nonrelevant. Mental fatigue is also a factor in the efficiency of the reception process. Thus the inefficiencies in our perceptive systems produce incomplete, fragmentary, and highly personalized views of what reality is all about. Since the stimuli received through the five senses are our only links to the real world, however, we must utilize them to the best of our abilities if we wish to adapt satisfactorily to our environment.

The mental images that the various stimuli create produce differing degrees of comprehension in our consciousnesses, depending on the amount of intellectual organization we can apply to those sensations. The ability to understand perceived phenomena is directly related to the degree of mental organization required to assimilate the stimuli properly: complex phenomena require a higher degree of mental organization for comprehension than simple phenomena. Improvements in the ability to organize sensory perceptions will consequently improve our cognitive abilities.

The process by which stimuli are organized into coherent mental images is known as the abstraction process. All we can really know are incomplete, imperfect concepts of the real world. Further, we tend to recognize only those stimuli that seem to apply and give meaning to particular objects, events, and processes in the abstraction process. Abstractions, then, delete many details of the actual phenomena but attempt to preserve their essences through the intellectual organizing process within the mind of the individual.

A model is an abstract representation of real phenomena that exist externally to our thought processes. Such models are real "things" that have independent existences both from the systems they are attempting to portray and from the images within the mind. Models, in effect, interpose an intermediate stage into the abstraction process that creates a more understandable image of a complex real-world situation. The objective of model building is not to portray or identify all aspects of phenomena, but rather to point out the significant elements and the salient interrelations in complex systems.

Models can fulfill many useful functions. The communication process in which complex ideas must be transferred can be made much more efficient by using appropriate models. Isolating and analyzing significant elements and their pertinent interrelations in a given system allows us to experiment with the system to further increase our understanding of its characteristics. Models may also provide a means for predicting and controlling the real-world systems they represent. In short, a knowledge of models and their structure, whether formalized or simply "understood," is a necessity for life in our present complex environment.

The following sections of this chapter will present a model classification system in which system models, especially business-related ones, are organized according to their degree of abstraction. The premise underlying this discussion is that complex real-world systems must be abstracted to model form in order to present forcefully the systemic elements and their interrelations. In this way we may appreciate and better understand the systems concept and systems analysis.

VERBAL MODELS

Verbal models constitute a loose category of models that rely on words to describe the elements and the interrelations of a particular system. Using words to define objects, things, events, and processes is both the most ancient and the most common approach to model building.

In either written or spoken form, words are especially well suited for communicating all manner of thoughts. The advantages of verbal models include their low cost, ease of construction, and ready comprehensibility. They are most useful where more sophisticated approaches to the description and analysis of routine affairs cannot be economically justified. Our modern industrial society currently places great emphasis on this method of model description.

The principal difficulties encountered with verbal models stem from the use of words themselves. Verbal descriptions of phenomena, in spite of our most exhaustive efforts, lack precision. Ambiguities and semantic difficulties are frequently present in verbal communication. Difficulties are also encountered when descriptions are incomplete or the reception of the verbal model is faulty. Each word is a potential source of misunderstanding. Thus the verbal model is an extensively used communication device but presents difficulties in transmitting systems information when it is used alone.

SCHEMATIC MODELS

All schematic models are ultimately based on the old adage, "a picture is worth a thousand words." Representing systems in pictorial form avoids many of the communication difficulties inherent in the use of verbal models. At the same time, it presents the systemic elements and principal interrelations directly and forcefully, with a minimum of ambiguity. The difficulties of internal abstraction are reduced since the mind may quickly grasp the main features and easily create the corresponding mental images. As a result, the use of schematic models greatly improves the efficiency of thought transfer and the effectiveness of the perception process.

Verbal models tend to be almost completely descriptive and explanatory in nature. Schematic models, which may be classed as the next higher level of abstraction beyond verbal models, are also strongly descriptive. The most frequent use of schematic models is to describe complex systems in summary form. Typically, schematic models are drawings or charts that present systemic elements or their attributes together with a single relation. In essence, a schematic model is a picture of a system.

Since schematic models must necessarily be limited to two dimensions in order to be drawn on a planar surface, the number of salient relations that may be shown is limited to one. This situation arises from the two-dimensional nature of the diagram. The x axis and the y axis may each describe one attribute of the system; their interaction yields only one interrelation. Common examples of business system relations that combine two systemic attributes are cost-quantity, cost-quality, and time-quantity. There are also examples of systems in which the systemic elements are designated and only one attribute is specified, such as maps and PERT charts. The inherent inability of schematic models to portray more than one systemic relation does not invalidate their use. It does require, however, that this limitation be kept in mind and that our expectations be reduced accordingly.

Analyzing a schematic model begins with an examination of the system's elements and their relations. This method of systems model analysis may be strengthened by examining in detail the *how, why, where,* and *when* of each perceived systemic relation. Analysis may be further improved by seeking other systemic relations that may also exist within the system but that might have been overlooked in preparing the diagram.

Systems synthesis is the creation of new systems models that postulate new systemic relations. Man-developed systems are the result of conscious planning effort to achieve one or more objectives. Preparing a systems model to describe a new system is required to develop an improved system of any type. As we shall subsequently discuss in detail, the information systems analyst must thoroughly understand the analytical approach (systems analysis) as well as information systems synthesis.

For presentation purposes we shall divide schematic models into three broad areas: (a) schematic models that depict a set of elements and their relations at a given point in time—static schematic models; (b) schematic models that portray flows of some description among the systemic elements—flow schematic models; and (c) schematic models that depict a transformation process—dynamic systems models. Although this classification system does not easily yield identifiable, mutually exclusive groups in every case, the exceptions may be handled on an individual basis. We will also encounter compound schematic models that incorporate, for example, both element flows and transformations.

Static Systems Models

Schematic models that apply to a given set of elements and their relations at a specific time may be termed static systems models. The time period, which must be finite, is not necessarily limited to a particular instant in time. However, it must be fixed, and may range from a fraction of a second to several years. The most important consideration in establishing the time base is that the relations expressed in the model be uniform and continuous throughout.

This subclass of systems models may exhibit only one type of relation within the model. The principal types of business-system attributes found in this type of model are space, time, quantity, cost, quality, and authority. Let us consider some business examples of each type of relation.

Maps are an excellent example of static systems models that emphasize the spatial relation. The elements are cities, towns, and geographic points of reference. The spatial relations among the elements are shown by their relative positions on the map. The scale of the map defines the proportional spatial relation. Other more directly business-related examples of spatial models are plant layout drawings, engineering drawings, and the pictures in product advertising. All of these models emphasize the spatial relation.

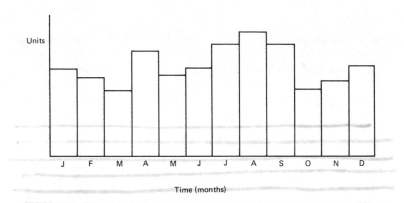

Units

J F M A M J J A S O N D

Time (months)

Fig. 2-1   Bar chart

The quantity attributes of a system are often shown as bar charts and graphs. Figure 2-1 depicts the quantity-time relations within a particular production system. In this example the production levels each month are the elements and the quantity is represented by the vertical length of the bar. Time is indicated on the horizontal axis.

The traditional Gantt chart is probably the most common business example of the time-activity relation in model form. These schematic systems models were originally developed by Henry L. Gantt and have been widely used for planning and controlling activities for almost half a century. Gantt charts provide managers with powerful insights into the interrelations (especially the time-based ones) among the activities of a process, an organizational unit, or a program.

The typical Gantt chart measures time in uniform units on its horizontal axis. Work activities, machine loads, or program responsibilities are designated on the vertical axis. Programmed work progress is shown as bars, lines, and other symbols extending from left to right across the chart. An example of a Gantt chart is shown in figure 2-2.

There are three basic types of Gantt charts that are widely used in manufacturing processes. The first of these, the load chart, shows the work assignments that have been made to an organizational branch, department, or a group of men and/or machines. Typically, such a chart will be used initially for planning and scheduling the work assignments, followed later by an evaluation of actual work progress to planned work progress. It may be revised and updated to make it current as required.

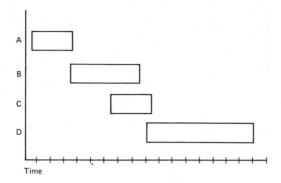

Fig. 2-2 Gantt chart

Another variety of Gantt chart is the record chart. Its principal purpose is to provide an easily understood record of the work activities of the designated group. It primarily emphasizes the presentation of historical data to communicate and evaluate systems efficiency and/or effectiveness and thus facilitates overall managerial control.

The last major type of Gantt chart is the program process chart, which shows the sequence of activities required to achieve a specific objective. It attempts to portray both activity time and sequence for programs that involve several different work groups. Its basic objective is to depict the time-based organizational interrelations in a total program (system). Most frequently, program process charts are developed in the planning stages of a program and are subsequently used as a basis for exercising program control.

The breakeven chart is the most familiar business-based schematic model in which the cost-quantity relation is expressed. The firm is the business system and the related systemic attributes are value and quantity of output. The chart expresses the model's fundamental relations by lines representing the variable costs, the fixed costs for a given period of time, and the revenue per unit. A typical breakeven chart is shown in figure 2-3.

This model may be quite useful for analyzing the basic cost/quantity relations and predicting the future behavior of the business firm. The production level at which all costs are covered but no profits are earned (breakeven point) is automatically developed by the construction of the chart. Anticipated profits (or losses) at any level of production may be estimated by the

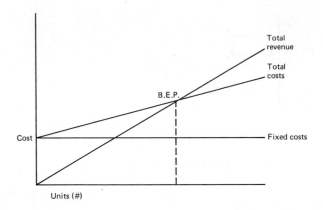

Fig. 2-3   Breakeven chart

length of the vertical line between the total revenue line and the total cost line. The model also suggests other areas for more in-depth analysis. Is the composition and level of the fixed costs really fixed? Is the total revenue line really a linear function or will unit price decreases be required to sell larger volumes of the products? Does the variable cost line reflect setup costs and capacity operation inefficiencies? These are typical questions a systems analysis of the breakeven chart will bring forth.

The final type of static schematic model relating to the business firm that we shall consider is the organization chart. The total system is, again, the firm. Individual managerial positions are its elements. The systemic relations that are portrayed are authority relationships, which may be of a line, staff, or functional nature. A typical organization chart is shown in figure 2-4.

Flow Systems Models

This class of systems models attempts to show flow, motion, or some other type of movement. It is this relation that binds the elements of the system together and gives these systems their unique character. The nature of the flow may be quite varied. It may be composed of physical materials or objects, such as liquid in a piping diagram or production units in a materials handling analysis chart, flow-process chart, or routing and assembly diagram. The flow of energy may also be shown in models of this type as, for example, an electrical circuit drawing.

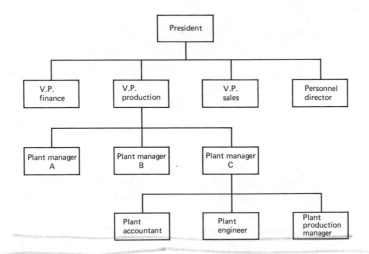

Fig. 2-4   Organization chart

Of special interest in the field of production management are systems models that describe the motions involved in the performance of work activities. Operator charts and multiple-activity charts are widely used to describe the sequential activity flow in the production process.

In recent years there has been substantial development of models for planning and executing large-scale programs. Several techniques, known as network analysis, have been developed that greatly assist these managerial efforts. PERT (Program Evaluation and Review Technique), PERT/COST, and CPM (Critical Path Method) are the best known and most widely used examples of network analysis techniques. The system as portrayed in network analysis models is the total program; its elements are the program's activities. The models attempt to depict the sequential, time-based relations among the individual activities. A typical small-scale PERT diagram is shown in figure 2-5.

The PERT diagram is often only the starting point for further analysis of the network systems model. Time, cost, and personnel resource estimates, when processed by various statistical techniques, produce a number of important insights into the system's structure. Important questions that may merit investigation are "What is the probability of completing the program within the allotted time span?" and "How can the available resources be substituted in the program?". The answers to these

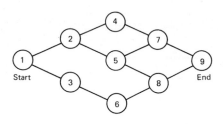

Fig. 2-5   PERT diagram

and other similar questions rely on mathematical manipulation of the data and are not readily demonstrable with the network model.

Program flowcharts represent the sequential flow of logical operations in a computer program. Their systemic elements are the individual instructions or operations for processing data. The relation among the elements are based on the orderly sequential flow of logic. It is the thread of logic that enables the computer to transform data into information. Most readers are, no doubt, very familiar with this type of model.

A closely allied flow systems model is the managerial decision tree. This particular model describes a decision system in which decisions and their results are plotted sequentially in a diverging pattern. The systemic elements are the alternate courses of action and the anticipated results. An example of a decision tree is shown in figure 2-6.

Flow systems models may also be presented in matrix form for convenience. The construction of a flow matrix is based on the *from-to* relationship between the elements as expressed in tabular form.

Construction of a flow systems matrix is begun by outlining the form of the basic matrix. According to standard convention the rows are $(1, 2, 3, \ldots, m)$ numbered or named and designated as flow sources ("froms"). In like manner the columns are designated as flow destinations ("tos") and numbered 1, 2, 3, $\ldots, n$ or otherwise identified. All of the flow sources and destinations within the system must be identified by a number or name. To indicate a flow from one element to another, an x is placed at the intersection of the source row and the destination column. A complete system matrix for the PERT diagram (figure 2-5) is shown in figure 2-7.

The usefulness of the matrix form of systems models may be increased by further defining the flow vectors within the ma-

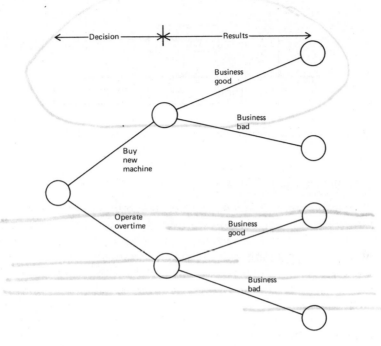

←——Decision——— ✳ ———Results———→

Business
good

Business
bad

Buy
new
machine

Operate
overtime

Business
good

Business
bad

Fig. 2-6 Decision tree

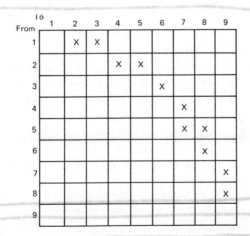

Fig. 2-7 Flow systems matrix

trix. Instead of designating the flow vector simply as x, a code
letter or short name may be inserted at the appropriate intersection to describe the nature of the vector. This technique may
also be extended to include vector quantity values.

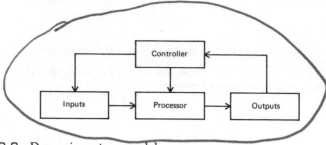

Fig. 2-8   Dynamic system model

Dynamic Systems Models

The outstanding characteristic of dynamic systems models is forceful, change-generating activity. This model form attempts to catch the essence of systems that are in a state of flux, where things are happening. The principal distinguishing feature of dynamic systems models (as opposed to flow systems models that also portray movement) is the presence of a self-regulating transformation process. In dynamic systems models the transformation process may alter the character or substance of the input elements so that they are scarcely recognizable in the system's outputs. These systems are termed "dynamic" because they exercise a measure of self-control over their performance.

The basic diagram for the dynamic systems model is shown in figure 2-8. The block on the left represents the systemic elements entering the system and are known as the *inputs.* The center block indicates the place where the inputs are converted and is known as the *processor.* The block on the right-hand side of the diagram represents the systemic elements that are produced by the processor and are known as the *outputs.* The block at the top represents the source of direction for the system and is known as the *controller* or program. Other features that may usually be found in dynamic models will be discussed in the following chapter.

The dynamic system converts the systemic inputs (the elements that enter the transformation process) into systemic outputs (the elements that leave the process). The number of inputs and/or outputs may vary from one to many thousands. An oil refinery, for example, may use only a single input—crude oil—to produce a large number of different end products. The situation may also be reversed. Several thousand different parts may be assembled by an aerospace manufacturing firm to build a single advanced weapons system.

Another characteristic of dynamic system inputs and outputs is that the inputs and/or the outputs may be either homogenous or heterogenous in nature. There is no requirement that all inputs (or outputs) must be similar to each other. The business firm, when considered as a dynamic system, requires the widely disparate resources of personnel, capital, and raw materials for systemic inputs. It may produce many different products and/or provide a number of different services for a broad variety of outputs.

The central block of the dynamic systems model is labeled as the processor. This is the site or environment where the interaction among the elements takes place. The processor may have physical dimensions ranging from a very small confined area to a very large ill-defined region. The processor of conceptual or thought systems may not exist as a location *per se,* but only in the minds of men.

The most familiar forms of processors are simple-to-complex physical objects such as machinery and electronic equipment. Another common type of processor is the biological units that perform life processes. Plants and animals consume nutrients to sustain the living being. The human mind is also a processor of sensory stimuli into thoughts, concepts, decisions, and activities.

The controller guides and directs the processor in the performance of its functions. We have previously noted that systems have objectives or purposes. To achieve them, the system's activities must be organized and function in a coherent reproducible manner. Likewise, stability is usually required for efficient operation. The controller establishes the systemic environment and regulates the inputs so that the system objectives may be achieved and system stability maintained.

ICONIC MODELS

Iconic models are static three-dimensional representations of physical objects. In a sense, they are the next higher level of abstraction above the two-dimensional models discussed in the preceding section. Although iconic models may contain moveable parts, they do not ordinarily attempt to represent a system's dynamic qualities. The third dimension enables the user to perceive certain relations, especially spatial ones, by direct observation. Since iconic models deal most frequently with physical objects, they are usually associated with the engineering and manufacturing activities of the business firm.

The scale of the iconic model must be known for it to be useful for communication or analytical purposes. Ordinarily, an iconic model is a small-scale replica of a physical object or system. Common examples of this type of iconic model range from small plastic airplanes to complex plant layout models. However, there is no requirement that such a model must be small-scale. Aircraft and automobile manufacturers normally prepare full scale mock-ups of their products as an integral part of new product design. The model scale may also be greater than the original object, as, for example, a scale model of a complex molecular structure.

The most common objective of iconic model building is to give the user a knowledge of the spatial relations of the real-world system. Iconic models can be very useful devices for instruction and communication purposes. They are also useful in disclosing potential problem areas in the production, maintenance, and use of manufactured products and plant facilities. The esthetic qualities of a product can be much more accurately portrayed with iconic models than by any other available technique. Further, although iconic models are not necessarily cheap or easy to build, they are usually less expensive, easier to construct, more easily modified, and more readily moved about than the real system.

ANALOG MODELS   *agree in one aspect will agree in others*

Analog models seek to describe the operational characteristics of other systems through the process of analogy. These models are built on the premise that the behavior of full-scale operating systems may be studied and analyzed by examining the behavior of other systems with similar characteristics. The results of the analog model investigation may then be applied to the actual system. The success of an analog model is directly related to the accuracy of the postulated systemic relation. Historical evidence and controlled experiments are frequently used to establish the exact nature of the analogous relation.

The most common type of analog model is based on a scalar relation. For example, prototype ship hull designs are frequently tested in special tanks where different wave motions may be simulated. One major oil company even maintains a model port facility in Europe complete with operating model tankers to train the ship officers of the tanker fleet. Wind tunnel testing of aircraft (iconic models) provides a wealth of knowledge about the flight characteristics of various aircraft designs. Pilot plant operations are frequently used in the chemical industry to establish the operating procedures for the manufacture of new products. All of these analog models rely on the knowledge that similar systems that differ from each other primarily in terms of scale will operate in the same way.

Other analogous relations may form bases for constructing analog models. The flow of water through conductors has been shown to be analogous to the flow of electricity through a wire. The use of analog computers is based on the existence of analogous behavior between the flow of electrical current through complex circuits and certain physical processing operations or mathematical computations. Systems simulation of business operations on digital computers, which usually require mathematical models in their preparation, is also based on the premise that there is an analogous relation between the model and the business operation. In all of these instances such a relation permits a processing system to be examined in model form.

The most immediate area of application for analog models is in research and development, product design, and plant operations. The behavior of the business firms as an analog-mathematical model has been investigated by Jay Forrester and is known as industrial dynamics.[1] The simulation of business problems (business games) is, of course, a well-recognized method of analysis and instruction.

MATHEMATICAL MODELS

Mathematical or symbolic models represent the highest level of abstraction in systemic model construction. Several of the barriers that constrain schematic, iconic, and analog models are breached by mathematical models that enable their users to extend their applications substantially. The fields of operations research and management science are devoted almost exclusively to developing and using mathematical models to provide man-

---

1. J. W. Forrester, *Industrial Dynamics* (Cambridge, Mass., and New York: The M.I.T. Press and John Wiley & Sons, Inc., 1961).

agement with more and better information for decision making.

Mathematical models offer a degree of precision that is limited only by our ability to count or measure. Mathematical relations may be stated in exact terms. Many systemic ones may not be accurately quantified, however, because of inadequate measurement techniques. In these cases, qualitative evaluations of the systemic relations must suffice.

The dimensionality restrictions of schematic, iconic, and analog models (two or three dimensions) do not apply to mathematical models. Thus the number of different systemic relations that mathematical models may describe is limited only by the perceptions of the model builder. In large-scale linear programming models, for example, the model dimensionality may be a thousand or even more. The elimination of the dimensionality restriction vastly increases the range and power of mathematical models.

Mathematical models may be more easily manipulated than any of the other model types. The structure of a mathematical model may be easily changed and the effects determined rapidly, especially with the use of computers. In an equation where the independent variables are known and the basic mathematical relations are specified, the dependent variable may usually be directly determined. In addition, the relation need not be completely determined (stochastic models) in order to be expressed.

Among the other advantages mathematical models offer are clarity and unambiguity. Standard, well-understood meanings are implicit in the symbology of mathematics, which substantially reduces the communication problem. Mathematical models also offer very concise, direct statements of a system.

Mathematical models may be categorized as either stochastic (probabilistic) or deterministic models. The former category may be defined as mathematical models that deal with uncertainties, both present and future, through the use of probability and statistics. The essence of these models is the description of a particular system in which the element of chance plays a significant role in the system's behavior. In order to define the relations that are subject to uncertainty or risk, system probability values must be established and incorporated into the mathematical model.

Deterministic models, on the other hand, do not recognize the element of chance in the description of the system. When the system's mathematical relations have been specified and the independent variables have been determined, the dependent variable may be computed with exactness. The assumption of absolute certainty in the mathematical relations is implicit in these models. Common business examples of deterministic models are breakeven analysis, economic order quantity determination, transportation problems, and linear programming.

Mathematical models may also be classed as either descriptive or optimizing in purpose. The basic objective of a descriptive model is to describe a single relation or, less frequently, a set of relations for a particular system. The expressed relations are usually of a fundamental and general nature; that is, they apply to a given system over an extended period of time under widely varying conditions. On the other hand, the practical use of descriptive models by substituting appropriate values for the several variables is limited to a single point in time. For example, the equation

$$A \text{ (assets)} = L \text{ (liabilities)} + NW \text{ (net worth)}$$

is a descriptive mathematical model of the financial resources and liabilities together with their application in the business firm and is commonly presented as the firm's balance sheet. The substitution of particular values for the individual accounts provides a description of the financial structure of the business system on a certain date.

The basic goal of optimizing models is to find the best possible allocation of scarce resources among competing opportunities. Their development is of relatively recent origin and is especially suited to large-scale complex business problems. Although optimizing models must necessarily incorporate a set of descriptive mathematical relations in their construction, their objective is to determine the systemic conditions that will best satisfy all of the systemic constraints. Linear programming and simulation are the best known examples of this type of model. Furthermore, an optimizing mathematical model is usually constructed to describe a specific system at a specific point in time and hence does not usually have the fundamental character of a descriptive mathematical model.

CONCLUSION

Constructing models to portray the various natures of systems is a very important part of the abstraction process. Reality is usually far too complex for man to assimilate a multitude of details, organize his thoughts, and make intelligent decisions without using abstractions. The development of models to help us conceptualize the many systems in our universe provides a means for intelligently grappling with reality. Through the use of models we may perceive systemic relations, postulate systems performance or behavior, and exercise some degree of control over our environment.

The different types of models presented in the preceding discussion are not mutually exclusive. The relations depicted in the breakeven chart, for example, may also be expressed with mathematical equations. Hybrid models may also be found, as in the analog-mathematical models of the business firm. Only the ingenuity of man is the limiting factor in model construction.

The application of model construction is a very important part of information systems analysis. Through the use of schematic models, we may more easily visualize information relations and note opportunities for systemic improvement. Model construction is one of the principal tools of the information systems analyst.

CHARACTERISTICS AND BEHAVIOR OF DYNAMIC SYSTEMS

In the preceding chapter we examined several different types of systems with their corresponding models. In the business world, dynamic systems may be found in many different forms and guises. This is due in large part to the fact that economic goods and services are created by processes and activities performed through human guidance and direction. In order to satisfy man's needs and desires, raw materials must be transformed into finished goods, seeds must be sown to reap the harvests, and natural resources (water power, coal, and petroleum) must be converted into usable energy. The concept of economic activity also implies that human resources be used not only as an energy source, but also to manage the process of creating goods and services that have economic value. As we shall see, efficient transformation processes for producing economic goods depend on the operation of many interrelated systems.

A dynamic system may be defined as one in which certain elements are altered in form through an ongoing, self-controlling process to create other unique distinct elements. Dynamic systems are isomorphic in character; that is, they differ widely in appearance but are composed of similarly related parts. Recall the basic dynamic systems model presented in chapter 2 (page 28). According to that definition, all biological units, both animal and vegetable, are dynamic systems. Each living thing requires some form of nourishment and other combinations of inputs such as air, water, sunlight, and certain minerals. These inputs are transformed through and directed by the life processes into activity, growth, and reproduction. Many manufacturing processes too may be structured as dynamic systems. In an aluminum reduction cell, for example, a large quantity of electric current is passed through a molten bath of cryolite containing dissolved alumina. Under the proper circumstances, these inputs are transformed into aluminum metal, which in form and substance is totally unlike any of the input elements. Process equilibrium in this case is maintained by electrical switches and control devices. Still another example of a dynamic system is the classroom. Here students and text material embodying concepts and ideas are brought together under the direction of a teacher and "educated" students are produced. Examination results provide a measure of feedback for the instructor. Additional reflection can yield many more examples of dynamic systems in everyday life.

Designating a particular system as a dynamic one implies the presence of a definite life-like quality in its operation. A dynamic system exhibits purposeful activity in the achievement of its goals and objectives. To a greater or lesser extent, self-regulation and self-direction in its operation make this type of system appear to be alive. In addition, a sense of process continuity is usually present, since most dynamic processes operate over a measurable and sometimes an extended period of time. Thus dynamic systems display to a greater or lesser extent the general attributes associated with living things: purposeful activity, self-regulation, self-direction, and predictable behavior under given conditions over time.

Dynamic systems do not necessarily involve life processes or biological units in their operation. In those dynamic systems where life processes or biological units are not present, however, we may usually discern human activity in the background. For example, input of raw data and workable programs into a computer system results in information that is useful to managers, engineers, and scientists. Although this dynamic system does not contain any biological units *per se,* the activity must be directed by a program that is a product of a human mind. Biological units or life processes are therefore not necessary requirements for the existence of a dynamic system. On the other hand, where biological activities are not involved in a dynamic system, the intellect of man is frequently present, creating and directing it.

Determining the exact nature of each element and the relations among the elements of a dynamic system is not always an easy matter. Dynamic systems in which the human element plays a relatively small role tend to be highly structured and amenable to detailed analysis. A computer, an internal combustion engine, or an electric generating system all display many specific determinable interrelations among their respective parts. In machine-like dynamic systems the output is a direct function of the input: the processor performs in a uniform repetitive manner and the controller maintains the system in a relatively stable equilibrium condition. Highly structured systems may therefore be sharply defined and rigorously studied.

Unstructured dynamic systems present many more difficulties with regard to definition and analysis. We may generalize by saying that as the human element in a dynamic system is increased, the more unstructured the resulting system is. An organizational unit in the business firm, for example, is a very unstructured dynamic system. Its inputs and outputs tend to be variable in nature and may sometimes behave erratically. The operations (processor) are not always performed in a uniform way. The manager (controller) will be able to maintain the system in a stable state only with great difficulty. Unstructured dynamic systems as a result are more difficult to analyze but may offer even greater rewards for the effort expended.

Underlying the behavior of all dynamic systems is the concept of predictability. Given a certain set of input elements, a reliable processor, and a discriminating controller, the output elements should appear in a predictable way. Dynamic systems should exhibit reasonable stability of operation even when environmental conditions fluctuate moderately. The law of cause and effect is presumed to operate in all dynamic systems analysis. The fact that such systems do not always behave in stable, predictable ways is evidence that they are not well structured and contain systemic elements or relations that vary for unknown reasons. Non-uniform behavior of a dynamic system is not a negation of the law of cause and effect, but rather is due to our inability to determine and control all of the significant systemic relations. Moreover, complex dynamic systems may even behave in a counter-intuitive manner because of the complex interrelations among their elements.

INPUTS AND OUTPUTS

To begin our discussion of inputs and outputs, let us define these two terms:

Input(s)—one (or more) elements in a given dynamic system that are consumed or transformed during the operation of a dynamic process, and

Output(s)—one (or more) elements in a given dynamic system that are created by the operation of a dynamic process.

By definition, every dynamic system must have one or more input elements and one or more output elements.

The identification of the individual input and output elements is usually the first step in analyzing a given dynamic system. Ordinarily, they are easily identifiable. The inputs are conspicuous because they are continually consumed and must be replenished or the process will slow down and/or stop. Likewise, the outputs may be readily recognized because they continue to appear and fulfill the purpose for which the system has been developed.

The input and output elements found in dynamic systems may be broadly classified as physical (material) elements, energy elements, or some combination of the two. This observation is based on the knowledge that the entire known universe is composed of matter and energy. The chemical elements in all of their forms and manifold combinations comprise the material inputs for dynamic systems. Not only may chemical composition vary over wide limits, but material form and structure are often just as important as chemical composition in the definition of systemic inputs. Energy inputs may take many different forms also, such as electrical, mechanical, thermal, and kinetic energy. The potential number of combinations of material and energy elements is virtually infinite.

Ideas, thoughts, concepts, and the spark of life are frequently present in dynamic systems but do not usually function as either inputs or outputs. These elements are more logically considered parts of the processor or controller since they do affect the transformation process but are not transformed themselves. An exception to this generalization may be the educational system in which concepts and ideas contained in books and lectures could be considered principal input elements.

Before assuming that a particular element in a dynamic system is an input, its behavior during the transformation process should be closely examined. Under certain conditions particular elements are required in order for transformation to take place, yet these elements do not change their form significantly during the process. A catalyst in a chemical reaction is an example of this phenomenon. It is necessary for the chemical reaction to proceed, but undergoes no apparent transformation itself. Likewise, a computer is a necessary adjunct of an automated data-processing system. Strictly speaking then, neither the catalyst nor the computer are input elements, but are instead parts of the processor.

As mentioned briefly in the preceding chapter, there is no requirement that all inputs or outputs be homogenous. There are examples of dynamic systems in which all the inputs or outputs are very similar in nature. For example, a self-regulating amplifier uses a power input and an amplification channel input, which are simply differing forms of electrical energy. The output of the self-regulating amplifier is a stream of electrical energy of constant magnitude. A more usual case in a dynamic process is that the inputs and the outputs are composed of combinations of matter and energy. For example, a living organism needs food, oxygen, water, and certain minerals. Food and oxygen, in this case, are the sources of energy, and the other inputs are material inputs needed to support the life process.

The definition of outputs given at the beginning of this section does not distinguish between those output elements that are sought through the operation of a dynamic system and those that may be created as by-products in its operation. Both types of outputs appear during the normal operation of many dynamic processes. We have many examples in technology today where the unwanted by-product has turned out to be quite useful and, in some cases, even more valuable than the original product. For example, the meat-packing industry has found uses for all of the by-products of the butchering process. No part of the carcass is simply thrown away. In other cases, the appearance of the by-product element may be a limiting factor in the dynamic process. The heat generated by an electrical motor, for example, in the transformation of electrical energy into mechanical energy imposes a major constraint on the available system output.

Another important concept in considering both inputs and outputs is the presence of input and output queues. Inputs may be entered into the system in batches as, for example, the consumption of meals by human beings, although in reality the digestive process is a more or less continuous affair. We may also note examples in which the input must enter the system in a continuous stream, such as in an electrical power distribution system. The important point to note is that dynamic systems ordinarily require a stream of inputs (either continuous or discrete) over a period of time in order to function properly. This same observation applies to outputs as well. Thus the input and output blocks should not be considered as solitary batches of matter or energy, but rather as flows of matter and energy to and from the dynamic system over a period of time.

One of the most important analytical techniques for the study of dynamic systems behavior is input/output analysis. What type and quantity of inputs are necessary to produce a given output? It is apparent that unless the relations between inputs and outputs can be specified with some precision, we cannot accurately predict the system's behavior. Moreover, the determination of processing efficiency in all dynamic systems is directly based on input/output analysis.

For simpler mechanical/electrical dynamic systems, the law of conservation of matter and energy prescribes a material and energy balance between the inputs and the outputs. For more complex dynamic systems, especially ones in which the human element is present and the inputs and outputs are measured in economic terms, a synergic relation frequently appears. The term *positive synergy* denotes the cooperative effect of two or more inputs to produce outputs of greater effectiveness or economic value than the sum of the inputs. On the other hand, negative synergy may exist in dynamic systems also. Increasing one of the system's inputs without limit eventually results in a reduction in the system's output. The law of diminishing returns is a general statement of this phenomenon. The presence of positive and negative synergic relations complicates, often substantially, the process of input/output analysis.

THE PROCESSOR

In order to establish a basis for a discussion of processors, we shall define this term in the following way:

> Processor—the site or immediate environment in which the dynamic process occurs, including all of the systemic elements (except inputs and outputs) that participate directly in the transformation process.

This definition specifically excludes input and output elements since they are the raw materials and product, respectively, of the transformation process. However, the definition of *processor* does include all of the elements that participate in the transformation process without an appreciable change in their basic natures.

From the definition given above, it follows that the systemic elements that make up the processor are almost entirely physical units or things that exist at specific places and points in time. The individual elements comprising the processor have many different interrelations (spatial, temporal, mechanical, electrical, and chemical, for example) that determine the exact way the processor operates. Restructuring the processor elements, of course, will completely change the system's operating characteristics.

The refrigeration process is an example of a dynamic system in which the role of the processor may be readily examined. The inputs to this system would be food, beverages, and water (for ice) at various temperatures as well as electric current. The output of the dynamic system is cold food, cold beverages, and ice. The processor, in this case, is the refrigerator composed of an electric motor, a compressor, a condenser, tubing, and the refrigerator case. The system elements of the processor are directly involved in the refrigeration process but are not transformed themselves except perhaps by very slow deterioration in their transforming capacity.

The analysis of the component elements of a processor can be a very difficult and baffling task. The determination of all the interrelations and their individual effects on the processor's functional characteristics requires the highly specialized knowledge of experts such as engineers, scientists, or physicians. Clearly, when systemic dysfunctions are present, systems expertise is required to correct the difficulties. We do expect the electronics engineer to know a great deal about electronic circuits, the physician to know about the body and its functions, and the manager to know how his organization operates. The amount of knowledge each of these individuals has is finite and limited by his intellectual capacity. However, individuals in each occupational or professional group may be viewed as systems specialists who use their particular systemic expertise to correct systemic dysfunctions.

For those not intimately involved in the operation of a dynamic system or for occasional users of particular dynamic systems, obtaining the high degree of expertise the specialists have is not possible and, often, not necessary. The user of the dynamic system under these circumstances is simply interested in the processor's overall behavior. Most automobile drivers, for example, are not especially interested in the fine details of internal combustion engine operation. Their approach is pragmatic: their main interest is driving the automobile from one place to another. The good driver, naturally, must be able to recognize when the automobile is not operating properly and get it into the shop for repair.

A particularly pragmatic approach to the analysis of a processor is to consider the processor as a "black box." This concept is drawn from the former practice of painting electronic equipment boxes with black paint for military applications. These boxes had clearly labeled input and output connections as well as operating instructions for their use. The users were not expected to know in any detail how the electronic gear actually worked internally or how to make more than very minor repairs. The black boxes were simply functional units that performed specific operations.

In the black box approach the processor is assumed to be unknowable or irrelevant because the analyst does not have the skill or time to delve into the complex interrelations that determine the functional behavior of the processor. The analyst takes the processor as a given reality and proceeds to observe the relations between it and the other parts of the dynamic system. The processor is thus defined in terms of its behavior.

The operational or behavioristic nature of a processor may be examined from several different viewpoints. First, we may specify the type of behavior that is expected from the processor. In this case processors that meet the desired performance specifications may be "plugged in" to the dynamic system with satisfactory results. If the specifications have been properly prepared, there will frequently be several processors from which to choose; the choice will be dependent on such factors as cost, processing efficiency, and availability. For example, many different computers are available today that could be used to perform a business firm's data-processing operations.

The second approach to the determination of processor behavior is through the use of analogy and similarity. Simulation studies may be used to study the performance of the dynamic system as a whole. As a matter of fact, the simulated behavior of the processor is perhaps the most fundamental part of the simulation model for the entire system. The study and analysis of similar dynamic system processors is a widely used technique for determining expected processor behavior. We expect processors that differ only in terms of scale to behave similarly. Small, medium, and large electric refrigerators cool their contents in much the same way. Most mammals process food to furnish the energy requirements for the body in a similar manner. Hence a knowledge of the elements and the interrelations of one processor may, with care, be extended to other similar dynamic system processors.

The third way we may determine the behavior of a dynamic system processor is by observation and experiment. Varying the input rate and the types of inputs into a system and noting the subsequent changes in its output rate and composition can yield valuable insights into processor behavior. This approach assumes that the transformation process is reproducible and relatively stable. When we have limited knowledge of the behavior of a certain processor, this method may be the best, or only, way to determine its operating behavior. The limitations of time and cost, however, are often constraining factors in the amount of experimentation that may be carried out.

THE CONTROLLER
AND THE FEEDBACK PROCESS

As we have defined the controller, it is the element in a dynamic system that controls the flow of inputs to the processor and establishes the processor's operating mode. In this sense, the controller actually determines the way the system will meet its objectives. We might also describe the function of the controller as providing the rules by which the entire system must operate to achieve predictable output of uniform quality and quantity. Consequently, the ultimate performance of the dynamic system depends to a great extent on the controller's design and operation.

The performance of the controller in a dynamic system is composed of two separate yet interrelated types of activity. First, it acts to regulate the flow of inputs in accordance with predetermined input/output relations to maintain a stable, dynamically balanced system. This function of the controller is directly dependent on the flow of sensory data from the system outputs for its performance. Second, it establishes the processor's overall operating characteristics by structuring the procedures and activities to be used in the transformation process. While we may distinguish these two different types of controller-related activity, the controller itself is only a single, though frequently complex, element in the dynamic system.

The first type of controller activity depends on data from the output of the dynamic system obtained through a sensing process. In this case, the system output attributes are measured by predetermined techniques. The controller then applies corrective action by altering one or more of the input streams to keep the system in balance. The action of the controller may be illustrated by the refrigeration process discussed in the preceding section. In this example the thermostat (controller) contains a bimetal strip that measures the air temperature inside the refrigerator case and closes or opens electrical contacts to start or stop the compressor motor. Thus when the ambient air temperature is above a preset limit, the compressor will be activated. When the lower temperature limit is reached, the bimetal strip will open the electrical contacts; the compressor motor will stop. The internal air temperature of the refrigerator will slowly begin to rise due to heat absorption until the cooling process is repeated. In this way the controller operates directly to regulate the electrical energy input to the refrigerator and to maintain a stable air temperature inside the refrigerator case.

The second type of controller activity, the direct control of the processor, may be illustrated by examining the operation of a computerized data processing system. In this example the computer program is loaded into the memory section of the central processing unit and provides the step-by-step instructions for manipulating the raw data inputs into information outputs. The computer program sets forth the exact operations the processor must perform in detail. Of course, the program must be prepared by an outside source—a programmer—who is seeking to prepare needed information outputs. The point to be emphasized, however, is that the computer program in conjunction with the computer control unit directs the processor's activities.

The thermostat in our refrigerator example also exhibits the second, or indirect, type of controller activity by regulating the operation of the compressor (processor) in the refrigeration system. Setting the thermostat at a particular temperature determines the proportionate amount of time the compressor must operate to maintain the required internal air temperature. Thus the operating ratio (time on/time off) of the processor itself may be controlled by changing the thermostat setting. In effect, the desired output of the refrigerating system is determined by the relative amount of processor activity. Additionally, the activity of the processor may be altered by changing the distance between the thermostat contact points. This action establishes the permissible air temperature range that the processor must maintain by controlling the length of the operating cycle.

Thus the total activity of the thermostat (controller) is directed toward accomplishing the basic objective of the refrigeration process—maintaining a specified internal air temperature—in two different ways. The thermostat directly regulates the input of electric current to the compressor motor and establishes the overall operating conditions for the refrigeration process. Most, if not all, dynamic systems operate with the controller performing the dual functions of input regulation and processor control.

As it is commonly used, the term *feedback* may have several different meanings. Feedback may sometimes refer to the data-gathering process, as in gathering information for managerial use in decision making. The term is more frequently used to denote the direct modification of the input stream by the output stream of the system without direct controller intervention. We shall use the term *feedback* in this latter sense. Diagramatically, feedback may be shown by a solid line connecting the output to the input of the system, as in figure 3-1.

Feedback, as defined above, may have an amplifying or reinforcing effect on systems performance. When the feedback signal has the same sign or direction as the output, it is known

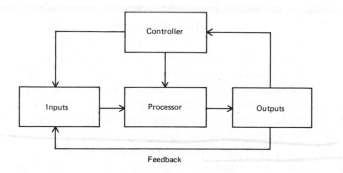

Fig. 3-1   Dynamic system model with feedback

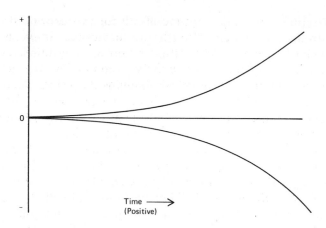

Fig. 3-2 Reinforcing (positive) feedback

as reinforcing feedback. In a public address system a shrill sound occurs when amplified sound from the speakers is picked up on the microphone and processed through the amplifier again and again. In the business world reinforcing feedback exists when advertising expenses are fixed as a percentage of sales volume (total revenue for the preceding time period), which is a frequent business procedure. Thus more advertising leads to greater sales (all else being equal), which, in turn, leads to greater advertising expenditures, and so forth. The continual increase in value of investments earning interest compounded is another example of reinforcing feedback in business.

Reinforcing feedback may also produce negative results by reducing, or throttling, the input stream to progressively diminish system .activity and output. When businesses are not profitable, budgets for new equipment and research and development are necessarily cut to a minimum. As a result, the business firm cannot improve operating efficiency or develop new products, which leads to lessening profitability. Reinforcing feedback in all dynamic systems tends either to increase or decrease the output stream at an ever increasing rate, as shown in figure 3-2.

Reinforcing feedback—either positive or negative—is found in many dynamic systems. To create stable self-regulating system performance, the effects of feedback must be counteracted by introducing compensatory adjustments through the control process. In the unprofitable business example above, manage-

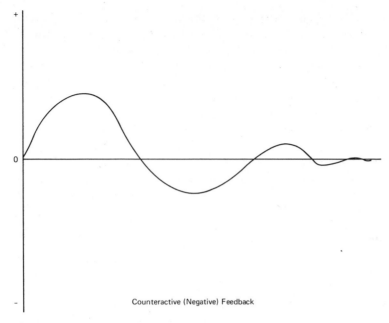

Counteractive (Negative) Feedback

Fig. 3-3   Counteractive (negative) feedback

ment must find additional financing or improve internal operations significantly to correct the situation. The effects of unde-
sirable feedback may be neutralized or even reversed in this way.

A second type of feedback may also be noted in dynamic
systems operation. Counteractive feedback has a sign or direction opposite to the output. The net effect of counteractive
feedback is to correct or reverse tendencies of the output to
deviate from the neutral state. When feedback response time
is relatively fast, counteractive feedback will stabilize output as
shown in figure 3-3. For example, when sales for a product line
begin to decline, management automatically reduces production
activity. If reaction time is fast and management does not over-
react, sales and production levels may soon reach a new equilibrium point.

The control of a dynamic system depends on the functional
quality of the entire control loop. In effect, the individual portions of the control loop—consisting of a data-gathering or
sensory section, the controller, and a system-directing or effecting section—each play an important part in maintaining stable
uniform system outputs.

The quality of the control loop performance depends first of all on the information derived from the systemic outputs. To be effective, the sensory process should accurately measure those attributes of the output stream that are most important in determining the degree of achievement of system objectives or that define the system operating characteristics most exactly. In the refrigeration system example, the attribute of temperature is the most important one in determining how well it is operating. Each dynamic system must be examined individually to determine the attributes that are most important for overall success; suitable measuring techniques must be incorporated into the sensory process to obtain the needed information to submit to the controller.

The frequency of measurement of the systemic output attributes will have an important bearing on the quality of sensory data sent to the controller. The measurement frequency may range from a continuous sampling to sampling plans that involve discrete samples taken over a period of time. Continuous sampling techniques are ordinarily the most desirable types of sampling plans for maintaining system stability. Since the output of the dynamic system is monitored at all times, the variations in systemic output that occur because of systemic malfunctions or feedback phenomena will be quickly detected and corrective action can be taken immediately. The thermostat in our refrigeration system monitors the temperature inside the refrigerator continuously. In this way, the instant a temperature limit is reached, the thermostat reacts to either start or stop the compressor motor. The time lag between sensing and effecting with continuous output monitoring therefore tends to be minimal and the degree of hunting or tracking is correspondingly reduced.

Man-machine systems, however, usually rely on some sort of discontinuous sampling plan. Obviously there are very few individuals who are able to check continuously the output from a machine. Usually the machine's output is checked on a relatively random basis as operators find the necessary time. Although this approach may be quite satisfactory for many man-machine systems, there are times when the systemic output is not checked often enough to assure adequate control. To overcome this difficulty, a sampling process in which samples of the systemic output are taken at frequent and uniform time intervals may be used. This approach overcomes the difficulty of operator non-attention and permits a more scientific evaluation of the systemic output. Process control charts, for example, use samples taken at uniform time intervals to maintain control over production processes.

The design of the controller must incorporate knowledge of system behavior based on the cause and effect relation for effective control loop operation: certain combinations of inputs must produce certain types of outputs. We have previously postulated that cause and effect relations underlie all the input/output relations in determining dynamic systems performance. In the refrigeration system example, the operation of the controller is based on the knowledge that operation of the compressor will decrease the internal air temperature. Since the basic cause and effect relation is well known, the thermostat used the input/output relation of electric current/cool air as the means for maintaining a uniform air temperature.

In more complex dynamic systems that involve human beings, the input/output relations forming the basis for adequate systems control are frequently very difficult to determine and are subject to many extraneous influences. This is due to the fact that a single measured effect (output attribute) may be due to several different causes. Diagnosis of the cause(s) for the complex system malfunction therefore requires that several different system attributes be measured before corrective action can be taken. For example, a physician must check a number of physiological attributes such as body temperature, pulse, and respiration rate before he can determine the nature of the illness. The multitude of attributes that reflect complex systemic behavior creates measurement difficulties and vastly complicates the design of the controller.

The final portion of the control loop is concerned with the actual control of the inputs. In some relatively simple dynamic systems the input stream may be regulated directly as a valve that may be open, partially closed, or completely closed. Its function is to regulate the flow of the input stream into the dynamic system. There is little difficulty in determining the proper valve adjustment when only a single input stream must be modified. However, severe input adjustment difficulties arise when multiple input streams must be controlled. Likewise, difficulties are encountered when the stream of inputs is discontinuous. In this case the controller may call for a given input that may not be available at that time, thereby introducing a time lag into the system and promoting overcorrection.

The entire control loop plays a critical part in the self-regulation of dynamic systems. If the control loop for the regulation of the inputs operates both directly and immediately, the system is called a *closed-loop system.* That is, the system is directly self-regulating and usually has a low response time to effect the input change. In closed-loop dynamic systems, changes in output or disturbances of any sort are immediately translated into directions for the input stream to change in order to regain a dynamically balanced condition. The degree of stability in closed loop systems is therefore normally high and correction time is usually minimal.

On the other hand, we may note other dynamic systems, especially those in which human beings act as the controller, where the control process is much less positive or almost completely absent. Dynamic systems of this type are called *open-loop systems.* The time between a change in system output and corrective input action may well be quite appreciable, leading to very unstable system operation. Overcorrection to compensate for the time differential frequently occurs in the modification of the input stream. Under these circumstances the system lacks a substantial degree of self-regulating capacity and its overall stability is significantly diminished.

The distinction between an open and a closed loop system is relative. A completely closed loop system would have an instantaneous response time and would be completely stable in its performance. Certain electronic systems approach such an ideal condition. In contrast, a completely open loop system would not use a control loop and would therefore not qualify as a dynamic system. In general, dynamic systems that use electrical or mechanical feedback tend to behave more as closed loop systems, while those that use human beings as the controller tend to behave more as open loop systems. To overcome the tendency of man-controlled dynamic systems to behave as open loop systems, systems designers must use every available means to modify control loop behavior to approach the performance standards of closed-loop systems.

The terms *open* and *closed systems* are often found in systems literature; they denote the degree of interaction between a given system and its environment. An open system receives and uses sensory data from extra-systemic sources exclusively in the control process. For example, a business firm that manufactures goods only on a customer order basis operates as an open system. A closed system, strictly speaking, does not use sensory data that originates outside itself in the control process. The refrigerator is an example of a closed system. Certain large-scale industrial operations, such as mining and petroleum refining, in which start-up and shut-down costs are very high, also tend to behave as closed systems.

In reality the operation of every system will to some degree be influenced by environmental conditions. Dynamic systems, however, must contain a direct or indirect output sensing device to provide a measure of system operating stability. Business-related dynamic systems usually contain the behavioral characteristics of both open and closed systems.

COMPOUND SYSTEMS

The preceding discussion has centered around the dynamic system as a single integral unit. In essence, this approach has considered the dynamic system as having sharply defined inputs, a processor, outputs, and a controller. This view may be applied to many simple dynamic systems. There are many others, however, for which this simplistic approach is inadequate. These systems may be called *compound systems* since they are composed of two or more distinct subsystems that operate together through the action of a unified controller. In other words, the processor, or black box, is subdivided into two or more separate units that must function together to achieve the objectives of the total dynamic system.

Although there are many examples of this phenomenon, they may not be recognized as compound systems. For example, the motive portion of an automobile, from a dynamic systems viewpoint, is an example of two separate subsystems acting in series under a unified controller. The automobile engine constitutes the first portion of the dynamic system. The engine, of course, is under the direct control of the driver, who maintains a desired level of performance by regulating the flow of gasoline to the carburetor. The second portion of the dynamic system consists of the clutch, the transmission, the drive shaft, and the rear-end assembly. This subsystem uses the mechanical energy the engine generates to drive the rear wheels. The driver may exercise control over the drive system through the clutch mechanism and the operation of the transmission as well as by regulating the engine speed. The output of the entire system

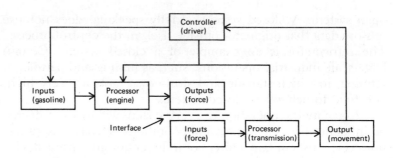

Fig. 3-4 The automobile as a compound system

is transportation for the driver and the riders in the car.

In the automobile example, the two processors acted in series with each other as shown in figure 3-4. That is, the output of the first subsystem became the input to the second. Although this example had only two subsystems operating together, more complex systems may have any number of processors operating in series. Interlinking data-processing systems in large computer operations often use the output of one information system as input to a second one and the output of the second one as input to a third, and so forth. In this way basic data that was input into the first information system may be found in subsequent systems. For example, purchase requisition data may be entered into a purchasing information system and one of the outputs— purchase orders placed—may become an input to the material receiving information system. Open orders received, which would be an output from the material receiving information system, would be introduced as one of the inputs into the accounts payable information system to generate voucher listings. The approved voucher listings could thereupon go to the check-writing system to prepare checks for payment of the materials. In this example we have followed a stream of data actually being transferred from one system to another on four separate occasions.

There is also another means of combining separate dynamic systems. When two dynamic systems operate independently of each other and their outputs are combined to furnish the inputs to another system, the first two subsystems are operating in parallel as shown in figure 3-5. There is no requirement that the outputs of the two parallel subsystems be similar. For the total system to be considered truly dynamic all three of the

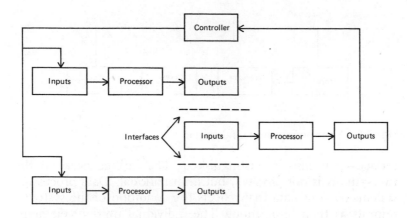

Fig. 3-5   Two subsystems operating in parallel

subsystems would have to be under the control of a single controller regulating the flow of inputs into each of the parallel subsystems and maintaining the proper balance between the inputs into the third subsystem. An example of parallel system operation may be found in electrical power generating and distribution systems. Electric power may be generated by falling water, fossil fuel, or nuclear energy generating plants. In any given electrical generating and distribution system any combination of these three power sources is feasible, depending on the physical facilities available. In this case, the output of the three types of parallel subsystems is homogenous and may be introduced into the power distribution subsystem without difficulty. Of course, the entire power and distribution system must be under the guidance of a complex control unit manned by human beings.

A special situation may be noted in compound systems in the area where two subsystems meet. The direct interface, as it is known, is the point where the output of one system becomes the input to a second system. This condition is explicitly noted in figures 3-4 and 3-5 where both output and input blocks are shown at the interface. The systems model may show the input/output interface implicitly, as in figure 3-6 where neither the outputs nor the inputs are specifically noted at the interfaces. Whenever two or more subsystems are joined there must be an interface between each.

A second type of systemic interface—the information in-

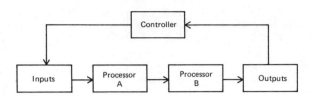

Fig. 3-6   Series-type compound system

terface—may also be distinguished. The linkage between the two systems is not physical, but informational. Data-processing systems use raw data that reflects the condition of the systemic outputs as their basic input. The individual units or elements in the system output, of course, will not be altered in any way by the measurement and reporting process. Yet the content of the information system mirrors the output of the dynamic one. As might be expected, information interfaces are most commonly found in control loop subsystems.

In order for several subsystems to operate together as a unit, the central controller must measure certain output attributes of each subsystem and use this information to regulate the flow of inputs into each. For effective operation of the entire dynamic system, the central controller must direct the flow of inputs throughout the entire system, although the individual subsystem control loops may continue to function. Thus control loops may be found for individual subsystems or combinations of them, in addition to the entire dynamic system. Naturally, as the number of feedback loops and the number of processing subsystems increase, the greater will be the difficulty in providing adequate control for the entire system. A model of a simple compound dynamic system is shown in figure 3-7, illustrating the control loop difficulties encountered with compound dynamic systems.

The practical difficulties encountered in exercising control over compound dynamic systems may be understood better by considering the control difficulties an automobile driver faces. He determines the behavioral condition of the engine by listening to it and observing the temperature gauge, the oil pressure gauge, and the ammeter. Because the drive system structure is simpler, its condition is determined by sound and "feel." As most new drivers will agree, learning to coordinate the engine speed, clutching, and shifting is difficult. The expert driver must

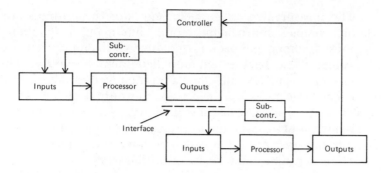

Fig. 3-7   Simple compound dynamic system

coordinate these activities as well as steer the car (steering sub-system) and apply the brakes (braking subsystem) to provide a safe and reasonably speedy trip under all sorts of driving conditions.

SYSTEMS EFFICIENCY AND EFFECTIVENESS

Dynamic systems involve transformation processes in which input elements are changed by an ongoing process into output elements. The system may be said to be efficient when the transformation process produces a minimal quantity of unde-sirable side-effects and takes place in a reasonably expeditious way.

More specifically, the efficiency of a systemic transforma-tion process may be expressed as a value computed by the ratio of input and output elements. In a physical transformation process this ratio may be expressed as

$$\frac{\text{Output}}{\text{Input}} = \text{Process efficiency}$$

Physical processes in which matter and energy are transformed may never have a value greater than 1, according to the law of conservation of matter and energy.

Efficiency ratios based on measures of physical units are quite common in business. Foundry and metal-working opera-tions, for example, use the metal efficiency ratio (pounds out-put/pounds input) as a measure of their manufacturing process efficiency. In this case a single element (pounds of metal) is transformed from a raw material to a finished product and the efficiency of the production process is imputed from this ratio.

The measurement of cost efficiency for the business firm is more complex and demands some simplifying assumptions. The most common approach is to reduce all the input elements to a single value by the common denominator money. The various input elements, including a reasonable return on investment, can be expressed as expenses; the output elements can be stated as gross sales or total revenues. The profit and loss statement most corporations prepare as a routine report presents total revenues and expenses for a given time period. The resulting values may be stated in the form

$$\frac{\text{Total revenues}}{\text{Total expenses + Profit}} \times 100 = \text{Financial operating efficiency}$$

A firm's financial operating efficiency may easily be computed once a mutually agreed-on profit value is substituted. Note that the value of 1.0 indicates that the operation is breaking even. The cost efficiency of the firm is deemed to be greater as the output/input ratio becomes larger.

The analysis of systems efficiency may sometimes be made more meaningful by measuring systems efficiency relative to a standard. Providing a guideline or yardstick for comparison introduces another element into the evaluation procedure, which makes the process more subjective. However, this criticism may be offset by providing a more understandable basis for efficiency evaluation. Such relative efficiency measures as

$$\frac{\text{Incurred costs (labor, materials, etc.)}}{\text{Standard costs}} \times 100 = \text{Relative production cost efficiency}$$

or

$$\frac{\text{Actual units produced}}{\text{Scheduled units of production}} \times 100 = \text{Relative production time efficiency}$$

may very well give a more accurate or realistic evaluation of efficiency.

The performance standards for determining systems efficiency may originate in several different ways. Many business managers establish goals and objectives in their operation plans that become, in effect, operating standards for the business system. Standards may also be developed through the use of accumulated (historical) information about systems performance. The accuracy and reliability of historical data varies, naturally, according to the reliability of data sources; it ranges from individual recollections to complete detailed records. Certain types

of systemic standards may also be developed by scientif-
ically-based standardized techniques, such as time and motion
standards or material yield standards. Systems efficiency may
also be evaluated by comparing the performance of one system
with another that has similar characteristics, as in the use of
industry averages.

In both the definition of the term *systems* and in the discussion of natural versus man-made systems the point has been
emphasized that purpose is present in virtually every system.
Man-created systems are simply organized means for achieving
specific ends. The measure of a system's effectiveness is directly
related to the degree to which the specific ends of the system
are being met. Unlike systems efficiency, which focuses on a
system's internal relations and operation, systems effectiveness
seeks to measure the external relations of a given system to the
other systems in which it is an elemental part.

The determination of systems effectiveness may be begun
with an explicit statement of all the goals and objectives for a
specific system, listed in descending order of importance, and
quantified wherever possible. Next, data about the system's performance over a period of time, in terms of actual results, with
regard to each of the stated goals and objectives must be developed. Finally, the actual performance must be divided by each
objective's potential performance to determine how effective the
system really is. The formula for the determination of systems
effectiveness is given by the following equation:

$$\frac{\text{Actual systems performance}}{\text{Potential systems performance}} = \text{Systems effectiveness}$$

The measurement of systems effectiveness for the business
firm may be in dollar terms for evaluation purposes. The first
step is to measure the total value of the system's outputs, which
will ordinarily be equated with the firm's total revenues. Next,
the potential revenue-generating capacity of the firm, based on
the constraints imposed by personnel limitations, capital requirements, raw materials availability, and production capacity,
should be estimated. The systems effectiveness may then be determined according to the following formula:

$$\frac{\text{Total revenues}}{\text{Potential revenues (at full capacity)}} = \text{Systems effectiveness}$$

Cost-benefit analysis is a special application of systems effectiveness evaluation. This type of analysis seeks to relate the

expected results of a projected program to its cost. Thus programs that measure benefits in the same terms may be compared to determine their. effectiveness relative to each other. The benefits are often computed in monetary values in order to assess more accurately the total impact of programs in which several types of benefits may be realized. Where the cost flow and the monetary benefit flow differ significantly over a period of time, discounting may be introduced to get the present values of program costs and benefits.

The verb *to satisfice* may be appropriately introduced into the discussion of systems effectiveness. This term may be defined as the satisfaction or fulfillment of needs, desires, or objectives only up to the point where there is insufficient motivation to expend further resources to achieve greater satisfaction. Many man-made systems perform in a satisficing rather than an optimal manner with respect to some of the systemic goals and objectives. As a result of the satisficing phenomenon, business firms do not often achieve the full measure of effectiveness in the pursuit of all of their objectives.

Thus the two concepts of efficiency and effectiveness are separate and distinct. The efficiency of a system provides no clue about the potential revenues that may be available from the system's operation. In like manner, a system's effectiveness bears no necessary relationship to the cost of operating it. Together, however, these two measures provide a means for evaluating total systems performance.

SYSTEM LIFE STAGES AND ENTROPY

Dynamic systems, perhaps due to their life-like character, exhibit various developmental stages from the time they first come into existence until they cease to operate. These are shown in figure 3-8.

The first stage, birth, represents the beginning of dynamic systems operation. Although the precise beginnings are frequently difficult to establish, nevertheless we recognize intuitively that all biological systems, all man-machine systems, and all electrical and mechanical dynamic systems must have had a beginning. We may define the systems birth period as beginning at that point in time when the separate existence of a particular dynamic system is recognized and continuing until it begins to operate on its own. Although this period cannot be

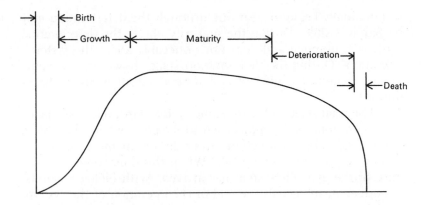

Fig. 3-8   Developmental stages of a dynamic system

precisely defined, it does provide a workable basis for determining the genesis of an individual dynamic system.

The second stage in systems development is identified as the growth, or development, stage. During this period the dynamic system begins to operate, producing outputs of the desired type and expanding operation up to its optimal level. For biological systems, the growth stage represents the period in which the individual organism is reaching maturity. For electrical and mechanical systems or man-machine systems, the growth process is more difficult to identify. A new piece of equipment may operate at a very high level of efficiency almost from the moment it is put into operation. Under normal circumstances, however, these dynamic systems must undergo a debugging period in which minor difficulties in equipment operation are resolved and the machine operators learn their jobs.

The third stage of the system life cycle is known as the maturity stage. During this time the system processes inputs into outputs at or near rated capacity. The overall efficiency will be well within design limits. In effect, it is during this stage that the system is truly fulfilling the purposes or objectives for which it was created.

Deterioration is the next stage in the cycle. After the system achieves the optimal level of output as determined by the initial design, it will begin a slow inexorable period of gradual declining activity. In the case of biological units, we call this process aging. With other dynamic systems, the machines themselves will gradually begin to wear out although the deterioration may be barely visible. During the maturity stage, the deterioration process is minimal and does not noticeably affect the system's operation. During the deterioration stage, however, the aging process becomes significant and system output is markedly reduced.

The final stage in the dynamic system life cycle takes place when deterioration has proceeded to the point where the system is no longer able to function physically or, in the case of machines, to operate economically. When this time comes, the demise of the dynamic system has arrived. With biological units, of course, death signals the end of the operation of the system. In the case of man-machine systems, however, repairs or other regenerative activities may coax the system back to a state of activity.

Note in figure 3-8 that the transition from one stage to another is indistinct and somewhat arbitrary. This occurs because the stages tend to merge into each other gradually. Under most circumstances attempting to make sharp distinctions between them will add little to our analysis of systems operation.

The second law of thermodynamics states that the unavailable energy within a given thermodynamic system tends to increase over time. This law was initially developed to study steam engine operation. The measure of unavailable energy, entropy, tends to increase in the steam engine's thermodynamic system because of heat losses from the engine to the atmosphere. The net result of increasing systemic entropy is to reduce the system's overall operating effectiveness. From our discussion of system maturity and deterioration above, the relation between increasing system entropy and systemic deterioration may be readily seen. A decrease in dynamic systems effectiveness does tend to occur over a period of time because of an increase in entropy.

To combat the increase in entropy for a given thermodynamic system, several options are available. The first calls for creating a higher level of input. Thus using more fuel will result both in higher energy levels within the system and in more available energy to produce mechanical work. With regard to biological systems, it is generally recognized that an athlete must consume a much greater quantity of food than a sedentary individual; the additional energy is required to sustain his substantially higher level of activity.

A second approach for reducing increasing entropy is the use of systemic operating adjustments. In the steam engine example, we may be able to change some valve settings or other parts of the thermodynamic system while the system is operating and thereby increase the mechanical energy output. The same process may be also observed with biological units such as man. The adage, "Work smarter, not harder," is excellent advice for the conservation of human energy.

Still another approach to reduce increasing entropy is to repair and maintain the dynamic system. To keep our steam engine operating efficiently, we must apply grease at the points of wear on a more or less continuous basis. The steam engine may also be shut down for overhaul. In our human example, medicines and drugs may be used to combat disease and other infirmities; surgery may even be necessary to correct very serious bodily dysfunctions.

Finally, the decline in system effectiveness may be stopped or slowed down by using certain regenerative techniques. The steam engine may be designed to exhaust steam over the water input lines to provide boiler feed water near the boiling point. In this case the waste heat from the exhaust is used to improve the quality of an input. We may use this same analogy for human beings by noting man's ability to learn from his mistakes and thereby modify his inputs to correct these errors. When an individual finds a food that does not agree with him, he will probably not knowingly eat it again.

In our following discussions of dynamic systems we will come across the concept of increasing entropy in many different shapes and guises. Increasing energy losses, decreasing systemic efficiency, and declining system output are difficulties the system designer and operator face continually. To a great extent, the effectiveness of system design is related directly to minimizing dynamic systems entropy.

4

SYSTEMS THEORY IN BUSINESS

Theory for the sake of theory is an interesting and perhaps satisfying activity for some individuals. Business students, on the whole, need a more pragmatic approach in which theory is related to the business world. Up to this point our discussion has centered around the development of the theoretical base for dynamic systems operations. In attempting to define and describe the many different aspects of dynamic systems, the application of systems theory and analysis to business examples has not been especially emphasized. If the theory that we have been discussing is valid, then its application to business-related examples should provide some insights into the operations of our free enterprise economy, business firms, organizational units, and managers.

Placing business activities in a systems context provides a convenient and readily comprehensible basis on which to examine and analyze business operations. The systems approach forces objectives and goals to become crystallized, component parts (elements) to be specified, and systemic relationships to be determined. Once the basic systemic analysis has been completed, systems modifications may be investigated to improve the efficiency and/or the effectiveness of the system. In this way business operations may be continually examined and refined to yield more successful enterprises.

In some of the following business-related systems applications, certain insights that can be discerned through the application of systems theory are already common knowledge to many management scholars. The fact that executives have recognized many of these relations and use this knowledge to make business decisions does not invalidate the systems theory approach. Rather, it emphasizes the common base of knowledge about business-related activities that may be recognized through the use of systems theory or through intuitive experiential insights.

THE MARKET SYSTEM

The free market system, as discussed in economic theory, emerged through a slow evolutionary process that grew out of feudalism. As a result of the new socioeconomic organization of society that appeared in the Middle Ages, several new institutions arose. One of these—the market system—became the most pragmatic means for the satisfaction of three basic economic questions: What will be produced? Who will produce it? Who will receive what is produced? In its present modified form, the market system continues to provide generally satisfactory answers to these basic questions. On the whole, it has provided the western world with the most convenient and efficient known means for the transfer of goods and services from producers to consumers.

Since the economic wants of man are insistent, recurring, and endless, the flow of economic goods from their sources to their destinations is a fundamental social activity. Consequently, the basic objective of the market system is to supply goods and services to individuals and organizations when and where they are needed. This sense of purpose in the market system arises directly from the desire of the producers to sell as well as that of the consumers to buy.

The field of economics uses many different schematic models to describe the different relations found in economic activity. Some of these familiar schematic models are the supply and demand curves relating price and quantity, total utility as a function of quantity (demonstrating the law of diminishing returns), and the Keynesian gross national product model. These static schematic models describe relations between certain attributes of the market system to present complex ideas in a readily comprehensible form. There are also economic models that attempt to show economic flows such as the money flow model

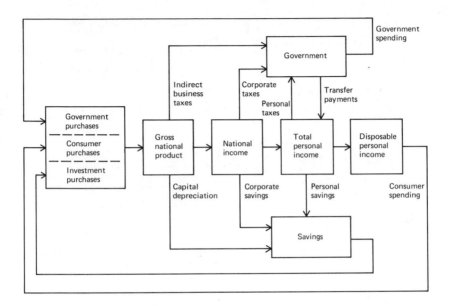

Fig. 4-1   The money flow model

shown in figure 4-1, which describes the origin, the economic accounts, and destinations of the value flows in our economy.

The market system may also be described as a dynamic system as shown in the model in figure 4-2. The left-hand block in the model represents the total aggregation of all business enterprises, which may range in diversity from agricultural units to small proprietorships to the large corporations employing thousands of workers, that operate in our economy during a particular time period. The outputs are shown at the right-hand side of the diagram and represent the destinations for the flow of goods or consumers. The processor block may be described, for the moment, as "the marketplace." The traders—both buyers and sellers—serve to regulate the flow of goods from producers to consumers through the action of price.

The economic production units, or inputs, create the goods

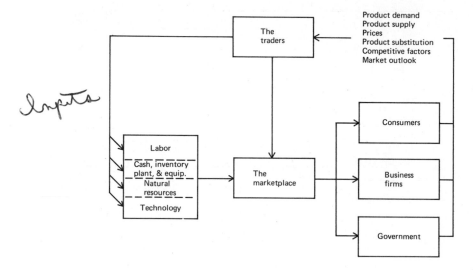

Inputs

Fig. 4-2   The market system as a dynamic system

and services that our society needs to function satisfactorily. We may classify these economic production units in several different ways. The legal form of organization may be the proprietorship, the partnership, or the corporation. Size of the organization is another appropriate classification scheme. Organization size may, of course, be measured in several different ways such as the total assets of the organization, the number of employees, the total value of sales or revenue, and the net worth of the business unit. We may also differentiate among economic production units by type of output: basic materials, semi-finished goods, supplies, consumer goods, services, or combinations of economic goods and services. Finally, we may also classify the economic production unit by customer type or geographic location. The classification scheme is not important in our analysis so long as we recall that business units may assume an almost infinite number of combinations of legal form, size (by several different measures), type of output produced, type of customer, and geographic location.

Each economic production unit must use a combination of supply factors to produce economic goods and services. The different supply factors are shown in the input block separated by broken lines. People, of course, must supply the energy or activity needed to create economic goods and services. Capital must be invested in the enterprise to purchase tools, equipment, and supplies; raw materials in the form of natural resources are needed by many manufacturing firms. Technology represents the accumulation of knowledge that is necessary to produce goods and services efficiently.

With reference to figure 4-2, we may note some peculiar circumstances that have been of substantial interest to economists in analyzing the market system. The situation in which we have only a single supplier of a particular good and/or service is known as a monopoly. When a small number of suppliers are the only source for a particular good and/or service we have an oligopoly. Monopolistic competition exists when we have several producers or sellers who provide similar goods and/or services. Pure competition is the opposite extreme from monopoly and occurs when we have many sellers of essentially undifferentiated products.

On the other hand, we may note certain markets in which there is only a single purchaser for a specific good and/or service. This condition is known as a monopsony. There are other examples in which only a few purchasers may exist.

Finally, we have the situation in which there are many purchasers. One of the principal activities in the field of economics is the study of the relations between buyers and sellers as a function of both the number of sellers and the number of buyers.

The control function is exercised by a group of individuals collectively known as "the traders." These individuals are owners and managers—representatives of the economic production units (sales personnel)—and the representatives of government, business, and the consumers who ultimately purchase economic goods and services. This amorphous group of individuals is in a constant state of flux. New buyers and sellers continually enter into the trading activity while others leave the marketplace. The roles of the traders are not fixed; buyers often become sellers and vice versa. Buyers and sellers may from time to time temporarily retire from trading activity by simply choosing not to trade. To all appearances the trading operation seems so disorganized and chaotic that the market system could scarcely function. Yet the symbiotic relationship between buyers and sellers is strong enough to overcome trade barriers most of the time.

The control loop in the market system depends on many bits and pieces of market information from diverse sources. Some of the information is readily available in trade journals, newspapers, promotional material, and information services. On the other hand, a substantial portion of more or less private knowledge about trade activities must be gained largely through exposure to the market system. The traders, collectively, use information about product demand, product supply, product substitution, competitive factors, and market outlook to establish the going prices for the various economic goods and services. The pricing mechanism is the primary means for implementing market system operation.

The overall operating efficiency of the market system depends on the flow of information from the producers to the consumers and vice versa. When the flow is restricted, there are opportunities for systemic dislocations. The producers, in this case, will be selling their goods and services to very unsophisticated buyers. In like manner, consumers may purchase goods and services from individuals who are unaware of their value. In either case, the market system is not functioning in the most efficient way possible.

The cost efficiency of the market system may be best evaluated by comparing it with alternative product-service distribution systems. Both socialism and communism generally require greater quantities of inputs to achieve the same levels of outputs as the free enterprise system. This is due in part to the substitution of bureaucracies for traders, which tends to be relatively inefficient because of the number of individuals associated with the decision-making processes. All too often, these individuals are more constrained in their activities than the enterprise managers in the market system. There is, perhaps, less personal interest in their managerial activities; they are not held directly accountable for the performance of their organizations; nor does the possibility of personal gain enter into the quality and timeliness of their decisions. There is, moreover, the ever-present possibility of graft, bribery, or other forms of malfeasance. For these reasons most businessmen and economists in the western world feel that the market system is, relatively, the most cost-efficient distribution system known.

Market system efficiency as a function of time also appears to be weighted in favor of the free enterprise system. Emergencies, unforeseen needs, and desires of the moment are always present in homocentric systems. If these needs must await satisfaction because of a time-consuming communication process between buyer and producer, then the distribution system will be slow. Most managers learn early in their careers that the quickest way to accomplish a particular task is to go directly to the individuals who perform the service or produce the economic goods. Busy executives' widespread use of the telephone amply demonstrates the reality of this observation.

If the market system may be faulted on any count, its effectiveness in satisfying the basic needs of the entire population will be the most probable cause. Both the money exchange system and the barter exchange system primarily emphasize the exchange of some object of value for economic goods and/or services. In contrast, a true communistic system attempts to equate the provision of goods and/or services to the individual's need for them. The contrast between these two approaches is quite substantial. In the former, a ready-made objective basis for goods and services exchange is present; in the latter, the basis for the exchange of goods and services may be largely subjective. In the case of objective criteria the decision is quite simple and straightforward—"If you have the money, you can purchase." When the decision must be based on subjective criteria, the whole process becomes disorganized and extremely difficult to administer. In recent years we have, of course, had a constantly increasing incursion of government into the mechanics of the market system. Welfare payments, for example, are designed to provide certain benefits to consumers who lack the financial means to purchase economic goods and services. In this way the basic operation of the market system remains intact, but its actual practice is more compatible with our expressed social objectives.

Earlier, we described the processor as the marketplace. As a first approximation this description is adequate. When economic goods are produced they must be distributed or transferred to the consumer. The processor's role in the market system is that of a pipeline. Goods are produced at one point in time and at one geographic location. The distribution process may require the producer and/or intermediaries to store the finished product, to physically transport it to one or more intermediate distribution points, and, finally, to transport it to the consuming unit. Accompanying the distribution process, a reverse flow of monetary value for payment of the goods or services takes place. Although there are many variations in the processor, the marketplace remains the activity center of the market system.

THE BUSINESS FIRM

On reflection, the business firm has the principal requisites to be classified as a dynamic system. It is composed of many separate parts or elements. Organizational units made up of individuals are one type of element; raw materials to be converted into economic goods are others. Plants, warehouses, retail outlets, and offices—each with its associated equipment—are also elements in the system. There are certainly unique relations among these elements that give each business its own special character. There is, moreover, a sense of purpose—a reason for being—present in each firm. Finally, each displays dynamic life-like qualities in its operation.

The business firm can be portrayed as a dynamic system with the block system model shown in figure 4-3. The three primary inputs—personnel, raw materials, and energy—are shown at the left-hand side of the diagram.

Money is also shown as a separate block on the left-hand side of the figure. It is not considered as an input *per se* because its real nature is economic value. While it may exist in many forms—that is, as cash, bank deposits, negotiable securities, accounts receivable, buildings, and equipment—the elemental substance, economic value, does not change and is not used up directly in the production of goods and services. Money should therefore more properly be considered as part of the processor.

The central block, or processor, is the immediate environment of the production/operation process. It includes the physical facilities as well as the available equipment—all the economic and technologic resources at the firm's disposal. The processor includes everything the firm uses to conduct business.

On the right-hand side of figure 4-3 is a block that represents the collective economic goods and services. This stream of

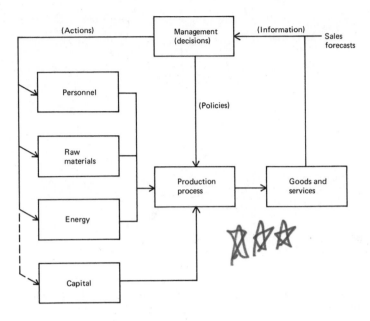

Fig. 4-3 The business firm as a dynamic system

outputs is the principal reason for the business' existence. The firm may, of course, produce other by-product types of outputs. Social benefits, community services and, on the negative side, pollution and ecological damage may also be viewed as outputs from some businesses.

The management of the firm acts as the controller in a dynamic system. In this role the manager should know what he wants the system—the business firm—to accomplish, especially with regard to the output of economic goods and services. These objectives or goals must be determined prior to the operating cycle. Secondly, the manager must assemble the proper inputs in the right amounts to achieve those objectives and goals. Finally, he must establish means (communication channels) to determine whether they are being adequately met.

In an ongoing firm, sales reports, forecasts, market research reports, and customer inquiries provide the manager with information about current marketing activities and give him insights for the development of new or revised products and services. This type of communication activity is analogous to the sensory portion of the control loop. The actual management information

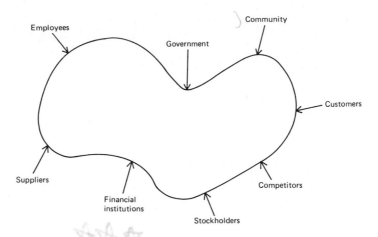

Fig. 4-4   External forces that influence a business firm

the sensors supply must next be compared to existing objectives, plans, and capabilities to determine whether corrective action is necessary. The management of the business firm performs this decision-making process.

If corrective action is required, managers have two basic options. They may directly regulate inputs by hiring or laying off personnel, by changing the quantity and/or quality of the raw materials purchased, or by changing the source or type of energy used in the process. Secondly, the manager may change the mode of processor behavior. Purchasing new equipment, changing the plant layout, or, perhaps most important, changing the policies and guidelines that affect the interpersonal relations between management and the workers.

The enterprise managers are the individuals who specify the purpose(s) for which the business firm was created and continues to function. The firm, however, is not an insulated, self-contained entity. It is a single element in the market system and exists only by fulfilling all of its obligations. The various external forces that influence its behavior are shown diagramatically in figure 4-4.

The owners or stockholders are the risk takers in any business venture. They supply the initial capital to finance the firm and are entitled to compensation for their invested funds. Further, the shareholders exercise their rights of ownership in the corporation by electing the board of directors, which, in turn, exercises fiduciary accountability for the firm's operation. In this way the rights of ownership are exercised at the highest level in the organization.

The firm's customers are an extremely important force that acts on it. The needs, wants, and desires of customers are the real reason why businesses exist. Only with satisfied customers will a good work force, modern facilities, and adequate financing produce a successful enterprise. Consequently, customer satisfaction must be an overriding objective of management.

The influence of the other forces of the firm are important also. The selection of employees will determine the degree of vitality in the work force. Managerial practices, of course, will also influence this input. In return, the business firm must perform certain obligations to its employees, such as pay wages and salaries promptly and provide certain employee benefits and reasonably good working conditions.

The suppliers of raw materials, semi-finished goods, and operating supplies also interface with the firm. The acquired goods and services must be paid for in a reasonably expeditious manner and often cooperative efforts may be required to resolve mutual product difficulties.

The corporate form of business enterprise has been given special rights and privileges in accordance with our legal and governmental system. In accepting these privileges, certain obligations are also incurred. The payment of taxes and the observance of laws, for example, are obligations businesses must accept. Most firms also recognize a general obligation to the community to be a good corporate citizen.

Financial institutions may exert special requirements on a business. Since most firms need to borrow funds from time to time, observing good financial practices is quite necessary. Long-term indebtedness especially makes use of restrictive covenants in loan agreements.

Finally, the actions of competitors play a major role in determining a business' actions. Many industries have associations of member firms who work together to establish product specifications, put on trade shows, and sponsor institutional advertising. These efforts establish a general climate for the whole industry and thus perform a valuable function.

The foregoing external influences on the business firm are reflected in its objectives and policies. To be successful over the long run the firm must satisfice (satisfy to the point where retributive action will not be taken) each of the external forces. To accomplish this formidable task, the sensory apparatus of management must be attuned to both internal and external information sources.

The efficiency of a business is most readily determined by its profit and loss statement. Given a certain level of operations, the primary focus of managerial activity is profit generation. To the extent that total costs are less than total revenues, profits will be earned. We cannot judge precisely the quality of management by the absolute, or even the relative, profits the firm earns. In a competitive market, however, reasonable profits cannot be earned with an inefficient production/operation process.

THE ORGANIZATIONAL UNIT

The preceding discussion centered on the firm from a macro viewpoint. It is also possible to consider the individual department or organizational unit within the business firm from a microsystems point of view. Although the same sort of model we described in the previous section could also be used to describe the department, perhaps a somewhat different approach might be more instructive here.

Individual departments are created by management to perform specific duties and to carry out certain functions. Ordinarily, management is loath to establish new organizational units without clear-cut pressing needs. The reasons are apparent. Each organizational unit is expected to make a positive contribution to the organization as a whole and contribute to its profit-making potential. To create new units that do not directly support these objectives is to disregard a basic responsibility of management. The basic objective of every organizational unit is therefore to perform one or more functions the organization needs in the most efficient manner possible.

A dynamic systems model of the organizational unit is shown in figure 4-5. The inputs on the left-hand side of the diagram are individual jobs, production orders, customers, business transaction records, or any other conveniently defined work unit. The flow of the work units into the department may be relatively quite uniform and continuous in nature or be grouped together in batches of substantial size. Regardless of method of receipt, the stream concept of input flows will be present.

The processor in this model includes the plant or office,

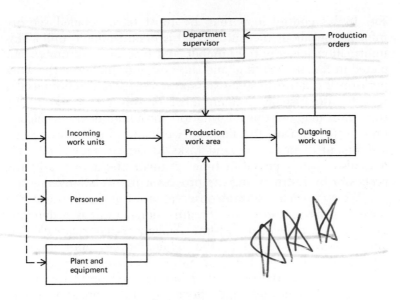

Fig. 4-5   A dynamic system model of the organizational unit

associated equipment, the departmental personnel, and the necessary energy from the utilities. From a departmental manager's
perspective, these items are given realities for the short run. Over
the long run, of course, the composition of the work group will
vary, the work quarters may be renovated, and new equipment
will replace the old. The transformation, or work, process may
exist as a single stage, as a group of stages in series (an assembly
line), as a group of stages operating in parallel with each other
(a sales department in a department store), or in some combination of the above. The almost infinite variety of tasks and task
sequences makes their structuring one of the supervisor's most
important job functions. In many manufacturing operations, the
task structuring (job sequencing) function is given to a separate
organizational unit, the production control department.

The output of the department is a completed or semi-
completed work unit. Due to the specialization of labor, which
is one of the basic reasons for the existence of departments,
it is not unusual to find that the department accomplishes only
a portion of the total task. The output stream from a particular
department must then be directed to other organizational units
for further processing.

The controller in this systems model is the first-line supervisor. In his control loop role, he must have detailed sensory information about the output of his organizational unit. This information includes the number and type of work units completed in the allotted time and the cost and quality of the work performed relative to some standard. Production reports (sales reports also) usually contain most of this information. The supervisor may use this information through a decision-making process to regulate the flow of work unit inputs, as in the assignment of new work unit tasks to certain individuals. He may also, over a period of time, regulate the activities of the processor by restructuring the processor interrelations.

We may make several observations on the basis of the preceding discussion of the organizational unit as a dynamic system. The individual first-line supervisor has relatively few alternatives with regard to the regulation of input flows. It logically follows then, that the major area of supervisory concern will or should be the removal of barriers and obstacles to performing tasks efficiently and effectively. This approach, sometimes known as the prop knocker theory of supervision, assumes that if you take away all the reasons why employees cannot do good work efficiently, then the supervisor should expect good work performed efficiently. There is, of course, a certain amount of wisdom in this theory, but it does overlook other important factors such as work planning, restriction of output by workers, and technological difficulties.

The quality of supervision is usually evaluated on the efficiency and effectiveness of the organizational unit. The underlying assumptions for this procedure are (1) that making good (effective) decisions will promote efficient organizational operations and (2) that making efficient (timely) decisions will promote stable (effective) organizational operation. These assumptions, based on dynamic systems theory, are valid to a large degree, but do not fully take into account the need for relating the quality of supervision to the achievement of organizational objectives.

The open/closed loop concept may be directly applied to the evaluation of managerial efficiency. The most efficient managers actively seek sensory data, make their decisions in a reasonable period of time, and implement them forthrightly. In so doing, the enterprise under the efficient manager behaves more as a closed loop system and enjoys greater operating stability. The business firm with inefficient management may not get all of the available facts, may take an unduly long time making decisions, and may implement them poorly.

The measurement of an organizational unit's or a production/operation system's efficiency may be approached from several different directions. Cost efficiency relates the cost of all the inputs such as labor, materials, supplies, utilities, and overhead expenses to the value of the goods and/or services produced. Inasmuch as input costs are regularly and systematically collected, this aspect of efficiency may be readily determined. Determining output value may be based on revenues or standard cost measures. As a matter of fact, measuring costs that are under the control of the supervisor relative to an organizational budget or cost accounting values is the basis for responsibility accounting systems. The growing use of such systems is due to their effectiveness as a managerial control device.

The second means of evaluating production/operation systems efficiency uses time as the principal criterion. In this case the manager uses time standards to evaluate the performance efficiency of the various organizational activities. Time for performance of activities may be compared to schedules established by higher management or to time standards developed from time and motion studies. In either case the objective is to determine how well the production/operation process is being performed with regard to time. In most business operations this measure of systems efficiency is almost as important as cost efficiency measurement.

Organizational operating efficiency may also be measured on a quantity scale. The number of pounds, gallons, or work units that enter the production/operation system can be compared to the number of pounds, gallons, or work units the organizational unit completes. After comparing the results of this approach with standard quantity-efficiency values, management has a measure of the system performance in processing the basic work units through its operation. This measure of efficiency is not universally used because in certain situations it may be difficult to measure the input and output quantities and because certain types of operations have no work unit losses.

The final means for measuring an organizational unit's operating efficiency uses quality as the principal criterion. In this sense quality has a direct influence not only on the acceptability of the final product but may also have an important influence on the price for which the product and/or service may be sold. Most manufacturing and clerical operations assume a certain number of errors will be made. Since mistakes inevitably cost money because of the additional time and effort spent to correct them, management usually tries to hold these errors to a reasonable level. Comparison of current quality levels to historical quality performance is the usual way the production/operation quality efficiency level is evaluated. Because measuring techniques for quality are often difficult to establish and because quality information is often difficult to collect, using such measures for determining of production/operation system efficiency is not as widespread as other means of evaluating efficiency.

Ideally, the best way to measure the performance efficiency of a production/operation system would be to use all the above measures. The development of management information systems, hopefully, should provide data about as many of these points as possible. As a matter of fact, one of the best measures for the quality of a management information system is how well these efficiency measures are incorporated in the system design.

A SYSTEMS MODEL OF THE MANAGER[1]

The general dynamic systems model, as shown in figure 4-6, may be adapted to the decision-making process executives use in the performance of their managerial functions. The output of the managerial decision-making process is, of course, decisions about the firm's activities. The processor (the central block) is the site where decisions are made—the manager's mind. The inputs are raw data and processed information that flow through the various communication channels. Directing this entire process is the sum of all the attributes of the individual manager.

Several different types of input information give managers the necessary information for making managerial decisions. The first source of information, according to our model in figure 4-6, is the periodic formal report. This report may be defined as one generated at uniform time intervals that contains specified information about the activities over which the manager has authority. This type of report is usually presented in a standardized format and is largely composed of numbers or values. The

---

1. The bulk of this section has been published. See M. J. Alexander, "Managerial Information Channels: A Systems Model," *The Journal of Business Communication,* Summer 1972, pp. 5–11.

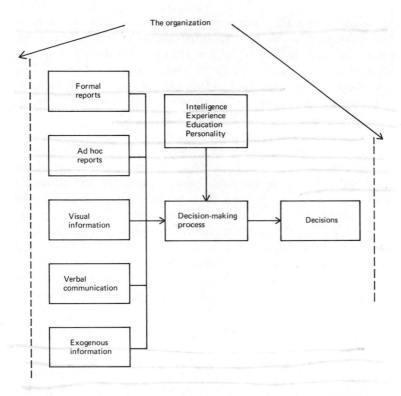

The organization

Formal
reports

Intelligence
Experience
Education
Personality

Ad hoc
reports

Visual
information

Decision-making
process

Decisions

Verbal
communication

Exogenous
information

Fig. 4-6   A dynamic system model of the manager

amount of expository writing is usually limited to column and
row headings or brief explanatory notes. The purpose of periodic formal reports is simply to provide an accurate picture of activities that have taken place in the organizational unit within
a specified time, the status of particular attributes of the organizational system at a particular point in time, or a combination
of these information types. Some familiar examples of this type
of information are balance sheets, profit and loss statements,
open order reports, late shipment reports, stock-out reports, and
employment termination reports. We should also note that
reports of this type are frequently amenable to electronic data
processing.

A second type of information input to the manager may
be termed *ad hoc* information. This category of information is
very broad and encompasses virtually all forms of written com-

munication that the manager receives on an occasional basis. Not infrequently this type of information covers only a single point and may be brief. *Ad hoc* information does not usually attempt to portray the status or describe the activities of an operating system. Examples of this type of information are business letters, written memos, customer inquiries and complaints, credit investigations, and formal study reports.

Visual perception is another source of information for the manager. Nearly every manager likes to spend some portion of his time simply observing the activities taking place in his organizational unit. These personal observations are important for managerial control because they provide direct data (impressions) about the organization's activity rate. The feelings that many executives derive from visiting the work area provide good background information for evaluating how well the organizational plans are being performed. Although personal observations seldom give the manager specific data upon which to base his managerial decisions, the information he gains from personal observation, when combined with verbal information, may be sufficient for making decisions.

The fourth type of managerial information input is verbal communication. Listening is a primary way of receiving information; most executives use this method a significant portion of the time. The circumstances in which the listening process is used in acquiring information range from the more direct approach, such as reports from a subordinate in response to direct questions to the bits and pieces of information received through the grapevine in the form of rumors and gossip. In this connection committees often serve as verbal communications devices in which the manager has the opportunity to hear other managers report on their activities, difficulties, and solutions to their problems. Listening and personal observation usually take place simultaneously and are most effective when performed together. As a matter of fact, about the only time that listening and personal observation are completely separated is during telephone conversations, and this too may well change in the foreseeable future.

The final managerial information input may be termed as exogenous input. This type of input refers to any information the executive receives that comes from sources outside the work environment. Televisions, radio, newspapers, magazines, and other literature are the primary media for such information. Although it does not usually relate directly to managerial decision making, this type of information does provide an enriched background that the manager may use when he makes decisions.

The processor in this system is the site where the internal mental processes are performed to arrive at managerial decisions. The location where this mental activity takes place can only be placed as somewhere in the manager's mind. The nature of the transformation process in which information is converted into decisions is so complex that we do not presently know how it occurs. The existence of the decision-making process is not in doubt, however; it may be readily verified through any manager's personal experiences. Further, the organizational chaos that results when no decisions are made over a period of time amply demonstrates that many decisions must be made in successful business firms.

The primary output of the system is managerial decisions that relate to the basic management functions. Managers must plan; they must organize; they must direct; and they must control the activities in their sphere of authority. However, such functions take place only as a result of many separate decisions made in response to a multitude of questions and problems. Information from all the diverse sources described above must be converted into guiding directions for the business firm to follow. The decision-making process is, then, the focal point for the manager's intellectual activity and the decision is its result.

Many, if not most, dynamic systems use some sort of intelligence or program for guiding their activities. Information, or experiences, about a system's operation must be stored and be available when needed. The processor must be directed to perform logical operations in a predetermined sequence at specified times. The control unit, operating from a program of some description, ordinarily performs the functions of gathering the instructions and data, storing them, and making them available as needed.

The principal attributes of the manager that influence the development of his "program" are intelligence, experience, education, and personality. The first ingredient that determines the nature of the managerial decision-making program is intelligence. Although psychologists are not unanimous in their definition of this term, we may equate it with mental agility. Individuals with quick, keen, perceptive minds are intelligent beings. Tests have long been available to measure this quality.

The relation between decision-making competence and intelligence is not known with a high degree of precision. Most management scholars feel that the potential for quality managerial decision-making is enhanced as the intelligence of the manager increases. This belief is apparently based on the assumption that the more agile and fertile minds can perceive and understand relations more quickly, can recall these relations over greater spans of time, and are able to apply them to new situations with more insight.

A second factor that influences the nature of the decision-making process is the managerial experience the executive acquires. Meaningful experience in performing managerial functions gives the manager a knowledge of how to apply management principles and techniques to individual situations. If he has successfully analyzed his previous managerial successes and failures, the lessons he learned from these experiences may be brought to bear on future problems.

The third feature of the manager's decision-making program is education. The acquisition of knowledge and the development of logical thought processes enhance his effectiveness and efficiency by providing him with the mental tools (vocabulary, technical information, basic concepts, and so forth), and a disciplined mind. Hopefully, the educated man has learned how to learn and is thereby enabled to derive meaning from the experience of others as well as his own.

The final ingredient that we will consider is the manager's personality. Its force may be felt in many different ways. Some managers are more aggressive than others; some may be more optimistic (or pessimistic); some tend to be more autocratic. These personality characteristics, in addition to other personality factors, influence the way an executive arrives at decisions.

The phenomenon of feedback also exists in the dynamic model of the manager. Managerial decisions call forth activity on the part of subordinates in the organization. This activity results in the performance of many different tasks to accomplish organizational objectives. Information about these activities is fed back to the manager through his information inputs and acts to revise or update his understanding of the total managerial situation. How well the feedback process operates is a function of the management information system's effectiveness and the manager's sensitivity to various information stimuli.

Several   interesting   points   about   the   decision-making process may be noted by examining this model. First, the role of the manager as a communication center is a central feature of the model. Not only must the executive be able to communicate his decisions to his subordinates and peers in a thoroughly understandable manner, but perhaps even more important, he must be a good information receiver. To accomplish this end, the good manager should endeavor to improve his reading and listening abilities to become a more perceptive individual. The effectiveness of the entire managerial decision-making process ultimately depends on the degree to which each manager is able to function as an efficient communication center.

In connection with the communication center role, the model also stresses the importance of the manager's establishing accurate, reliable, and timely communication channels both within his firm and with the external environment. A well-structured management information system is essential to provide the basic information about current operations. The development of good personal relations with subordinates and peers is very necessary for getting group behavior information. Nor can any manager afford to overlook the events and developments that are taking place in the world today as they may possibly relate to his firm. In the end, all the information inputs must be balanced against each other to provide the optimal input mix.

Another feature of this systems model that is worthy of analysis is the nature of the manager's program. We have noted that this is shaped by many different factors—intelligence, work experience, education, and personality. The existence of so many complex ingredients necessarily means that determining probable managerial success is a very difficult affair. Only when the total intellectual, physiological, and psychological profile of the prospective manager is considered may any reasonable prediction be made of his future performance.

The final point in the analysis of the systems model concerns the focal point of all management activity, namely, the decision-making process. It is at that point that the quality of management is ultimately determined; the success of any manager depends on how good his decisions turn out to be. The executive cannot shirk this reality. The decision-making process, therefore, is the final determinant in the quality of his professional performance.

Conclusion

The foregoing discussions of the dynamic systems model in business-related activities and processes demonstrates that basic systems concepts may be applied to these areas. By depicting the free enterprise economy, the business firm, the department, and the manager as dynamic systems, we may more readily appreciate the significant operational characteristics and basic systemic interrelations within the enterprise.

In particular, the essential nature of the controller as a regulator of inputs and creator of processor environment becomes more apparent. To build more efficient and effective organizations, managers at all levels must strive to mold their organizations as closed loop systems. This may be done by providing proper training for their employees, developing decision-making procedures, and delegating appropriate authority to subordinates. These activities will help the organization become both more stable operationally and more responsive to outside influences.

The systems approach emphasizes the role of information and information systems in the organization. Managers must receive a sufficient quantity of accurate current information to make sound decisions. Further, this information must be communicated to the users to be useful. Effective information and communications systems are fundamental for a well-managed business firm.

5

INFORMATION SYSTEMS IN THE BUSINESS FIRM

Many managers (and many information systems analysts also) fail to realize the existence of the many different information systems that operate continuously within business firms. These different information flows play a vital coordinative role in all organizational activities. All individuals within organizations need a wealth of information in order to perform their respective duties efficiently. As we discussed in the systems model of the manager, the need, or necessity, to know what is happening forces each manager or operating employee to establish his own communication channels. To a certain extent, each of these channels is tuned into one or more different information systems.

To place these different information systems in proper perspectives, let us examine the more common information systems found in medium- and large-scale business firms. As we shall see, each of these information systems has a distinct character all its own and plays a unique role in fulfilling the organization's total information needs. By defining the objectives, the operational modes, and the general content of these different information systems, the relations between the various systems may be examined and, especially, their complementary natures may be understood.

COMMUNICATION SYSTEMS

The term *information* implicity assumes the existence of usefulness (utility) as distinguished from data (facts) that do not necessarily have any apparent utility. Further, information utility may be realized only when information is transmitted from

one data-processing or information-generating system to another. Information when transmitted assumes an economic
value because it can modify the behavior of the second system.
Thus communication systems or networks are designed to transmit information among many different systems within the organization.

A basic communication system may be defined as two or
more distinct information-generating subsystems operating in
series with each other. These subsystems may be either human
beings or electronic data-processing equipment. Under this arrangement the output of the first subsystem becomes the input
to the second. The interface between the two is linked by the
message that is transmitted. When additional information-generating subsystems are present in the total communication system, there will be an output-to-input interface between each
pair of information subsystems in the series. In this way the total
communication system may be viewed as a large complex of
interrelated subsystems. The objective of the resulting supersystem is to impart knowledge, thoughts, ideas, perceptions,
qualities, properties, or organized data among the individual
systems.

The individual elements in a communication system are,
as we have pointed out, systems in themselves. Each of them
is, in reality, a data-processing system of some type or other.
(Human beings may be considered as a special type of data-processing system.) The individual system elements may serve a
data-gathering role in which their primary function is to gather
data from diverse sources for subsequent transmission to another
system. Examples of electronic data-gathering systems are remote inquiry terminals, data phone installations, and the various
peripheral input devices found on computer systems.

Another function communication system elements perform
is the processing of data. In this role the system element processes data into information, as we will discuss later in the section
on data-processing system operation. The function may, of
course, be performed by individual human beings, groups of
individuals using various mechanical aids, or computers. Regardless of form, each of these data-processing systems performs
a vital role in the communication system.

The final function of a system element in the communication system is concerned with the conversion of information into a useful form. The output devices found on com-

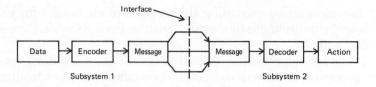

Fig. 5-1   A model of the communication process

puters, such as high-speed line printers and cathode ray tubes, perform this function. We also find examples of this type of activity being performed by individuals, as in report writing, public speaking, teaching, and translating foreign language. In all of these instances, the role of the communication system element is to put the derived information into a form that has utility.

Under ordinary circumstances, communication systems do not function as dynamic systems. Naturally, the difficulty of managing two or more data-processing systems in series and/or parallel is substantially more difficult than for a single one. Since there is no explicit control process, communication networks are usually viewed as flow systems in which information is transmitted from one point to another through the entire system.

Figure 5-1 shows a model of the communication process. On the left-hand side of the diagram the message-creating portion or subsystem is shown. On the right-hand side of the diagram the message-receiving subsystem is depicted. Between the two we find the interface of the communication system. It may in reality be composed of several information channels. Some of the more common ones involve writing-reading, speaking-hearing, or gesturing-seeing, which take place both between individuals and between individuals and machines. The channel in this sense performs a linking service by connecting the information source with the information user. Between two electronic data-processing systems the communication channel, or interface, may be bridged by electronic pulses sent through the air or through wires.

The interface between the two data-processing systems is frequently subject to interference, known as static or noise. The presence of static tends to reduce the efficiency of the communication system by decreasing the reliability of message reception and requiring many controls to insure its accuracy. Static, of course, may be reduced between the individual information systems by increasing the number of channels—for example, permitting simultaneous visual as well as verbal communication.

In a very simple communication system, some feedback may be generated in message sending. For example, if an individual sends a message to a second individual, the message sender may examine the behavior of the message receiver for signs that the message was understood. If it was not, the sender may retransmit the same message or transmit a restated one. Asking the receiver to repeat the message is an excellent way to determine whether it was received correctly.

The presence of many communication systems in every organization is ample demonstration that substantial communication takes place. There may be some doubt, however, that communication systems are always effective. The effectiveness of a particular communication system depends on several factors. The two information systems must, of course, use a common language. This observation applies not only to individuals but also to different pieces of equipment that might be found in a computer system. Historically the problem of equipment compatibility has been a source of considerable irritation to many data-processing managers.

Another factor that significantly influences the effectiveness of the communication process is the internal operating efficiency of the message-sending and -receiving systems. The message-sending subsystem may send as many messages as it wishes, but this will be of no avail if the receiving subsystem is not operating simultaneously. Since both units must function together in a coordinated way, the effectiveness of the communication system directly depends on their degree of coordination.

Insofar as feedback may be incorporated into a communication system's operation, overall system effectiveness will be improved. Feedback, of course, reduces the opportunities for systemic malfunctions. Direct feedback, which occurs when using direct observation and questioning, promotes higher or greater effectiveness.

THE INFORMAL INFORMATION SYSTEM

The informal information system is the ubiquitous information network established and maintained through informal interpersonal contacts among the firm's employees. Informal communication exists to a greater or lesser extent in all types of organizations under nearly all circumstances. By its nature, a very loosely organized, poorly defined system functions in a sporadic manner. Management exerts very little direct influence on the operation of such a system and can control it only in a very indirect way.

We may identify two separate aspects of the informal information system. The first arises from personal contacts and acquaintanceships among the firm's employees and is directed toward filling their work-oriented information needs. It is manifestly impossible for all the necessary or useful information to be passed through the formal organizational channels of communication. It is so much simpler to ask a coworker for information that most employees first seek information help from their peers before asking their supervisors. For the most part, employees at the lower organization levels are willing to offer advice and help to other members of their peer group and are somewhat more reluctant to provide information to those in higher and lower positions.

Henri Fayol noted the existence of work-oriented informal information systems many years ago.[1] Fayol's Bridge is an informal communication link between two employees in different parts of the same organization. A production foreman, for example, will simply call the maintenance foreman to arrange for minor machine repairs rather than pass a request up through the formal channels of communication to the manager of both functions (plant manager) and back down to the maintenance foreman. This form of interpersonal communication link is shown in figure 5-2. It should be noted that this communication linkage is perfectly acceptable, even desirable, as long as the respective supervisors are aware that it exists and are generally kept informed of the information flows across it.

The other aspect of the informal information system is the grapevine. The rumor transmission process arises from the deep-seated need of each employee to know what is happening in his environment. This fundamental need is so strong that employees, even those at the lower organizational levels, will go to great lengths to obtain such information. The grapevine is simply a response to a collective employee need.

---

1. Henri Fayol, *General and Industrial Administration*, (London: Sir Isaac Pitman & Sons, Ltd., 1949), pp. 34–36.

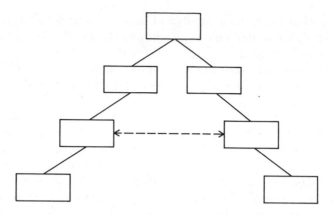

Fig. 5-2 Fayol's bridge

Grapevine activity seems to vary inversely with the degree of employee satisfaction with the information obtained through other means. Rumors, for example, appear quite frequently in departments where the manager deliberately withholds information as a means of exercising power and control. Thus management can decrease grapevine activity by supplying as much valid information to the employees as possible. In this way each employee's information needs will be more fully satisfied through information passed on through formal organizational information channels and the grapevine will become less important.

Rumors seem to do at least as much to subvert organizational goals as to foster them. They tend to stir up dissension, arouse emotions, and stiffen resistance to change. They are also often contrary to fact. Sixteen of thirty rumors in one study were found to be false.[2] Quite naturally, this type of information produces a very poor effect on the behavior of any organization.

The grapevine model of the rumor transmission process, figure 5-3, depicts a typical rumor transmission network. The transmission of gossip and rumors is performed by a special group of individuals that we may call *communicators*. These individuals are the primary links in the transmission of information through the network.

The communicators, or rumor transmitters, appear to be

---

2. R. Hershey, "The Grapevine—Here To Stay But Not Beyond Control," *Personnel,* vol. 43, no. 1 (1966), pp. 62–66.

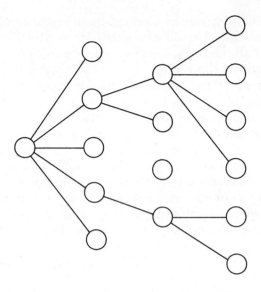

Fig. 5-3   The grapevine (rumor transmission process)

unique individuals who often have several different identifiable characteristics. First, these employees tend to cultivate the communicator role in order to satisfy their somewhat greater than normal need for approval from their peers. Supplying needed or desired information to fellow employees undoubtedly creates a sense of personal social approval for the communicator since his fellow employees will usually be happy to see him and visit with him. Many communicators also feel that rumor "improvements" will enhance their approval by others, and thus they exaggerate rumors. Secondly, these communicators frequently have jobs that require movement within the organization. In order to function most effectively, they must come in contact with a wide range of different individuals. In this way, they may generate more sources of information and can more readily disseminate rumors and gossip to a large audience. A third characteristic of rumor transmitters is a strong sense of peer group loyalty. These individuals often identify strongly with their peer group in the organization. This behavior pattern naturally follows from the communicator's desire for approval from his fellow workers and may explain why rumors tend to flow laterally through an organization much more quickly than vertically.

Another feature to be noted in figure 5-3 is the existence

of isolated individuals who have no consistent informal information system links. Not all individuals are part of the grapevine network at all times. New employees, physically isolated ones, and independent thinkers are often excluded from the grapevine. This fact reduces the grapevine's reliability and effectiveness in transmitting information to all employees.

Many management scholars feel that the grapevine can be used to disseminate certain kinds of information under unusual or peculiar circumstances. However, any deliberate use of it for information transmission diminishes, even ever so slightly, the supervisor's leadership role. He becomes no longer regarded as the primary source of information because "good" information has also been transmitted through the grapevine. If this situation occurs frequently, the supervisor is placed in a very awkward position.

With regard to systems efficiency, informal information systems are relatively efficient means of transmitting information. The cost of operating the system is nominal—and unavoidable. People need to cross-communicate and will almost certainly do so when given the opportunity. The time efficiency measure (speed of response) of an informal system is outstanding. A few well-placed communicators can transmit information to an entire organization in a very short time. Only with respect to quality is the informal information system suspect. Information inaccuracies and exaggerations do occur rather frequently.

The effectiveness of the informal information system is quite good. The informal cross-talk in an organization does satisfy many information needs. The great danger appears to be that the informal information system will become too effective and will thereby erode the effectiveness of other information systems. When this situation occurs, the total effectiveness of the combined information systems will be reduced.

The informal information system is not a dynamic system in any sense of the term. Correction or control of information inputs does not exist. Misinformation and falsehoods may only be corrected with great difficulty and after they have done most of their damage. To combat these inaccuracies, managers must be honest and forthright with their subordinates. They must pass on all the information that has been cleared for dissemination. Such devices as rumor clinics, which attempt to provide accurate and timely answers to current rumors, may be established to correct these untruths. The best solution to the problem of untrue rumors, however, is to prevent them from starting around the grapevine by supplying employees with valid and current information as soon as possible.

ORGANIZATIONAL INFORMATION SYSTEMS

Organizational information systems encompass all of the information flows down from top management and the responses of lower-level employees up to top management. The managers at all organizational levels are ultimately responsible for planning, organizing, directing, and controlling the activities of their organizational units. Managerial directives must be communicated from the top-level managers, perhaps through several managerial levels, to the employees of the firm. In order to exercise control, there must be a reverse information flow to give management feedback about the activities being performed at the lower levels. The organizational information system then is simply a collection of different channels or media for transmitting information from the top of the organization to the bottom and back up to the top once more. A schematic model of an organizational information system is shown in figure 5-4.

Organizational information systems are very closely related

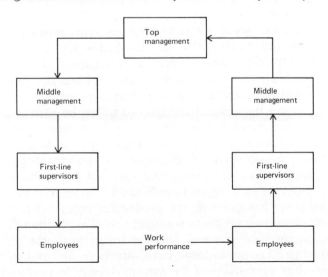

Fig. 5-4 Organizational information system

to management systems. The principal purpose of management systems is to provide organized direction for a business' activities. The principal purpose of the organizational information system is to transmit these organizational directions to their ultimate destinations and to provide feedback to top management. The management system without a satisfactory organizational information system will not produce satisfactory results. Conversely, a good organizational information system will not make up for a lack of planning, organizing, and controlling on the part of top management. In this way management systems and organizational information systems complement each other.

The messages sent through organizational information systems are concerned with the objectives, goals, plans, policies, operating practices, procedures, and directives to carry out the necessary tasks in producing the firm's goods and services. From the lower levels of the organization the primary types of information that are sent upward are activity reports, status reports, progress reports, *ad hoc* reports, and oral reports. Special employee concerns, such as grievances and suggestions, should also be forwarded up through the organization when appropriate. We can conclude from the wide variety of information that must be passed downward and upward through the various organizational levels that there must be communication difficulties in nearly every firm.

The informational content of the messages sent downward through the organization may be classified as (1) specific directions or instructions and (2) general background information. Basic directions must ultimately emanate from the board of directors and top management. It is their responsibility to establish the course they expect the firm to follow by setting objectives, determining corporate strategy, and formulating policies. Proceeding downward through the organizational hierarchy, a transition from generalized direction to specific instructions usually takes place. We usually find also that authority to issue instructions may be assigned to individual managers or to particular functions. For example, the production control department is expected to issue production orders to the production departments; engineering drawings become instructions for product manufacture. Communicating both directions and instructions is most often accomplished by writing (typing or printing), by verbal orders, or by both.

General   information   requires   many   different   communication channels to communicate this information down to the lowest levels of the organization adequately. Among the more common media for transmitting general information are company magazines and newspapers, meetings for groups of employees, letters sent directly to the home or mailed to the employee through inter-company mail delivery, pamphlets on information racks, employee handbooks and manuals, bulletin boards and posters, news bulletins, and memoranda. Each of these information channels individually has limited effectiveness. When the channels are properly combined, however, the total effectiveness of the downward information flow may be improved substantially.

The principal types of upward communication media are those listed in the systems model of the manager section of the preceding chapter: formal reports (showing system activity over a period of time, system status at a particular point in time, or a combination of both), *ad hoc* reports, and direct verbal/visual reports. Each of these channels again has relative advantages. In addition to these techniques, top management may also employ employee attitude and morale surveys, suggestion systems, employee grievance procedures, and an ombudsman to facilitate communication from the lowest levels of the organization to the top.

The effectiveness of organizational information systems depends on many different factors. The selection of channels, as discussed above, will influence the effectiveness of the communications process. The most effective method for information transmission is a combination of oral and written messages. Next in effectiveness is oral messages only, followed by written messages only. Fourth in relative effectiveness is the bulletin board, followed, finally, by the grapevine. In addition to the choice of communication channels several other factors influence the effectiveness of the organizational information system. The development of a bond of trust and confidence between employer and employees fosters the ready communication of information. Further, the willingness of management, as demonstrated over a period of time, to provide relevant, accurate information to the employees will influence the system's effectiveness. Of course, unless management does attempt to provide sufficient valid information, there cannot be a high degree of effectiveness in the organizational information system.

Although the effectiveness of top-down information systems

is often good, the flow of information from the bottom of the organization to top management is frequently very poor. Perhaps the most important reason for the ineffectiveness of upward communication is a natural reluctance on the part of individuals to volunteer information that may reflect adversely on their personal performance. For this reason the bulk of information flowing upward through the organization must be generated by the formal information reporting system. Exceptions to this observation may be found where lower-level employees wish to achieve a degree of recognition either for jobs well done or for poorly performed jobs that are certain to be noted by their supervisors, and, finally, where information about the poor performances of other supervisors has adversely affected a supervisor's own performance. These three types of messages normally circulate upward without any obstruction. Employee suggestion systems and grievances filed through the union also go up the organizational ladder with little difficulty. All other information must be dug out by the inquiring manager, lest the facts remain buried forever.

The efficiency of organizational information systems is also a function of the channels or media that are used for information transmission. Thus the use of committees composed of many individuals may be a relatively efficient communication technique in terms of time spent on the communication process, but very inefficient from a cost standpoint due to the considerable expense of the managers' time. Conversely, there are also examples where the cost may be somewhat lower but the time required for communication may be longer, as in sending out interoffice memoranda.

The organizational information system is primarily a flow system and does not exhibit any control mechanism *per se.* Although information flows down through the organization and back up, this does not constitute a control loop in the usual sense of the word. Management uses the return information, of course, to review operations and establish a basis for the revision of organizational plans. As in the systems model of the manager, individual managers may function as the controller in the organizational information system. However, the behavior of these systems is usually far from that of the idealized closed system.

OPERATING INFORMATION SYSTEMS

The primary function of business firms is the production of an economic good or the performance of a service. As we have already noted, not all of the firm's activities are devoted to these ends. Many other tasks that are not directly related to production but are absolutely essential to the efficient performance of its primary function must be performed. Product design, plant engineering, maintenance, personnel services, production control, and quality control are some examples of these necessary auxiliary services. Clerical operations that involve manipulating data to maintain business records are also necessary auxiliary services. Customer orders must be recorded and filed, raw materials and supplies must be ordered, production orders must be prepared and released, inventory records must be kept current and accurate, customer invoices must be prepared and sent to the customer, and records of customer payments must be posted to the customer's account. These are some of the major chores that are concerned solely with the record-preparation and record-keeping activities of the business firm.

Operating information systems may be defined as the information systems that collect, maintain, and utilize basic business data to satisfy a business' record-keeping requirements and furnish the basic data for its operating decisions. The purpose of operating information systems is simply to prepare and maintain the necessary records in order for the firm's primary functions to proceed efficiently. Many different types of records must be kept accurate and up-to-date to satisfy the requirements of operating supervisors as well as other external systems such as the stockholders, the different levels and branches of government, customers, suppliers, and employees.

The earliest operating information systems were maintained entirely by hand. All of the effort was strictly clerical in nature and because of the relatively high expense per record transaction and the small number of business transactions, the systems tended to be quite simple structurally. Only those records that were absolutely essential for the operation of the business were maintained. This approach was the prevailing method of maintaining operating records until the beginning of the twentieth century when machine methods first began to appear. Today, of course, computers are widely used to perform the record-keeping function.

Introduction of the computer also altered another feature of the record-keeping process. Formerly, records tended to be kept in a more decentralized way. Individuals or groups responsible for particular operations kept their own records of account. Under these circumstances it was very difficult to consolidate the various records to prepare combined files or reports. Thus the usefulness of the record files tended to be somewhat limited. In contrast, the introduction of the computer has brought about a strong movement for centralizing record-keeping activities. No longer is it necessary or desirable for individual organizational units to maintain their own private files; these operations can now be done centrally on computerized equipment. Moreover, consolidation of the various files has eliminated duplication of effort and file utility has been increased.

It is in the area of operating information systems that the introduction of the computer has produced the greatest impact and gained the quickest acceptance. Consider the herculean task of trying to maintain the accounts-receivable records for a major oil company with some five million gasoline credit-card customers. An army of clerks would scarcely be able to perform this task. Putting these records on the computer, however, permits the customers' accounts to be updated daily and their monthly bills to be prepared automatically.

The substitution of electronic effort for human effort is now a familiar story. The reasons for the rapid acceptance of computer mechanization in operating information systems are threefold. First, operating information systems are the most readily visible users of clerical effort. Second, the expenses and the potential cost savings associated with these clerical systems can be quite significant. Finally, computers with their high levels of speed and accuracy were readily adaptable to the data-processing requirements of operating information systems.

The cost of maintaining operating information systems is usually considered as part of the cost of doing business, an overhead cost. As such, a reduction in the operating cost for an operating information system will have a direct influence on the firm's profitability. Every dollar of operating information system expense saved will add a dollar to gross profits. Consequently, cost efficiency is one of management's major concerns in evaluating operating information systems efficiency.

For many business firms the time efficiency for operating information systems is not an especially critical factor as long as operations are conducted in a reasonably expeditious way. Certain other firms, however, are more interested in time efficiency than cost efficiency. For example, airlines must be able to make flight reservations while the customer is on the phone. Improving both the cost and time measures of efficiency are important managerial goals. Unfortunately, there is usually a tradeoff between cost and time efficiency—low processing costs usually mean a longer processing cycle time and vice versa.

The effectiveness of an operating information system must be measured against the objectives for the entire business. Do the operating information systems significantly aid and foster the firm's efficient production of economic goods and/or services? We should expect each of the individual operating information systems to support the production/operation system fully by supplying needed information in a timely manner. On the other hand, there is no point in accumulating mountains of records in any of the operating information systems unless there is a clear-cut need to maintain them. The collection and maintenance of records is a very expensive task and may add very little to the operating information system's overall effectiveness.

Under normal circumstances, operating information systems are not dynamic, since they do not initiate action to regulate their raw data inputs. However, the information in their files may be used for input data in a decision-making process, especially at the lowest organizational levels. For example, if the inventory level for a certain item falls below a predetermined value, this fact could be used to trigger a decision to replenish the inventory stock by preparing a purchase requisition. Also, operating information system files may be occasionally accessed to answer specific management queries about a particular file item. However, these cases do not constitute a closed control loop as we have been using the term.

MANAGEMENT INFORMATION SYSTEMS

Managers must have complete, accurate, and timely information to make sound business decisions. Having a wealth of good management information available does not guarantee that the manager will make intelligent use of it to make his decisions. However, without good management information available, he is at a serious disadvantage. For our purposes we may assume that if a manager has sufficient relevant information, he will be able to make reasonably sound management decisions.

A management information system may be defined as any information system that provides a manager with information on the activities and pertinent interrelations about the current status of the production/operation system over which he has authority. From this definition the basic system objective is evident—namely, to provide the manager with complete, accurate, and timely information relating to the performance of the organization.

A schematic model of the relation between the management information system and the production/operation system is shown in figure 5-5. As shown in the model, the management information system measures attributes of the production/operation system, processes the data, and prepares management information reports. In reality, the management information system is a part of the control loop that maintains dynamic control over the business firm.

The inputs to management information systems are simply raw data collected from strategic points in the production/operation system. Very often the raw input data is collected in connection with or extracted from operating information systems rather than being specifically collected for management information systems alone. Using the same input data for operating and management information systems permits substantial economies in system operation. The selection of the proper raw data inputs is a critical process since they must be chosen to reflect the condition of the production/operation system to management. Further, not all items in selected raw data types will necessarily be useful in management information systems. Thus input data selection is a most important consideration for management information systems.

The quality of the raw data is especially important in management information systems also. Erroneous input data will necessarily result in erroneous management information reports, leading managers to base their decisions on incorrect information.

Managers need two basic types of information about the production/operation system's performance to appraise accurately what is taking place in their organizational units. The first type of required information—activity reports—is needed to define the activities that have taken place in the organizational unit during a certain period of time. The various resource

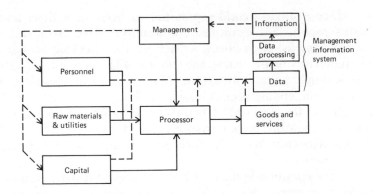

Fig. 5-5 The management information system and the
          production/operation system

streams (labor, raw material units, utilities, and equipment) must
be monitored to determine the resources that have been used
to produce the goods and/or services. The output (jobs, work
orders, batches, products, and so forth) must also be monitored
to determine what the production/operation system has accomplished during a given time. The comparison of input and output
data that reflects production/operation system activity with predetermined standards, such as budgets or schedules, provides
the manager with useful information that allows him to determine his organizational unit's efficiency during a specific period
of time. Examples of relatively common activity reports are profit
and loss statements, shipping and receiving reports, sales reports,
and a host of others.

  The second basic type of information managers need to
determine the conditions of their production/operation systems
is the status report. Such a report indicates or specifies the state
of a particular element or group of elements in a production/
operation system at a given point in time. Comparing the level
of a particular element at the present time with its level at various
past times is an excellent way to identify trends taking place in
the production/operation system. For example, if the end-of-
the-month inventory values have been increasing over the past
several months, the manager should be alerted to an unusual
condition that may require additional investigation and perhaps
action. Examples of status reports are the corporate balance
sheet, inventory listings, employee rolls, and present accounts-
receivable balances.

  These two different types of reports are sometimes combined

to produce a single hybrid report that is both an activity and a status report. For example, computer-prepared bank statements usually list each check written on the checking account and all deposits made during the month. This part of the statement is simply an activity listing. Most statements also have a beginning and ending account balance. These two values define the status of the account at two different points in time. As a result, the monthly bank statement provides a clear picture of what has happened in the checking account and what its balance is at the present.

A very common feature of both activity and status reports in most management information systems is data summarization. Many management information systems have vast quantities of raw data available for processing. Since managers usually have only a limited amount of time available for reading and reflecting about their management reports, data summarization becomes almost a necessity if the reports are to have any real value for managerial decision making. Consequently, the use of subtotals and the condensation of detail transactions are common features of management information systems reports.

The use of the exception principle, in which the only data reported to management is that which falls outside some predetermined limit, is also a common reporting feature in management information systems. In this way the manager has the system activities that are most apt to need remedial action brought to his attention. Generating such reports is, of course, quite easy for electronic data-processing information systems.

The efficiency of management information systems is very difficult to judge. In general, these systems require somewhat more data-processing time per record and per report type than operating information systems. This is due to the larger range of data sources, greater data manipulation or computation times, and special report formats. We should note that these systems are not usually processed independently from the operating information system. They both use much common data, which results in management information reports often being created as operating information systems by-products. Hybrid information processing systems of this sort are sometimes known in information systems circles as management operating systems.

The reports management information systems generate are one of the most effective means available for supplying managers with information about the activities and current status of their organizational units. Perhaps because such reports have not always been available, the true value of management information systems is not always appreciated. Management information reports must be timely in order to be effective. The more quickly the manager is aware of systemic dysfunctions, the better he will be able to correct the underlying conditions that cause them. Accuracy and reliability of the report data will also strongly influence the effectiveness of the managerial reports. Ultimately, however, the effectiveness of the management information system must be judged by how well its reports define the condition of the production/operation system and thereby enable the manager to make sound, prompt decisions.

DECISION-MAKING INFORMATION SYSTEMS

Decision-making information systems are special information systems that process data to make one or more decisions resulting in actions to bring the production/operation system back into a predetermined stable condition. In essence, such systems supplant the manager as a decision maker and make decisions necessary to correct out-of-balance conditions within the business firm.

The contrast between operating information systems, management information systems, and decision-making systems may perhaps be best explained by considering an example. In a rudimentary raw material information system, the operating information system keeps track of the inventory receipts and disbursements so that the current balance of each item is known at all times. It might also prepare a list of items to be reordered. The management information system extracts information from the inventory records to give management background information about unusual or peculiar conditions or trends. A decision-making information system automatically recalculates economic order quantities and reorder points to reflect activity changes and prepares purchase orders for those items below the reorder point. In this way the decision-making information system seeks to maintain inventory in a balanced, stable condition.

From this example we may conclude what the objective of a decision-making system is: to convert the managerial control loop from an open-loop type of performance to a closed-loop one, thereby creating a truly dynamic system. If the decision-making information system can be designed to handle the major contingencies, the production/operation system will be under much closer control and will operate more efficiently and effectively.

However, not all decisions are amenable to an automated decision-making process. The terms *programmed* and *nonprogrammed* have been used by Simon to designate two classes of decision making:

> Decisions are programmed to the extent that they are repetitive and routine, to the extent that a definite procedure has been worked out for handling them so that they won't have to be treated *de novo* each time they occur....
>
> Decisions are nonprogrammed to the extent that they are novel, unstructured, and consequential. There is no cut and dried method for handling the problem because it hasn't arisen before, or because its precise nature and structure are elusive and complex, or because it is so important that it deserves a custom-tailored treatment.[3]

Programmed decisions, therefore, may be developed to handle repetitive, recurring decision-making situations in which problem structures are similar and well defined. Since rules may be established for programmed decisions, these decisions can actually be made before a particular decision situation arises. Further, this type of decision making is readily adaptable for use in an electronic data-processing information system.

Nonprogrammed decisions, however, require human intervention. Decision rules have not been developed for nonprogrammed decisions because the problem situations are unique; or because it is not economically feasible to develop the decision rules; or because the problem variables are unknown, too complex, or too numerous; or because some combination of these factors exists. The purpose of management information systems is to provide the manager with background information for making such decisions.

The distinction between programmed and nonprogrammed decisions is not always clear. Decisions that are structurally simple and repetitive may be formalized as programmed decisions. However, there are many examples in business today where decisions of this type have not been expressed as a set of decision rules. It is more correct, perhaps, to think of decision

---

3. Herbert A. Simon, *The New Science of Management Decision,* (New York: Harper & Row, Inc., 1960), pp. 5–6.

Fig. 5-6   Decision complexity continuum

complexity as a continuum that ranges from the very simple to the extremely complex as shown in figure 5-6. Thus those decisions at the low end of the complexity scale would be amenable to programmed decision-making techniques while those at the upper end would be more appropriately classed as nonprogrammable in nature. For decisions of intermediate complexity, the principal classification criterion would be, "Is there sufficient economic justification to conduct the decision structure investigation and develop the appropriate set of decision rules?"

A possible point of confusion may arise when comparing an operating information system that contains programmed decisions and a true decision-making information system. Certainly many operating information systems do have decision points in their programs to determine the program path. However, if we go back to the basic purpose of the decision itself we can usually discern the difference between the two types of decisions. The question that must be answered is, "Is the purpose of the decision to process a record or to initiate basic, remedial systemic action that will bring a production/operation system back into equilibrium?"

The overall efficiency of decision-making information systems is excellent from a time vantage point. As should be expected, eliminating the human element will increase the speed of the decision-making process. With regard to cost, the picture is not quite so clear. Certainly eliminating managerial attention to certain decisions should decrease the cost of decision making. Offsetting this cost reduction, however, are substantial cost outlays for complex programs and sophisticated equipment necessary to implement a full-blown decision-making information system. As a result, system projects of this type must be approached with a great deal of caution before the economic advantages can be determined.

Decision-making information systems represent the final stage in the evolutionary development of information systems. Their effectiveness is still limited to a great extent by the restriction of their use to lower, less complex levels of decision making.

Simple, highly structured decision-making information systems have proven to be very effective in controlling certain production/operation systems. There are many examples of computers being used to control complex industrial operations, such as oil refinery operations, much more effectively than human decision making ever permitted. As the level of decision complexity rises, however, there are fewer examples of effective decision-making information system applications encountered. The results of a bad decision in these cases are usually felt to be too far-reaching to merit this high degree of trust.

While the area of decision-making information systems applications to higher-level management problems is still largely unexplored, there are some signs pointing to a pressing need for more research in this area. "The intuitive judgment of even a skilled investigator is quite unreliable in anticipating the dynamic behavior of a simple information-feedback system of perhaps five or six variables. . .the human is not a subtle and powerful problem solver."[4] As more knowledge is gained about the behavior of the business firm as a dynamic system, managerial decision-making abilities must be improved to remain competitive. The production/operation system and the other subsystems of the business firm must perform more as closed dynamic systems. This is the challenge of the future.

DATA-PROCESSING INFORMATION SYSTEMS

Another type of information system frequently discussed is the data-processing information system. By definition, a data-processing information system simply transforms raw data from one or more sources into one or more types of information. To a certain extent the use of the word *information* in the section heading is redundant and has only been used to emphasize that data-processing systems comprise one type of organizational information flow—a formalized, frequently mechanized, type of flow. Data-processing information systems are also of considerable interest to information analysts because computer technology may often be applied to them.

The basic objective of a data-processing information system is to transform raw data into comprehensible, useful information

4. J. W. Forrester, *Industrial Dynamics,* (New York: The M.I.T. Press and John Wiley & Sons, Inc., 1961), p. 99.

in the most efficient way possible. In such a system the principal concerns are the collection of data, the conversion of raw data into information, and the presentation of the information to the users. The fact that we wish to accomplish this in the most economical way introduces the need for organized procedures. If the system is computerized, the computer program is the organizing agent. For lower-level data-processing systems, the operating instructions or paperwork procedures serve to organize the system.

The systemic inputs for a data-processing system are simply bits and pieces of fact about a particular element or relationship (activity) in the business firm. There is, however, an underlying structure to the raw data inputs that must be present in order to process any of them. A price of $9.95 or a quantity of twelve has no meaning without an item description (name or number). Nor would we be any wiser unless we also knew what sort of activity was represented by the raw data. For example, twelve units of a certain item priced at $9.95 per dozen does not have any meaning unless we also know whether it was sold for cash, sold on account, returned for credit, or adjusted for price. Thus data-processing system inputs, usually known as unit records, must contain an element identifier (employee number, order number, part number, and so forth), one or more element modifiers (price, quantity, color, size, model, and so forth), and activity, or transaction, identification (sale, customer return, record change, and so forth).

The data-processing system's output is whole, or complete, facts and knowledge about some phase of business operations. There is an implicit notion in the concept of information that the status or activity of a system element will be defined. "There were six units of part number 123456 in raw materials inventory last Friday midnight." "Gross sales for the month of November were $1,234,567." In both of these examples the information reveals a sense of completeness that leads to improved understanding of the condition. Ordinarily we also assume that data does not become information until it is communicated to someone. Consequently, data collected and stored in files does not really become information until it is presented for use to management.

The processor in a DP system performs the familiar data-processing functions. The raw data (unit records) must be collected from many diverse sources. The data must be classified and perhaps sorted to facilitate processing and reporting. The unit records may require data manipulation, checking, and calculation. Data aggregates may be summarized by class or type. Finally, reports must be prepared to communicate the information to selected receivers.

Data-processing systems range in complexity from very simple small record-keeping or tally systems to large ones that involve thousands of different types of input records and hundreds of different output reports requiring many different intervening operations. The number of different data inputs and output reports does not vary directly with the size of the organization, although large organizations naturally have a greater variety of them than small firms.

Data-processing systems also vary widely with regard to the degree of mechanization they use. For small, simple tally systems, manual system operation is probably preferred. On the other hand, very large DP systems virtually require the use of computers for reasonably efficient operation. Data-processing systems exhibit an almost infinite variety between the extremes of completely manual operation to large-scale modern computer operation. To be rational and objective, the information systems designer should not always assume that every data-processing system requires a computer. There will probably always be some DP systems that would be best operated manually.

The application of data-processing systems technology to operating information systems is a well-established practice today. The functions of collecting, classifying, sorting, calculating, and reporting are very conveniently performed on electronic equipment. Moreover, operating information systems applications are more likely to have the volume of transactions necessary to justify the expense of electronic equipment. Typically, the first DP applications are made to operating information systems by simply substituting electronic data processing for the older and slower electromechanical or manual data-processing information systems.

The application of electronic data-processing technology to management information systems occurred as an outgrowth of computerized operating information systems activity. Management has long been aware that operating information systems contained a wealth of information about company operations. Formerly, the laborious and expensive task of extracting comprehensive and meaningful information from the operating information files was difficult to justify economically. For years, managers had to be content with rudimentary reports that gave little insight into the status and activities of the company's operations. Consequently, the ready availability of masses of information that could be sorted into many different sequences, summarized at several different levels, and reported in a variety of different formats has created the managerial information explosion during the past decade or two. All of these wonderful management information reports were available with very little or, in many cases, no need for additional raw data inputs, and at minimal cost! It is a small wonder that many managers succumbed to the temptation to receive too many reports containing more information than they could digest.

The adaptation of electronic data-processing technology to decision-making information systems is still on the horizon. At the lowest operating levels there are many examples of computers that perform routine decision-making tasks with great precision and reliability. Although these applications are usually related to the maintenance of production process control conditions, decision-making information systems may also be found in conjunction with operating information systems. An automatic inventory reorder system, for example, can be designed to create a purchase requisition automatically when the quantity level for a particular item falls below the reorder point. In this case an incomplete decision-making information system is linked to a raw materials inventory operating information system.

At the mid-management levels of the organization we do find a few examples of computers assisting in the managerial decision-making process on a regular basis. The use of linear programming to optimize the allocation of scarce raw materials between competing business activities is practiced in certain industries—for example, in meat packing, metal processing, and gasoline refining. Complete reliance on the results of the automated decision-making process, however, is usually withheld by requiring an operating manager to validate the computer decision. At the upper management levels, simulation studies of complex operating systems may be used to assist managers in their decision-making processes by providing more information about the nature of their present or planned production/operation systems.

The efficient operation of a data-processing system with regard to cost per record transaction is a major management concern. The operation of data-processing systems is an overhead cost that does not contribute directly to the utility of the product and/or service produced. For this reason cost-conscious managers have pursued the mechanization of data-processing operations vigorously. The results in many cases have been excellent. For example, a major airframe manufacturer was able to reduce the number of employees in the material division (purchasing, receiving, and inventory management) from fifteen hundred to six hundred over a span of ten years while it doubled the number of purchase orders and items carried in inventory. The direct labor cost savings substantially exceeded the additional computer cost, while at the same time the order-processing time was also reduced.

Mechanized data-processing systems are usually more effective than manual ones. Electronic DP systems give management more accurate and timely information. Management reports may be tailored to individual requirements to facilitate the use of the information. Enabling the manager to make better decisions more quickly will substantially increase the quality of management. Thus mechanized data-processing systems can improve managerial effectiveness.

CONCLUSION

Information flows are found in all organizations. Well-functioning information systems are a vital ingredient for the successful performance of the business firm. The managerial activities of planning, organizing, directing, and controlling depend on the collection, preparation, and dissemination of information. To satisfy the manifold information needs of the organization, the many different information systems discussed in this chapter must be used. Some of them (informal information systems and organizational information systems) appear spontaneously. Others must be created, often laboriously. We may indeed postulate with little reservation that the success of the business firm in meeting all its obligations is a direct function of the efficiency and effectiveness of its various information systems.

THE INFORMATION SYSTEMS STUDY

As we have seen, managers desperately need accurate, timely, and well-organized information to make sound decisions. Without a reliable flow of information the manager is forced to make his decisions in an intellectual vacuum. The quality of such decisions must necessarily be rather low; the infrequent successes encountered will be due more to chance than anything else. To satisfy this information hunger, nearly all managers are anxious to obtain more, better, and more timely information.

Unfortunately, many managers are only vaguely aware of the deficiencies in their informational inputs. Further, they often tend to be unaware or unconcerned about the different sources of managerial information. In addition, the time available to develop sound information to base decisions on is often limited by other demands on the manager's time. Knowing what information is really required to furnish a sound basis for a decision is, indeed, a difficult task for any manager. Common sense and intuition may fail to provide the manager with sufficient insight into his real problems to adequately define them and enable him to develop good decisions.

The development of efficient and effective information systems, therefore, should be a top-priority item for managerial attention. Since the development of sound information systems will require the cooperation of many individuals within the business firm, the roles and responsibilities of the primary ones must be clearly understood. Only when all members of the organization appreciate their interdependencies may successful information systems be planned and implemented.

SYSTEMS STUDY PREREQUISITES

Many firms have been disappointed to find that computerized data-processing installations and techniques have produced much less than satisfactory results. The evolution of data-processing operations from the old manual and EAM procedures to computers has frequently not fulfilled managerial expectations. The reasons for the lack of success in computerizing such operations often go back to the time when the data-processing efforts were begun. Errors in judgment and execution, many of them quite small and seemingly insignificant at the time, later caused gigantic difficulties in the successful implementation of computerized systems. The responsibility for the failures, of course, ultimately rests on top management's shoulders. All too often, computer installation programs have not received their full managerial support; neither did management appreciate the effects that a lack of commitment will eventually produce. As a result, ill-conceived and poorly executed plans for computer systems have led to costly failures and setbacks.

The first step, then, in implementing a successful computerized data-processing program is to gain full management commitment. To do this, the extent to which present operating difficulties are due to a lack of good information must be brought directly and forcefully to the top managers' attention. They must recognize that computerized data-processing systems have the potential for reducing operational difficulties, cutting costs, and improving their products/services. In this regard a rudimentary knowledge of data-processing technology can be very helpful. All too frequently in the past, managers have been reluctant to investigate the feasibility of computerized operations until the inefficiencies in their present information systems have produced an adverse effect on the performance of their production/operation system. Attempting to introduce computerized operations into the organization in times of crisis will, of course, compound the existing difficulties. Positive benefits from the implementation of computerized data processing cannot be readily realized under these circumstances, and the new operations will produce unsatisfactory results for a longer than normal period of time.

Before a data-processing system is formed, the top managers in the organization should be fully aware that there will be many difficulties in installing it. They should be well advised that overnight successes are only infrequently achieved and that successfully implementing the system may well take a substantial length of time. Further, they should appreciate that the ultimate cost savings for the investment of company funds and efforts will take several years to be realized. They should also realize that there must be substantial personal involvement on their part lest the installation programs fail to meet their needs completely. In short, top management should not be oversold on the benefits of computerized information systems or underinformed about the real costs.

For maximum effectiveness the managerial commitment to such a system should be demonstrated in several different ways. The expenditure of funds for the purchase/lease of a computer together with the necessary peripheral equipment is a major indication of commitment. Substantial sums of money must be allocated at the beginning of the program, and there will be a continuing liability for many years to maintain and improve the equipment. Ideally, one would like to begin the financial commitment with a relatively inexpensive computer configuration. As the number of applications within the business firm expands, hopefully, additional equipment modules or larger units may be added. In this way the computer may continue to serve the organization without major interruptions and the overall financial commitment can be minimized.

Top management must also demonstrate their commitment by allocating sufficient funds to support a data-processing organization. Well-qualified personnel must be hired and trained, if necessary, to staff it. Direct and indirect payroll costs for starting operations will be sizable and these expenses continue indefinitely. The space requirements for the computer installation will be an expense item and should, if at all possible, permit expansion as the size of the organization increases. Operating supplies comprise another unending stream of expenses for a data-processing department. Consequently, adequate funding of this department is both a basic and a necessary requirement for a successful computerized data-processing system.

With regard to the selection of personnel, top management exercises one of the most important parts of their commitment to DP operations. It has long been recognized that managerial quality is an extremely important factor in the success of any business activity. Just as top management establishes the operating environment for the entire business firm, so will the choice of the data-processing manager establish the environment for the data-processing operation. The selection of a well-qualified supervisor is imperative if the DP department is to function as an effective organizational unit. This manager should have excellent qualifications in the area of computer and data-processing technology since he must serve as the final arbiter for many technical decisions. He should also be quite familiar with the organizational structure of the business firm and be personally acquainted with many of its managers. Finally, he must possess a substantial degree of executive talent to guide and direct the members of the organization to achieve objectives. Compromising these requirements in the selection of a data-processing manager can introduce many additional difficulties into an already difficult situation.

The full commitment of top management should be well understood and fully appreciated by the other employees of the firm. Top management, therefore, must communicate the extent of the commitment to the rest of the organization. Formal statements and news releases are often used to announce the start of a computer installation program. Staff meetings, interoffice memos, and even short training sessions for management personnel will help convey the importance and the urgency of the data-processing program.

Introducing advanced data-processing technology into the firm will produce changes in the organizational structure and the balance of power among the departments. Top management must recognize that these organizational realignments will occur and direct them, insofar as possible, into productive patterns. Any new functional relationships between the DP department and the balance of the organization should be carefully defined, documented, and communicated to all members of management. In this way irritating difficulties and personality clashes may be minimized.

A peculiar difficulty, which occurs infrequently, exists when major organizational units have their own systems and procedures personnel. These employees may easily find themselves at odds with the personnel from the data-processing department since their duties overlap to a considerable extent. Top management must make decisions that clarify the relationship of these staff assistants to the department. It may be advisable to transfer them to that department or, alternatively, to give them certain line duties in their respective organizations. If the latter course is chosen, these employees may provide invaluable service as coordinators of the information systems within their organizational units.

A final step that top management should take to emphasize their commitment is to delegate specific authority to the data-processing department for the development and implementation of all DP information systems within the entire organization. Failure to recognize the need for centralized authority over the regular formal information flows within the organization will almost inevitably create bickering and confusion. By specifically recognizing that the data-processing organization has the authority to establish information operating procedures, potential conflicts between it and the balance of the firm can be minimized.

DEVELOPMENT OF THE OVERALL PLAN

The creation of an overall plan for implementing computerized data-processing systems is a very critical stage in the development of a satisfactory information system structure. The first step in building a house, after selecting the building lot, is preparing a set of plans and specifications that set forth the boundaries of the house and specify the component parts together with their interrelations. In this way the contractor can proceed to build the house with a minimum of waste and with the knowledge that the completed house will meet the requirements of the future owner. So it is with information systems. If we wish to develop a well-functioning information system that will truly serve the needs of management, then a comprehensive plan that shows the interrelations among the different information subsystems is imperative.

Historically, the development of an information system structure typically has not been based upon well-developed, comprehensive plans prior to the installation of computerized information systems. The need for a quick payoff has all too frequently forced scarce systems analysis resources to be allocated to those operating management information systems that were most easily implemented. A common first application has been the payroll system, in which wage and salary computations are transferred to the computer simply because this option was immediately available and could show some cost savings. Unfortunately, this approach often leads to future difficulties as other information systems are developed.

Another common error in the historical approach to implementing of data-processing systems has been the simple mechanization of clerical operations. As we have seen in our short discussion of management information systems, this approach may eliminate clerical effort but quite often does not give management any additional insights about the operation of the business firm itself.

Many firms have belatedly begun to recognize the fallacy of the piecemeal approach. After a number of different information systems have been implemented, they have realized that the individual information systems are very difficult to tie together into any sort of integrated data-processing system. As a result, many firms have had to retrace their steps and spend a great deal of time, effort, and money to establish an overall plan for information system implementation. Not only has there been a substantial expense, but in many cases the existing operating systems have required substantial rework before they could be integrated into the overall plan.

A comprehensive plan for the implementing of computerized data-processing facilities is a very practical concept. Not only does it permit the organized allocation of scarce systems resources to achieve maximum productivity from the data-processing system, but it also enables the business firm to implement all future systems in the most expeditious ways possible. It is not necessary for such a plan to contain specific time periods for program implementation, since future developments may require substantial modifications. Better is the use of an elastic time frame that simply sets forth the planned sequence of implementation. In this way, the overall plan will not become an unbearable constraint for systems implementation.

The time, effort, and expense for developing an overall systems implementation plan should be made at the beginning of the total program. The effort involved will require that the available systems personnel initially spend the bulk of their time on this program. The time required to develop a well-organized program may range from several months to as much as one year. Unfortunately, there will be little direct measurable productivity in the form of new information systems applications during this time. For this reason, top management is frequently reluctant to pursue this particular avenue. They want to see results from their commitment of money and effort. Yet any such results are apt to be very shortlived without a good foundation program.

Once the overall plan is developed, individual information systems must be selected for implementation. The most obvious or natural areas for mechanization may not be the best choices. The best criterion for selecting areas for information systems implementation is profit potential. Areas that offer such potential are usually related to those business functions that are performing below par and where management has the least amount of control. Also, they usually are those areas in which management makes its most important decisions and utilizes its most important resources. In short, the best areas for the implementation of new information systems yield significant contributions both to profits and to competitive survival.

Using the criteria of maximum profitability the areas that consistently yield the greatest benefits are:[1]

1. Planning and control of finished goods in the distribution network

2. Planning and control of materials, machines, and labor in manufacturing operations

3. Planning and control of the material procurement function

These high-payoff areas should receive primary attention and emphasis in the planning of a computer-based information system. Personnel information systems would receive lower priority and attention, for example, since the cost benefits are more indirect.

Within each of these three areas, there will be many separate, yet closely related, information systems. The need to establish a precedence relation among all the different information subsystems is very important in the development of the overall plan. Ordinarily, a single area that is expected to yield the greatest contribution to profit will be chosen. Once the information system for this particular area has been completed, other areas will suddenly appear quite deficient in their operation. The

1. Joseph Orlicky, *The Successful Computer System,* (New York: McGraw-Hill Book Company, 1969), p. 96.

selection of succeeding subsystems for implementation will be most easily accomplished if adjacent (from the standpoint of operating sequence) systems are chosen next. In this way, the growth of the system can be most readily achieved with the smallest degree of systemic dislocation.

In a manufacturing operation the following information subsystem areas will usually be found:[2]

1. Forecasting
2. Materials planning
3. Inventory control
4. Manufacturing operations scheduling
5. Shop order release
6. Dispatching
7. Collection of production data

If manufacturing operation scheduling is chosen as the first information system to be developed, the next project should be either inventory control or shop order release. In this way, the orderly growth of the manufacturing information system may be most readily accomplished. Thus the selection of the first project is not of super-critical importance in developing an integrated information system since, in time, all of the other functional areas will also be included.

During the planning stage the primary objectives and the boundaries of each of the information systems must be clearly established. If possible, the information interfaces or flows of data across individual system boundaries should be established during the planning phase. In this way the logical progression and growth of the integrated system can be readily perceived and appropriate steps may be taken in the initial information system design to prepare for later development.

Along with the development of the overall plan, the need for standardized terminology should be recognized. The identification of records, forms and, especially, the names of individual items in these records is critical. A standardized list of terms designating each information element will both provide a solid basis for future systems growth and prevent semantic difficulties in discussing individual data items.

---

2. Ibid., p. 95.

THE INFORMATION SYSTEMS ANALYST

The information systems analyst seeks to fill the manager's need for information in his role as an information specialist. The systems analyst is expected to know in detail the various information flows present in the organization. He must be very familiar with the various techniques for gathering, organizing, and communicating information within the organization. He must be able to recognize a manager's information needs perhaps even before the manager himself is aware of them. In short, the information systems analyst is an information specialist who attempts to bridge the communication gap between the organization and the manager.

Obviously, the role of a systems analyst is rather complex. First, he must be a technician. Before he can perform his function effectively, he must know the capabilities of various communication and data-processing methods and techniques. Ordinarily he must have a substantial knowledge of computer technology as well as the characteristics of the available computer equipment. He must understand cost implications and operational constraints for all types of data processing. Although it is not mandatory, a working knowledge of one or more programming languages is quite helpful.

Secondly, the information systems analyst must be an organizational expert. He must be thoroughly familiar with the structure of the organization, including its lines of authority and communication. A knowledge of basic company policies, procedures, and rules is a standard part of his repertoire. In addition, he should have a reasonably thorough understanding of the organization's basic objectives and goals. A good knowledge of the various production processes is also a very valuable asset.

Finally, the information systems analyst must be a human relations expert. He must deal with many different types of individuals—managers and supervisors, hourly employees and technical specialists, as well as staff experts in accounting, finance, personnel, and engineering. He must be a good salesman, since he is in reality selling better communication to the organization. The systems analyst should also be a competent teacher since he will probably train employees to use the new information systems. Consequently, he must be a very unique individual, possessing technical talents, organizational expertise, and a large measure of human understanding.

Naturally enough, competent information systems analysts are difficult to find. The extensive background provided by a good formal education has been found to be very helpful in this type of work. For this reason many firms prefer systems analysts to have an MBA degree. Extensive on-the-job training is also needed to provide a satisfactory background about the organization's data-processing operations. This knowledge is normally best acquired by working (programming) for a period of time in the data-processing department. An active interest in people—another requisite for a good systems analyst—is an innate characteristic possessed by some, but not all, individuals. There is good reason for saying good systems analysts are both born and made.

DEVELOPMENT OF GENERAL BACKGROUND MATERIALS

After the overall plan for systems implementation has been developed and the personnel for the systems investigation are selected, the systems analyst must gather general background material about the production/operation system. This material provides a backlog of information about the operating environment against which the conventional information systems analysis will be made. Until the systems analyst has investigated this background, he cannot be expected to know or to understand the information dimensions of the production/operation system.

Quite frequently the systems analyst has performed other duties or held other positions in the firm. One of the great benefits from this approach for training systems analysts is that the analyst develops general organizational expertise. While performing other tasks in the business firm, he meets many other individuals; he begins to learn something about the firm's products and services; and he begins to develop insights into the actual operations of the business firm itself. Gaining this background of experience is a natural by-product of employment; it occurs even though there is no well-developed, standardized training program. The fledgling systems analyst who has not had this opportunity may acquire much of this background by keenly observing current operations and asking questions of the operating personnel.

On the other hand, the informal and haphazard training

that has just been described is often quite insufficient in itself
to provide the systems analyst with sufficient background knowledge. He must, of necessity, deliberately seek out additional
sources of information to complete his understanding of the total
business environment. The following records and documents,
when available, offer a rich source of additional background
information for the prospective systems analyst. Although some
firms may not have current publications of each type, the systems
analyst, somehow or other, should locate all of the information
available.

Policies and Procedures Manuals

A well-written policy manual contains a wealth of information
about the organization. As a rule, a policy and procedure manual
sets forth the guidelines for managerial decision making in nearly
all of the business' functional areas. More often than not, these
manuals emphasize the procedural aspects more than the broad
guides or bases for decision making. Statements of overall corporation objectives, as contained in press releases, may also
provide useful background information. Specific goals and objectives of operating divisions or departments may also be available when the business firm uses the managerial technique of
management by objectives. Guidelines for preparing operating
and capital budgets may also be useful if they are available.

Some of the information sources cited above are located
in rather inaccessible places. Regardless of the location of the
data, the alert systems analyst must pursue the development of
his background information with considerable zeal. For him to
think of designing information systems without a strong foundation of background knowledge is to place him at a tremendous
disadvantage.

Organization Charts

Another source of information for the systems analyst is the
firm's organization chart. Ordinarily, the organization chart
depicts the authority relations and the direct communication
channels through the organizational hierarchy. Unfortunately,
many firms do not keep their charts up to date by recording
both personnel changes within the organization and the realignments of the lines of authority that take place during reorgani-

zations. The systems analyst should keep these two difficulties in mind as he may find it necessary to develop his own organizational chart. In addition, he must also keep in mind that the organizational chart may not show functional lines of authority and other informal relations that are vital parts of the functioning organization. These understandings can only be derived by purposeful investigation.

Production/Operation System Flowcharts

Product flowcharts are schematic systems flow models that show the primary movement of the different products as they move through the various organizational units. In most manufacturing operations, the different raw materials are processed through successive departments in either a series or parallel system configuration to produce one or more final products. If the information systems analyst can trace the various production stages by preparing a product flowchart, not only will he gain a better understanding of the production/operation process, but he will also gain insights into the firm's communication problems.

Product flowcharts use the following symbols to present the various activities in the production process:

Operation   The performance of work in the manufacture of a product. Ordinarily, this task is assigned to a single work station and describes only a single activity. An explanation of each activity ordinarily appears just below the symbol.

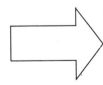

Transportation   The movement of the product or its parts among the various locations where work is performed. When the product moves from one department to another, two parallel lines through the arrow may be used.

Storage   Intervals during which the product, or any part of it, awaits further processing. When a *T* appears in the triangle the storage is only temporary. Permanent storage is designated by a triangle containing a *P* and indicates a delay of several days or more.

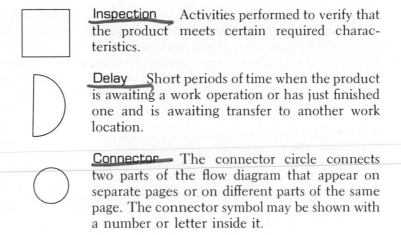

Inspection   Activities performed to verify that the product meets certain required characteristics.

Delay   Short periods of time when the product is awaiting a work operation or has just finished one and is awaiting transfer to another work location.

Connector   The connector circle connects two parts of the flow diagram that appear on separate pages or on different parts of the same page. The connector symbol may be shown with a number or letter inside it.

Employee Activity Descriptions

Job descriptions may also be a valuable source of information for the systems analyst. In many firms, especially where unions are present, job descriptions are readily available for clerical and operating employees. These normally list all of the activities the individual is expected to perform. They usually also include a description of the equipment the clerk or operator must use in the performance of his task.

Personal Interviews

The most widely used and the most important source of both general and specific information for the systems analyst is the personal interview. Most analysts find early in their careers that the bulk of the information about organizational activities and behavior has never been written down. It exists largely as independent fragments of knowledge in the minds of the people in the organization. The only feasible means for gathering this information is through the personal interview. The successful systems analyst, therefore, must become quite skilled at interviewing in order to extract this otherwise unavailable information.

The systems analyst will find that interrogation is a very useful means for developing both general background information about the firm's activities as well as detailed information needed in the information systems investigation. In developing background information he will be attempting to broaden his knowledge of company policies, procedures, and general operations as well as that of the human interrelations within the firm. Almost anyone who might possess reliable knowledge is a potential information source. When the analyst begins asking questions, he will quickly find that some individuals are very helpful and others are reluctant to provide any information. To provide broad coverage and reduce information bias, he should gather his information from as many different sources as possible.

Perhaps the best way to acquire general background information is simply to ask direct questions. Short, *why-when-where-what-how-who* type questions can usually be answered quickly and are the least likely to irritate the responder, provided he knows the answer or will admit ignorance. If the advice, "Ask an intelligent question every day and then go find the answer to it," is conscientiously followed, a wealth of general background information can be acquired in a surprisingly short period of time.

Using the interview to gather information for a systems investigation must necessarily be more planned and orderly than the gathering of general background information. In such an instance the systems analyst is attempting to determine the exact nature of the existing information system. The flows and transformations of information within the system must be precisely defined. The information supplied to management must be compared to actual needs. The difficulties and bottlenecks in the present information system must be examined and their causes determined. Such information is most readily found through a formal interviewing approach.

The following points will greatly aid the successful conduct of the interviews in an information systems investigation:

1. Develop as much background material on both the individuals and the activities of the organization as reasonably possible before scheduling any interviews. If proper research and preparation have been done, the interviewing time may be spent investigating the more important points in greater detail.

2. Interview the manager of the organizational unit first. He should have a great deal more detailed information about the overall operations than any individual and thus should

be able to provide the best insights into current information system difficulties. Moreover, if a degree of rapport can be established with the manager, the entire investigation will proceed much more smoothly. The other employees in the organization will catch the cooperative spirit from the manager and reflect it in their behavior.

3. Prepare specific information goals before the interview. Try to establish the general boundaries of the subject before the interview is made. In this way direct, probing questions may be readily formulated, all of the necessary information can be collected at one time, and the analyst may assess the quality of the responses quickly.

4. Schedule the interviews in advance. The analyst needs the wholehearted attention of the manager or employee during the interview. Making an appointment will help ensure that he will be able to conduct the interview at the most convenient time for the manager and, hopefully, that there will be a minimum number of interruptions.

5. Make a record of the interview. Some analysts take copious notes during the interview; others are content with only a few notes. Regardless of the quantity of notes, the analyst must not rely completely on his memory for the facts at some later date. Interview notes may also be used to summarize the findings with the interviewee at the conclusion of the interview.

6. The interviewer must do his utmost to stay on the subject of the interview and not wander off to other operational problems or dead-end topics. This tactic will enable him to collect his data in the minimum time without additional interviews.

7. The analyst must be especially careful not to subvert the interview by his own behavior. Displaying a superior attitude, using technical jargon, introducing personal opinions, and talking too much will all reduce the effectiveness of the interview to a very low level.

In order for the systems analyst to gain the greatest insights into both the operation of the existing information system and the information needs of the managers and the employees, he must consciously empathize with each interviewee as much as possible. If he can really see their difficulties and feel their information hunger, he will appreciate the importance and the delicacy of the task before him. Failure to see matters from the respondant's viewpoint makes communication more difficult and often reduces the amount of rapport.

After conducting all the interviews, the analyst is faced with the difficult task of integrating the diverse results into a coherent understanding of the existing information system. Putting together all of the pieces to make a single picture of the real situation will tax his conceptual abilities. The techniques for accomplishing this task will be taken up in the following chapter.

AN OVERVIEW OF THE INFORMATION SYSTEM DEVELOPMENT PROCESS

The preceding discussion has centered around the general requirements for developing new information systems. The firm's managers must first recognize the inadequacies of their present information systems and the necessity of developing improved ones. This recognition, of course, must be backed up by a commitment of resources. In addition, the necessary personnel, in particular systems analysts, must be available to design and implement the new systems. Before the information systems analysts may begin their tasks they must, naturally, understand the general business environment of the firm and its peculiar missions.

Once the commitment has been made and personnel requirements have been met, the actual work of developing an information system may be begun. For explanatory purposes we shall divide the information system development process into three separate phases as shown in figure 6-1. These three stages follow the general chronological systems development pattern. However, some scholars prefer to combine the first two phases or to further subdivide the systems implementation phase according to individual preferences.

The first phase may be termed the systems analysis phase. In this portion of the development cycle, the systems analyst is principally concerned with developing a detailed personal knowledge of the existing information system. He will, of course, draw heavily on the accumulated background information that we have discussed in this chapter. However, the principal thrust of his effort will be to gather as much information as possible about the operation of the existing information system. This

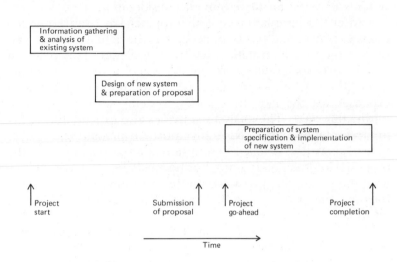

Fig. 6-1   The information system development process

knowledge may then be used to examine its individual segments and understand thoroughly the reasons behind any peculiarities he may find. In other words, he must completely analyze the existing information system before he is in a position to consider the development of alternative ones.

For convenience the singular term systems analyst *is used to designate the individual or individuals performing the systems analysis activity. For smaller-scale information systems, the most common practice is to assign a single analyst to perform the entire project. As the scale of the project increases, more analysts may be assigned to it. Since the total number of analysts assigned to a project may vary according to project size and other factors, the singular form will be used in subsequent discussions to cover both situations.*

In most cases there will be no sharp demarcation between the completion of the analysis phase and the beginning of the design phase for the improved information system. During the second stage of the cycle, the systems analyst will put together his bits and pieces of knowledge about the existing information system into a framework for an advanced one. He will attempt to improve the existing system's efficiency and effectiveness.

These efforts will culminate in the preparation of an information systems proposal for management consideration.

After the information system proposal has been presented to management and has been accepted, the actual implementation of the new information system may begin. This phase of the cycle is somewhat more complex and involves personnel from other organizational units. A major portion of the total expenses for the new information systems will be expended during this stage. The analyst's activities also expand during the implementation phase. Not only must he prepare the system specification (the detailed description for the operation of the proposed information system), but he must also work very closely with the programmers, the computer operating personnel, and the operating personnel in the department that will use the new information system.

The entire systems development process is both expensive from a cost standpoint and, frequently, lengthy from a time standpoint. There are no magic formulas or shortcuts that will yield reasonably satisfactory results with any degree of certainty. Only by proceeding with measured thoroughness through the information system development process will the results live up to the expectations of the systems users.

CASE STUDY: EUTECTIC ALUMINUM CORPORATION

The Eutectic Aluminum Corporation manufactures a complete line of aluminum extrusions. The principal markets for its products are the aircraft industry and the automobile industry; another market is selling building contractors and homeowners doors, storm windows, and screen frames.

Extrusion billets are purchased in two sizes (6″ and 8″ diameters) and three aluminum alloys (the first alloy is 2024 alloy—copper is the primary alloying element; 5356 alloy—magnesium is the primary alloying element; 6061 alloy—magnesium silicide is the primary alloying component). After the billets are received from the primary producers, they are stored in the raw materials storage area until needed for particular orders.

After production orders are released, the billets needed to fill each order are moved to the press department. The 6″ diameter billets are heated and extruded on a 1700-ton extrusion press, and the 8″ diameter billets are heated and extruded on a 3000-ton press. Immediately after extrusion on either press, all shapes made from 5356 alloy and 6061 alloy in the T5 temper are stretched to straighten them.

As soon as practicable, all extruded shapes are moved to the finishing department and placed in temporary storage. The 2024 alloy ordered in the T4 temper must be solution heat treated (heated to about 900° F. and quenched in cold water) and allowed to age at room temperature to gain maximum strength. Where maximum formability of 2024 alloy extrusions is desired (0 temper) the shapes are heated to 700° F. and slowly cooled in the annealing oven. The 5356 alloy extrusions do not require any thermal treatment. The 6061 alloy extrusions ordered in the T6 temper require solution heat treatment followed by an artificial aging treatment (around 300° F.) in the annealing oven. Sometimes 6061 alloy orders must be produced in the T5 temper, which requires only artificial aging in the annealing oven.

After the appropriate thermal treatment, all extrusions not already stretched must be stretched for straightening, cut to finished length, hand straightened (if necessary), and inspected for dimensions and defects. The finished extrusions are then moved to the shipping department where chemical coating treatments may be applied (if necessary). The extrusions are then ready for packaging and shipment to the customer.

Prepare a product flowchart for the entire operation.

INFORMATION SYSTEMS ANALYSIS

After the information systems analyst has acquired a general background of information about the organization and its operations, he may begin to study its individual information systems. In this stage of the analysis, he will be attempting to determine the essential nature of present information flows. Documenting them establishes a conceptual base both for the detailed analysis of the current system and the subsequent development of the improved one.

No production/operation system can exist without information flows to guide, direct, and control the operations. However, this does not necessarily mean that a formal information system of any type must be present. Some very simple production/operation systems function without the benefit of a formal information system. Under these primitive circumstances some sort of informal information system is present, since it is inconceivable that any production/operation system can function effectively in a total information vacuum. The systems analyst must be alert to the existence of both types of information flows (formal and informal) in his investigation.

In this chapter we shall examine how information flows may be defined and how information systems may be analyzed in terms of their objectives, boundaries, interfaces, elements, and functional relations. Any analysis of a current information system should include an evaluation of the present system's efficiency and effectiveness. In short, the analytical stage is ultimately concerned with the thorough documentation and study of the existing information system.

DETERMINATION OF INFORMATION SYSTEM OBJECTIVES, BOUNDARIES, AND INTERFACES

Ordinarily the first step in the analysis of any existing information system is to determine its objectives. An information system exists, of course, for many different reasons and for many different purposes, which constitute its objectives. Underlying the existing information system is the need for the operational manager and the employees to know those activities that have taken place, those that are currently being performed, and those that must be performed. Neither the employees nor the manager could possibly be expected to function efficiently or effectively without this knowledge. It is apparent, therefore, that each existing information system must have certain objectives that ultimately serve to satisfy the information needs of the individual managers and employees.

In many basic information systems there is an overriding objective for the whole system. This objective, known as the primary objective, spells out in general terms the principal reason for the information system's existence. For example, a purchasing information system has as its primary objective the orderly, efficient flow of requisite information for the purchase of materials at the lowest possible cost to be delivered to the firm in a timely manner. Similarly, other information systems may be described in terms of the functions they perform relative to the operation of the production/operation system. Inasmuch as the existing information system has been created for a specific purpose, the determination of that purpose becomes the first task in the information systems investigation.

Underlying the principal purpose or objective of the information system, we usually find one or more subsidiary objectives. These subsidiary, or secondary, objectives relate to specific information forms that operators or managers of the production/operation system currently receive and use in the performance of their duties. For example, in a purchasing information system the preparation of purchase orders containing all of the appropriate information to identify the order completely must be recorded and sent to the vendor. Other copies may also be used to advise the receiving department of the incoming shipment and to file in the purchasing department for a record of existing financial liabilities. In this example, the secondary objectives of the purchasing information system are to furnish notification to the vendors and receiving department as well as to provide a hard-copy record of the outstanding purchase orders. The individual copies of the purchase order are simply the means by which the vendor, the receiving department, and the purchasing department satisfy their information requirements.

The existing information system must be examined very closely to determine whether it satisfies information needs for each individual associated with it. Both the operating personnel and the organization managers have information requirements that the systems analyst must determine. The operational users of the information system will be concerned primarily with the information system as an operating information system. In this sense their interests will be closely related to the day-to-day operating function. The information furnished to managers will be substantially different from that for operating personnel. In contrast, managerial personnel associated with the information system will use information from it to perform the tasks of planning, organizing, directing, and controlling the production/operation system.

The information systems analyst, after determining which employees get what information, must determine the extent to which the existing formal information system is satisfying their total information requirements. Ordinarily, he will find that the information requirements are currently being satisfied through a combination of information received from both the formal and the informal systems. To the degree possible, he should examine the informal information system to determine the exact nature and extent of the information carried in it. Since this information from the informal system is obviously needed by both operating and managerial personnel, its content should be documented as completely as possible.

During the initial stage of the systems investigation, the analyst will probably begin to receive certain insights into information needs that are not currently, or only partially, being satisfied with existing information flows. Quite often the individuals being interviewed will volunteer comments about difficulties they currently have with the information system. From his own work experiences, the systems analyst may also note information deficiencies in certain areas. These insights are invaluable and may be put to very good use during the subsequent development of an improved information system.

The boundaries of the present system should also be examined during the initial investigation stage. Ordinarily, the first phase in the approach to this subject is to determine, in a general way, the principal information flows. This will establish the overall information area with which the present information system is concerned. In the second phase of system boundary determination, those information flows that are specifically excluded from the present system are set forth. Needless to say, the only information systems that must be specifically defined as being outside the existing one are those that might conceivably be included in it. Those other information systems, which clearly do not have any relationship with the present information system, do not, of course, need to be defined specifically. For example, in determining the system boundaries for a purchasing information system, we should include within them the preparation of purchase orders, the closing out of completed purchase orders, and other directly related activities the information system performs. On the other hand, the purchase requisition system and the accounts payable system must be examined to determine whether they are actually a part of the purchasing information system. The personnel information system, since it bears almost no relation to the purchasing information system, does not necessarily need to be distinguished as being outside it.

The next stage of the initial system study is the specification of information system interfaces. Many information systems rely, in part, on other information systems to supply a portion of their data requirements. To transfer information from one system to another, there must be an interface between the two. Moreover, the present information system may supply certain information to other systems across an interface. In this way the information requirements for the second system may be supplied with information that is already available. Collecting basic transaction data only once will result in the more economic collection of data and will tend to reduce the introduction of errors.

DOCUMENTATION OF THE EXISTING INFORMATION SYSTEM

Ideally, the systems analyst should be a collector at heart. This statement is particularly true in the documentation stage of the systems investigation. To be most effective, the analyst should collect samples of all the documents and records used in the information system and thoroughly document all the system's activities. In this way he can develop a firm knowledge of the exact nature of each information element in the entire system. Without this supporting documentation, he will subsequently have no way to determine the system's informational content and processing behavior.

The order in which he collects documents or records is relatively unimportant. The principal requirement is only that a sample of each document or form be collected sometime during the investigation. Included on the document sample should be the required data that must be entered on the form as well as the optional data. A description of the record form and its information content in this way will be quite useful to him later in the preparation of an improved information system design. A record of the activity levels (average number of records of each type input to, or output from, the system per unit of time) should be developed since it will also be quite useful during subsequent analysis.

Beginning with the inputs to the information system, the systems analyst will usually find two major types of inputs. The first type is the source documents that describe the initial business transactions. They may, of course, take many different forms, such as sales receipts, employee time cards, purchase requisitions, or bank deposit slips. All of these source documents possess certain characteristic data that defines the business transaction. The second type of input records are the actual record forms used to input data directly into the information system. Examples of this type of input are punched cards, paper tape records, and optical scanning records. The various data fields should be clearly noted for each type of input data record.

The outputs from the information system may be classed in a way similar to that for input transaction classification. Output reports, including reports to managers, other individuals outside the production/operation system, and employees in the operation system, must be collected. In this way the present method of reporting business transactions may be properly noted. The second class of outputs is intermediate data records, such as punched cards, which are transmitted to other information systems for subsequent use. Examination of the information content of these two types of outputs will establish the nature of the elements that must be input to the information system. That is, we cannot expect any data-processing system to produce information that is not based in some direct way on a corresponding input element. Computers cannot create information without proper input data.

Next, the processor, or the processing operations, must be examined. The individual clerical (data-processing) operations performed on the raw data must be recorded to establish the precise means by which the data transformation process takes place. This information may be obtained from the clerical job instructions, from the work procedures for a particular job, or from direct questioning of the operators themselves. It is usually best not to rely on a single information source to describe the processing activities. This observation is valid for any of the various information sources for processor activity. The analyst should be wary of uncooperative employees omitting or confusing pertinent activities in job descriptions.

Especially important in documenting processor activity are the decision points in the information system. When a decision must be made with regard to the type of processor activity to be performed, the criteria for it must be explicitly stated. For low-level decision-making activity, which is typical for many clerical operations, the decision table format is particularly appropriate. Not only is it compact in form and size, but it enables the analyst to verify that he has indeed satisfied all the possibilities present in a decision-making process. If he uses this technique, he is not likely to overlook any loose ends in his investigation.

Another portion of the information system that the systems analyst should document carefully is the information files used in the information system itself. The filing sequence, or file key, is very important for locating information within a given file. Although each record in a particular file usually contains much information, it can be located only with great difficulty without some index identification. For example, if a vendor file in a purchasing information system is in vendor number sequence, information can be located quickly when the vendor number is known. When the number is not known, locating information about a certain vendor will require a search through the entire file. To circumvent this difficulty, cross listings that link certain information elements may be prepared. In the case of the vendor file example, a separate list in vendor name sequence may be prepared to provide the corresponding vendor number.

In file documentation the systems analyst should note, in particular, how long information is retained. Some files act only as temporary depositories of information; information is purged from the file after it has satisfied its purpose. For example, an open purchase order file contains copies of outstanding purchase orders. When a purchase order is completed, the purchase order document is removed from the file in order to keep the basic file constantly updated. On the other hand, certain files are intended to maintain documents permanently. The closed purchase order file, which contains copies of completed purchase orders, is meant to retain these records indefinitely and thus to provide an historical reference.

Also important in file description is the source of information. In some cases the files simply hold documents or information prepared during the normal course of system operation. In other cases they may contain unique information collected solely for use in the file. The open purchase order file previously discussed contains documents (purchase orders) prepared by the normal processing operations of the purchasing information system. In contrast, a vendor file, which contains a variety of information about vendors, requires special information to be collected especially for it.

Finally, the systems analyst should document the control techniques used to maintain the integrity of the present information system. Hash totals (a count of the number of transactions in a batch of data) provide a check for the number of raw data inputs entering an information system. Sometimes special documents are prepared to verify the accuracy of information contained in different parts of the system. Control sheets of this sort, such as trial balance sheets, are extremely useful and are widely used in financial information systems to keep the information within the system accurate. Also important in maintaining system integrity are procedures for checking the validity of systems information against the production/operation system for which it is designed. Physical inventory counts may be taken at fixed time intervals to verify the quantity listed. In this way, the information system truly mirrors the actual condition of the physical inventory.

DEVELOPMENT OF THE INFORMATION SYSTEM FLOWCHART

After the existing information system has been documented, or in conjunction with its documentation, the information systems flowchart should be prepared. Its essential purpose is simply to provide a pictorial model of the information flows to facilitate subsequent analysis. In this sense the flowchart of the present information system is a working paper and may not appear in the systems proposal or the systems specification.

The American National Standards Institute (ANSI) has prepared a recommended list of symbols for computer-related information systems flowcharting. The shape of each recommended symbol, its meaning, and an example of its use is shown in figure 7-1. The figure also shows, some other commonly used symbols.

ANALYSIS OF THE EXISTING INFORMATION SYSTEM

After the systems analyst has determined the present information system's objectives, thoroughly documented the system, and developed its flowchart, he is ready to proceed with the analysis. The objective of the analytical stage of the investigation is to break down the individual components and activities that comprise the information system into their most elemental form. Only after the existing information system has been completely dissected can the improved one be designed.

The analysis may be begun by determining the answers for each part of the existing information system to the following questions:

What activities are performed in each step of the system?

Why are they performed in their present way?

When must they be performed?

Who performs them?

Where are they performed?

Some of these questions may have been answered, at least partially, during the documentation stage. In the analytical stage, however, they are directed to each activity in the information system. In other words, at this point the systems analyst must

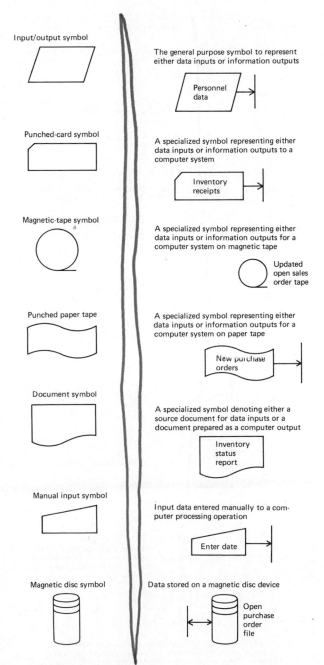

Input/output symbol

The general purpose symbol to represent either data inputs or information outputs

Personnel data

Punched-card symbol

A specialized symbol representing either data inputs or information outputs to a computer system

Inventory receipts

Magnetic-tape symbol

A specialized symbol representing either data inputs or information outputs for a computer system on magnetic tape

Updated open sales order tape

Punched paper tape

A specialized symbol representing either data inputs or information outputs for a computer system on paper tape

New purchase orders

Document symbol

A specialized symbol denoting either a source document for data inputs or a document prepared as a computer output

Inventory status report

Manual input symbol

Input data entered manually to a computer processing operation

Enter date

Magnetic disc symbol

Data stored on a magnetic disc device

Open purchase order file

Fig. 7-1   Flowchart symbols

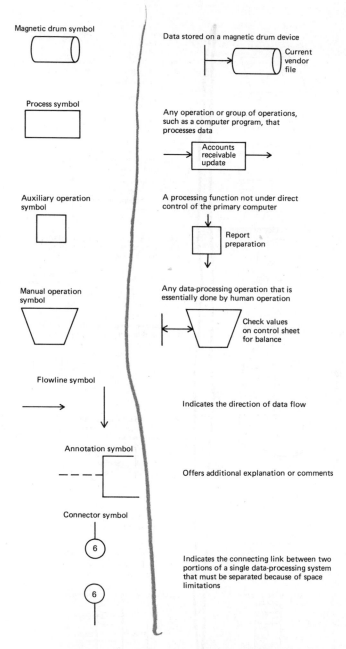

Magnetic drum symbol

Data stored on a magnetic drum device

Current
vendor
file

Process symbol

Any operation or group of operations,
such as a computer program, that
processes data

Accounts
receivable
update

Auxiliary operation
symbol

A processing function not under direct
control of the primary computer

Report
preparation

Manual operation
symbol

Any data-processing operation that is
essentially done by human operation

Check values
on control sheet
for balance

Flowline symbol

Indicates the direction of data flow

Annotation symbol

Offers additional explanation or comments

Connector symbol

6

6

Indicates the connecting link between two
portions of a single data-processing system
that must be separated because of space
limitations

In addition to the ANSI symbols, several other symbols are
sometimes used in flowcharting manual and clerical information
systems. These symbols have not been standardized, but are
used by many systems analysts in their information systems in-

Fig. 7-1 (cont'd)

vestigations. This lack of complete agreement should not deter us, since the ultimate purpose of the information systems flow-chart is simply to facilitate understanding of the existing information flows within the organization.

The following symbols may also be used for information systems flowcharting.

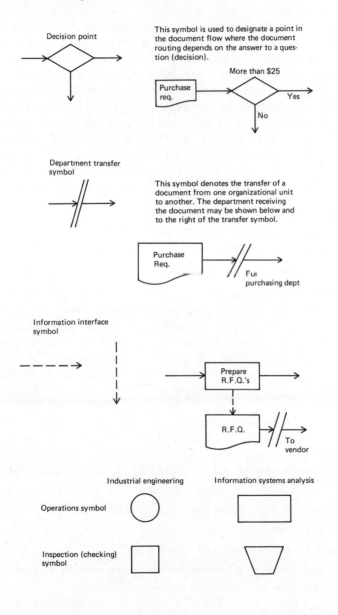

Decision point

This symbol is used to designate a point in the document flow where the document routing depends on the answer to a question (decision).

Department transfer symbol

This symbol denotes the transfer of a document from one organizational unit to another. The department receiving the document may be shown below and to the right of the transfer symbol.

Information interface symbol

Industrial engineering

Information systems analysis

Operations symbol

Inspection (checking) symbol

Fig. 7-1 (cont'd)

determine the exact nature of the information system and thoroughly understand its behavior.

Because so many operating information systems have been developed piecemeal over an extended period of time, the analysis stage may require extensive effort. Sometimes the reasons for particular practices may be found in policy statements and memos, but most frequently the reasons behind certain practices can only be found by careful interviews with long-service employees. Quite often the analyst will find that the more or less superfluous activities in the present system were instituted in the distant past to take care of difficulties encountered then or to provide safeguards against potential abuses and human errors. Careful and thorough analysis should bring out all of these facts.

During the analysis of the information system, the systems analyst should continually keep searching for means to improve the performance of the existing system. Each operation in the system should be subjected to the following four questions:

Can the operation be eliminated?

Can it be combined with another?

Can it be simplified?

Can its sequence be changed?

The answers to these penetrating questions will offer the analyst many insights for improving the information system.

The systems analyst must continually be on guard against quick, superficial answers to the above questions. There may be good valid reasons why the present operations must be performed in a certain way. When there is any doubt about the answers for a particular operation, questioning several different long-service employees may provide more information.

The decision-making processes in the information system must be subjected to the same level of scrutiny as the operations. The same type of questions that were asked in analyzing the operations must also be asked about the decision-making processes.

Can the decision-making process be eliminated?

Can it be simplified?

Can it be formalized as a set of rules?

Can the making of decisions be delegated to operating employees?

The preparation of formal decision rules (decision tables) is an excellent means for structuring the decision-making process. The inexorable logic that must be used to prepare them forces one to consider each possible situational variation and the resultant decision needed to accommodate it. Thus establishing decision rules, whether in table form or not, facilitates the study of the decision-making process.

One point of special concern in analyzing decision-making processes are the decision points reserved for special managerial attention. (These decision points are sometimes known as pre-action control points.) The existence of such decision points indicates that management is not delegating authority. For example, a few years ago the former president of one of the major airlines reputedly required his personal authorization for all purchase orders of more than fifty dollars, except for food and fuel. Examples of this magnitude are fortunately rare today. However, there are still many instances in which managers are loath to delegate authority to operating personnel. Inevitably this leads to bottlenecks in the information system.

The solution to the problem of authority delegation rests with managerial planning. Establishing operating plans, budgets, and structured decision rules to screen out the truly exceptional cases will reduce this difficulty to a manageable level without losing control over the operating system. Further, adequate and timely managerial reports will dispel the anxiety felt by managers who are concerned about losing personal control.

Virtually every operating information system is subject to "short circuiting" when two or more individuals who perform different operations or functions work together. For example, when a machine breakdown occurs and the purchasing agent cannot be reached, managers who have a good working relation with the purchasing agent may take matters into their own hands. They give the vendor a call and get the necessary parts, promising to have a confirming purchase order sent the following day. Emergency action of this sort is justified, at least in the operating manager's eyes, by the pressing need for the replacement parts. On the other hand, such action is clearly a violation of the purchasing procedures top management has established. If the relation between the operating manager and the purchasing agent is good, these procedural breaches will likely never come to the attention of top management. In this case the operating information system has been short-circuited.

Operating information systems are short-circuited much more frequently than most managers wish to acknowledge. Upper-level managers usually make strenuous efforts to keep these occurrences to an absolute minimum. Failing to follow prescribed procedures may even result in disciplinary action against the offenders. The procedural violation will then become a source of interdepartmental squabbling and name-calling.

The systems analyst should recognize that extraordinary circumstances will arise from time to time and that short circuits will occur. He should attempt to ascertain the nature and frequencies of these emergencies and, for his own records, the individuals most frequently involved in them. This type of information will help him determine the effectiveness of the existing controls in the operating information system and provide insights for ways various operations and decision points may be eliminated, simplified, or combined.

EVALUATION OF THE EXISTING INFORMATION SYSTEM'S EFFICIENCY

The final stage of the existing information system investigation seeks to establish the system's relative efficiency and effectiveness. The purpose of this portion of the investigation is to determine a basis to compare the existing information system with alternative ones. A rational evaluation of both system efficiency and effectiveness is essential to establish the relative merits of any new information system. Without an objective comparison, the proposed information system will be dependent on subjective feelings, and management will not be able to assess properly the impact of the new system on the firm's operation.

The evaluation of system efficiency uses the same criteria that we previously discussed in evaluating organizational efficiency. The total cost of operating the existing information system per time period and the cost per record transaction must be determined. The efficiency with respect to time required for record processing is also an important consideration. Likewise, the quality measure of efficiency, the ability to keep errors from entering the information system, and the accuracy of the system's information must also be assessed. The quantity measure of efficiency does not usually apply when evaluating existing information systems, since there is only a remote likelihood that input data will be accidentally lost. When errors of this sort do appear, they will be reflected in the relative quality of the information system. Thus quantity measures of efficiency assume an insignificant role in the evaluation of the present information system.

Cost Efficiency

Cost is usually the major factor in the analysis of information systems efficiency. Ultimately, the most convincing arguments either for or against a proposed information system are related directly to expense.

The measurement of cost efficiency for an information system may be approached from two different directions. First, the total cost for operating a given information system over a given period of time provides a measure of absolute cost efficiency. Second, the cost efficiency for a given information system may be approached by determining the cost associated with the processing of each individual record. This approach yields a more relative value since it discounts the effect of transaction volume. Both these approaches are usually combined to provide a complete appraisal of cost efficiency.

Determining tangible costs for the operation of the existing information system is a relatively straightforward procedure. Tangible costs are defined as those costs with which a dollar value may be easily associated. The largest tangible cost, the direct labor expense, may be determined by taking the combined wages and salaries for those individuals who directly perform the operations in the present information system. Salaries of clerks, typists, data-processing machine operators, and other personnel who play direct roles in systems operation should be included in the determination of the total labor cost. Not infrequently, these individuals spend only a portion of their total working time directly engaged in the operating functions of the information system. The normal practice in this case is to prorate their wages and salaries for the amount of time they are actively working in the system. Information about wage and salary rates may usually be readily obtained from the personnel or payroll department.

The second type of tangible cost is that of the data-processing equipment. The depreciation expense and the equipment rental cost of typewriters, keypunchers, verifiers, unit record equipment, and other equipment normally used in the operation of the information system must be included. Naturally, when the equipment is used in two or more different information systems, its expense will normally be divided or prorated on the basis of relative usage. Equipment rental charges and depreciation costs may be obtained from accounting department records.

Although the cost of operating supplies and services may not at first seem significant, they should also be included in determining the total information system cost. These items include paper, printed forms, miscellaneous supplies, and equipment maintenance expenses. The cost of the supply items may be obtained from the purchasing department; maintenance cost figures, if any, may be obtained from the equipment maintenance contracts, which are also in the purchasing department.

Overhead costs are special costs allocated to various organizational units to prorate collective costs that are not directly assignable to individual operations. These costs include all of the administrative expenses for the operation of the information system; that is, the management costs for supervisors and the fringe benefits for the operating personnel involved in the system. In addition, cost allowances for the space used by the operating personnel and the utility costs for the operation of the information system should be included. The accounting department has the basic data from which these costs may be developed.

Determining the intangible costs associated with the present information system is a much more difficult problem. By definition, intangible costs are those with which a dollar value cannot be readily associated. By their very nature they must be based on subjective estimates. For example, determining the cost when a customer sale is lost because an item is actually out of stock is at best difficult to ascertain. The fact that errors exist within a given information system and result in erroneous managerial action will certainly result in additional operating expenses for the firm. When intangible costs are developed, they should be clearly designated as estimates and the basis for the estimate should be set forth in a footnote.

Ordinarily the total cost for operating the existing information system for a certain period of time is usually determined first. The collection of various total costs per time period discussed above is most easily done before the cost per transaction is computed by simply summing up the individual costs of each type for a specified period. The cost per transaction may then be determined by dividing total cost by the number of transactions during that time. The basic cost values thus computed become the basis of comparison for all proposed information system modifications.

Time Efficiency

The time efficiency values for the information system are also very important measures. The objective of such measurements is the determination of the average time required to process a given type of business transaction. For example, after a purchase requistion has been prepared and submitted to the purchasing department, a certain period of time will elapse before the purchasing order is placed with the supplier. The average time required to place a purchase order thus becomes a measure of time efficiency for this portion of the purchasing operating information system. Likewise, the timeliness of the management reports generated by the purchasing information system, such as the listing of open purchase orders, has a very important bearing on how quickly purchasing department management can take corrective action. Both of these time measures are therefore important in assessing time efficiencies for the operating information system.

Since many operating information systems perform several different functions and process many different types of information, a better measure of time efficiency may be made by considering each type of transaction in relation to each operating function. In other words, each type of transaction should be traced through the operating information system and actual process times for each process step should be collected. After the various types of information transaction times for each function have been measured, a total time efficiency for each type of transaction may be prepared.

The systems analyst must measure the process times for a sufficient number of information transactions to determine a reliable average time required to process each type of transaction. If a large number of transactions ordinarily take place during a particular period, the best approach may involve taking a sample for the determination of the average process time value. If a relatively small number of a particular type of transaction ordinarily take place, the best approach may be to measure the types of all of the transactions made during that time. In either case, sufficient data must be taken to assess or measure adequately the time efficiency for each major type of transaction.

The timeliness of managerial reports prepared from operating information system data is another important consideration in determining the system's time efficiency. In this case, the analyst measures the time required to prepare the necessary management reports. Since it is very difficult to measure the cost benefits of more timely reporting, he must usually be content with making time efficiency measures for managerial reporting. Inasmuch as managers generally recognize the need for timely information, the time efficiency value for each type of managerial report is usually a very important managerial consideration.

Quality Efficiency

The measurement of quality efficiency is perhaps the most difficult of all the efficiency measures. However, some assessment must be made in order to evaluate this form of systems efficiency. The objective of such measurement is to evaluate the degree to which the information system is prone to develop and propagate errors.

Human beings make mistakes from time to time in the performance of their functions. These mistakes, while individually not of outstanding significance, collectively create many difficulties in managing the business firm. The number of informational errors that must be present in order to impair efficiency seriously does not have to be large. As a matter of fact, a value of one or two percent error will seriously impair the credibility of the information system's data. It naturally follows that substantial efforts must be taken to reduce the number of potential errors if the system is to be reliable.

Examining an information system to determine the reliability of its internal data is made more difficult because errors are often not recognized. Operating employees and managers are usually aware of mistakes that have been brought to their attention as error conditions. However, there may be many other errors in the data that are not recognized as such. These errors will continue to exist indefinitely and gradually will erode the quality of the information system. Some errors are never brought to managers' attention because the involved employees and other outside users of the information system may take advantage of these mistakes. For example, a customer who receives an invoice or bill for less than the agreed upon price of the merchandise is not likely to voice a complaint. Nor are employees and supervisors likely to complain when errors are made that reflect creditably on their performance. Further, there is a significant tendency for most personnel to bury their mistakes: in other words, mistakes that are not likely to be discovered simply remain hidden.

Therefore the direct measurement of quality efficiency is a most difficult endeavor. While the systems analyst may be able to collect fragmentary data about data quality in the present information system, this approach will yield only inconclusive results.

The indirect evaluation of quality efficiency may be a better or more fruitful approach. While the indirect measurement of quality efficiency does rely to a great extent on subjective evaluation, the results often provide a more accurate evaluation of the data quality within the existing information system. The indirect approach relies primarily on analyzing a current information system for various error detection procedures. For example, using a verifier operation after keypunching data on a unit record card is a quite efficient error detection method. Using control techniques such as hash totals, cross footing, and the like can also indicate that the data within the information system is of a reasonably high quality. Further, substituting machine effort for human effort in the various data-processing activities (classifying, sorting, listing, and calculating) tends to minimize the errors present in the information system.

When both the direct and the indirect approaches for evaluating data quality are combined, the analyst gets a more realistic appraisal of the information system's quality efficiency. The results of this evaluation, unfortunately, are difficult to express in quantitative terms. Consequently, the expression of quality efficiency is usually made in subjective terms, such as *excellent, very good, acceptable,* and *poor.* These terms, as applied to each portion of the existing information system, reflect only an approximate evaluation of the system's quality efficiency.

EVALUATION OF THE EXISTING INFORMATION SYSTEM'S EFFECTIVENESS

Evaluating the present information system's effectiveness consists of comparing its explicit and implicit objectives point-by-point with its actual accomplishments. In this stage of the evaluation we are seeking to determine how well the system actually achieves the purposes for which it was created. Defining both the primary and secondary (explicit) objectives, of course, was necessary before the investigation could be conducted. Now that the initial investigation has been completed, there is sufficient information both to determine the system's success in meeting its explicit objectives and also how well it is fulfilling its potential as an operating, management, and decision-making information system.

With regard to the system's primary objectives, we usually find that the existing system is at least minimally effective; that is, that it functions in a way that achieves its primary purpose in a reasonably satisfactory manner. Of course, there will usually be a certain amount of dissatisfaction with the present information system or else the systems investigation would never have begun. On the other hand, the system must have been achieving the basic objectives, at least partially, in order for the firm to produce goods and services. For example, a purchasing information system must operate moderately well to provide the necessary raw materials and supplies for the production process. No business firm could possibly operate without some means for obtaining these raw materials and supplies in a reasonably expeditious manner. Thus we may usually assume that the existing information system does function at least minimally well.

Since the secondary objectives of the information system are more specific, evaluating it for effectiveness in achieving them can be more specific. Each of the secondary objectives should be compared individually with the degree of achievement actually obtained. Questions such as, "Does the present information system adequately describe and define the flow of information?" and "Does the current information system provide management with sufficient, appropriate, reliable, and timely reports?" should be asked. In short, just how well is the existing information system meeting the purposes for which it was originally designed? The answers to questions of this nature will give the systems analyst insights about the system's effectiveness.

The current information system may also be evaluated against idealized objectives for information systems of its particular type. Thus the analyst may compare the actual achievement of objectives against the objectives that a given type of information system may theoretically achieve. This approach demands that he have a strong knowledge of each manager's information requirements and the demands for information by operating personnel working with the current system. Because managers are often unable to articulate their needs to the systems analyst, he must be able to anticipate and conceptualize those needs without too much help from either the managers or the operating personnel. Briefly, the analyst should strive to know more about the real information needs of the organization than any other individual in the organization does before he can fully evaluate the system's effectiveness. However, recognizing that this objective is awesome should not deter us from trying to conceptualize the information needs of the operating manager. Both the product flowchart and the systems flowchart provide the analyst with much useful background information for determining such needs.

The evaluation of information systems effectiveness is most apt to be deficient not in the processing of data (operating information system), but in the preparation of management information reports. This aspect of the effectiveness evaluation, therefore, deserves the most extended consideration.

Let us turn our attention to the departmental work flow model shown in figure 7-2. This model presents a simplified view of the major work unit stream found in the production/operation system. Analyzing the individual components in the production/operation system reveals several information areas that are very useful to the manager. The numbers in the figure are keyed to the following discussion:

1. Forecast of input work unit activity. The firm's top management as well as the supervisors of each organizational unit must have information about the future flow of inputs to the system. Managers cannot plan their future activities without some knowledge of the activities their organizational units will be performing in the future. The sales forecast seeks to provide this information for the entire business firm. As customer orders are received during each period, variances between forecast and actual activity may be com-

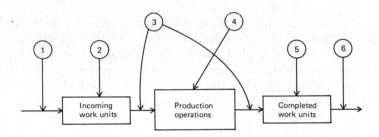

Fig. 7-2 Departmental work flow model

puted and used to update operational plans. In this way the business firm may become more responsive to external market forces and achieve greater stability also.

When forecasts of future input activity are broken down to the organizational unit level, the forecasting problem may be somewhat simplified. Organizational unit forecasts usually emphasize shorter periods rather than the long time spans found in corporate forecasts. Due to the long lead time required to manufacture many products, it is often possible to prepare adequate forecasts of work unit inputs into individual departments well in advance. PERT and line-of-balance techniques may be used to break down the total work requirements into separate activities and provide realistic work schedules for each organizational unit in the entire project or program. Consequently, forecasting input unit activity into individual organizational units may be more precise.

2. Input work unit status. Once incoming work units have been identified and the activity requirements specified, the manager may use this information to make the immediate processing plans. The backlog of work units, together with their schedules for performance and completion, form the basis for allocating personnel, materials, supplies, plant, and equipment in the production process. The backlog in this case represents the work units that may be processed at the manager's discretion. Thus the status of work unit inputs ready for processing is an important part of the manager's information needs.

3. Processor activity. Once activity is begun on a particular work unit, the manager needs to know the level of effort

or the degree of activity that has been expended on the work unit over an appropriate period of time. In this way he may be continually appraised of the activities of his organizational unit relative to scheduled work and monitor them.

The difficulty in defining the activities of the organization is compounded when there are several distinct and separable processes within the organizational unit. Thus, describing the activity of each work unit by process center may be necessary in order to describe the processing activities precisely enough to serve a useful managerial purpose.

The usefulness of process activity reports increases greatly when appropriate system efficiency measurements are included. Cost performance by work unit, raw materials utilization by work order, work schedule achievement by work unit, and quality level attainment give the manager much more usable information about his organizational unit's activities. Including standards for comparative purposes will enable him to assess both the efficiency and the effectiveness of the operations being performed.

4. Processor Status. The status of each work unit at particular points in time within a given organizational unit is a very important managerial control device. Here the manager's interest will be focused on the determination of the current status of each work unit being processed. This information can serve both as a means of locating a given work unit and of checking the progress of the work units relative to the schedule.

Both process activity and process status reports are amenable to exception reporting. Those work units that are currently within the specified cost, time, quantity, and quality standard limits do not need to be reported to management. The manager's attention may then be more properly directed to the determination of exceptional conditions; that is, those work units that do not meet the allowable constraints (cost, time, quality, and quantity), thus indicating a need for managerial action. In this way the manager's valuable time may be more readily directed to investigating extraordinary (both good and bad) conditions.

5. Output status reports. This type of management report gives the status of completed work units that remain in the organizational unit manager's area. Insofar as the individual

organizational unit is concerned this report is analogous to the finished goods inventory report for the business firm. Although this information may not directly concern a particular operating manager, to the succeeding manager in the process this information is, in reality, his input status report. Thus the output status report from one organizational unit is also the input status report for the next unit in a sequential production process.

6. Output activity reports. Most managers need a record by time period of the work units that their units have completed and released. The data in these output activity reports may be organized by individual process within the organizational unit, by work unit, by product type, or by customer, depending on the manager's needs. These reports will give him a record of the accomplishments of his organizational unit. Moreover, they allow him to assess the relative cost, time (schedule), quantity, and quality efficiency of his unit. This information may also be analyzed to reveal important systems relations and thereby provide a basis for improved operational planning.

   The managerial information requirements shown in figure 7–2 are also related, in a manner of speaking, to the traditional managerial functions. The work unit input status and activity reports are closely linked to the management planning functions and may be termed planning reports. The processor status and activity reports provide management with information about current system activity, thus permitting resources to be restructured or reallocated on a short-term basis. These information flows are vital ingredients for the ongoing, dynamic organizing process. Finally, the output status and activity reports (including appropriate historical data) may be used as an information base for system performance analysis. The knowledge thus derived will be invaluable for accurately appraising the current *modus operandi* of the system and for managerial control. In this way these historical information flows are closely related to the traditional concepts of management control.

   The individual manager's information needs in each of the areas discussed above may be satisfied in several different ways. First, the data may be presented simply as listings of work units in status or activity formats. This is the most complete approach; however, it presents the manager with more information than he may be able to use within his allowable time limits for reading and reflection. Secondly, the data may be summarized according to some convenient plan to present concise statements of work unit status and activity. Third, the reports may be prepared using predetermined criteria for the detection of exception conditions. Finally, the manager may wish to know only the activity or status of specific work units in his organizational unit. This type of information is best made available through separate inquiries to a random-access auxiliary storage unit.

Not every operating unit manager will need all of the different report types discussed above to manage his operation intelligently. Sometimes, for example, the incoming activity may be of such unvarying magnitude and composition that this type of information does not really enhance his ability to manage his organizational unit. Sometimes also, the work units that have been completed are immediately moved to another organizational unit and are no longer of any concern to the original manager. Output status reports would then be superfluous for him.

In summary, the effectiveness evaluation of the current information system is a subjective collection of statements that relate current system performance to the desired system objectives. Deficiencies and shortcomings that are noted may be used as reference points in evaluating the effectiveness of proposed information systems. The preparation of detailed existing information systems efficiency/effectiveness studies should be an important part of every information systems investigation.

CASE STUDY: THE PLAINFIELD WATER BOARD (A)

The city of Plainfield, located in the Midwest, has a population of about 50,000. Water sales and services are handled by a separate organizational unit known as the Water Board, which is a unit of the city government.

A director of operations manages the board's operations. There are four departments—water pumping and distribution, construction and maintenance, meter reading, and office—each with their own department head. The purchasing agent serves under the office manager and has three clerks assisting him.

The purchasing system procedures have been in use for some time and are currently under investigation. The procedural steps in the present purchasing system are:

1. A purchase requisition is originated in a department by the department head and is submitted to the director of operations for approval.

2. The director of operations either approves or disapproves the requisition. If approved, the requisition is forwarded to the purchasing department for action. If disapproved, it is returned to the originating department.

3. (a)   Items under $25—The purchasing agent contacts an appropriate vendor for all items under $25 and records the vendor's name and address on the requisition form.
    (b)   Items over $25—A request for quotation (RFQ) form is sent to three potential vendors for all items over $25. The names and addresses of all vendors are recorded on the purchase requisition form in the space provided.

4. After the vendor is selected, the requisitions are sent to the accounting department where they are coded with the account to be charged (asset, expense, and so forth).

5. The requisitions are then returned to purchasing where prenumbered purchase orders are prepared with distribution as follows:
    (a)   Original   —To vendor
    (b)   1st Copy   —To current vendor file along with purchase requisition to await material received report (filed alphabetically by vendor)
    (c)   2nd Copy—To originating department
    (d)   3rd Copy —Permanent file (filed by purchase order number)

6. The vendor invoice from the vendor and the material received report from the storeroom are filed temporarily in the current vendor file until both forms are received. Upon receipt of both, all items in the current vendor file are pulled and attached together to form a vendor set (the first copy of the purchase order, the purchase requisition, the vendor invoice, and the material received report).

7. The vendor sets are audited by the clerks, who perform the following operations:
    (a) Vendor prices and quantities are checked between invoice, materials, received report, and the purchase orders.
    (b) Extensions and footings on vendor invoices are checked.

    If the vendor invoice is found to be in error, the vendor is notified and the set is again placed in the current vendor file to await the corrected invoice or credit memo.

8. Upon completion of the audit operation above, the vendor set is recorded in the vendor set log with purchase order number, vendor name, invoice number, and total invoice amount. This list is used to prove that the vendor set has left the purchasing department.

9. The vendor set is sent to the accounts payable unit.

10. Upon completion of a payment voucher by accounts payable, the vendor set is returned to the purchasing unit and the vendor set log is updated to record the vendor set transfer.

11. The vendor set is filed in a permanent file (the closed purchase order file) alphabetically by vendor name. Currently the system processes an average of twenty completed purchase orders per working day (twenty working days per month). The average time for the completion of a small order (less than $25) is ten days and for large orders (greater than $25), twenty-six days. The average monthly cost of operation for the purchasing system including salaries, supplies, and overhead is $4,000.

What are the primary and secondary objectives of the present purchasing information system?

Prepare an information system flowchart.

Analyze the purchasing information system. Critique

Evaluate the efficiency and effectiveness of the present purchasing information system.

THE DESIGN OF NEW INFORMATION SYSTEMS

The design of a new information system is the activity that follows the investigation and analysis of the existing information system. When information system analysis and systems design are treated as separate activities and performed by different individuals, as may occur in some large data-processing organizations, systems design will be an entirely separate and distinct activity and will follow systems analysis. However, when the same person performs both of these activities, the design of the new information system may actually be started during the analysis stage. As the shortcomings of the existing information system become more apparent, the systems analyst will gradually shape a new information system design in his mind to resolve the difficulties. Hence the two processes—information systems analysis and design—often overlap each other in actual practice. In the subsequent discussion we shall assume that the systems analyst performs both the analysis and design activities. As previously stated, we shall use the term *systems analyst* to designate one or more individuals.

The design stage of the systems investigation demands that the analyst have a high level of technical and conceptual skills. The major objectives for the new information system, as well as the subobjectives for the operating and management information systems, must be identified to develop a unified set of goals. In addition, the systems analyst must have a thorough knowledge of the available data-processing equipment for the new information system. He also needs substantial expertise in recognizing human constraints (resistance to change) that will be present during the implementation of any new information system. Finally, he must understand certain principles of information systems design that specify the management of information during the various stages of data processing. Each of these factors play a significant role in the creation of every new information system.

OBJECTIVES OF THE NEW INFORMATION SYSTEM

The overall objective of the new information system is simply a general statement of the aims and goals that it seeks to achieve. In some cases the statement of the new objective will be very similar to the old one. The old objective furnishes an excellent starting point for developing the new one. The systems analyst should, of course, modify the general system objective for the existing information system with the planned system additions and expansions suggested by the systems analysis.

After the statement of the general system objective has been completed, the systems analyst should develop the specific subobjectives for the operating information portion of the new information system. In considering the subobjectives for the operating information subsystem, system efficiency will likely receive more attention than system effectiveness. The emphasis on efficiency occurs because the effectiveness of the operating information system is usually already passably good.

Specific operating information subsystem goals that are often sought in the design of a new information system are:

1   The automation of clerical functions
2   The development of centralized information files
3   The elimination of superflous decision points
4   The improvement of data input timeliness and accuracy
5   The standardization of work procedures
6   The elimination of superfluous control procedures

Achieving any of these goals will contribute to reducing operating costs, processing of business transactions faster, and improving the accuracy of the data within the information system. Attention to these checkpoints will help the analyst set the operating system subobjectives for an improved information system.

The statement of subobjectives for the management information system section of the new information system will probably differ greatly from those of the management information system section of the existing system. This is a natural result of the need for information system improvement being concentrated more in the management information area. Managers must have more complete, more timely, and more accurate information about the activities of their organizational units and of the business firm to improve the quality of their decisions. If their information requirements were being moderately well met with the existing information system, there would not be the urgent managerial interest so frequently found for new information systems. Thus the emphasis of the subobjectives for the management information system section will usually be directed toward improving systems effectiveness.

Both status and activity reports for the work unit inputs, work units processed, and work unit outputs may be demanded from the new information system. The basic organization of the reports (complete listing, exception, or summary) as well as their frequency may be specified at this time. Analytical and efficiency reports of the organization and its activities are also quite helpful and informative. The timely preparation of these reports will substantially improve the information system's effectiveness. The efficiency of the management information section is usually not stressed since it is understood that the reports should be prepared in the most efficient way possible.

If managerial decision making is to be supplemented or supplanted by the new information system, this should be stated as a subobjective also. Included in this statement should be a definition of the decision-making process.

DATA-PROCESSING CONSTRAINTS

The availability of data-processing equipment imposes very real restrictions on the design of the new information system. This is especially true where the new system depends on the use of a computer and other allied equipment. Needless to say, there is no point in designing a new information system that will use data-processing equipment the firm does not presently have or cannot reasonably anticipate acquiring if needed. It is therefore necessary for the systems analyst to be quite familiar with the firm's equipment configuration—either the present equipment or that which can be available in time for the system installation.

The systems analyst may begin his equipment configuration appraisal by considering the existing data-processing equipment first. This examination should include not only the equipment available but also its capacity to handle new applications. Two questions must therefore be answered: "What types of data-processing equipment are on hand?" and "Does the available equipment have sufficient capacity to process the new system's additional workload?" The answers to these two questions will, in large measure, establish the initial parameters for the new system's design.

To obtain the answers to the above questions, the analyst's attention should be directed toward the individual elements in the data-processing system. An inventory of the available computer hardware and software will quickly show where limitations are. The following list of commonly available DP equipment will provide a guide for assessing the present equipment availability limitations.

I.   Unit Record Equipment
     A.   Keypunch machines
     B.   Verifiers
     C.   Sorters
     D.   Collators
     E.   Interpreters
     F.   Reproducers
     G.   Accounting machines
     H.   Calculators

II. Input Devices
     A.   Punched card readers
     B.   Punched paper tape readers
     C.   Magnetic ink character recognition devices
     D.   Optical character recognition devices
     E.   Magnetic tape units
     F.   Remote inquiry/input terminals

III. Central Processing Unit
     A.   Core storage (fast memory) capacity
     B.   Software

IV. Auxiliary Storage Devices
     A.   Disc storage units

     B.   Drum storage units
     C.   Miscellaneous storage devices (CRAM, Data cells, and
          so forth)
V. Output Devices
     A.   Magnetic tape units
     B.   High-speed line printers
     C.   Cathode ray tubes
     D.   Data plotters
     E.   Card punch units
     F.   Paper tape punch units
     G.   Remote output terminals

After the systems analyst has determined whether each type of equipment listed above is in the computer system, he should determine whether it has sufficient capacity to include the data-processing requirements of the new information system. Three different types of equipment capacity restrictions must be evaluated to accurately assess the capacity question:

1.   Time constraints. (Is there sufficient open processing time to handle the increased workload from the new information system?)

2.   Equipment power constraints. (Does the existing DP equipment have the internal processing ability to accomodate the new application? For example, the availability of sufficient core storage is often a limiting factor in time-shared applications.)

3.   Software constraints. (Is the software available to integrate the new application readily into existing operations?)

Each of these constraints limits the ability of the existing equipment to handle new applications. At this stage of the system design it may not be possible to evaluate precisely whether a particular element in the computer system will be a real constraint. These facts should be noted in the system proposal and a more definitive study undertaken during the preparation of the system specification.

The availability of equipment and the capacity limitations discussed above should not necessarily eliminate all consideration of other equipment configurations. For example, simply because there is not ample disc or drum storage capacity does not mean a new application is not feasible. It does mean, however, that the new information system must contain adequate economic justification to obtain the additional equipment. If this seems likely, the systems analyst will certainly wish to include the possibility in his assessment of the overall data-processing capabilities.

HUMAN CONSTRAINTS

All information systems rely on human beings for their preparation, operation, and use. The managers, the operating employees, and the data-processing personnel each have a set of unique problems and frustrations. Therefore, during the design stage the systems analyst must take into account the special characteristics of the individuals who will be associated in any way with the new information system. Their expectations and attitudes as well as their technical abilities will determine to a great extent the new system's success. During the design stage the analyst has the opportunity to structure the new system to minimize these human problems.

Balancing all of these divergent viewpoints and arriving at a sound information system design is not an easy task. To achieve a workable design, the analyst must closely examine the innate capacities and human qualities of each group. Compromises with idealized system design may be necessary and may, in fact, speed the implementation of the whole information system.

The data-processing personnel and in particular the programmers are most likely to have difficulties of a technical nature. The question of programming competency is important, but may be overshadowed by hardware and software difficulties. For example, if the new system uses remote input terminals and multiprogramming software routines, the programmers and operators will be faced with computer operating system debugging problems in addition to the task of preparing the operating programs. It would probably be inadvisable in this case to attempt installation of a complex data-processing system in a single giant step. Rather, the new information system should be designed for implementation in a series of steps to allow the personnel time to solve their problems one by one.

The availability of sufficient programmers is an additional consideration in designing a new information system. Programming talent is often in short supply. New information systems should be designed around or take into account both the number of programmers that can be assigned to the new system and their technical competencies. Each new DP system must, naturally, be meshed into the existing capabilities of the personnel and the present work schedule.

The operating employees who prepare the inputs and use the outputs of the information system may have unique problems also. To begin, there are often fears of job displacement when a new information system is introduced. Employees are also likely to have a certain amount of anxiety about the new status of their jobs. Yet their active cooperation is needed to make the new system a success. With these thoughts in mind, the analyst should structure the new information system to introduce as many job-enriching qualities as possible. If possible, operating employees should not be expected to perform only a single task. Rather, individual tasks should be combined in such a way as to enlarge the scope of each job.

The systems analyst should also try to assess the degree of the employee's resistance to change. Of course, a certain amount of resistance is to be expected. On the other hand, if the resistance to change is expected to be large, the implementation schedule should, perhaps, be divided into several steps. It may also be advisable to include more stringent controls over both inputs and outputs to forestall accidental and intentional tampering with the system.

The wishes and desires of managers present the widest assortment of difficulties for the analyst in designing information systems. The problems encountered with managers range from the over-enthusiastic manager who wants a sophisticated new information system complete with bells and whistles to the conservative or even hostile manager who thinks his present system is the best of all possible ones. Most managers, fortunately, are somewhere in between these two extremes. They are realists who want both an efficient (especially cost-wise) and an effective information system. They regard an information system as a means to an end rather than an end in itself. Because they tend to be results-oriented, the analyst may wish to design the system to achieve some quick payoffs. If the quick payoffs are a part of a comprehensive system design and can be integrated later into a complete system, this strategy may be appropriate. The analyst must never, however, lose sight of the overall plan for information systems implementation.

THE SYSTEM PROPOSAL

The system proposal is a report to management on the results of the investigation that has been conducted. Its purpose is to provide the interested managers with the details of the existing and proposed information systems. Before more time and money are spent, the concerned managers must decide whether to proceed with the development and implementation of a new information system. The decision as to whether to proceed is, of course, one for which management alone is responsible.

Contrary to the practice of some system investigations, the purpose of the system proposal should never be to hardsell a new information system. The dangers associated with "overselling" cannot be overemphasized. Cost and time budgets that are subsequently grossly exceeded will cause untold harm to the reputation of the data-processing group. Management reports that do not actually help the manager make better decisions will ultimately lead to disrepute of system investigations. The reports the new information system will generate must be accurate and timely. As a result, the systems analyst should approach the system proposal with the intent that the information contained in it be both factual and objective. To the extent possible, the proposal must be a full disclosure of the benefits, the costs (financial and otherwise), and the potential problem areas for the new information system. Half-truths and misleading statements must be avoided at all times.

There is no standard format that is universally used for all system proposals. The following general format presents the major topics and issues that are usually discussed in systems proposals. The sequence of topics may, of course, be rearranged to suit the organization that prepares the proposal or for which it is intended. Thus some proposals might start with the conclusions and recommendations section, since this format permits the managers to get the major points of the report without considering a detailed examination of the existing and proposed information system. The following topics are normally included in the systems proposal:

   I. Systems investigation background
  II. Description and analysis of the existing information system
 III. Description and analysis of the proposed information system

System Investigation Background

In this section of the report the historical background of the information system study is presented. This information usually includes the person or persons who requested the initial study, their reasons for seeking the investigation, and some of the more important problems they were facing at the time. Details about the investigation itself are also usually included. These items include the name or names of the individuals who conducted the investigation, the time when it was actually begun, and any other pertinent information that was encountered during the study. In essence, this section of the systems proposal simply provides general background information about the circumstances surrounding the original investigation.

Description and Analysis of the Existing Information System

This section of the system proposal outlines the present methods and/or procedures in the existing information system. The various items discussed in chapter 7 may be presented in this part of the report. Ordinarily, a flowchart of the existing information system is included in this section to facilitate the presentation. Operating costs as well as the other measures of system efficiency (time, quantity, and quality) should also be included. A discussion of system effectiveness is also appropriate in this section of the systems proposal.

Description and Analysis of the Proposed Information System

In this section, the objectives and subobjectives of the new information system must be presented and discussed. The various constraints should be set forth to establish the basis for the system's design. A flowchart of the proposed information system will aid greatly in showing the major streams of information. Some of the more pertinent details of the system design should also be presented, especially the output reports that the managers receive to assist their decision making. The full costs and benefits of the proposed information system must be discussed completely.

Discussion of the Existing and Proposed Information Systems

In this section of the system proposal, point-by-point comparisons of the existing and the proposed information system are presented. Here the systems analyst has the opportunity to discuss the major advantages and disadvantages of the two systems. The particular points for which comparisons are appropriate are cost, information systems processing time, quality of the information contained in both systems, and the capacities for expansion or expanding activity in both systems.

Conclusions and Recommendations of the Investigation

This portion of the system proposal presents the conclusions the analyst reached during the course of the investigation of the new system's feasibility. If appropriate, the analyst may wish to make recommendations for the acceptance of the new system. He may also wish to make certain recommendations about the operations of the present information system that might improve its efficiency and/or effectiveness. There should be no inference that the recommendations are anything more than recommendations.

An appendix prescribing the details for the implementation of the proposed information system is quite often included in the system proposal. The purpose of this appendix is to set forth the plan for developing and installing the new system. The various activities together with the individuals responsible for their performance should be included in the appendix. Time estimates for the completion of each activity may be included to establish checkpoints for gauging the progress of the new installation. A convenient method of presenting implementation programs is the PERT chart. Another important feature that should be included in the appendix is a detailed cost analysis for the implementation of the new system. These cost values may subsequently be used to establish budgets for the performance of each activity. In this way, the operating managers may follow the cost progress of the installation program.

After the system proposal has been completed and distributed, many firms present the systems investigation to the managers (and sometimes the operating employees also) in an oral summary report. This report offers each manager the opportunity to discuss the relevance and accuracy of the conclusions and recommendations. Most systems analysts feel that the oral presentation offers a final opportunity to present their views to the managers, as well as to receive feedback from the managers themselves. The oral presentation is usually regarded as the conclusion of the system investigation.

Normally, the decision about implementing the new information system will be made a short time after the presentation. Budget approvals must be granted, which may take an appreciable length of time. After the decision to go ahead has been reached, all the pertinent details of implementation should be announced to the operating personnel. Such an announcement will help them understand the implementation plans and will promote their cooperation during the implementation process.

INFORMATION SYSTEM DESIGN

The Outputs

The formal process of information system design is usually begun by specifying the desired information outputs first and then proceeding backwards through the system to determine the raw data sources and their content, the necessary data-processing steps, and the structure of the supporting data files. This approach emphasizes the importance of the system outputs as the principal reason for the creation of a new information system. Beginning with the analysis of the outputs also leads naturally to determining the information system elements and their peculiar interrelations rationally and logically. For these reasons this approach is most often followed.

Other approaches to system design may be used under special circumstances. When modifying an existing information system, for example, it may be practical to start with the present information system inputs and files to determine the various types of outputs that could be generated by restructuring the processor operations (reprogramming). In this way the current information system would provide a base for the development of the "new" information system and there would be a minimum time delay for the system to become operational. Since these quick and dirty design jobs usually do not fully consider the operating and managerial information needs and are often difficult to integrate with other information systems, they should be regarded only as temporary expedients.

The secondary objectives for both the operating and management information system portions of the whole information system, which are set forth in the introductory section of the system proposal, furnish a convenient starting point for determining the desired outputs. Such subobjectives, if they are properly formulated through extensive discussions with managerial and operating personnel, specify the general information requirements for the system. To meet these expressed needs, the new information system must generate outputs (reports, messages, documents, and special listings) that contain the required information. In this stage of system synthesis, the analyst will probably be well advised to spend greater effort in developing management information rather than operating information. The reasoning behind this advice is that the management reports will be evaluated by a relatively few individuals while many people will offer comments on the operating reports.

Report names that are truly descriptive of their contents and identify the function of the report may be assigned to each system output after it has been identified. A master list of all the reports may also be prepared to serve as a guide or checklist in the subsequent preparation of the design for each report

Next, each general information output must be analyzed in depth to determine the content that is needed to satisfy the information needs implicit in the corresponding subobjective. Initially, the analyst may wish to include all conceivable information items. He should do this with the realization that cuts will probably be necessary later to achieve a practicable report. Using the knowledge gained during the information-gathering stage of the system investigation, follow-up discussions with key managerial and operating personnel, and his own insights, the analyst should gradually be able to piece together the items of information that are truly needed to fulfill the individual subobjectives of the new information system. Ultimately, of course, this synthesis must lead to a specification of the report contents and a layout for each type of output.

In designing system outputs there has been a tendency, especially when computers are first introduced into business firms, to flood managerial and operating personnel with many thick computer printouts. Computer system analysts and data-processing managers have acted as though the benefits of the computer were directly proportional to the quantity of output prepared. Since a single modern high-speed printer can prepare over 75,000 pages of hard copy each day, it is quite easy to prepare many more and much larger reports than management can possibly use effectively. Once managers have been confronted with this avalanche of paper, they are likely to react negatively to computerized information systems. In fact, these thick reports may even tend to produce greater confusion and uncertainty than existed before the introduction of the system. The systems analyst, therefore, must continually strive to provide the information users with sufficient information to satisfy their needs, but he must resist the urge to provide all of the information available.

A widely used technique for reducing the size of output reports is exception reporting. This technique requires that only extraordinarily good or bad results be reported. In this way the manager receives only information that requires action. He does, however, receive the full records for all of the exceptional items, since they are worthy of his attention.

Implementing exception reporting requires, first of all, that standards of good and bad performance or conditions be established. The computer program then outputs only those informational items that are outside the preset limits. The resulting report is thus composed only of items that may require a management decision.

Also of great importance in this stage of system synthesis is the specification of the information sequence in the various output reports. If, for example, we wish to prepare a status report for the open purchase orders, the sequence of the items in the report may be by purchase order number, by vendor number, by item name, by item identification number (part number), by shipment due date, by ordering department, by account number to be expensed, or by purchasing agent placing the order. Although the information content of the open pur-

chase order report might well be the same for all of the sequences above, the item sequence will strongly influence the
report's usefulness and should be directly related to the user's
needs. In addition to specifying the major reporting (sorting) sequence, the systems analyst may also wish to specify intermediate and minor sorting sequences as well as subtotals, totals,
and special notation symbols to make the individual reports
more useful.

The final step in the output synthesis is the development
of the report formats. The report title and other suitable heading information for easy identification should appear at the top
of each page. Column headings and the data spacing patterns
must be established. The prevailing practice by nearly all systems analysts is to place the sequence-specifying information
items (major, intermediate, and minor sort keys) on the left-
hand side of the report and the attribute-identifying information
items on the right-hand side. This arrangmennt facilitates locating the individual information items. For the preparation and
presentation of report layouts, special printed forms are used.

The Inputs

The next stage in the design of a new information system is
to determine the various input data streams and specify their
contents. A primary source of input messages will probably be
the operating personnel who are performing the activities about
which data is being collected. For example, reservation clerks
in an airline reservation information system make seat status inquiries and passenger flight reservations; time clerks prepare
time sheets for the payment of personnel in a payroll information system; service station operators prepare charge forms for
credit gasoline sales.

Staff personnel who have specialized information needed
by the information system may also originate input messages.
Thus flight schedulers must establish flight identification
numbers, departure and arrival times, and total number of seats
available for each flight in an airline reservation information system; personnel department employees must assign employee
numbers and input social security number, number of dependents, pay rate, and payroll deduction data for a payroll information system; accounts receivable clerks must prepare custom-

er addition and deletion forms in a credit-card accounts receivable information system.

Finally, input messages may sometimes be originated by computer personnel and managers. Computer operators may be required to enter such information items as date and job number as well as input messages to correct certain error conditions; managers may enter item status inquiries. Regardless of origin, the identification of the different input data streams must be established before the contents of the information stream can be specified.

The determination of the raw data requirements for each type of input is generally a straightforward, logical procedure. For every item of information in each output report, there must be a corresponding source of raw data entered into the information system as an input. Thus the specification of the output reports and their contents determines the information inputs the system needs.

A technique that is sometimes useful in specifying data input items is classifying each output information item according to one of the following categories:

I items—nontransformed, in-and-out items
C items—computed items
K items—constant items

Recognizing a specific output information item as belonging to a particular class can assist in the determination of the most appropriate source. For example, K items are more appropriately derived from job setup cards and program constants than transaction data.

The systems analyst may vary his efforts over a wide range in this portion of the systems investigation. At one extreme, he may wish to limit them to a careful item-by-item check of each output report to satisfy himself that the various streams of input data can include all of the necessary data. In this case he simply wishes to make certain that there are adequate and sufficient data sources for each output. At the other extreme, he may wish to specify the data content and format completely for each type of input message. The former level of effort is, perhaps, more typical for a systems proposal, while the latter course must be followed in a systems specification.

The Processor

There are two separate, distinct approaches to the design of the processor section of a computer-based information system. The choice between the two is critical since the selection of one data-processing method or the other establishes the essential operating system's *modus operandi.* The first approach—batch processing—is characterized by a periodic (daily, weekly, monthly, quarterly, or other convenient time unit) processing of the accumulated transactions pertaining to a certain information system. The second approach—online processing—is characterized by the immediate processing of individual transactions as they occur. Although these two approaches to processor design tend to be mutually exclusive, there are occasional examples of batched data transactions being input on online systems.

Batch, or periodic, data processing, from an historical point of view, has been the most widely used method for automated data processing. Early computer systems, as well as unit record (punched card) systems, achieved their levels of cost and time efficiency by processing batches of similar records at regular time intervals. Batch processing is still a widely used data-processing technique and will probably remain important into the foreseeable future.

Hardware improvements within the past decade, especially with regard to remote input/output terminals, improved auxiliary storage devices, and expanded core storage, have hastened the development of information systems that maintain the status of production/operation information systems on a current basis. Moreover, there appears to be a continuing trend toward developing larger and more complex online, or continuous, data-processing systems. Thus the importance of online information systems is growing and we may confidently expect many more online system applications in the future.

There are practical differences between batch and online data-processing systems in each of the following areas:

Data preparation and collection Typically, batch systems have separate, identifiable data collection and preparation activities such as keypunching source documents to punch cards, preparing magnetic tape from punch cards, record sorting, and so forth. Online systems, on the other hand, usually collect data as business transactions occur and transmit it directly to the computer without any intervening operations.

Processor set-up   Batch processing often involves reading the appropriate program in to core storage and performing certain housekeeping activities before the data can be processed. Processor set-up activities are minimized in an online system since the system is actually maintained in a state of constant readiness.

Input data accuracy control   Raw data audit techniques to maintain accuracy may be readily incorporated in batch processing systems, as found in the separation of keypunching and verification activities. Input accuracy may be more difficult to control with online processing systems, although most remote input terminals do provide immediate feedback to the sender.

Processor efficiency   In batch processing every single master record must be read into fast memory (core storage) for record key comparison with the current transaction record. If the number of transaction records is small relative to the total number of records in the master file, processor efficiency may be rather poor. Under the same circumstances online processing is more efficient, since only the active master records are actually accessed. An additional consideration is the problem of idle computer time when no transactions are entering an online system. Overall, batch processing makes somewhat more efficient use of processor capacity than online processing.

Computer equipment   Batch processing usually requires fewer types and smaller capacity equipment than online systems. Remote terminals and auxiliary storage capacity are not necessarily required with batch systems, but are normally needed for online systems. The processor capacity of online systems may need to be larger also in order to handle peak transaction activity loads.

Software   The computer operating control systems for online systems tend to be more complex, expensive, and troublesome.
    The choice between batch and online data processing depends on the evaluation of several factors:

Cost   Batch processing systems tend to have a slightly lower cost per transaction, which is the result of more continuous use of the computer and reduced hardware/software requirements. Online processing systems may be able to overcome some of the cost disadvantages by running batch processing jobs concurrently and performing other operational economies such as file consolidation.

Quality   Since it is difficult to check online inputs for accuracy, there is a tendancy for such systems to contain more errors than batch systems.

Timeliness   Since data is processed at specified intervals in batch systems, the information is never really current. This situation is not particularly disadvantageous under certain circumstances. Most financial reports and many management reports depend on data accumulations to provide sufficient information for trend analysis. On the other hand, there are many instances where data timeliness is crucial to the success of the information system. An airline reservation system, for example, would be of little value without immediate access to the current status of all scheduled flights.

The design of the actual data-processing operations may be viewed as three distinct phases—the collection and preparation of the raw data inputs for entry into the processor (computer), the primary data-processing operations, and the preparation of the various outputs. In relatively simple DP systems, these three phases tend to be distinct and individually identifiable. In large scale integrated DP systems, however, the outputs from one system often become a portion of the inputs to another. Thus output preparation may also be input preparation and the distinction among the phases becomes blurred. For the purposes of our discussion, however, we shall consider these three phases separately.

Data gathering and preparation operations are a necessary prelude to the main data-processing operations. Raw data, as contained in source documents, is often not in a form suitable for direct entry into the system. The first requirement, therefore, is the collection or transfer of raw data into a machine-processable form. This activity may be accomplished for batch data processing systems in several different ways: keypunching (and verification) of punch cards, paper-tape punching, magnetic tape keyed data recording, optical or magnetic ink character recognition, and direct keyboard entry. Online data-processing systems may also use any of the techniques above but usually rely on remote terminals for collecting and transmitting data inputs.

Principle #1   Raw data inputs must be placed in the most appropriate machine-processable form for entry into the data-processing system.

The determination of the most appropriate machine processable form will be subject to many considerations. When raw data is available only from handwritten source documents, keypunching into punched cards is the most common transcription method. When source data can be made available as a by-product of source document preparation, some or all of the data transcription process may be eliminated, which results in both cost and time savings as well as improves data accuracy. Although the present availability of different types of input equipment is important, the long-run benefits and cost savings from other input equipment should be thoroughly explored.

Principle #2   All raw input data for which accuracy is an important consideration must be separately checked by a verification process before it is entered into the main processing operations.

Every reasonable precaution, of course, must be taken to make certain the raw input data is as accurate as possible. However, certain types of data, such as financial data, are especially critical and must be checked by verification before being entered in the system to insure the accuracy of the resulting outputs and maintain system integrity. Input records that must be verified are usually punched on cards by one operator and checked on a verifier by a different operator. Other forms of raw data inputs may be checked by various means. For example, remote terminal inputs (typewriter type) prepare typed copies of the input messages, which may be examined for errors before they are released to the computer.

Principle #3   All raw data inputs must be edited for accuracy and completeness before the main data-processing operations are begun.

Editing programs may be incorporated at several places in the preparation of inputs. For example, editing programs may check data as the original machine-processable records (punched cards or paper tape) are being transcribed to magnetic tape or auxiliary storage. Under other circumstances it may be easier to perform editing just before the main processing operations for each record. The important point is not the placement of the editing operation but rather its presence.

> **Principle #4** For the most efficient batch-type data processing, all of the separate but similar input data streams should be gathered together and transcribed into the most efficient form for entry into the main processing operations.

The transformation of raw data into machine-processable form does not complete the raw data input preparation phase. In general, different types of transaction records may be batched together, provided they have the same record keys (employee number, part number, purchase order number, and so forth) and a transaction code that identifies their natures. At the same time the records are being grouped, they may also be transcribed into the most efficient form for entry to the computer (auxiliary storage or magnetic tape). In this way input data may be entered into the computer as quickly as possible and the program may move from one input record to the next with minimum delay, minimizing the main processing operations cost.

This same concept is also used to a certain extent with remote terminal, online data-processing systems. Raw data inputs are held temporarily (buffered) and entered into the system as a discrete batch or group of electronic impulses. In this way valuable computer time is not wasted simply waiting for the completion of an input message.

> **Principle #5** For all batch data-processing systems, the input transaction records must be sorted to a specified sequence (major, intermediate, minor) before the main processing run.

Virtually all business-oriented operating information systems reference one or more master information files with current transaction record inputs. The common denominator for these bodies of data is the record key. To develop efficient batch data-processing operations all transactions that relate to a single data record should be processed consecutively. Further, the progression from one record to the next should be orderly and follow a logical plan to minimize programming difficulty and operations cost. Sorting current transaction data to a specified sequence and maintaining tape and auxiliary storage master files

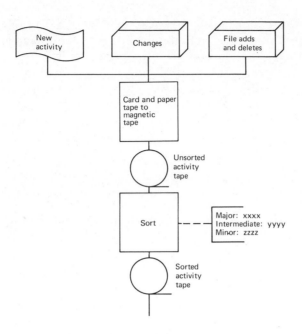

Fig. 8-1   Generalized model for batch processing

in the same sequence is the most direct means for obtaining efficient internal DP operations.

A generalized information systems model for a batch processing operation that shows the application of the principles above is shown in figure 8-1. An example of the data collection and transmission activities for an online system is shown in figure 8-2.

In a majority of business and commercial data-processing systems, the processor functions may be viewed as file updating and/or file interrogation tasks. In a typical file updating operation, business transactions are collected and posted to one or more master record files. The master records, which may be stored on either magnetic tape or in auxiliary storage, will then contain the most current information available for each record in the file. For example, the file updating process in a simple batch inventory information system would process all of the receipts, disbursements, and adjustments for each part number against the part number master record and maintain the current inventory status of each part number. Most business firms have

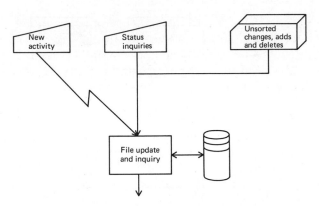

Fig. 8-2   Data collection and transmission in an online system

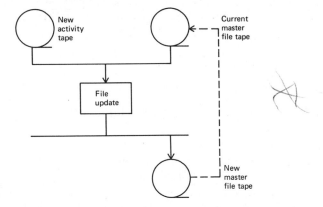

Fig. 8-3   Updating a magnetic tape master file

many different files (such as customer, vendor, open purchase order, raw material inventory, personnel, and so forth) that must be kept current to provide essential operating and managerial information.

Principle #6   When magnetic tape master files are used, current magnetic tape master file(s) will comprise one (or more) input stream(s) and corresponding new magnetic tape master file(s) must be created during the file updating run. (This principle is illustrated in figure 8-3.)

File interrogation, or file consulting, tasks are also very common data processor operations. In these tasks data from the master files is extracted and appropriate action is taken according to the program. Selected information from the master record may be manipulated or output to furnish information for operating and managerial personnel. A simple monthly billing system, for example, would interrogate the customer master file, extract selected information (customer name, address, purchases and payments during the past thirty days, and so forth), and print the monthly statement.

It is not at all necessary for file updating and file interrogation operations to be performed in separate processing runs. When the situation warrants, which is quite often, the two tasks may be combined and much greater processing efficiency realized.

> **Principle #7**   Individual records within the data files stored on auxiliary storage (disc, drum, and so forth) devices must be addressable from data within each transaction activity record.

The application of this principle ordinarily causes no difficulty with magnetic tape master records since the master records are already sequenced by record key. When master records are stored on auxiliary storage devices, however, record location difficulties may arise. A logical, linking relationship between the record key and the auxiliary storage address of the master record must be established. Otherwise there will be no way to locate the master record. While the solution to this difficulty is usually reserved for the system specification, the system analyst must keep this problem in mind as he designs the master file structure of an information system. An example of individual master files with their address-related key is shown in figure 8-4.

> **Principle #8**   Computer output information streams should utilize the most efficient output devices available.

Obtaining high levels of computer operating efficiency is one of the most important goals for data-processing personnel. Since most business applications are input/output bound, it logically

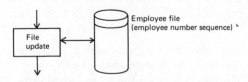

Fig. 8-4   Individual master files with their address-related key

follows that every effort should be made to output information as fast as possible. Decoupling both input and output preparation operations from the main processing operations permits the highest input/output transfer rates and will usually improve operational efficiency.

The practical application of this principle produces more significant results on large scale DP systems than small. Thus, in a large-scale installation the bulk of the main frame output, as well as input, would be on magnetic tape that would subsequently be processed on a small computer (slave unit) to prepare the hard copy reports. In this way the large computer would not need to idle along driving high-speed printers and wasting valuable computation time.

> **Principle #9**   An activity listing of all accepted transaction activity inputs should be prepared during every file updating run.

Although this principle is sometimes violated to reduce the amount of hard copy preparation and file storage costs, omitting activity listings can lead to unfortunate misunderstandings and difficulties. Suppose, for instance, a customer claims to have paid his bill and has a cancelled check to prove it. In all probability the payment was credited to someone else's account when the customer accounts were updated. The question that must now be answered is "Which customer account has been erroneously credited?" The easiest way to trace a difficulty such as this is to prepare and file an activity listing for each master file updating cycle.

The purpose of an activity listing is to provide an audit trail for tracing any individual activity transaction that enters the information system. Without an input activity listing there is no feasible way to determine the reason or source of errors in the information system. For this reason auditors often insist on having this type of output. Input activity listings, of course, may be prepared for both batch and online data-processing systems.

> **Principle #10**   Spurious messages discovered by the editing program should be output on an exception (input error) report.

Errors from incorrect input entries and spurious transmission signals can quickly destroy the effectiveness of an information system. Incoming data checks performed by the edit program, however, can eliminate a portion of these errors. The

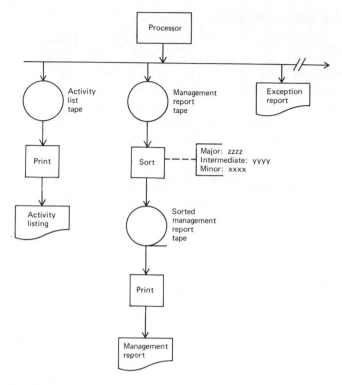

Fig. 8-5   Output section sample of system flowchart

purpose of this report is simply to list input transactions that were not processable for subsequent followup. The detailed discussion of the data-checking techniques to be used in a given information system is ordinarily not discussed in the system proposal, but is reserved for presentation in the system specification. However, the systems analyst should include an exception report in the outputs if he intends to perform any input data editing in the information system.

   Principle #11   Output reports in different record key sequences from the master record key sequence must be sorted before report preparation.

   The output information stream must necessarily have the same sequence as the master file from which it was drawn. To present the information in another sequence will require a sorting operation.

   A system flowchart incorporating examples of the last four principles appears in figure 8-5.

ECONOMIC ANALYSIS

The development, design, implementation, and operation of a new information system requires the use of scarce economic resources. Funds must be spent; manpower must be assigned; facilities and equipment must be leased or purchased; and time will be required. Prudent management cannot allocate these economic resources to new information systems without realizing a return from their investment. To ignore the economic aspects of this management decision would be truly irresponsible behavior by any manager.

The only rational basis on which to decide is that the value to the business firm of a new information system must exceed the total resource cost for the installation and operation of the new system. There are three separate approaches for evaluating this problem—cost analysis, cost-benefit analysis, and dimensional analysis. Each of these has its merits. The systems analyst should select the particular type(s) of analysis that most objectively presents the situation to management for their decision.

Each information system proposal should contain, therefore, a section that deals with the economic analysis of the new information system. The analyst should use his best abilities in preparing the economic evaluation section of the proposal. An ill-conceived and ill-prepared economic evaluation will substantially reduce the proposal's chances for acceptance. He must present the economic evaluation in terms that clearly and completely present the economic impact of the new information system on the organization's primary activities. The following approaches for presenting this information in the systems proposal can clearly portray the economic advantages and limitations of a new information system.

Cost Analysis

Perhaps the most basic and widely known technique used to justify the installation of a new information system is the cost displacement, or cost savings, approach. In this approach the analyst compares the continuing cost for operating the present system with the cost for implementing and operating the new one. The difference between the total cost for the new system with the cost for operating the present information system over the same time period will, hopefully, produce a net cost savings

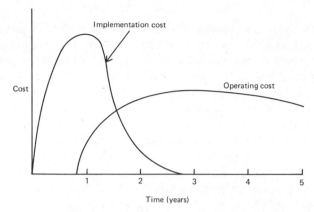

Fig. 8-6 Characteristic pattern of implementation and operation
cost elements

to the business firm. If there is a net cost saving, this fact can
be used as a powerful argument for the installation of the new
information system. On the other hand, if the total cost is
greater, management will be able to compare the additional
services provided by the new information system to the incremental cost.

The implementation and operation cost elements of information systems exhibit a characteristic pattern, as shown in
figure 8-6. The implementation cost is a nonrecurring cost for
the design, programming, debugging, and installation of the new
system. To use good financial practice, the total initial cost
should be prorated over the system's expected life. The installation expense recovery time normally ranges from three to as
many as eight years. The second cost element, operating cost,
is the total cost for operating the new system and includes the
continuing expenses for labor, equipment, facilities, and operating supplies. Both the implementation and the operating costs
must be determined to present an accurate appraisal of the
expected cost of the new information system.

Another approach, although based on fallacious reasoning,
has also been used to economically justify otherwise indefensible
expenditures. This approach dwells on the magnitude of the
costs that would be avoided by purchasing a particular product
or service. The argument is similar to the reasoning sometimes
attributed to wives when they purchase a new dress or husbands
when they purchase an automobile. The dress has been marked
down from $90 to $50 and therefore $40 has been saved by buying

the new dress. Assuming that the purchase of that particular dress was, in fact, necessary, there has been a cost saving. The real question to be answered, however, is whether the product or service is worth the actual cost to the purchaser, assuming he has the ability to pay for it.

Some systems analysts have used this approach to justify the installation of new information systems. Their line of reasoning usually traces the following pattern. The manager needs more information; he needs it more quickly. The present information system can be expanded to provide it at a substantial increase in cost. A new computer-based information system could supply it at a lower cost. Therefore, the computer-based information system should be installed and the additional expense will have been avoided.

The reputable systems analyst should be extremely hesitant to justify the cost of the new system solely on the grounds that it can provide these services at a cost below that which would be incurred by expanding the present system. Rather, he should relate the value of the additional information services to their incremental costs for a defensible decision-making base.

Data-processing time savings, under certain circumstances, may be used to justify the installation of an improved information system, For example, airline reservation systems have been justified because they provide immediate responses to customer inquiries about flight reservations. There is no objective way in which the speed of response may be precisely correlated with cost. Determining the costs of lost sales, poor decisions, and lost customer goodwill and relating them to the cost of the new information system is a very difficult task. Most managers intuitively realize that certain decisions must be made quickly if they are to be effective. Time, therefore, is sometimes used in justifying the proposed information system.

Information quality is another feature that may be used to justify the installation of a new information system. The important consideration in this case is the cost to the business firm for data manipulation errors in the system. Banks, for example, must be extremely careful to maintain the data of their accounts in near-perfect order. The superhuman level of accuracy attainable with computerized information systems has been a very strong argument for installing data-processing systems in the banking industry. Even without cost and time considerations, the improvement in information accuracy may be used in certain instances to justify new computerized information systems.

Cost-Benefit Analysis

In recent years cost-benefit analysis has become an important tool for evaluating new projects. In essence, this approach attempts to relate the cost of the program with the benefits to be derived from it. Thus if the benefits from a new program clearly exceed its cost, then the new program may be readily justified. Although this approach offers an easily understood means for evaluating new programs, there are also difficulties and limitations that must be appreciated.

The determination of cost, as mentioned previously, may be undertaken with a substantial degree of precision. The tangible costs for the installation and operation of a new information system may be determined by considering each cost element in turn (direct labor, facilities expense allocation, equipment expense, operating supplies expense, and the prorated systems development expenses.) The intangible costs, of course, are more difficult to assess for the new information system than for the existing one. The total cost for the new information system is simply the sum of these two costs.

The benefits that the new system, hopefully, will provide are much more elusive and difficult to determine. Ordinarily, the benefits of the new information system must be expressed in dollar terms to provide a common denominator. In this way the dollarized benefits from the new system can be directly compared with its cost.

When the systems analyst attempts to reduce the benefits expected from the new information system to specific dollar values he faces substantial risks and difficulties. If he overestimates the dollar value of the benefits, he exposes himself to the charge of overselling the new information system. If he underestimates the value of the benefits, the proposal may be rejected. Thus he finds himself in a dilemma in which it is inevitable that some people will disagree with his evaluation. This situation may and should be avoided by persuading management to supply their estimates of the expected benefit value of the new information system prior to the preparation of the proposal. The final decision by management on the system proposal must ultimately rest on their evaluation of the value of the benefits. Under no circumstances should the systems analyst attempt to force management to use a financial benefit schedule he has developed to make their decision.

The analyst may determine the dollar values for each of the benefits for reference purposes. Thus any direct cost savings

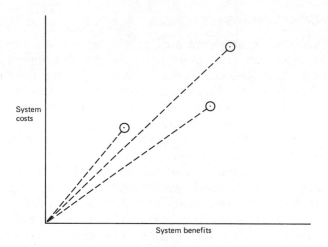

System costs

System benefits

Fig. 8-7   Three information system proposals

(or dissavings) expected from the new information system should first be determined. Next, dollar benefit values for each new system output and/or capability (increased speed, increased accuracy, and so forth) should be estimated through discussions with operating and managerial personnel. Finally, all of the individual dollarized benefits for the new system are added together to produce the total dollar benefits. Again, the total dollar benefit value should be clearly identified as an estimate lest the analyst appear to usurp management's decision-making prerogatives.

When several different information systems are under consideration for the same application, cost-benefit analysis may be presented in graphic form to express more clearly the cost-benefit relationships. In figure 8-7, three different information systems proposals have been designated by points reflecting their cost and their respective estimated benefit dollar values. If the point representing each system proposal variation is connected to the origin, the proposal with the lowest cost-benefit ratio may be identified by the line with the smallest slope. Other things being equal, the selection of the proposal with the smallest slope will yield the greatest benefits per unit of cost.

Dimensional Analysis

The evaluation of information systems, as we have discussed above, is subject to many difficulties because of estimating the

TABLE 8.1
Evaluation of a Hypothetical Information System

Decision Parameters	Present System	Small System	Large System	Index Number
Direct annual cost (labor, overhead, depreciation, supplies)	70,000	100,000	200,000	4
Utility of output for decision-making	5	2	1	5
Timeliness of output	5	4	3	3
Data accuracy	3	2	2	3

cost benefits of intangible items. Cost benefit analysis reduces all of the various dimensions to a single common denominator, dollars. In this way dollar comparisons provide a means for evaluating different proposals. However, this approach may be criticized because of the subjectivity involved in the reduction of intangible benefits to dollars.

Dimensional analysis is a mathematical technique that seeks to unify the decision-making process by structuring the decision in a manner that eliminates the various dimensions of the decision (cost, timeliness, quality, flexibility, and so forth).

Let us consider an example of dimensional analysis as applied to the evaluation of information systems. Assume that there are three possible information system configurations. The first configuration will be the existing information system. The second will be a small-scale, temporary system, and the third will be a complete and fairly expensive system. These hypothetical information systems have been evaluated as shown in table 8.1

The various parameters of the decision-making process are listed in the left-hand column. The expected benefits and costs are shown under the columns Present Information System, Small Information System, and Large Information System. Within the table relative weights or costs (savings) must be established for each proposal within each decision dimension. A relative scale from one to ten may be used in which the number one represents the best possible result and the number ten is the worst possible outcome.

The index number shown in the last column represents the relative importance of each dimension used in the evaluation. The values assigned to the index number indicate each parameter's relative importance to the circumstances existing in the firm at a certain time and range from one (least important) to ten (extremely important). The analyst may derive the exact index number values assigned to each parameter from his discussions with the individuals concerned with systems operations. Such values may, however, also be assigned by averaging the estimates of the individual managers or by using an amalgam of values agreeable to all individuals concerned. To be most useful, all of the participants in the systems investigation should agree on the weighting factors.

The preference for each proposal using the dimensional analysis approach may be expressed as the product of all individual proposal parameters raised to their respective index number powers. In this way, the plans may be compared by determining the product ratios with each other. The general statement for this approach is:

$$\frac{\text{Preference for proposal 1}}{\text{Preference for proposal 2}} = \left(\frac{D_{11}}{D_{21}}\right)^{f_1} \left(\frac{D_{12}}{D_{22}}\right)^{f_2} \cdots \left(\frac{D_{1m}}{D_{2m}}\right)^{f_m}$$

The product of the various ratios is a pure number that has no dimensional characteristics. In effect, dividing the relative weights of each proposal eliminated the various dimensions from the final result.

Let us examine the problem stated in table 8.1. Comparing the first plan with the second yields the mathematical expression

$$\left(\frac{70,000}{100,000}\right)^4 \left(\frac{5}{2}\right)^5 \left(\frac{5}{4}\right)^3 \left(\frac{3}{2}\right)^3 = 89.3$$

The product of this expression is a value greater than one. Its significance is that the new small-scale system is preferable to the existing system by the margin of 90:1. Using the same approach in the comparison of columns three and four (new small-scale systems vs. new large-scale system) produces the following mathematical expression:

$$\left(\frac{100,000}{200,000}\right)^4 \left(\frac{2}{1}\right)^5 \left(\frac{4}{3}\right)^3 \left(\frac{2}{2}\right)^3 = 4.74$$

The product of this mathematical expression is also greater than one, indicating that the large-scale system would be the optimal choice. A product value less than 1.00 would indicate that the first proposal was preferable to the second.

CONCLUSION

The system proposal is the culmination of the entire systems investigation. Not only is it a definitive statement of the present information system, but it is also a complete blueprint for an improved system—a plan for achieving better communication in the organization.

In connection with the publication of the system proposal, the major results of the investigation and an outline of the proposed system may be presented at a meeting of the concerned managers. These presentations afford the systems analyst the opportunity to present the proposal in a summary manner and to answer questions posed by the audience. It is simply not possible to explore all avenues in the proposal itself.

After the publication and presentation of the system proposal, the analyst must await the decision of management. Ordinarily it is more prudent not to proceed with the implementation of the system until the project has been approved by top management. If the project is important and needed, approval will normally be granted within a short period of time. If the project is deemed less urgent, approval may take longer. In the former case, relatively little time will be lost, and in the latter case no further expenses will be incurred that would require explanation if the project were cancelled.

In the system proposal, the presentation, and subsequent discussions with management, the systems analyst must simply provide the facts as he finds them and leave the decision making to management. Naturally, he will experience a substantial measure of emotional involvement with the project. It is most difficult to be rational and objective under these circumstances. It is, nevertheless, the responsibility of management to weigh all of the factors and make the final decision.

CASE STUDY: THE PLAINFIELD WATER BOARD (B)

Two years ago the city of Plainfield leased a complete computer system. Although Plainfield has implemented several applications, only the customer billing operation (preparation of the monthly bills from data supplied by the meter readers and the accounting group) has been implemented for the Water Board. The office manager has recently suggested to the purchasing agent that some of the available computer capacity could, perhaps, be used to mechanize a portion of the purchasing operation.

Mr. Simms, the systems analyst, has conducted a systems investigation of the existing purchasing information system as discussed in Plainfield Water Board (A). In addition, he has developed the following information:

1. There is ample computer capacity to handle the proposed application. The present computer configuration includes a card reader, three magnetic tape drives, disc storage, and a high-speed printer.
2. There is an experienced programmer available to work on this system.
3. The purchasing agent would like more information about late shipments but is unsure whether he needs other types of reports.
4. Using a computerized information system, the average length of time for the completion of small orders can be reduced from ten to eight days and for large orders, from twenty-six to twenty-one. The implementation cost is estimated to be $10,000 and the monthly cost for operation is estimated to be $2500. The new system must pay for itself in five years.

Is the purchasing information system a good choice for the continuing mechanization of operations? Why?

For a computerized purchasing information system

A. What outputs do you think are necessary? desirable?
B. What input streams of data will be needed to provide for the outputs?

Prepare a computerized purchasing information system flow-chart.

Give a brief economic analysis of the two information systems.

THE INFORMATION SYSTEM SPECIFICATION

The successful implementation of a new information system or the revision of an existing one is the ultimate goal of every information systems study. The systems analyst's ideas as presented in the system proposal are general concepts that must be refined and thoroughly documented to provide a satisfactory base for creating an efficient operational information system. The analyst should, therefore, be well aware that the overall task is only well begun with management's acceptance of the system proposal and that much additional effort will be necessary to bring the project to a successful conclusion.

A successful information systems implementation program is usually composed of several distinct phases or activities, each of which contributes directly to the achievement of the end result. A system specification, the basic design document that defines the inputs, the processor functions, the data file structure, and the outputs for the new information system should be prepared. The implementation plan, which is often included in the systems specification, sets forth the activity schedule and designates the individuals or groups responsible for carrying out each implementation activity. The preparation of the computer programs is, of course, a major activity in the implementation of every automated data-processing system. Testing and checking the new information system out must be completed before it is truly operational. Training programs for the associated personnel should precede and/or accompany information system testing and check-out. Finally, the follow-up stage picks up and inter-weaves any apparent loose strands in the new system and may conclude the project with a formal evaluation report after a suitable period of time. Adequate and sufficient attention to each of these stages will substantially improve the probability of both an early completion date and a successful, operational information system.

THE SYSTEM SPECIFICATION

Just as no construction project should be begun without a complete set of plans and specifications, so should no information system be installed without a detailed specification. Like many management principles, the wisdom of this statement has been demonstrated directly and forcefully by breaching the advice. Thus installing an information system without thorough and complete planning will nearly always cause numerous and severe difficulties in both the implementation and operation stages of the system's life cycle. Preparing a complete system specification will not, of course, guarantee that the new system will function as desired. On the other hand, information systems for which detailed plans have not been prepared and used will almost always produce unsatisfactory results.

There is also a corollary observation directly related to the necessity for adequate planning. If the plans are inadequate, then there must necessarily be inadequate performance stand-ards and, hence, inadequate project control. Effective project control depends directly on the development of well-conceived plans. This observation, of course, is not restricted to informa-tion systems implementation programs but applies to all types of organizational programs.

The purpose of the system specification is to crystallize and record the new system's complete structure. As the final author-ity on the details of the information system, the systems specifi-cation becomes the central reference point for joint action by all of the project participants. Moreover, it furnishes the basic historical record for the reference file used to record all future changes and modifications in the information system. In the event that the original systems analyst should ever be separated from the project for any reason, the availability of a thorough system specification will enable the new analyst to continue the project with minimum delay and confusion.

One of the principal differences between the system proposal and the specification is the level of detail in the description of the information system. While the system proposal discusses the information flows through the system in general terms, the system specification presents a much more detailed treatment of the flows. Specific points, such as field location, size, and character type (alphabetic, numeric, or alphameric) for each data item in every record must be clearly defined. Expected record activity levels and program controls must also be specified in the system specification to assist the computer programmers. Ideally, the specification contains all the information necessary to prepare efficient computer programs, secure the necessary supplies (forms), train the personnel who will be operating the system, and manage the implementation of the information system.

Although there is substantial variation in the form and content of system specifications prepared by different organizations, the principal parts (sections) of a typical specification are:

1. Introduction
2. System Inputs
   A. Source documents (forms design)
   B. Computer input design
3. Processor Design (detail system flowcharts)
4. Data Base (File) Design
5. System Outputs

In the following sections of this chapter we shall examine these topics in detail.

Introduction

The introductory section of the system specification is normally rather brief and simply recaps the background and objectives of the new system. A short discussion of the historical development of the project is especially appropriate if the specification is to be widely distributed. Pertinent document references may also be included to provide additional information sources for interested personnel.

Source Document Design

A source document is the initial form on which data about a particular business transaction is recorded. The purpose of a source document is to collect transaction data to furnish a permanent record and/or to introduce such data into an automated business information system. For example, sales slips are source documents the seller prepares at the time merchandise is sold. They provide a record for both the customer and the business firm of the sales transaction and may also be used by keypunch machine operators for transcribing sales data into a machine-processable form. Other examples of source documents are purchase requisitions, material receiving memos, time cards, personnel data forms, 1040 (income tax) forms, bank deposit slips, hospital admission forms, and university course drop slips. These source documents and a host of others serve the dual functions of providing hard-copy records of transactions and being data sources for computer-based information systems.

The data content of each source document is directly related to the information requirements of the various output reports. Each item of output information must have one or more corresponding raw data inputs. The source document data requirements, therefore, may be ascertained or verified by pairing each output information item with one or more raw data input sources. Specifying the different types of data (I, C, and K items) as discussed in the preceding chapter is a valuable aid during the data-pairing process.

A corroborative approach to determining the data content of each source document is to consider the requirements needed to completely define the nature of the respective transaction. Thus a sales slip (source document) should distinguish definitively each particular sales transaction and would, therefore, minimally contain such information items as date, customer name, quantity, merchandise description, unit merchandise price, total price, and perhaps other pertinent data. The inductive approach stresses the need for a complete definition of the various attributes, or descriptors, that comprise each transaction. This approach might also suggest the collection of certain data that would be useful to preserve in the records but might not be needed for the computer-based information system at the present time. The best results in source document design are usually achieved through a combination of the inductive and deductive approaches.

The layout of the data requirements on the source document is often a compromise between the ease of form completion and the ease of data entry into the automated information system. Source documents that can be quickly and easily completed by operating personnel are often difficult for keypunch operators to use. The data entries in this case have probably been arranged for the convenience of the form preparer. On the other hand, source document forms that keypunch operators can readily use may be difficult for unsympathetic employees to prepare. The usual solution to this difficulty is to establish a priority relation between the form's preparer and its user. If preparation is deemed the most important, then the design of the form may properly reflect this emphasis and vice versa.

The controversy between document preparers and users may be resolved by using combination or concurrent data collection techniques. For example, purchase order documents must ordinarily be prepared for all purchases with one copy being forwarded to the data-processing department for keypunch transcription. A creative solution to the double preparation dilemma is to prepare the purchase order documents and a punched paper tape of the typed entry data simultaneously with a specially equipped typewriter. Subsequently, the punched paper tape data may be entered into an automated data-processing system without the need for a separate keypunch operation. Another widely used and very familiar application of concurrent data preparation is the recording process used with gasoline credit card sales/purchase transactions.

Through the concurrent collection of data, a system's operating efficiency may often be significantly improved. Net cost reductions in system operation by eliminating duplicate activities, decreasing processing time, and improving data input accuracy are the major advantages found with combination data collection techniques. The benefits of simultaneous source document and input data preparation must, of course, be balanced against any additional data collection equipment costs to determine the best method.

Input data accuracy, a persistent problem in every information system, may be improved through the use of good forms design. When the same input data is needed by two or more users, multipart forms (forms having two, three, four or more copies combined with the original) will eliminate the need for copying the data more than once. The exact data needed and its placement may be made most explicit by using a box design with internal labels as shown in figure 9-1. Open-ended questions requiring variable-length answers should not be used if there

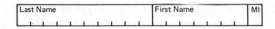

Fig. 9-1   Placement of data with internal labels

are any other alternatives. Arranging data requests in familiar sequences (number, street, city, state, and zip code) will also promote accuracy.

To help ensure that responses will be complete, arrangement of the questions on the form is very important. The sequence of responses should be from left to right and top to bottom, since this is the way the respondent reads and writes. To the extent possible, the data requirements should be clustered in one general area of the form rather than scattered over its entirety. The best practice is to use only one side of a form lest the respondent overlook the reverse side. To avoid omitting data, the respondent's memory may be jogged by using exhaustive multiple choice lists as shown in figure 9-2.

The final step in the source document design process is the specification of the form itself. The weight and color of the paper, the dimensions of the form, the number of copies per form, the style of type, the method of reproduction, and the quantity to be ordered must all be determined. Ordinarily the answers to these questions are closely related to form preparation

	Chickenpox
	Measles
	German measles
	Diphtheria
	Scarlet fever
	Typhoid fever
	Other (list)

Fig. 9-2   A multiple-choice list

costs and may require technical expertise. Printing shops and business form preparation firms are usually happy to assist the systems analyst in making the best selection.

Computer Input Design

Computerized information systems normally use several different types of input messages in their operation. The input messages as classified by their function are (1) transaction inputs, (2) user inputs, and (3) system inputs. The message characteristics of each type of input message must be known to the programmer in order to establish message priorities, necessary program subroutines, and other technical programming details. Since each of these message types plays a unique role in the operation of an information system, let us consider them in detail.

In terms of input volume, transaction inputs are the most important type of input message. Transaction input messages include all of the data used in the information system that ultimately results in information output from the computer. Items of transaction data include all of the inputs familiar to automated data processing systems—personnel data, customer orders, purchase order data, financial data, production data and many other similar items of data. The data in all of these different types of input messages have one thing in common: they are the individual data building blocks for all of the many reports that the system will generate.

Very often transaction data inputs are data from the organization's current operations and activities. However, transaction input messages may also be used to update internal data files. For example, the current data input for a purchase order contains such data items as vendor code number, merchandise description, unit and total price, delivery schedule, and other associated data. On the other hand, file data of a more permanent nature, such as vendor file data, contains the name, address, and other data for a particular vendor and is filed in auxiliary storage under a vendor code number. In this instance, file data might appear in output reports but would not require that all vendor data for each purchase order be separately entered.

The second type of input message is known as user input; it is created by the user to communicate with the information system. Examples of this type of input message are requests or questions through which the user is able to extract specific data from the information system. Interrogatory message capability is especially important for modern online management information systems.

The final type of message input is known as a system input message. Virtually every computerized information system is subject to overall control by a computer operating system. The job control parameters, console typewriter instructions, and other features necessary for the physical operation of the information system are established through the computer operating system. System analysts rarely get involved with this type of message input, but it is an essential part of data-processing operations.

Each message type must be identifiable both to individuals who use the information system and to the computer program itself. A natural requirement, therefore, is that there be a unique transaction record name that, preferably, is related to the general nature of the particular transaction. Such descriptive names are usually already in existence for the major types of transactions. Purchase orders, sales orders, stock-out slips, receiving memos, and many other terms describe particular types of transaction records and may readily be applied to the corresponding computer input messages.

While these descriptive terms are quickly recognized by individuals who use the information system, they would be recognizable only with an unnecessarily complex bit of programming by the computer. Rather than referring to different transaction records by name, program preparation is much more simple using a transaction code number to distinguish each transaction record. A short (two- to five-character) code is usually sufficient to identify the type of input message and, if desirable, the major information system using this input record as well.

Establishing a transaction code structure is also a necessary prerequisite for determining the individual program segments. Large-scale programs that involve many different input records require a different set of program instructions for each type of data input. The transaction code can be used both to identify the various program branches and as the principal means for switching to a given branch. The computer program may then reference the transaction code to determine the required processing operations.

The transaction code is often a very useful device for sequencing or ordering the different transactions that enter the information system. For example, file maintenance input data (basic record additions and changes) for each file record should be processed before the current transaction messages. Thus the transaction code creating a new purchase order record in auxiliary storage should have a lower transaction code number than the receiving memo transaction code number. In this way a purchase order record will be present should merchandise be received the same day a purchase order was issued.

The format design for input messages must be clearly defined in the system specification. The fact that a given information system may easily have a dozen or more different types of input messages emphasizes the need for structural uniformity in the format of the input messages. The alignment principle recognizes this need for uniform message input structure. The same data items or information fields must be placed in the same relative message positions for each input to a given information system. Not only does the application of this principle make the initial preparation of the data more simple, but the ease of programming will also be substantially improved by the consistent application of this principle. The alignment principle, of course, must always be applied to the key information elements, including the transaction code, used to determine the sequence of items in batch data-processing operations.

The data within each individual field must be placed in the most compact form possible. The process of compacting data into a form that is readily machine-processable (encoding) will reduce an information system's operating expenses. While the costs for processing and storing a single, larger-than-necessary data field are very small, the slight additional cost applied to many records, processed many times over, may be quite appreciable. In addition, there may be physical limitations related to the computer—for example, the number of characters per disc segment track—that further underscore the necessity for data compaction.

The use of codes to compress data fields offers other advantages in information system design. Codes may be structured to reveal certain unique relations, or characteristics, that would not otherwise be apparent. For example, an organizational unit code system in which the first digit refers to a major organizational branch (manufacturing, marketing, and so forth), the second digit refers to a major division within the branch (plant, geographic area, and so forth), the third digit refers to a major department within the division, and the final digit refers to a unit within the department has a structure that identifies a unique internal relation. This particular four-digit code not only defines individual organizational units but also defines the principal authority relation present throughout the entire organization. Moreover, items coded in this way may be readily summarized by organizational level to provide other insights.

The properties and attributes of items may also be incorporated in a coding system. A lumber yard might well use a code such as *2x4x8F* to identify stock items. In this case the first two digits are the lumber dimensions in inches; the third digit is the length in feet; and the final letter designates the type of wood as fir. Knowing the code key permits the ready identification of the item from the code or, conversely, the preparation of the proper code for each type of lumber.

For best results all new coding systems should be coordinated through a central group. Coding systems developed by one organizational unit to fit its particular needs sometimes overlap with the coding systems of other units. Further, the *ad hoc* approach to coding system development makes organization-wide integrated coding systems impossible to implement. For example, consider the difficulties that would be encountered daily if the engineering department used their own coding system to identify engineering drawings, if the part numbers on the engineering drawings had their own unique coding structure, and if the tools used to manufacture the parts had their own separate numbering system. A great deal of confusion would certainly result from such an arrangement and the difficulties in implementing a production planning information system or a standard cost system would be substantial.

Processor Design

The overall design of the processor section of the information system has been partially developed in the system proposal. The principal information streams, the input media, the processing runs, and the various outputs were outlined for management consideration to demonstrate the feasibility of the automated data-processing system. Consequently the processor section of the system specification is simply concerned with the final definition of the processor activities for the programmer(s).

To provide the programmer(s) with sufficient information to prepare their programs with a minimum of difficulty, each run or individual program must be succinctly and accurately described. Ordinarily the program name, the objectives of the run, and the activities necessary to accomplish the run objectives are set forth. Special requirements, such as the identification of exception conditions, subtotals, and totals and special notations must also be clearly identified. In short, all of the information needed by the programmer(s) to prepare an efficient operating program must be included in this section.

For relatively simple processing runs, sufficient information to specify the run activity may be entered in the annotation symbol adjacent to the processor symbol in the systems flowchart. In the first run (sorting run) of the batch type purchase order information system (see the case in chapter 8), for example, the necessary data could be shown in figure 9-3. This information will be quite ample to establish the parameters for the utility sorting program (a standard software item.)

When the number of separate activities performed during the run becomes larger, the directions must be defined in narrative form within the system specification. In the activity listing and file update run of the batch type purchase order information system (see the case in chapter 8), the instructions might be presented in the following way:

Activity listing and P.O. file update run. List all of the activity that passes the program edit checks. Prepare new P.O. records as required in the master P.O. file. Update master file P.O. records by overlaying data. Compute total number of transactions in each T.C. (transaction code) group and entire run. Prepare dollar totals for each T.C. group and entire run. Identify with an asterisk those P.O.'s that have been completed by receipt of either the receiving memo or the invoice. Dump P.O. master file weekly to magnetic tape and save for four weeks.

A description of this sort should give the programmer sufficient information to prepare the working program.

Additional information may be helpful or required to prepare the program. Start/stop procedures, error conditions, operator messages, entrance and exit parameters for multiprogramming, and other special points should be discussed with

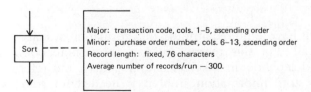

Major: transaction code, cols. 1–5, ascending order
Minor: purchase order number, cols. 6–13, ascending order
Record length: fixed, 76 characters
Average number of records/run — 300.

Fig. 9-3   Specifying run activity

the programmers for possible inclusion in the system specification.

As a general rule, the fewer the number of computer runs,
the more efficient the overall data-processing operations will be.
This generalization must not, however, be applied indis-
criminately to all data-processing operations. Combining two or
more processing runs will reduce setup time and may eliminate
one or more passes of a data file. Because many business data
processing systems tend to be input-output bound (speed of input
and output being the limiting factor in data-processing efficiency), combining processing runs can improve the overall
efficiency.

As the number of internal processing operations is increased, however, a shift will eventually occur and the data-processing operations will become processor bound (internal processing speed will become the limiting factor). When this point
is reached, the advantages of run consolidation disappear and
increasing operating inefficiency results. As a result the systems
analyst should strive to find the best possible balance between
peripheral and internal data-processing operations. At times it
may even be advisable to segment certain processing runs because of equipment limitations, such as limited core storage or
tape units, to achieve high levels of operating efficiency. Again,
programmers can offer invaluable assistance in determining the
optimal balance before the systems specification is written.

Many large-scale computers today have sufficient internal
processing speed and core storage capacity that it is feasible to
process two, and sometimes more, separate runs from two or
more different information systems at the same time. Through
multiprogramming, the computer flips back and forth among
the programs very rapidly, giving the appearance of simultaneously processing the programs. The purpose of multiprogramming, of course, is to take advantage of the tremendous compu-
tational power of these large computers.

File Design

Most individuals have a limited amount of information available
for instant recall. For this reason we use notes, notebooks,
address books, telephone directories, encyclopedias, and reference books to store information until it is needed for some
purpose. We then know (hopefully) where to go for the facts.

The same situation exists with automated information systems. Only a finite amount of information can be maintained in core storage for immediate use. However, the system's power is extended enormously through access to information files that contain previously recorded data. To state this idea even more forcibly, the data files in an information system ultimately determine its capabilities and capacity. To obtain the maximum benefits from any data-processing system, the systems analyst must have an adequate knowledge of file creation, organization, access, processing, and maintenance as these concepts relate to automated information systems.

Perhaps the best way to define the term *file* is to consider it from a perspective of data hierarchy. The most elemental data form is the character or byte. At the next higher level, groups of characters with an internal relation are known as fields. Continuing upward to the next level, a group of interrelated fields form a record. Finally, a set of records with one or more common fields located in the same record positions is a file. The records may be ordered or not. The records may have the same number of fields or not. They must, however, have a mutual identifier composed of one or more fixed-length fields located in the same record positions known as the record key.

One of the most important decisions the systems analyst will make with respect to file creation is to choose the file medium. Files for automated data processing may, of course, be created in several different forms. Punched cards, paper tape, magnetic tape, and auxiliary storage (disc storage, drum storage, data cells, and so forth) are the most commonly used file media in automated data processing systems. Each of these has certain characteristics that makes it more suitable for certain applications than others. Table 9.1 summarizes the outstanding characteristics for each of the major types of file media.

A second consideration in file creation is the length of the record to be filed. When the record length is fixed (when it always contains the same number of characters in each field and the same number of fields in each record) the records are much easier to manipulate, but file space may be wasted. An inventory file, for example, could easily be structured with a fixed format in which each field in the entire record contained the same number of characters and the fields had identical locations within the record. The program instructions in this case would be relatively simple to prepare and individual data fields could be

TABLE 9.1
File Media

	Advantages	Disadvanatges
Punched Cards	Easily prepared and verified; inexpensive	Suitable only for temporary files
Paper Tape	May be prepared as a by-product of other data collection activity; inexpensive	Cannot be sorted, good only for temporary files
Magnetic Tape	Easily processed, permanent; relatively inexpensive	Usually requires inter- mediate preparation step; requires computer
Auxiliary Storage	Records easily; quickly accessible	Relatively expensive

easily accessed or changed. Empty record spaces, however, would be needed to make up the balance of the eighty characters in a punched card of the 200 characters in a disc track sector. In addition to the cost considerations for the unused portion of the record storage space, the programming instructions will require nonproductive data movements as when moving disc track sectors into and out of disc storage.

The alternative way of handling this difficulty is to use variable-length records. The length of the records might vary because of the size of individual fields within them, the number of fixed-length fields within them, or both. An example of the latter case would be a single purchase order record that might contain one or many items. There would be certain common information (vendor name and address, terms, delivery date, and so forth) on each purchase order, but the total length of the purchase order record would be directly related to the number of items on the order. Putting all of the record data at one file location would eliminate the need to repeat the common pur- chase order data that otherwise would be required if each item were filed in storage as a separate record. This would permit valuable storage space to be saved for other uses. However, pro- gramming difficulties and record manipulation problems be- come formidable tasks under these circumstances.

The resolution of the fixed record length–variable record length dilemma must be set forth in the system specification. The constraints of computer hardware, programmer sophistica- tion, operating personnel capabilities, and system operating costs are the major determinants in the selection of one type of record over the other. Since the problem is so closely related to the actual operation of the system, the systems analyst should discuss it at length with the programmers and arrive at a consensus before specifying the solution.

The final major consideration in the file creation process is the temporal nature of the file itself. Files may be categorized as either temporary or permanent files. A magnetic tape, for instance, that contains the new purchase orders and changes used to input this data to the information system would be considered a temporary file. Temporary files are most often used to facilitate data movements into and out of a central processing unit and are found in almost every data-processing system. Their distinguishing feature is that they do not usually maintain their separate identity for any appreciable length of time.

The function of permanent files, in contrast, is to maintain a basic store of data for an extended period of time. The individual items within the file often change with time, but the file itself retains its identity within the system continuously. An open purchase order master file could be set up on punched cards, magnetic tape, or direct-access storage. It could be composed of either fixed- or variable-length records. The actual records within it would change gradually over a period of time. The open purchase order master file, however, would always be maintained as an integral part of the purchase order information system.

The other aspect of file organization that must be specified is the sequence of the record key, or absence of it, in consecutive records. When numeric records are sequenced from one to infinity and alphabetic records are placed in alphabetic order, the resulting file organization is known as ascending order. This is, by far, the most common ordering sequence. The opposite case—descending order—may also be specified but is used infrequently.

A record file must not necessarily have any sequence or order. Random files, as unordered files are known, occur frequently when a group of similar records are first brought together. As discussed in the preceding chapter, one of the very first operations performed in batch processing (and sometimes also with online data processing) is sorting the records to a predetermined sequence. Once the sorting operation has been completed, further processing operations can usually proceed much more efficiently. Random files may also exist in direct-access storage devices. While it is not mandatory for direct-access storage files to be stored in any particular sequence, the random location of records is determined by programmed instructions, not by chance alone. Random auxiliary storage files, though widely used, are not the most common means for storing records in auxiliary storage. Most auxiliary storage files rely on sequenced records with programming variations to handle certain accessing difficulties.

The organization of the various files in a data-processing system must always be specified in the system specification. File organization may be defined as the relation of key fields in consecutive records. All files must have one or more fields located in the same relative positions to serve as a means of identifying individual records. For example, the white pages in the telephone directory list every subscriber by his last name (major key), first name (intermediate key) and middle name or initials (minor key). Each subscriber is listed in alphabetic sequence with the full record key occupying the first three variable-length record fields. Knowing the person's full name usually makes finding his telephone number an easy affair because we are very familiar with this method of file organization. Thus a knowledge of the file organization makes the files usable and the access of individual records quite straightforward.

The yellow pages section of the telephone directory is also a record file that has its own unique file organization. Business classification is the major key and subscriber name comprises intermediate and minor keys as discussed in the preceding paragraph. Changing the file organization, as in the yellow pages in the telephone directory, makes the file useful to fulfill a different purpose. File organization, through the selection of the record keys, reflects the purpose for which the file was developed.

In connection with random sequence files, there is a special technique used to establish a sequence between succeeding or related records, known as *chaining.* Records are chained by setting aside within the record or some other designated storage area specific field(s) specifying the succeeding or related record key and its location. In this way a record file may actually be ordered internally, but present the outward appearance of random sequence.

For any file to be useful, individual records within it must be accessible for data processing. Particular records in an interpreted punched card file may be located with a quick manual search. Individual records in paper tape or magnetic tape files may be found only with a record-by-record search of the complete file from one end to the other. A complete file scan, however, is a very inefficient means for locating a single record and should be avoided whenever possible. One of the really great advantages of auxiliary storage devices is their ability to locate individual records within the file very quickly. They make their greatest contribution to information systems design when this capability is exploited fully.

However, there is a major difficulty in using this equipment feature. The central processing unit places and retrieves auxiliary storage records not by record key, but by auxiliary storage address. Some sort of link must be established between the storage address and the record key, otherwise there is no immediate way to locate a particular record. Computer manufacturers have recognized this obstacle and have developed four different techniques to overcome it.

The first technique, known as full indexing, uses an index that gives the general storage address (often called a bucket) for each record in the file. Once the general storage location is known, each record in the area is examined in turn until a record key match is found. The computer program can then prescribe the necessary operations. The full indexing method has two major disadvantages: (1) when the number of records becomes large, the index itself becomes very unwieldy and cannot be maintained in core storage for immediate access and (2) auxiliary storage space is wasted because sufficient storage space must be allocated initially to accomodate the maximum number of records foreseen. For these reasons and because of the need to prepare a new sequentially sorted index for every processing run, this method is not widely used.

The second method used to locate the addresses of particular records is known as partial indexing. Each item in a sequentially sorted record key index contains the general storage location for the record. A fine index at the beginning of the general storage area specifies the exact address of the record sought within the general storage area. This method is actually a two-stage index operation and provides very fast access. It suffers from the same disadvantages as the full indexing method above.

The third method, self-indexing, uses all or a portion of the record key itself to determine the general storage address.

The individual record is then located by checking each record in the general storage area until a record key match is found. This method is rarely used because the addresses of the available storage areas seldom coincide with the numbers in the record key.

The last method for linking record keys to auxiliary storage addresses, known as address generation, uses an algorithm to convert the record key into a general auxiliary storage area address. A record-by-record search is then used to locate the record within the area. For example, a five-digit record key might be squared and the middle three-digit positions added to 1500 to establish the general auxiliary storage area. The objective in this instance would be to store all of the records in a uniformly distributed manner in the general storage areas 1500 through 2499. Rather complex algorithms, often made available by computer manufacturers, may be needed to achieve reasonably uniform and compact record files.

The address generation method is especially prone to a peculiar type of difficulty—record overflow. Even when extreme care is taken in developing the algorithm for establishing general storage addresses, certain general storage areas are likely to have too many records assigned to them, which causes a record overflow condition. When this happens, the searching operation must be directed to another general storage area (chaining) and the search must be continued. As the auxiliary storage record file locations become more completely filled, record overflow difficulties increase and the record access time becomes longer.

None of the preceding methods for linking record keys and storage addresses are adequate under all conditions. Selection of the best method is, at best, a difficult task. In many cases an indexing method is arbitrarily selected because adequate software is available and the programmers are familiar with a particular method. This situation, however, does not relieve the systems analyst of his responsibility to determine and specify the best method of indexing.

The processing of record files consists essentially of read/ write data movements between core storage and the record file. The input processing mode (read mode) simply transfers a portion of the record file (one or several records) into core storage. Most computers are designed so that the original data in the record file will remain intact after the transfer; that is, the record file data is duplicated in core storage and is not wiped out of the original record location. The mechanics of the read operation are essentially the same for all of the different file media.

The output processing mode (write mode) moves individual records or portions of a record file from core storage to one of the file media devices. The destination of the data movement, however, does have an influence on system design and operation. The data may be moved into a new, clean area, which creates, in reality, a new record file. This is the situation when a new master file magnetic tape is prepared during a file updating operation or when a new record is added to a record file in auxiliary storage. On the other hand, a revised record may be overlayed on the original record with auxiliary storage devices and the original record contents will then be obliterated. When this situation exists, the systems analyst must tackle the problem of file security. If the record is updated with erroneous data, how can the original be preserved or recaptured? If the problem is deemed significant, the systems analyst may need to develop special security measures to prevent the loss of the original data.

Data files must be accurate and up-to-date if they are to fulfill their roles in the information system satisfactorily. The effect of error accumulations, whether due to the input of incorrect data or simply not keeping the files current (errors of commission and omission), is to gradually destroy all confidence in record data integrity. Preserving file accuracy is known as file maintenance and consists of the procedures and practices incorporated into the information system operation to retain the information integrity of the file. This task requires continuous effort at a high level to gain the benefits that accurate, up-to-date files provide.

The seriousness of file data errors depends to a certain extent on the uses to be made of the data. If the file simply maintains data for reference purposes, the effect of data errors within it may not be too great and a higher error level can be sustained without impairing its usefulness. For example, a misspelled street name for an employee in the personnel data file would probably cause little harm. Not posting employee data to the personnel file promptly would be, of course, much more serious. When the file data is used in programmed decision making, file data errors and omissions can have much more far-reaching consequences. Inventory quantity errors could cause materials to be ordered that were not needed or needed materials not to be ordered. In either case file inaccuracies would create major operating difficulties. Thus the intended use of file data will determine how much effort should be spent in file maintenance.

The systems analyst must forestall the introduction of errors into the formation system and its record files by all of the means at his command. This feat may be accomplished by establishing thorough data collection and acquisition procedures, by instituting sound data handling procedures during input, by establishing data checking (editing) practices at critical points within the information system. File auditing and verification procedures should also be established to reconcile erroneous data with actual conditions. All of the procedures and practices used in file maintenance are ordinarily outlined in the system specification.

The file maintenance task begins with the collection of data for input into the information system. Making the personnel who prepare source documents and data inputs aware of the total system will pay excellent returns by assuring that all pertinent data is collected and entered in the proper form locations. Each employee should fully understand the significance of his efforts and the extreme importance of accurate source data to the information system and the business firm. Educational programs that promote a sense of employee participation in the operation of the system will encourage personal responsibility for inputting accurate data.

In addition to employee training, management must also be prepared to exercise disciplinary measures, where appropriate, to secure employee cooperation. The use of employee identification codes or some other means to determine sources of excessive errors may be advisable. Just as important as its concern over erroneous input data should be manangement's insistence that all completed transaction data be promptly reported. All transaction records that affect each file must be input immediately upon completion to assure a proper data flow. Unless management is willing to demonstrate strong leadership through continued interest, slovenly and tardily prepared inputs can soon wreck even the best-designed information system.

The systems analyst with the assistance of a resourceful programmer can incorporate many system checks into the computer programs to promote data input accuracy and catch certain errors that may enter the system inadvertently from time to time. Input data editing is usually the first checking operation and involves testing input data for certain accuracy standards as well as for reasonableness. For example, checking price and quantity fields to make sure they contained no alphabetic characters is a routine editing operation. Checking the number of hours worked by an employee to see if it is less than 168 would be an edit check for input data reasonableness. Between these two approaches to input data editing, many errors can be prevented from entering the information system.

Data checks may also be incorporated into the operating programs to check on the reasonableness of data developed or derived from other data. For example, the weekly payroll check writing system could contain a limit of $500 to $1000 on the amount paid to an hourly employee for his weekly wages. Or a negative inventory balance would indicate an impossible condition that should be brought to the inventory manager's attention. Instituting program checks for peculiar conditions such as these will help managers and operating personnel locate erroneous data.

Even in the best designed information systems errors will accumulate over time. Provision must therefore be made to purge these accumulated errors through a reconciliation process. Many firms rely, for example, on a periodic (quarterly, semi-annual, or annual) physical inventory check. A count is taken of each inventory item quantity for comparison with the item quantity contained in the record file. Discrepancies between the actual count and the record are investigated and the inventory record is corrected. An alternative to a complete inventory count would be to select specific inventory items for checking based on some criterion, such as all inventory items that fall below the reorder point during the preceding week. Regardless of the technique used, every information system must contain provisions for adjusting file data when error conditions are identified.

System Outputs

To most operations managers, one of the most interesting and understandable portions of the system proposal is the output section. Consequently system proposals nearly always deal at length with the reports, and define their contents and format as well as their frequency of preparation. In view of this, the

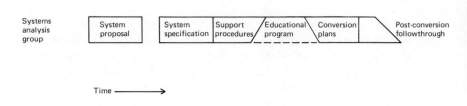

Fig. 9-4   Implementation activities required of the systems analyst

system specification need only reiterate the basic information already presented in the proposal with, perhaps, some technical details to round out the presentation.

THE INFORMATION SYSTEM IMPLEMENTATION PROGRAM

Up to this point we have considered only the activities of the systems analyst or systems analysis group as developers of a new information system. The systems analyst must also perform many activities after the completion of the system specification before the information system is truly operational. These activities are shown with their sequential relations in figure 9–4. Quite often there will be no definite demarcation line between activities; that is, the activities will actually overlap. This aspect is indicated in figure 9-4 by slanted demarcation lines between activities.

After the completion of the systems specification, the systems analyst will usually begin to prepare the support procedures for the operation of the new information system. Ordinarily these procedures contain the detailed operating practices and, are documented as a system users' manual for distribution to the operating and computer personnel. The actual preparation of the new procedures should be performed by the systems analyst in order to provide a central coordinating point and to maintain uniformity of style. The users of the system should have a voice in the preparation of the supporting procedures to make certain all items have been covered. In addition, after the supporting procedures are prepared, they should be discussed with the operating personnel to insure that the procedures are both understandable and practical to follow.

The new procedures should be tested with trial runs before the system becomes operational. Because so many difficulties usually arise during the conversion from the old information system to the new, it is good practice to identify and eliminate as many of the potential difficulties as soon as possible. Any errors or procedural difficulties that appear in the trial runs may thus be corrected before conversion crises occur.

The activity that usually overlaps and follows the development and checkout of the supporting procedures is the education program. Its purpose is to provide the operating personnel with some basic understanding of data-processing technology as well as the objectives and operating characteristics of the new information system. A thorough education program will also help employees overlook minor operational difficulties and inconveniences until the new system is functioning properly. Further, through an educational program the operating personnel will be given sufficient insight to offer suggestions for improving the system and will know the systems analyst well enough to freely communicate such suggestions and ideas.

The systems analysis group is responsible for preparing the educational materials (flip charts, slides, handout materials, and so forth) and conducting training sessions. Every effort must be made to include all the operating personnel in the program. Any individuals who are not included are likely to resent their apparent neglect deeply and withhold their cooperation. Classes are best held on company premises and during regular working hours, although other arrangements may also be satisfactory. If non-exempt personnel are required to attend after working hours, they should be paid overtime since the company is the principal beneficiary of the training program.

Inasmuch as the preparation of educational materials will involve substantial expense and effort, such materials should be retained for educating new employees hired after the system has become operational. Although new employees will learn the system's operation by contact with their coworkers and managers, the original education materials may also be used to supplement their job education.

As the educational program is being completed, the systems analyst will turn his attention to the development of specific conversion plans. Conversion from one information system to another is almost always a traumatic experience for everyone involved. Specific plans, therefore, to implement the conversion process will make the experience much more bearable. The use of Murphy's law (if anything can go wrong, it will) is especially appropriate in planning for the conversion process. When adequate preparations have been made for all possible contingencies, conversion may be consummated with little difficulty. Experience has shown that difficulties are most likely to be encountered with computer equipment, computer programs, and, to a lesser extent, with information logistics.

Backup procedures (for handling hardware and program failures) must be developed before the conversion process. If the new system fails or proves to be inadeuate, the backup system will provide an alternative means to enable business operations to continue. For example, if the remote input terminal section of an online information system should fail to perform satisfactorily (have input terminal or transmission difficulties), data collection and input procedures using punched cards or paper tape should be ready. If the regular central processing unit goes down in a real-time system, provision must be made to switch data-processing operations to a backup computer. If everything goes wrong, it may be necessary to go back to manual data-processing methods temporarily. Thinking ahead and trying to envision all of the possible calamities before they occur will enable the systems analyst to devise countermeasures without crisis pressures.

Another area of potential difficulty in the system conversion process relates to data security and recovery. The computer program may contain unforeseen errors that cause data-processing operations to halt in midstream. Data files may be wiped out, lost, or improperly updated. Restart procedures must be developed to handle all interruptions. File regeneration procedures will assure that file data can be recovered if it should be mishandled in any way. It is the systems analyst's responsibility to prepare adequate plans to cope with all manner of operation problems.

The systems analysis group must follow the new information system for a time after it has become operational, at least until it is known to be operating satisfactorily. The systems analyst should retain close contact with the operating personnel and expedite minor programming or system operating modifications during the break-in period. In a sense a systems analyst never really yields his responsibilities for the continuing operation of both an efficient and an effective information system that he has designed.

One feature of the post-conversion followthrough that is too frequently overlooked is the preparation of a post-conversion system evaluation report. The purpose of this report is to evaluate the actual results and impact of the system on the firm's operations. Determinations of systems efficiency and effectiveness are very appropriate topics for inclusion in this report. Hopefully also, the post-conversion evaluation report will substantiate the benefits set forth in the system proposal and thereby improve the credibility of future proposals.

While the systems analyst plays a major role throughout the development of a new information system, many other groups enter into the later stages of the implementation program. The different activities of these associated organizational units must be closely coordinated to avoid delays. When each organizational unit understands the program interrelations and its individual responsibilities in the implementation of the new information system, a smooth conversion process will result.

Figure 9-5 presents the primary organizational units that are involved in implementing a new information system together with their major activities and relative temporal relations. The various organizational groups are listed on the left-hand side of the diagram and their activities are shown as a function of time. The systems analysis group has been interposed between the computer-oriented organizational units (programming and computer operations) and the operations groups (operations personnel and operations management) to emphasize their coordinating role.

After the preparation of the system proposal, operations management must consider the cost-benefit relations in the new information system, evaluate the impact of the new system on organizational operations, and make the final decision for the organization on the selection, or rejection, of the proposed information system. If the decision is made to proceed with the development of the new system, the system specification is prepared as discussed in the preceding sections of this chapter.

The preparation of the necessary computer programs is the first major activity to be started outside the systems analysis group. Initially, the programmers will offer assistance and advice to the systems analyst during the design of various portions of the new information system. Once the system specification has been completed, programming activity may be begun in ear-

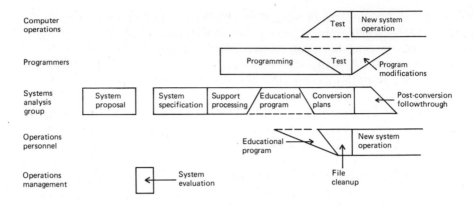

Fig. 9-5   Implementing a new information system

nest. The advantages of a well-written, thorough specification will be immediately apparent as soon as programming begins. Program preparation is not difficult and may proceed rapidly if the programmers understand the system's operation precisely. When the system specification is ambiguous and omits pertinent details, the programmers will spend a disproportionate amount of time searching for the facts and recoding sections of the program to accomodate undiscussed details.

As the program segments are completed they should be run on the computer to locate the "bugs," or program errors. The first program tests are usually made with specially prepared data that simulates both typical transaction data and all kinds of erroneous data. Once the programs function properly with the specially prepared data, the individual program segments are checked with actual transaction data. Finally, the individual program segments are combined and the entire information system is checked as a unit with both actual and spurious transaction data.

Once the system becomes operational (after conversion) other programming errors will probably appear, especially in complex programs. These errors are not reflections on the programmers' abilities, but are due to the almost infinite number of variations and combinations found in raw transaction data. As these programming errors are found, corrections and modifications must be made. Some of the errors will be discovered by computer operations personnel who can relay the facts directly to the programmer concerned. Other program errors will be found by the operating personnel who should pass the information to the systems analyst and thence to the programmers. Complete records, of course, must be kept of all program changes together with the reasons for them.

During the final program testing, the computer operating personnel will have the opportunity to work with the complete information system for the first time. Together with the programmers and systems analyst they may review their section of the system users manual. This would also be the best time to discuss their role in the cutover to the new information system and the conversion contingency plans. Computer personnel will also need some time to make job schedule adjustments in anticipation of the additional workload the new information system will create.

The operating personnel will begin their adjustment to the new information system with the education program conducted by the systems analyst. Many of these individuals will have substantial fears that their jobs are in real danger and that they are going to be replaced by a computer. The education program, therefore, must be opened with a strong forthright statement by operations management reassuring the operating personnel that they will not lose their jobs. Employees should be told that their job duties will probably change significantly and that a few transfers may be necessary at a later date. There is ample evidence that employee attrition without subsequent replacement will solve most of the surplus employee situations within a reasonable time. Thus operations managers may safely go on record that there will be no layoffs without undue risk of later contradiction.

Data files are an integral and very necessary part of virtually all information systems. Before the new information system can become operational, the associated data files must be prepared. Some of the new data files may not have a counterpart in the old information system and must be created from scratch. However, many of the new files will have counterparts in the old information system and will only have to be transposed to the new data form. In either case the new files must be complete in numbers and content before the cutover to the new information system.

The transposition of the data files to the new form provides an excellent opportunity, or necessity, to verify the old file data and make necessary corrections. There is little point in starting the new information system without purging erroneous data from the files. A thorough file cleanup can remove another major obstacle to the successful operation of the new system.

The operating personnel are normally responsible for preparing the data inputs for the generation of the new data files. Ideally, completing the data transposition should coincide with starting up the new information system. When the data is transposed too slowly or must wait for the cutover, provision must be made for an interim file maintenance operation. In this case the records that have already been transposed must be updated manually to reflect their current status.

The actual cutover to the new information system is usually a tense moment for everyone concerned. The direct cutover (cold turkey approach) simply switches abruptly from the old information system to the new, as shown in figure 9-6. Since the old information system is discarded entirely, the new one must be made to function satisfactorily one way or another. The drastic nature of the direct cutover usually restricts its use to relatively simple systems and those that are not critical in nature.

The parallel system type of conversion is shown in figure 9-7. This approach seeks to maximize security by continuing to operate the old information system until the new one has demonstrated its ability to perform satisfactorily. This approach is especially applicable where both systems have the same or very similar outputs, such as payroll information systems. Where the outputs are not really comparable, parallel systems operation will produce indecisive results.

Phase-in/phase-out conversion, shown in figure 9-8, is a very effective method that eliminates some of the undesirable characteristics of the preceding methods. This method simply picks up all of the current activity on the new information system and lets the old information system gradually wither away. For example, the conversion of a manual open purchase order system to an automated one, all new purchase orders beginning

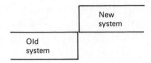

Fig. 9-6   Direct conversion

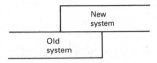

Fig. 9-7   Parallel conversion

Fig. 9-8   Phase-in/phase-out conversion

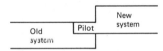

Fig. 9-9   Pilot conversion

on a specified date would be processed by the new system. As the old purchase orders were closed out, the old manual system would be slowly phased out. On the whole this conversion method, where applicable, provides the smoothest transition from the old to the new system.

The final cutover method, pilot conversion, converts a selected portion of the old information system for a period of time. While the old information system is still operating, the new one can be thoroughly checked out and any necessary modifications can be made. When the new system has demonstrated satisfactory performance for an appropriate time, the remaining portion of the original system will be cut over to the new system. In situations where the phase-in/phase-out method is not applicable, this method may be used to smooth out the conversion process.

CONCLUSION

The successful implementation of a computerized information system is ordinarily not an end in itself. Rather, it is simply a stage in the evolutionary development of improved organizational information flows. Once a particular plateau has been reached, others appear. New managerial demands and new technology combine to create new information requirements. For the present, there appears to be no end to the evolutionary process.

The following chapters will present certain basic, widespread computer applications in business firms today. While only a sample of the fundamental applications can be presented here, systems investigation, analysis, and design are the basic tools for the development of all information system applications. Once the basic concepts have been mastered, additional applications may be recognized and new ones may be envisioned.

FINANCIAL INFORMATION SYSTEMS

The financial subsystem (hereafter referred to as the financial system) is one of the five major subsystems comprising the typical business firm. Although this system may not be the most important, it definitely occupies a central role in sustaining the operation of the other subsystems. All business organizations and, indeed, most other types of organizations make use of funds, either directly or indirectly, to achieve their objectives. In this sense the analogy of money as the lifeblood of business has considerable merit since a flow of monetary value supports all business activities. Thus both an efficient and an effective financial system is vital to a firm's short- and long-term success.

The financial system is concerned with the flows and transformations of monetary values in the operation of a business. The field of accounting is devoted primarily to maintaining historical financial records through accepted practices and procedures. The field of finance, on the other hand, emphasizes the planning and organizing activities as related to monetary flows. In effect, the financial information systems in the business firm embody both the areas of accounting and finance.

A basic understanding of financial system operation is a prerequisite for the study of financial information systems. As is true for information systems in the other functional areas of the business firm, the financial information systems must provide the comptroller (financial manager) with the information necessary to plan, organize, direct, and control the activities of the financial system.

We shall postulate that financial managers who thoroughly understand the inner workings of the financial system and receive adequate, accurate, and timely information about its performance will be able to make excellent financial decisions.

THE FINANCIAL SYSTEM

The basic objective of the financial system is to meet the firm's financial obligations as they come due using the minimal amount of resources commensurate with an established margin of safety. The system must provide the firm with sufficient continuing support for performing its primary activities through the prompt payment of liabilities. The total amount of funds required to meet the firm's present and anticipated financial requirements must also be adequate to maintain a satisfactory level of activity. Collecting funds and subsequently disbursing them in an orderly, efficient, and timely way to the firm's various activities is the basic function of the financial system.

A dynamic system schematic model of the financial system for a typical business firm is shown in figure 10-1. While the financial system is directly concerned with cash flows, its most important function is the transformation process in which funds are collected and then exchanged for goods and services. The financial system schematic model follows the conventional pattern in which the inputs appear on the left-hand side of the diagram and the outputs appear on the right-hand side. Control may be exercised over the system through information about past, present, and anticipated future funds flows that give the financial manager a knowledge of the system's operational behavior. He may then use this information to alter the balance among the several inputs into the system and thereby obtain the desired performance.

The boundaries of the financial system have been designated by the two major interface lines shown in figure 10-1. For our purposes the input boundary has been established to include only those financial inputs that are one step away from conversion to cash. Where credit sales exist, which is the usual case, inventory would not be considered an integral part of the financial system. On the output side of the diagram, the boundary is determined through the payment by check for goods and/or

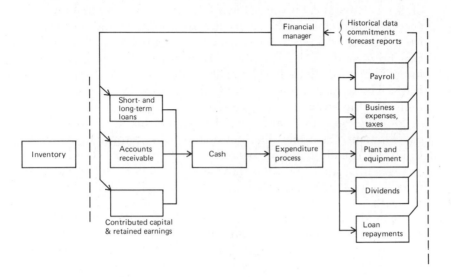

Fig. 10-1   Schematic of a typical financial system

services. All of the activities that take place within these limits are a part of the financial system.

As discussed in the preceding paragraph, inventory is not, generally speaking, a part of the financial system, but it does play a crucial role in the firm's financial structure. The inventory block in this diagram may represent either in-process inventory for the manufacturing firm that does not maintain an inventory of finished goods or finished-goods inventory for the business that maintains a stock of goods for direct sale. A knowledge of the quantity of funds invested in inventory provides an indication of the investment level in this asset account and of potential accounts receivable. Hence the financial manager must have information about the inventory levels in order to manage the financial system properly.

The major inputs to the financial system have been designated by three input blocks: contributed capital plus retained earnings, accounts receivable, and short- and long-term loans. Contributed capital represents the initial funding or permanent financing of the business firm as accomplished through the sale of common and preferred stock. As the firm achieves a certain

degree of financial success, a portion of the profits may be rein-
vested in it as retained earnings. The counterpart of this block
on the balance sheet is the net worth section. The second block,
accounts receivable, is the main ongoing input of funds derived
from the sale of goods and/or services. Accounts receivable may
also be viewed as the liabilities of customers to the business
firm. The third block has been labeled short- and long-term
loans. This system input represents funds from financial institutions that the business uses to augment its liquidity temporarily
or to provide longer-term financial resources for its growth and
development. Seasonal fluctuations in the requirement for
funds are usually handled through short-term loans. Long-run
changes in asset structure usually require financial adjustments
that involve long-term loans, contributed capital, and retained
earnings.

The three major inputs must be converted into cash before
the firm can use these funds constructively. In the case of short-
and long-term loans and contributed capital, the time between
the completion of the financial transaction and the receipt of
cash is usually quite short. The receipt of money from the sale
of goods, however, may be a more lengthy process, although
it usually does not exceed a period of several months. The cash
itself is usually held in the form of bank deposits. Petty cash
funds are sometimes used to handle minor financial transactions
of a nonrecurring nature.

The next block in the financial system schematic model is
known as the expenditure process. This is the point where the
financial manager exercises his decision-making capacity to allocate the available funds to the system's various outputs. In large,
well-organized firms the expenditure process may be performed
on a routine programmed decision-making basis for budgeted
expenses. In smaller firms where the financial resources may
be more strained, the process may be reviewed on an individual
expenditure basis.

The outputs of the financial system are indicated by the
five blocks on the right-hand side of the diagram. Payroll expenses are an ongoing liability and are usually administered in
a routine manner. Since the payroll information system is composed of repetitive calculations, it is often one of the first infor-

mation systems to be mechanized in new computer installations. Business expenses, including taxes, are indicated by the second block and constitute for most firms the major portion of their expenditures. Some decision-making discretion may be given the financial manager in the payment of business expenses; that is, he may have the option of quick payment to take advantage of cash discounts or deferral of payment until the end of the credit term period. He may also defer payments, if the firm is willing to risk a poor credit rating.

The remaining three blocks on the output side of the financial system model are plant and equipment investment, dividend payments, and loan repayments. Investment for new plant and equipment is usually handled through the capital budgeting process in which top management directs the allocation of funds among competing investment opportunities. The proper allocation of funds to various projects provides the basis for the firm's sustained growth and development. Dividend payments represent returns to the stockholders for the use of the contributed capital that they have supplied. Under ordinary circumstances the dividend decision is established by company policy, subject to quarterly review by management. Finally, loan repayments must be made to reduce outstanding indebtedness as required in the loan agreements. While the decision to make loan repayments may be subject to a limited amount of managerial discretion, under ordinary circumstances loan repayment schedules are determined at the time the loans are made and become strongly binding liabilities.

Although the financial manager will normally be granted sufficient authority to direct the system's daily operations, top management usually retains a substantial degree of authority in this area. The financial manager, of course, must have sufficient, accurate, and timely information about the current status of the entire financial system to plan and control its activities properly. Through his knowledge of the details of the system's operation, he is in a position to make adjustments and corrections to maintain the system in the desired state of balance. A knowledge of the business's applicable empirical financial ratios, experience in the financial operations of a particular business firm, and a sound knowledge of financial theory should give the manager

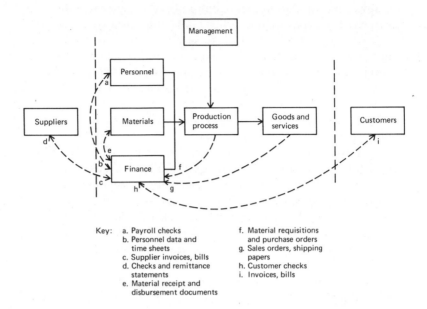

Key: a. Payroll checks
        b. Personnel data and
           time sheets
        c. Supplier invoices, bills
        d. Checks and remittance
           statements
        e. Material receipt and
           disbursement documents

        f. Material requisitions
           and purchase orders
        g. Sales orders, shipping
           papers
        h. Customer checks
        i. Invoices, bills

Fig. 10-2   Interfaces of the financial system with other systems

the background necessary to make sound financial decisions.

Many of the decisions he makes will be guided by long-standing company policies. These policies represent the directions established by top management and should be designed to achieve the firm's objectives efficiently. Implementing the financial policies, however, is the financial manager's responsibility, and his activities must reflect the guidelines laid down in the financial policy statements.

The financial system has certain interfaces with each of the firm's other major systems. These interfaces with their respective information transfer documents are shown in figure 10-2.

The relation between the financial system and the personnel system is found in the payroll interface. Money is needed to meet the firm's financial obligations to its personnel. Under normal circumstances this is done through the transfer of time cards, time sheets, or some similar payroll authorization record to the payroll accounting department. The payroll accounting subsystem uses these records to determine the financial payments due each employee on a regular time schedule.

The payroll accounting subsystem completes the interface by preparing and delivering payroll and personal expense checks while making, as required, appropriate entries in the proper accounting records.

The financial system interface with the materials system is similar to the personnel system interface. Raw material must be purchased and payments must be made to the suppliers. The materials system normally interfaces with the financial system through material receipt and disbursement documents sent to the accounts payable subsystem. However, this is not to say that all items processed through the accounts payable subsystem are necessarily raw materials for the production process. Payments may be required for many items that are not raw materials and do not actually enter the production process such as supplies, capital goods, and business expenses. There is no standard counter document that would be sent from the financial to the materials system. This function is performed indirectly, however, when checks for payment are sent to the supplier.

The financial system has only a weak interfacing relation with the production process. In some respects the production process may be viewed as a continually changing reservoir of committed funds. Responsibility and profitability accounting subsystems attempt to relate the expenditure of funds to the organizational units to provide a means for determining managerial accountability. In this way, management may monitor the entire production process's financial dimensions.

The marketing system interfaces with the financial system through sales orders or shipping documents to the accounts receivable subsystem. Because accounts receivable represents one of the major sources of funds for the financial system, a well-structured accounts receivable subsystem can serve as a monitor of marketing system operations. Reports of product activity, customer activity, and marketing organization activity may give management major insights into the firm's relations to its external business environment.

The efficiency of the financial system cannot be determined by the conventional output/input relation. Obviously, all of the funds that enter the system are available for disbursement or use, and therefore, the output/input ratio must always be equal to one. The system's efficiency is most readily evaluated on the basis of liquidity maintenance and operating cost. On the input side, an efficient financial system will turn over accounts receivable into cash as quickly as possible. Credit investigations to reduce bad debt losses, good collection procedures, and the use of local banks of deposit are some of the techniques to increase input turnover rates. On the output side, the efficient financial system will take full advantage of the terms of payment offered by suppliers; that is, it will not pay its obligations until they mature. When the financial system is efficient, the maximum liquidity will thus be achieved.

Since the system's basic objective is to meet the firm's financial obligations as they come due using a minimal quantity of financial resources to maintain an established margin of safety, the evaluation of systems effectiveness must be based on how well the basic objective is being met. The first part of the system objective may be readily evaluated. Is the business firm presently meeting its financial commitments on time and does it appear likely that it will continue to do so in the future? An affirmative answer to this question indicates that the firm is satisfying this part of the basic financial system objective and that its financial resources are at least adequate. The second part of the basic objective focuses on whether the financial resources are being utilized in the best possible manner. Cash is an idle resource. While a certain amount is necessary to balance out the ebbs and flows through the system and provide a margin of safety against unforeseeable circumstances, cash in excess of this amount represents a lost opportunity for investment. The inadequate use of debt (financial leverage) represents a failure to use the firm's credit resources.

The preceding outline of the financial system emphasizes the need to integrate the systemic elements of the financial system into a cohesive, balanced, and smoothly operating system to achieve satisfactory results. The accounts receivable and accounts payable subsystems occupy a dominant position in the financial system and determine to a great extent its efficiency and effectiveness. These two subsystems must function properly if the financial system is to meet its established objectives. Both the accounts receivable and the accounts payable subsystems will be examined in detail in following sections of this chapter.

The financial system, moreover, must furnish management with cost-attribute information about the entire production system. This information is vital to managers at all levels to form a basis for intelligent decision making. Responsibility accounting systems provide the financial information about the activities managers control and, in this way, enable them to better execute their managerial functions. Such systems will also be examined in a later section of this chapter.

The Accounts Receivable Subsystem

Since almost ninety percent of the financial transactions in this country are done on credit, the accounts receivable subsystem is one of the fundamental elements in the financial system of nearly every business firm. Essentially, its basic objective is to facilitate the transformation of sales transactions into cash. Many companies are vitally dependent on cash inflow from accounts receivable to meet their current expenses and maturing obligations. For all firms that offer goods and services on a credit basis, efficient and effective accounts receivable subsystems are necessary for successful long-term business operation.

The maintenance of the customer records of account for merchandise sold or services rendered on a credit basis is one of the accounts receivable subsystem's principal functions. The integrity of customer accounts is vital to the company in order to provide a sound basis for conducting business transactions and to furnish accurate information for making managerial decisions. Accurate accounts promote customer goodwill by removing points of potential conflict between the customer and the firm. Generating statements regularly to facilitate the collection of accounts is a natural product of the accounts receivable subsystem. Another of its functions is to provide the credit department with information about delinquent customer accounts to minimize the losses from bad debts. Finally, this subsystem should give management analytical information to define the unique behavior of the business firm as a dynamic system.

The activities of the accounts receivable subsystem are especially amenable to the substitution of machine (computer) effort for human effort. The bulk of the work is clerical in nature and the level of decision making, for the most part, is relatively low. As the number of transactions increases, significant cost

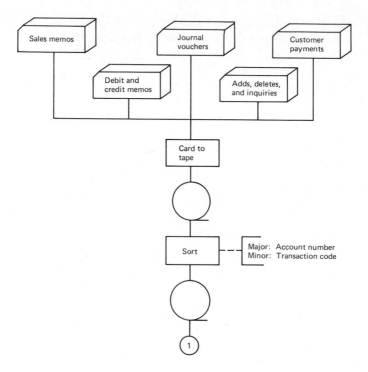

Fig. 10-3   A typical accounts receivable data-processing system

savings may frequently be effected by using unit-record equipment or computers to perform the more routine tasks of posting and billing. A thorough economic evaluation of the system requirements and available equipment system configurations will reveal the best possible overall systems design.

A typical, but simplified, accounts receivable data-processing system (A/R system) is shown in figure 10-3. This particular systems model uses daily batch computer processing as would be encountered in a medium- to large-scale application. A multitude of variations on this general model exist in practice to meet the special requirements of business firms and the available computer equipment. The main features of this model, however, are incorporated in most A/R systems.

The four basic types of entries to the A/R system are shown at the top of the diagram. The first of these is the record-of-sale document. Records of sale (also known as sales memos, sales slips, or sales tickets) are classed as source documents and are

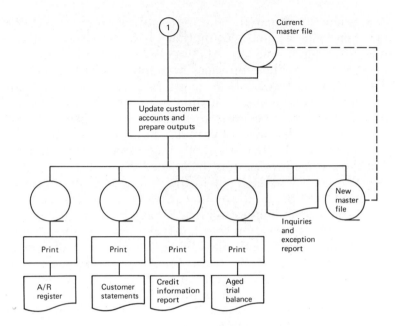

Fig. 10-3   (cont'd)

usually prepared at the time the merchandise is transferred to the customer. Following the unit record concept, each line item in a record of sale or each sale individually is considered as a separate transaction for input into the A/R system.

Credit and debit memos are the second type of data input. Credit memoranda are issued to adjust the customer's account for merchandise returns, short shipments, billing errors, and certain allowances. Debit memoranda, on the other hand, are adjustments to the customer's account where insufficient charges were initially made, such as billing and invoice errors. In order to provide a central point of contact with the customer and reduce the opportunity for abuse, the authority to make adjustments is normally delegated sparingly to individuals outside the financial system.

Journal vouchers are special inputs used primarily to adjust small account differences and write off bad debts. The accounting department usually prepares them monthly to keep the record of accounts accurate and to reflect the current status of the accounts receivable.

Payments on customer accounts must be entered into the

A/R system to maintain their current status. Proper identification of the customer and the account that is to be credited sometimes presents a minor difficulty. Many A/R systems use a customer code number as their principal account classification device. Thus when payments are received that do not contain this identifying code number, a manual search through the master customer list must be made to find it. This problem may be compounded if the payment must also be linked to specific items or transactions. In this case, both the customer code number and the specific invoice must be located manually.

The final types of input to the A/R system are customer additions, deletions, and inquiries. After a credit check has been made and a credit limit established, a basic data record containing the customer code number, customer name, address, salesman, territory, credit limit, and other pertinent information must be entered into the A/R system. Similarly, provision must be made to update or delete each customer record if present circumstances change. Credit information on specific accounts may also be needed from time to time; provisions for providing this information must also be incorporated into the system.

As indicated in figure 10-3, all of these source documents are keypunched into eighty-column cards for entry into the A/R system. After the cards have been processed to yield magnetic tape records, a sorting operation is performed to place the transactions in a specified sequence. The major sort key is usually customer code number, although customer name can be used if precautions are taken to insure proper format structure. The intermediate sort key is usually the transaction code number. The transaction code identifies the type of input, establishes the sequence in which the data-processing operations will take place for each customer record, and specifies the subroutine to be used for processing each record. For example, the transaction coding system should process customer account additions before any sales transactions are processed. In this way, sales transactions made the same day a new account is opened will be properly posted to the new customer account. Otherwise, the sales transactions for a new customer account could be entered before the customer account was established, yielding an error situation. If a minor sort key is required, invoice and item number may be used. The entire sort sequence key is invoice number within transaction code within customer number.

The activity file is now ready for the main processing run

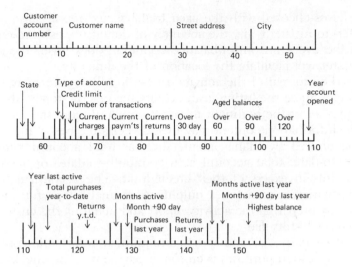

Fig. 10-4 Typical layout of data fields in a master customer file

with the master customer file. One of the principal functions performed during the main processing run is the updating of the master file with all of the current activity, resulting in the creation of a new master file. A typical layout of the data fields in the master customer file is shown in figure 10-4. The second function of the processing run is the preparation of output data that will be used for different types of printed reports or inputs into other data-processing systems.

The number of different types of information outputs that may be generated during a single processing run depends on the computer equipment configuration. Smaller computer systems may require several runs to prepare all of the reports needed by management, requiring that the primary program be segmented.

The first type of information output prepared during each processing cycle is known as an activity report or, alternatively, as the accounts receivable register. Some A/R systems are designed to produce both reports, although such reports have substantial information overlap. Each sales record, credit/debit memorandum, journal entry, and customer payment is listed on this report together with the total transaction amounts to provide a permanent record of accounts receivable activity. This report may serve as an audit trail for all entries into the A/R system. Moreover, the summary values from this report may be cross-checked with the aged trial balance report (discussed later) to further verify the accuracy of the customer's accounts. In the event an out-of-balance condition does arise, the A/R register will facilitate the location of the difficulty.

The format of the activity listing or A/R register may vary widely. Since the listing is an activity record, the report should supply all of the pertinent information about each transaction. The information content may include certain types of information desired by management, such as total account activity year-to-date, total account activity month-to-date, or account amounts in excess of their credit limit. The account activity information is sometimes output on magnetic tape for subsequently preparing the activity report and updating the customer account history file.

One of the A/R activities that requires an information output for verification purposes is customer payments. The checks and cash payments received daily on customer accounts must be closely supervised. The total amount of both checks and cash deposited each day must equal the total amount credited to customer accounts. A daily check on receipts listing of all payment activity is often used to verify the accuracy of the total daily bank deposits.

Another of the major outputs of most A/R systems is periodic statements to customers with outstanding balances. In some firms that sell primarily to other businesses, customer statements may not be absolutely required since the accounting procedures use the invoice as the principal device for presenting customer liabilities. These firms have the option of using only invoices for billing purposes or a combination of invoices and periodic statements. On the other hand, there are many other instances where customers do not pay until statements are rendered. The preparation of statements at regular intervals, even when not explicitly required, will notify the customers of the amounts due and, in the absence of a response, serve to verify the account balance.

The determination and followup of late-paying accounts is an especially important feature of most A/R systems. It is very important to identify delinquent accounts as soon as practicable since they become more difficult to collect as they grow older. If the volume is sufficiently large, delinquent account information may be output on magnetic tape for subsequent processing by the credit information system, as will be discussed in chapter

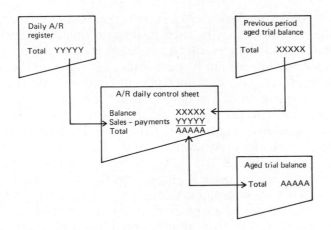

Fig. 10-5   Aged trial balance report format

14. When the volume of delinquent accounts is relatively small, a simple listing of the delinquent accounts grouped or sorted according to the length of delinquency or the amount owed will be sufficient for credit department followup.

Some business firms also need to identify customers who suddenly build large balances or exceed the specified credit limit. While increased account activity does not necessarily signal approaching collection problems, the credit manager may wish to investigate the cause for the increased activity. Customers who exceed preestablished credit limits must be notified. This type of information may be incorporated in the delinquent account output discussed in the preceding paragraph.

Accurate cash flow forecasts are necessary for good financial planning. Additionally, unforeseen increases in the total amount of accounts receivable may create cash flow difficulties for many firms. One approach to the solution of this problem is to analyze delinquent accounts with an aged trial balance report. This report lists each active account with the amount owed separated into several columns, depending on the time that portion of the total debt was created. The format for a typical aged trial balance report is shown in figure 10-5. The preparation of an aged trial balance report also has the additional advantage of providing an information source for the development of an A/R system control procedure.

Finally, output provisions must be made for customer credit inquiries and the ubiquitous exception (input error) report. If the output volume for these two report types is low, the computer console typewriter may be used to prepare them. Otherwise, a separate output channel will be needed to prepare these reports.

One other important feature of the A/R system is the maintenance of accurate customer account records. Rather than correct errors as irate customers bring them to attention, the best practice is to use control procedures to maintain the A/R system's integrity. Figure 10-6 depicts a standard procedure designed to eliminate or severely reduce the chance for errors. The total amount of the A/R customer accounts from the preceding period or cycle is entered on the A/R control sheet. Next, the net amounts (gross sales minus payments and returns) for the current period are entered on the A/R control sheet and added together. The total amount from the A/R control sheet will equal the total amount from the aged trial balance report if the accounts are in order. Discrepancies must be located by reference to individual accounts in the activity register and aged trial balance report.

Up to this point our discussion has centered largely around the general features found in most A/R systems. In order to consider further some of the special difficulties that are encountered in the design of A/R systems, we may divide A/R systems into two major subclasses —balance-forward and open-item A/R systems. Each of these has certain characteristics that strongly influence the ultimate design of a satisfactory A/R system for a given business.

Balance-forward A/R systems are designed to process open charge accounts that involve many relatively small purchases made over a period of time. These systems do not bill each sales transaction individually; they group all sales transactions to a particular customer for a certain time, such as one month, and submit one bill that covers all purchases. The unit record in this type of system reflects a total sales transaction made to a customer at one time and place. Typically, balance-forward A/R systems are found in firms that deal directly with consumers— department stores, gasoline companies and other firms that use credit cards, and utility companies.

The balance-forward type of A/R system must contain provisions for processing partial payments since customers sometimes do not pay their accounts in full during a billing cycle. The usual practice is to credit payments against the charges for the earliest period and apply the balance against the charges

CUSTOMER	ACCOUNT NUMBER	SR	SALES MAN	BALANCE	CURRENT	OVER 30 DAYS	OVER 60 DAYS	OVER 90 DAYS
CRANDAL & COMMINS	46346	1	44	50 3.42	50 3.42			
CULVER CONSTRUCTION CO	58607	1	19	1696.34	1315.67	380.67		
CUMBERLAND DAIRY	32264	3	72	379.05	379.05			
CUTTERBILL INC	88211	1	68	791.22	602.19	189.03		
CUYENSTAHL DIE WORKS	10910	1	43	4537.29	4537.29			
DADAROLA CONTRACTING	19777	1	11	55.80			55.80	
DADE & FORSTERMAN INC	20791	2	3.	747.65	737.65			10.00
DAHL DAHL & YONKO	49382	2	19	921.0	921.0			
DARCHESTER PLATING CO	11071	1	84	146.43	146.43			
DEAN HARDWARE CO	52086	1	26	875.0		875.0		
DEI LEVIN SUPPLY CO	14125	1	44	1727.77	1727.77			
DEVENY AND SONS	22767	1	11	54.83	54.83			

AGED TRIAL BALANCE — DATE 04/30/6-

Fig. 10-6   Aged Trial Balance

in the next period. Some A/R systems contain provisions for adding a finance charge, such as 1.5 percent per month on the unpaid balance, when the accounts are not paid in full within a specified period. Many balance-forward A/R systems also produce output for preparing and updating customer mailing lists as a byproduct of the system. Finally, the need for a customer history output file is more pressing in this type of system in order to provide management with sales analysis information.

The other subclass of A/R systems, the open-item A/R system, is designed to process specific items within each sales transaction. The unit record for this type of system is the line item within each invoice; the identity of each line item must be maintained throughout the entire data-processing cycle. Customer billing is performed by invoicing the customer for each sales transaction rather than by monthly statement. Payments are usually made on the basis of the total invoice amount, although occasionally payments will relate only to certain items on an invoice. Open-item A/R systems are most often found in businesses that sell to other businesses, such as business equipment manufacturers, wholesalers, and jobbers.

The open-item type of A/R system must maintain a separate record of each item within each invoice for each customer. This requirement substantially increases internal record-keeping difficulties and programming problems. Moreover, the need to credit payments against specific invoice items further complicates internal data-processing requirements.

Another feature frequently found in open-item A/R systems is the cash discount, such as one percent ten days, net thirty days. This incentive for early payment necessitates additional entries into the accounts receivable records to record discount terms, amount discounted, and whether the discount was earned. Standard discounts offered to various classes of customers and trade discounts are usually computed during invoice preparation and do not require any additional A/R system program activity.

Some firms use special billing practices that are peculiar to certain industries. The use of dating terms, for example, is common in the jewelry, toy, and garment industries where sales are highly seasonal. Merchandise may be sold and delivered to the customer several months before the seasonal surge in sales occurs. However, payment is not required until the beginning of the sales season. In this way the manufacturer may balance his production and shipping schedules and reduce his inventory storage requirements. The customer for his part is not expected to pay for the merchandise until the seasonal selling period begins. The A/R system in this case must recognize the liability of the customer on the periodic statements, yet not actually bill the customer until the proper time.

An A/R system's efficiency is directly related to the cost of performing the accounts receivable functions and the time required to perform them. In many cases efficiency may be improved by mechanizing some of the system's activities. Where the volume of accounts is several thousand or more, installing and operating a computerized A/R system shows substantial cost savings by reducing the processing costs per record. Further, such a system may permit a significant reduction in the overall time for posting, billing, and report preparation.

The effectiveness of an A/R system is concerned with how well its basic records are administered and how adequate the management reports it generates are. The accuracy of the basic records is directly related to the performance of the control procedure. A well-implemented control procedure keeps errors to a minimum and improves record reliability. The second part of the A/R system effectiveness evaluation criterion is more difficult to examine directly. The financial manager must have several different types of information reports in order to relate the accounts receivable subsystem activities to the operation of the entire financial system. The following management information reports must be designed to give him sufficient feedback to be able to plan, organize, and control the accounts receivable subsystem and the financial system activities.

A/R activity and status summary report   At frequent intervals the financial manager must receive summary reports of the activity within each input classification; cash sales, payments on accounts, credit/debit memos, and journal voucher entries. In addition, such reports should contain the current status of the A/R subsystem with the amounts due the firm broken down by age (0–30 days, 30–60 days, and so forth). Historical data from past years is very helpful as a basis for comparison.

Delinquent account feedback report   The credit manager needs information about late-paying accounts to determine whether corrective action is necessary. Without a stream of information about the status of current delinquent accounts, effective action to collect the accounts cannot be taken.

Aged trial balance report   This report, which contains an age distribution of the accounts receivable, provides a basis for comparative analysis to reveal trends in account payment practices and estimates of future cash inflows. As previously discussed, it also serves as a valuable internal control device for keeping the records of account accurate.

Customer activity history reports   This type of report focuses on the activity level for each customer in order to determine the firm's more important customers as well as those who have not been active recently. Good customers may be singled out for special consideration, such as advance notices of sales, to demonstrate goodwill. Inactive customers must be purged from the account file and the mailing list.

All of the management information reports discussed above are intended to increase the A/R subsystem's effectiveness using existing data to provide improved managerial insights into its operation. Only by using the accounts receivable subsystem's available information resources may this aspect of financial decision making be improved.

The Accounts Payable Subsystem

Raw materials, supplies, and services are some of the major systemic inputs to the business firm. The materials management function, which may be performed by a separate organizational unit in some large manufacturing firms or by a part of the production organization in smaller ones, creates financial liabilities for the firm by purchasing these inputs. The firm must also pay other financial liabilities, such as taxes, insurance, and internally generated expenses. The accounts payable subsystem maintains surveillance of these liabilities from the time they are created until they are discharged by payment.

The first main objective of the accounts payable subsystem is to maintain a record of all liabilities for the purchase of materials, supplies, and services. This process is begun by establishing a basic record of liability at the time the purchase order is placed with a vendor, which creates a conditional liability for the firm. After the goods have been received, checked for quantity, type, and quality, and approved, the liability has been validated. Next, the liabilities must be posted and the balance of the ledger account determined. Finally, a check must be written, the payment recorded, and the basic liability record (purchase order) closed out.

The subsystem's second main objective is to allocate and analyze the expenses for the firm's operation. In order to provide managerial control over the operations of the business, the accounts payable subsystem relates each item of expense to some business activity. Numbered ledger accounts in any desired level of detail are established to collect the charges for each activity. Ordinarily, the basis for the system of numbered accounts is the types of expense categories found in the ledger accounts.

These two objectives are not usually of equal importance to business firms. In wholesale firms, for example, the volume of invoices may be quite large but the distribution of expenses to different activities may be quite simple. In this instance, the disbursement objective dominates the distribution objective. Industrial firms, on the other hand, frequently find the number of purchase orders to be relatively small and the distribution of expenses to business activities to be much more important. In this case, the distribution objective would assume greater importance.

The accounts payable subsystem, like the accounts receivable subsystem, may be adapted to substitute machine effort for clerical effort in the operation of the system. A schematic model of a rather primitive (by present standards) accounts payable data-processing system (A/P system) is shown in figure 10-7. In contrast to the computer-based batch processing A/R system, this particular system configuration utilizes punched cards and unit-record equipment. A/P systems design may, of course, range

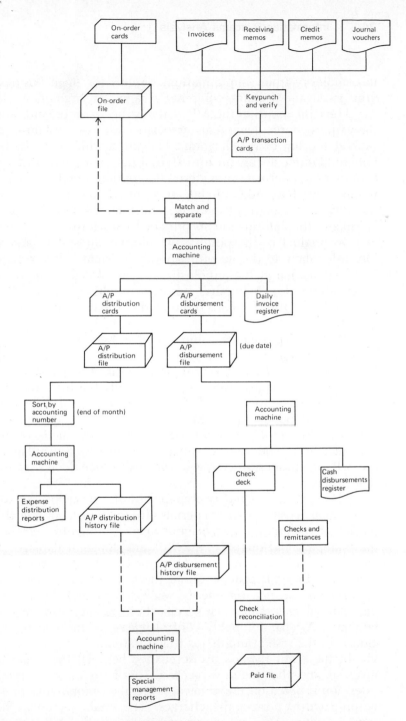

Fig. 10-7   Schematic of a typical unit record accounts payable
            data-processing system

in complexity from simple manual systems for small business firms to advanced online computer systems for large ones.

The basic inputs to the A/P system—the on-order cards and the various source documents associated with the system—appear at the top of the diagram. The purchasing order is the initiating source document for external purchases and contains certain basic information: material description, vendor, vendor number, purchase order number, account number, date needed, quantity, price, point of delivery, and material specifications. Normally, this information in punched card form is prepared as a by-product of the purchasing information system and is forwarded daily to the accounts payable system. After receipt by this department, the punched cards are placed in the open order or on-order file in purchase order number sequence. The open order file thus contains the record of the firm's conditional liabilities.

At the time suppliers ship merchandise, a copy of the packing slip and/or shipping papers as well as an invoice (bill) will be sent by mail to the purchasing firm. The packing slip copy and the shipping papers serve to notify the firm that the materials listed on the packing slip have been shipped as indicated on the shipping papers. Most frequently these documents are forwarded to the purchasing or receiving departments of the customer firm. The invoice, however, is usually forwarded to the A/P organization since it is a principal source document for that system.

The receiving memo is prepared by the receiving department upon receipt of the materials. In addition to noting the receipt of materials, the receiving memo frequently includes information about quantity, quality, and shipment damage. A copy of the receiving memo is forwarded to the A/P group for input into the A/P system. Some firms, especially those that perform defense or governmental work, must check the incoming material against material specifications before payment will be made. A separate quality control release memo can be included in the system inputs for this situation.

In the event there is a discrepancy between the quantity invoiced and the quantity received, or if an error in price extension is noted on the invoice, a credit memorandum must be prepared to correct the charges. The credit memo is the source document for entering corrections into the A/P system.

Payables are also originated within the business firm and

hence are not supported by a purchase order. These expenses are established with a journal voucher that describes the expense item, lists the account numbers to be debited or credited and their amounts, and shows an approval signature. The petty cash fund, a small cash fund for miscellaneous expenses, is replenished as required through the use of a journal voucher entry. Payments for taxes, insurance, and travel expenses are also entered into the system through journal vouchers.

After all of the supporting documents have been received and verified by the accounts payable organization, the firm's liability has been fully validated. At this time all of the documents relating to each transaction are gathered and the A/P group assigns the transaction a serial number. The serial number is known as the voucher number and becomes the transaction's identification key during the subsequent record processing.

The source documents are then keypunched and verified, to prepare the transaction cards. These cards are next matched against the on-order deck to remove the on-order cards that have been closed out. In this way the on-order deck will represent only outstanding purchase orders that have not been completed.

Next, the transaction cards are processed through an accounting machine to produce a daily invoice register, the distribution cards, and the disbursement cards. The daily invoice register is a simple listing in voucher number sequence of the validated transactions for a single day. This permanent record of validated liabilities permits any transaction to be reviewed without reference to the original documents. The total amount from the daily invoice register also provides one of the entries to the daily control sheet (see figure 10–8).

The distribution cards are accumulated for the monthly accounting period in the payables distribution file. At the end of the month, the payables distribution file is sorted in account number sequence and processed by an accounting machine to produce the expense distribution reports. The distribution cards may then be placed in the distribution history file for subsequent use in preparing the annual expense distribution reports.

The format of the expense distribution report varies according to the purpose for which it is to be used. The accounting department frequently requires an expense distribution report in summary form for allocating expenses to individual ledger accounts. Operating managers use such reports to follow the purchases and/or expenses that have been charged to their

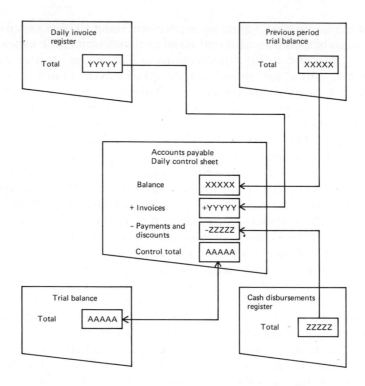

Fig. 10-8   Control procedures in an A/P system

departmental activities. In some respects the expense distribution report may serve as a primitive responsibility accounting report, which is the subject of the next section of this chapter.

The disbursement cards from the daily A/P invoice register operation are sorted by payment due date and merged into the A/P due date file. Filing the disbursement cards in the due date (ledger) file is the equivalent of posting the transaction in the ledger, since the file itself is the ledger. The A/P due date (ledger) file should be sorted by vendor number and listed at the end of each accounting period to determine the obligations that remain unpaid (trial balance). The A/P due date file may be listed by due date and summarized to prepare a cash requirements forecast report if required by the company treasurer. Alternatively, a daily listing of the vouchers to be paid may be submitted to the company treasurer for his information and approval.

The disbursement cards should contain both the gross

amount due the supplier and the net or discounted amount also. The most common discount allowance with which A/P systems are concerned is the cash discount, a cash incentive normally offered for prompt payment of the invoice. Terms, such as two percent ten days, net thirty days, provide a substantial inducement (amounting in this case to an annual rate of interest for the additional twenty days of approximately thirty-six percent) for the prompt discharge of the liability. Cash discounts may be offered by firms not only to turn over their accounts receivables quickly, but also to encourage purchasers to buy certain types or quantities of merchandise and make purchases during certain seasons of the year. In view of the financial benefits to be gained by taking advantage of the cash discount, A/P disbursement cards should be filed according to the latest date for which the discount may be taken.

The accounts payable disbursement cards are removed from the due date file as payments come due and entered into the check writing subsystem. Since check writing is an especially vulnerable area for employee malfeasance, rigid administrative controls must be established to safeguard company interests. The current payables due cards are processed by an accounting machine to prepare a cash disbursements register, remittances, and checks, and a check reconciliation card deck. The cash disbursements register is an activity listing of all disbursements and earned discounts taken each day. The total from this register is entered manually into the A/P daily control sheet, as indicated in figure 10-8. Remittance statements explaining the liabilities being discharged by the check normally accompany it and may be prepared from data contained on the A/P disbursement punched cards. Preparing the checks on punched cards greatly facilitates machine comparison of cancelled checks to the check reconciliation deck. Outstanding checks and any discrepancies may be noted on a check clearance report and handled on an exception basis.

After the checks are prepared, the A/P disbursement cards are placed in the disbursements history file. This file is complementary to the history file prepared from the distribution cards and contains, in addition, information about discounts taken and lost. The analysis of the disbursement history file is a source of valuable management information. Sorting accounts payable data by vendor, type of expense, organizational unit, or product enables the manager to discern diverse relations that exist among the different phases of the business operation. The volume of purchases from each vendor, the delivery reliability of different vendors, and material rejection problems may be more precisely defined by using data in the A/P disbursement history file. The efficiency of the accounts payable subsystem may be evaluated by noting the amount of cash discounts lost over a period of time. Cash requirements planning may also be improved through analysis of accounts payable data. These analytical reports are shown in figure 10-7 as special management reports.

The institution of control procedures is particularly important in A/P systems since check preparation is an integral part of the system. Control of the overall A/P system is centered in the preparation of the accounts payable daily control sheet shown in figure 10-8. The trial balance from the previous day is the starting point in the procedure and is the first entry on the control sheet. Next, the total amount of all invoices, credit memos, and journal vouchers as shown on the daily invoice register is entered on the control sheet. Cash payments and earned discounts totals taken from the cash disbursements register are entered and subtracted from the sum of the preceding values. The resulting value is the control total and must equal the sum of all the transactions in the A/P due date (ledger) file. Assuming an initial in-balance condition from the previous day's operations, system input and/or output errors may be located by examining the daily invoice register, the cash disbursements register, and listings (trial balances) of the previous and current A/P due date file.

The efficiency of an accounts payable subsystem is measured by the degree to which the system meets the financial commitments of the firm while maintaining maximum liquidity. In this sense the subsystem is operating at maximum efficiency when current obligations together with earned discounts are paid on the dates that they fall due. The efficiency of the system is judged by evaluating the total actual operating cost as compared to that of other methods of operation. As noted with the A/R system, cost benefits with improved management information and better controls may be gained by mechanization. The nature and extent of these benefits may be determined only through investigation of all the alternatives.

The effectiveness of the A/P system may be evaluated by noting the degree to which it fulfills its various functions. The timely preparation of checks, the accurate maintenance of liability records, and the stewardship of cash assets may be judged with relative ease. The quality of information available for managerial decision making is more difficult to determine. However, this is the area in which A/P system effectiveness is most apt to be deficient. Forecasts of cash expenditures, for example, should not only include items in the due date file but also time-expense estimates taken from the on-order file. In this way the financial manager makes relevant use of all the data contained in the system. Other opportunities for providing management with valuable information are also present in the disbursement history file. The analysis of management information needs coupled with the availability of data can substantially increase the A/P system's overall effectiveness.

The following management information reports are some of the more common and important types of information that A/P systems provide financial management:

A/P activity and status summary report This report summarizes the new validated liabilities of the firm as well as a summary of other adjustments made to the accounts.

Cash disbursement summary report This report is a simple listing of cash disbursements for a particular period, including earned discount data for each remittance.

Cash expense forecasts These are summary reports of conditional and validated liabilities according to the period when payment is due.

Expense distribution reports These are reports showing the breakdown of expenses for each business activity or organizational unit.

Special management reports These are special reports based on the analysis history file data.

Consistent and reasonable use of the data available to the financial manager from the A/P system will permit a manager to make better decisions and to gain improved insights into the structure and operation of the accounts payable system.

RESPONSIBILITY ACCOUNTING SYSTEMS

One of the most frustrating experiences that a manager faces is the realization that his subordinates are performing activities without any real knowledge on his part of what is really going on. A manager is usually physically unable to supervise the activities of each subordinate directly. General directions and sufficient authority must be given to subordinates to accomplish the necessary tasks. After this has been done, the manager must establish control procedures to determine whether the basic objectives are, in fact, being met.

The financial subsystem interfaces with all of the other major subsystems in the business firm, as was shown in figure 10–1 at the beginning of the chapter. The financial dimensions of business activities provide a common denominator for establishing an information base to evaluate each major subsystem's operations. Thus measuring the financial attributes of the production/operation subsystem can give management appropriate information for developing satisfactory control procedures. In this way the activities of the production/operation subsystem can be effectively monitored.

Responsibility accounting systems (R/A systems) are information systems designed to provide the manager with the knowledge of how well his organization is meeting its objectives (budgets). The direct expenses generated in manufacturing goods and performing services form the basic inputs to the R/A system. This expense data is then sorted, classified, and summarized to yield information reports to management about the operation of the production process.

Responsibility accounting systems seek to determine the relative efficiency of organizational operations rather than their effectiveness. Total organizational effectiveness is most likely to be achieved when each of the organizational units is operating efficiently. There is an underlying assumption in this approach that the objectives of the business firm have been established by top management and have been communicated through detailed plans to the individual operating units. Therefore the principal effort of lower-level executives becomes the achievement of the highest possible level of efficiency in the performance of their designated duties.

Cost accounting techniques in manufacturing enterprises are directed at three major objectives: determining product cost, inventory pricing, and manufacturing cost control. In general, cost accounting systems provide an adequate means for determining product cost and inventory pricing. The control of manufacturing costs, on the other hand, is a neglected area in many cost accounting systems. Responsibility accounting systems attempt to meet all three of these objectives by emphasizing cost control primarily and using cost control data for developing product costs and inventory pricing. Thus responsibility accounting systems and cost accounting systems are both directed toward the same ends. The difference lies in the order of priority of the different objectives and the techniques by which each of them is satisfied.

The managerial control process is composed of several steps: establishing standards, measuring performance, comparing performance against the standard and, finally, taking corrective action to improve systems performance. The R/A system follows this pattern. Budgets are the standards: performance is measured with expense data; the values are compared to yield variances. The appropriate corrective action is left to the discretion of the manager.

In the case of R/A systems the departmental operating expense budgets are the set of standards against which current performance is evaluated. Individual expense items the supervisor exercises direct control over are analyzed for past periods and projections (forecasts) are made for subsequent periods. Experience has shown that the best results are obtained when the individual manager and his supervisor work out the projections together and arrive at a mutual consensus on the budget. The target values must be realistic and attainable. In this way the supervisor develops an emotional committment to his budget and will exert maximum effort to meet the goals.

Budget values may be developed by either of two approaches: fixed budgets or variable budgets. In the fixed budget approach the budgeted amounts for the coming periods are determined in advance for each expense classification and are not usually subject to major revision throughout the periods covered. There is a tacit assumption that the level of organization activity will remain approximately constant within the projected periods. Variable budgets, on the other hand, seek to relate directly the amount budgeted by expense class to the level of activity in each period. In this case it is assumed that all of the budgeted costs are variable costs related directly to the activity level and are therefore controllable by the supervisor as the activity level changes. As might be expected, variable budgets are somewhat more difficult and expensive to develop than fixed ones. They do, however, provide for much greater flexibility with regard to unplanned changes in the activity level and product mix.

The business firm must have a well-defined organization chart before an R/A system can be developed. The formal organization chart is a systems model of the organization that depicts the lines of authority extending from top management down through the entire organization. Each individual normally reports to a single supervisor. The reports generated by an R/A system follow in reverse the lines of authority in the organization chart. The first-level supervisor recieves reports of the activities of each of the first-level departments for which he is responsible. The third-level manager receives a summary report dealing with the organizational activities of each second-level manager who reports to him. The reporting process simply follows the lines of authority back through the entire organization to the chief executive officer.

The preparation of reports for each responsible manager depends on the development of an organizational coding system that enables the computer to allocate the expenses to the appropriate department and to prepare the summary reports for the higher levels of management. Assuming there are four levels of management and not more than ten organizational units reporting to any one manager, a three-digit code may be used to define the lines of authority. A number in the hundreds position would designate each third-level manager. The second-level managers who report to each third-level manager would be designated by a number in the tens position. A number in the units position would designate a first-level supervisor reporting to a second-level manager. Using a major/intermediate/minor sorting operation, the computer could automatically group the expenses for each organizational unit and prepare the summary reports for the upper levels of management.

Controllable expenses must also be organized into a standardized coding system to expedite recording and allocating expenses. Although there are several different ways this coding system may be developed, such a system usually follows the ledger account numbers in the accounting system. Among the items most often considered as controllable expenses are:

Supervision expense
Setup expense
Productive labor
Down time

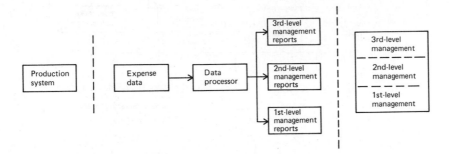

Fig. 10-9   Summary system model of the R/A system

Repair and rework
Overtime premium
Supplies
Utilities

The controllable expenses do not represent all of the department-mental expenses, only those over which the supervisor can exercise a degree of control. This is the criterion by which every item must be judged for inclusion as a controllable expense.

The organizational budgets, the organizational coding system, and the controllable expense classification system are combined in the report-building process to create the various R/A reports. Each of the controllable expense items is grouped and sorted by organizational unit together with the corresponding departmental budget values to produce detailed reports for the first-level supervisors. The summary of actual expenses, budget, and variance values for each organizational unit are then combined to produce the second-level management R/A reports. The summary values from each second-level organizational unit report become the detail values in the third-level management reports. In this way the different information elements of the R/A system are combined to give the managers at each level sufficient information to monitor the activities in their respective organizational units without any extraneous detail.

The summary system model of the R/A system is shown in figure 10-9. The production/operation process for which ex-

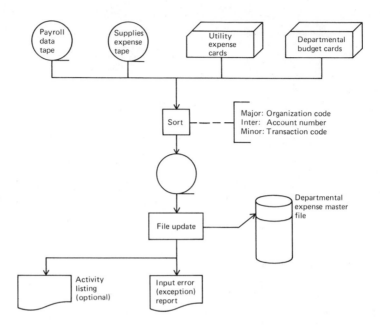

Fig. 10-10   Typical R/A system flowchart

pense data must be collected appears on the left in the diagram; it is broadly defined as the operations performed by every organizational unit in the entire firm. Using this all-inclusive definition, operations that might not ordinarily be considered as part of the production process (that is, finance, marketing, engineering, and research and development) would be included in the interface of the production/operation process with the R/A system.

The second interface, which appears on the right-hand side of the figure, involves the transfer of information generated by the R/A system to management. Three different report types are shown, but the number required depends on the number of management levels in the firm. Essentially, the differences among these reports is the level of detail included in each. Thus the first-level supervisor's report contains all of the detail necessary for him to identify and control his individual departmental costs. The R/A reports for the management levels above contain

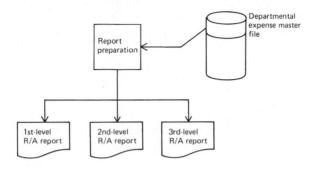

Fig. 10-10   (cont'd)

less primary detail at each level and stress summary information more.

A typical R/A system flowchart is shown in figure 10-10. This particular flowchart is based on the configuration of a medium-sized computer installation using disc files for master record storage. Another feature that should be noted in the flowchart is the use of segmented programs. The first processing run is essentially a file maintenance operation in which the master file is updated with current data. Subsequent processing runs prepare the individual report types.

The inputs for the R/A system must be gathered from several diverse areas. Labor expenses by type within each organizational unit will originate from the payroll system. Premium (overtime) pay is usually separated by labor expense category, and is included as a separate line entry. Supplies and miscellaneous expenses may be developed by either the materials management information system, the accounts payable system, or by both. The exact data source will depend on the types of data available in each of the information systems and the ease of extracting the required supplies and miscellaneous expense data from them.

Utility cost data will probably originate within the plant engineering organization. Readings from departmental utility measurement stations must be combined with unit utility cost values to produce these inputs. Inasmuch as supervision of the plant utility system is usually delegated to plant engineering, this organization is most able to supply the data. The final type of R/A system input data, budget data, is usually supplied by the budget section of the accounting department, which serves as a central point for budget administration.

The input data from the various sources must be placed in sequence before the file maintenance processing run can be performed. The major sort key is the three-digit code that reflects the basic organizational structure. The minor sort key is the account number or other coding system that identifies the types of expenses used in the R/A reports. Sequencing the data in this way permits each type of expense within each organizational unit to be summarized.

The file maintenance processing run updates the master file records, which contain the historical expense records and the budget data for operations during the current fiscal or calendar year. An activity listing with appropriate summary values is also prepared at this time to serve as an input audit trail. The exception report for erroneous input data may be incorporated in the activity listing or output as a special report.

The R/A reports may be prepared in one or more subsequent computer runs after the master file has been updated. If sufficient core storage is available, the second- and third-level R/A reports may be prepared in the same computer run as the first-level ones by temporarily storing the summarized information for these reports. On the other hand, the report preparation program may be simplified substantially and the core storage requirements may be reduced if a separate computer run is used to generate each report type. The systems flowchart in figure 10-10 depicts the former case, in which all of the R/A reports are prepared in one computer run.

An example of a first-level R/A report is shown in figure 10-11. In order to make the report more understandable, names have been substituted for the organizational code number in the report heading and for the account numbers in the body. This substitution is accomplished by a table lookup subroutine in the program. Notice also that budget figures do not appear directly in the report. The difference between the budget and

Punch Press Costs

Controllable Expenses	Amount		(Over) or Under Budget	
	This Month	Year To Date	This Month	Year To Date
Supervision	700	2800	—	—
Setup	410	1630	(10)	(30)
Repair and rework	380	1685	20	(85)
Overtime premium	360	1340	(40)	(60)
Supplies	240	980	10	20
Utilities	520	2100	25	90
Miscellaneous	395	1320	(45)	80
Total	2905	11855	(40)	15

Productive Labor:	Standard		Variance	
	This Month	Year To Date	This Month	Year To Date
Amount	$7224	$32480	$350	$920
Hours	2580	11600	20	240
Per Hour	2.80	2.80	.05	.08

Fig. 10-11   First-level R/A report

actual amounts (variance) is more immediatly significant in evaluating operating efficiency.

An example of a second-level R/A report is shown in figure 10-12. This report also uses a table lookup subroutine to convert organizational codes into proper names. Second-level R/A reports are basically summaries of the first-level reports with substantial portions of detail omitted. Second-level managers who wish detailed information may, of course, receive copies of their first-level supervisor's reports. Third-level reports present summaries of the second-level reports; third-level managers may also receive the second-level reports of their subordinate managers if they wish.

Another form of information that may be prepared from the data in the master files is the controllable expense and labor cost information for the cost accounting and financial accounting systems. Much of the data the R/A system collects is directly usable in conjunction with uncontrollable expense data to prepare the cost of production and sales reports and the state-

Production Department Cost Summary
(General Superintendent)

Controllable Expenses:	Amount		(Over) or Under Budget	
	This Month	Year To Date	This Month	Year To Date
General sup'ts office	$ 2,160	$ 8,340	$ —	$ 100
Punch press	2,905	11,855	(40)	15
Drop hammer	1,835	7,300	15	100
Milling machine	1,710	7,155	(30)	(365)
Screw machine	2,120	8,400	(60)	(800)
Heat treat	1,260	5,360	50	(290)
Assembly	4,190	16,200	70	620
Painting	905	3,830	(15)	45
	$17,085	$68,440	$(10)	$(575)

Productive Labor:	Standard		Variance	
	This Month	Year To Date	This Month	Year To Date
Punch press	$ 7,224	$ 32,480	$ 350	$ 920
Drop hammer	6,405	25,290	(120)	(380)
Milling machine	6,030	24,380	80	140
Screw machine	6,925	27,710	195	475
Heat treat	3,880	16,695	(210)	(860)
Assembly	11,360	49,205	605	(1210)
Painting	4,815	17,315	(45)	360
	$46,639	$193,075	$ 850	$(555)

Fig. 10-12   Second-level R/A report

ments of income and expense. Inventory prices and product costs may be determined from the controllable expense data, the labor cost data, and the uncontrollable expense data to complete the information requirements of a satisfactory cost accounting system. Placing primary emphasis on organizational unit expense control through an R/A system does not preclude the development of a good cost accounting system.

The operating efficiency of the R/A system depends, in part, on the availability of input data in the proper form from other information systems. Output records from the supporting systems must be accurate, readily available, and in a form suitable for processing in the R/A system. Payroll data, for example, must be classified by type of work performed (that is, productive, down time, set-up, repair and rework, and personal). Expending large amounts of effort to prepare input data will decrease the system's cost efficiency substantially.

The amount of fast memory plays a smaller role in R/A system cost efficiency. As discussed previously, the availability of sufficient core storage permits all the R/A reports to be prepared simultaneously in one computer processing run.

The R/A system's effectiveness must be measured against the results the system achieves. Its reports should enable the operating managers to exercise more intelligent control of costs in their respective organizational units. Such reports do provide a convenient and accurate means for evaluating managerial effectiveness. The ultimate answer to the question of R/A system effectiveness rests with the use that managers at all levels make of the information in R/A reports.

PERSONNEL INFORMATION SYSTEMS

The development of data-processing systems related to the personnel area in the typical business firm has usually lagged behind information systems such as payroll, accounts payable/receivable, production control, and inventory control. The principal reason for this situation appears to be that data-processing systems in these other areas showed substantially greater cost savings than a personnel information system could demonstrate. It was only natural, then, for managers to place higher development priorities on those projects that could yield a higher and more immediate financial return.

A second reason for the somewhat slower development of data-processing systems in the personnel area has been the requirement that every personnel record be accessible immediately. The ability to access random records did not become a practical reality until the commercial introduction of disc and drum auxillary storage devices during the early 1960s. Before that time, computer records of all sorts could only be stored on magnetic tape and records could be accessed only during the periodic processing operations.

Vestiges of this situation linger to the present. However, the business and industrial community today has recognized that computer-based personnel information systems can provide more accurate, more timely, and better organized information for management at less cost than the older manual systems. Increasing federal regulation and the administration of complex labor contracts have also hastened the transition to computerized sys-

tems. In this chapter we will first examine the operating characteristics of a typical personnel system within the context of our
dynamic system model of the firm. Specific areas within this
subsystem will then be examined for computer-based data-processing applications.

THE PERSONNEL SYSTEM

The various activities personnel departments perform have
sometimes been labeled the *personnel process*. This approach has
considerable merit since it considers the entire personnel function as a dynamic, ongoing operation with many different interrelations within the firm.

Let us extend the personnel process concept, however, to
the operation of a dynamic system, the personnel system. Our
discussion in chapter 4 of the business firm as a dynamic system
viewed personnel as one of the system's basic inputs. People,
both managers and non-managers, provide the great force that
converts raw materials of some description into finished goods
and/or services. In short, to perform a useful economic function,
a firm requires effort from individuals with many different skills.

There has always been a need for human activity to accomplish organizational objectives. Human beings in former times
were considered to be commodities that could be purchased,
used, and discarded according to the whims of "management."
Through the centuries, however, there has been a gradual
evolution in the importance of people as unique contributors
to the achievement of organizational goals. This became more
clearly recognized during the first part of the twentieth century.
The advent of labor unions, the increasing requirements for
highly skilled technologists, and the results of employee motivation research have resulted in greater emphasis on personnel
as a primary input into the production process.

Within the overall system concept of the business firm, its
personnel function may be examined as a separate unique system
as shown in figure 11-1. The basic input for the system is people;
that is, new employees who have just joined the firm. Hiring
new employees occurs when the level of activity within the firm
is increased, when new skills are needed, and when terminated
employees must be replaced. These new employees will have
an infinite variety of skills, personalities, physical characteristics,
educational backgrounds, and work experiences. In nearly all
cases they will have expressed an implicit acceptance of the

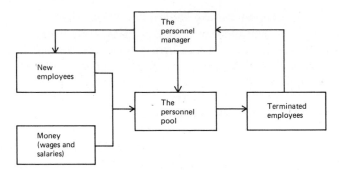

Fig. 11-1   The personnel system

subordinate's role in the superior-subordinate relation and will expect to work toward the firm's objectives in their own personal ways. Before they can assume active roles in their assigned work activities, they will probably need to be oriented (given basic information about the operation of the firm) and, perhaps, trained to perform the tasks associated with their position.

The other major input to the personnel subsystem is money. If we expect employees to perform satisfactorily, they should be paid a reasonable wage at scheduled intervals. In addition to direct wage and salary costs, all indirect costs such as fringe benefits are included in the firm's total personnel compensation costs.

The central portion of the dynamic system model (processor) is a reservoir of trained, competent individuals, both managers and workers, actively engaged in the performance of their duties. This group of motivated individuals actually provides the human effort that was previously described as the personnel input in the systems model of the firm.

As suggested by the fact that new employees are continually being added to the work force and other employees are being separated from it, the makeup of the processor is constantly shifting. The innate characteristics of the work force also slowly change due to the continual growth and development of individuals working for the firm. Individuals grow in maturity, intellectual breadth, and work experience. Thus the work force's capacity to accomplish tasks in a changing business environment evolves over a period of time. As a result, the personnel pool (processor) must be viewed as a dynamic entity with constantly changing characteristics.

The output of the personnel subsystem is those employees

who are permanently separated from the active work force. Voluntary resignations, retirements, firings, and permanent-type layoffs due to changing technology or economic conditions are the most common examples of permanent reductions in the labor force. Absences due to health reasons (sick leave), vacations, attendance at formal educational programs, temporary layoffs, and other absences that are only temporary reductions in the labor force should not be considered as output of the system. Company policies and procedures usually establish guidelines to distinguish one group from the other.

The personnel manager functions as the controller of the personnel subsystem. His principal information inputs are the forecasts of employee terminations not related to level of business activity (retirements) and forecasts of changes in manpower requirements due to fluctuations in the level of business activity or changes in the nature of the business. By integrating these two information streams, he may develop plans for recruiting, placing, and training (if required) new employees. In effect, he regulates the flow of inputs (number and quality of new employees) to balance the firm's total anticipated manpower and skills requirements.

Quite frequently the personnel manager must also perform other duties that relate indirectly to the performance of the processor. The administration of the fringe benefit program, labor contract negotiation and administration, wage and salary administration, personnel evaluation program administration, training program administration, and other programs that may be assigned to him for administrative purposes (food service, safety, plant security, and so forth) are all programs designed to implement the firm's personnel policies. In this connection we should note parenthetically that seldom does any other area of the firm have as many policies, together with their associated procedures, as the personnel function. Thus through the administration of various personnel-related programs as well as through the regulation of quantity and quality of the work force, the personnel manager exercises a major directing influence on the performance of the personnel system.

The efficiency of the whole personnel system is best evaluated through a series of relative comparisons with pre-established standards. In the measurement of cost efficiency, for example, the wage and salary rates for each job classification could be compared with those for similar job classifications in the immediate area, the industry, and nationally. To the extent that current wage and salary rates are lower than the comparative values, the cost efficiency is good. Of course, this analysis must be evaluated with subjective factors in mind also. Company policy, effective manpower utilization, and cost/productivity trends exert a strong influence on the final cost evaluation of personnel system efficiency.

Labor turnover is the best relative index to a time measure of personnel system efficiency. The labor turnover rate is usually computed as the number of quits during the month divided by the total number of employees at mid-month:

$$\frac{\text{Number of quits}}{\text{Total number of employees}} = \text{Employee turnover rate}$$

If the labor turnover rate is high relative to a historical or industry standard, then we may conclude that the work force is composed of proportionately more less-experienced personnel. From this conclusion we may infer that the overall productive capacity of the personnel system is below a desirable level and hence is less efficient. Conversely, if the labor turnover rate is low, we may infer that the time measure of personnel system efficiency is quite satisfactory. Moreover, recruitment and train- ing costs as well as the higher costs of production attributable to new employees may also be noted in cost measures of the system's efficiency.

More exact measures of personnel system efficiency are difficult to ascertain. Perhaps the best guide for the quantity measure is the fluctuation in level of employment over a period such as one year. Substantial differences in employment levels would indicate a less efficient personnel system, while a relatively uniform employment level would indicate a more efficient one. This factor, of course, may not be controllable due to the seasonal nature of the business.

The quality measure of personnel system efficiency may be surmised from the organization's recruiting success. The firm's ability to attract employees who fully meet the job specifications for open positions will exert a powerful long-run influence on the quality of employees in the personnel system. An efficient personnel system can only be built with an adequate flow of well-qualified new employees.

The system's effectiveness may be evaluated subjectively by comparing the actual performance of the manpower pool with its expected performance. The personnel manager, in all fairness, can be held responsible only for those aspects of employee performance over which he exercises authority and control. He is thus responsible for acquiring and maintaining a sufficient number of employees who have the skills required to perform the scheduled workload. This facet of personnel system effectiveness may be most easily evaluated by noting the organizational positions that are currently filled with very marginally qualified or unproductive individuals. An effective personnel system should have few employees of this type.

On the other hand, the other aspects of the system's effectiveness, the motivation of the employees, and the proper management of the human resources are the responsibility of the firm's managers. Studies by Herzberg, for example, have shown that management itself exercises the dominant influence in the determining of employee commitment and job motivation.[1] To achieve a truly effective personnel system, both the personnel manager and the other managers must perform their respective functions effectively and cooperate fully with each other.

The Data Base

As we have previously noted, business-oriented computer programs operate on two broad classes of data—transaction data that reflects current business activities and file data that relates to collected or previously processed data. In simple information systems, input transaction data streams are processed with data from a single file to develop both operating and management reports. In advanced or integrated information systems, we often encounter situations in which data from a single transaction is needed to update two or more files or where data files with extremely long records must be subdivided to be manageable. These situations require a fresh approach to data file design.

The term *data base* is widely used to denote data collected and maintained in two or more coordinated data files that may be utilized by one or more information systems. One data file that is used by two or more information systems is also called a data base in some of the information system literature. Regardless, the term always refers to data files, not transaction data.

---

1. Frederick Herzberg, *Work and the Nature of Man* (Cleveland: World Publishing Company, 1966)

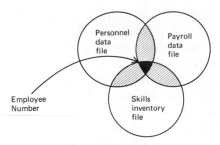

Fig. 11-2   Employee number as a record access key

In order for two or more data files to qualify as a data base, they must have a common denominator (that is, have one or more common data fields). In the simplest case, all records comprising a data base within the files are accessible with the same record key. In a personnel information system, for example, employee number could serve as the record access key for the personnel data file, the payroll file, and the skills inventory file, as illustrated in figure 11-2. The black central area represents employee number data, the shaded area represents duplicate data contained in each pair of data files, and the white area represents data contained only in one file. In this example any record in each of the three files may be updated or accessed through the employee number. In this case the data base would be structured as shown to avoid very lengthy individual records.

The second type of data base structure is more complex and involves linking together data files with different record access keys. This situation is illustrated in figure 11-3. The open purchase order file uses the purchase order number as the record

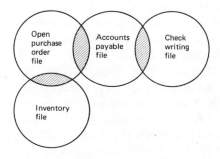

Fig. 11-3   Linking data files with different access keys

access key and also has record fields for item identification number and voucher set number. Thus when the purchased item is received, the open purchase order information system program could also access the inventory file and update the quantity field with the number of units received. This feat is possible because both the open purchase order file and the Inventory file have a common data field—the item identification number—that could be used to link them. In the same way, the open purchase order file could be linked to the accounts payable file through the voucher set number. The check number can link the accounts payable file to the check-writing file.

The application of the data base concept to information system design usually implies random-access capability. While random accessibility of data is not an absolute requirement for a functional data base, irksome and time-consuming data manipulation difficulties are usually encountered when data files are maintained on magnetic tape. Multiple-entry record keeping in which data from a single business transaction is simultaneously entered in two or more files is virtually impossible when magnetic tape files are used. For this reason, random-access auxillary storage devices must be used to gain all of the benefits a data base affords.

The creation of a data base composed of several related files is often a compromise between two conflicting objectives—the minimization of data duplication and the optimization of data accessibility. The first objective calls for eliminating as much duplicate and redundant data as possible. This may be accomplished by storing individual data fields at only one location within the whole data base. By reducing duplicate data fields to a minimum, the total amount of file storage for the data base and, therefore, the equipment cost will be the lowest possible. Further, file maintenance will be a simpler task under these conditions, which will lead to operating cost reductions.

The conflicting objective—data accessibility—produces a countervailing force in data base design. If we are seeking information from a data base, we would prefer to have all of the pertinent information stored in only one of the files. When two or more different record files must be accessed to provide all of the needed information, the searching process is more cumbersome and time-consuming. Resolving these conflicting objectives usually results in a modest but manageable amount of data redundancy within the related data files.

Another aspect that is implicit in the data base concept is application independence. Although the data base may be designed initially for use in a single information system, it should be viewed as a separate and distinct entity apart from any particular system application. Applying this viewpoint, the files within a data base become a common data foundation that is available to any information system in the entire firm. Moreover, the application independence idea must be extended to cover future information systems as well as existing ones. When the independence of the data base is not fully recognized and provisions are not made for collecting and storing relevant, related data, introducing new information systems will likely require extensive reprogramming.

Extension of the application independence idea produces another revelation of great importance. A data base is not the exclusive property of any organizational unit or business function. Historically, data files of all descriptions have been created, maintained, and administered by individual departments to serve their needs alone. Simply transferring a file to a computer-usable form (magnetic tape, disc, drum, and so forth) often does not reduce the department's proprietary interest in it. However, when computerized data files are incorporated into a data base, departmental autonomy ceases. This transformation usually involves eliminating duplicate and redundant data, reorganizing the file's contents, and consolidating files. The departmental proprietary relation over the data files can no longer exist. The individual departments are still required to maintain the files by supplying current transaction data, but they must give up all control over record content, record format, and data base administration.

Naturally when departmental managers recognize this point, they often become very apprehensive and reluctant to pursue data base implementation. They are justifiably concerned that their freedom and ability to plan, organize, and control their departmental activities will be jeopardized. Moreoever, the authority they relinquish will necessarily be consolidated and vested in a new organizational power center, the information systems department and the data-base manager. Thus the organizational and political changes that result from the implementation of a data base program are likely to have far-reaching consequences among the firm's management.

To counteract the inevitable opposition to a data base implementation program and establish a sound basis for its success, several things must be done. First, the information systems department manager must realistically assess the quality and capacity of both the departmental staff and the computer hardware/software that can be obtained. There is no point in undertaking a data base implementation program without adequate and sufficient resources. The consequences of a major system failure will be disastrous for the business firm as well as for the information systems department. Secondly, the systems analysts assigned to the task must perform an especially thorough investigation and design of the new data base. Finally, top management must forcefully and completely support the program, including restructuring the organization if required.

Data base security is ordinarily a more difficult problem and requires more safeguards than simple data file security. One of the important characteristics of data bases is that they can be accessed by one or more information systems and/or one or more organizational units. Thus input errors may be introduced by many different input sources; fixing the accountability for them becomes a much more difficult task. In addition, the confidential nature of certain data files, such as personnel, payroll, and cost files, demands that data base access be limited to individuals who have a demonstrated "need to know." The additional security requirements for certain data base files may, in some cases, limit their utility by restricting access and imposing security regulations.

The Personnel Information System

The management of the personnel function in business organizations is intimately related to the collection, storage, and use of data concerning all aspects of personnel. Historically, personnel-related information has been maintained as record files located in various branches and departments of the organization. Basic employee data and, sometimes, appraisal data have been maintained by the personnel department. Wage and salary data has been maintained by the personnel department. Employee appraisal data has been stored in the manager's files. The insurance and medical departments have maintained insurance data and medical files, respectively. Moreover, certain types of data, such as recently acquired skills and educational data, have frequently been known only to individual employees, and no current record exists anywhere within the firm. Thus the division of employee data among separate record files has resulted in sporadic and incomplete usage of collected information for managerial purposes.

Computerized personnel information systems are designed to collect, maintain, and make economic use of personnel data for managerial purposes. The realization of this goal has become possible only in recent years with the development of random access storage devices. The further development of remote input/output terminals connected online with the central processing unit and its data files has further improved the feasibility of placing personnel data into computer-processable form. Present data-processing systems provide a feasible means for collecting, maintaining, and using comprehensive personnel data.

One of the primary functions of a modern personnel information system is to collect and maintain basic personnel records. Rather than have many separate files in different locations, random access storage devices can maintain a data base that may be readily accessed by an employee identification number. As personnel activity occurs, the personnel data base (also known as the personnel data bank) may be updated quite readily. The establishment of formalized data entry procedures and the relative ease of updating the personnel data base have resulted in substantial improvements in the accuracy and timeliness (as well as the completeness) of all personnel records. As personnel information is needed by management, inquiries may be made to the data base and immediate responses may be obtained. The personnel data base may also be used to prepare both current activity and status reports for the entire personnel system and furnish basic data to other information systems, such as the personnel information system. For these reasons, a computer-based personnel information system with a well-designed data base can offer significant advantages for record keeping.

One of the most difficult tasks facing personnel management is the analysis of the personnel data base to determine the attributes and characteristics of the firm's employees. The personnel data base, through the use of special programs, can produce many different personnel analysis reports, such as wage and salary administration reports and educational attainment reports. These may be prepared by sorting selected data into special sequences to examine particular attributes of the employee population. In addition, the personnel data base may be searched to identify employees who have particular skills, attributes, and abilities. Through the unique capabilities of an automated personnel information system, these special analytical reports can satisfy certain government report requirements as well as special management information needs.

The personnel data base also performs a valuable function in supporting information requirements for other systems. The payroll system may use it to supply personnel data such as social security number, address, number of dependents and, perhaps, special deductions. The insurance information system may also access it to supply a portion of its information needs. Medical information systems, pension information systems, responsibility accounting systems, and skills inventory information systems can all make excellent use of information contained in such a data base. In this way, a substantial amount of redundant personnel data is eliminated from the supporting record files. Further, data changes in one record file are immediately available to the supporting systems. Consolidating personnel data files that will make accurate, up-to-date information available to all the supporting information systems is easily the most efficient way to process personnel data.

The users of the personnel information system and its related data base are most frequently restricted to members of the personnel department, managers in other departments, and certain employees in other personnel-related information systems. The confidential nature of data contained in the personnel data base demands substantial security measures to insure adequate protection of employee data. There are nearly always access restrictions in personnel information systems. Not only is record access limited to those with a demonstrated "need to know," but the entry of input data must be closely supervised also. The reasons for these safeguards are especially apparent in the payroll system; for example, an unauthorized change in the salary level could result in an employee being overpaid.

An example of a computer-based personnel information system is shown in figure 11-4. The general outline for this information system is very similar to others we have already examined. First, various input data streams are transcribed into data-processable form and are combined for entry into the central processing unit. Next, the processor updates the personnel data base. Finally, the information stored in the data base

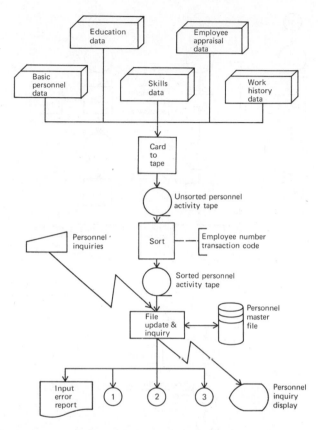

Fig. 11-4   Computer-based information system

is used to prepare a variety of operating and management information reports. A unique feature found in this personnel information system is the ability to prepare special outputs or reports
upon request.

The first input data stream is composed of basic personnel
data. This data, which is largely collected at the time of employment through the personnel application form, includes such
items as full name, social security number, birth date, mailing
address, home telephone number, name and address of next of
kin, sex, race (to be used only for statistical purposes), skills
aptitude test data, citizenship, military data, security clearance,
job title, assigned work area, number of dependents, and salary.
During the course of employment, some of this data may require

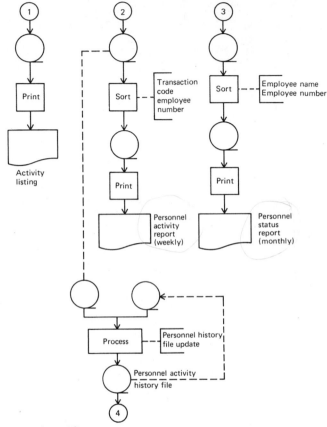

Fig. 11-4   (cont'd)

updating to reflect changes in the employee's current situation. Additional data may also be collected to handle special circumstances, such as sales quotas, commission rates, drawing account limits, and the like. An example of a basic personnel data input card is shown in figure 11-5. It is the data collected in this input stream that is most likely to be duplicated in other personnel-related information systems.

The second input data stream is concerned with the employees' educational backgrounds. Although this data may in many cases be collected on the original personnel application form, it is sufficiently important to warrant separate identification and treatment. This data includes number of years of school attendance, whether the applicant has graduated from high school, year graduated, colleges, universities, or vocational

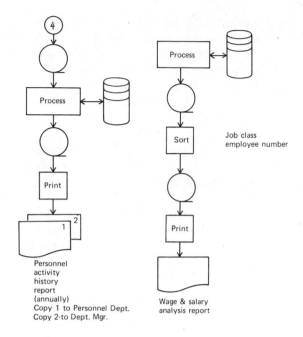

Fig. 11-4   (cont'd)

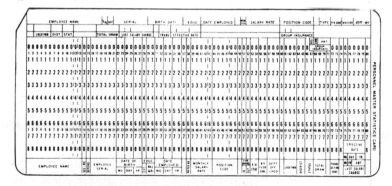

Fig. 11-5   Basic personnel data input card

schools attended, degrees received, major study areas, and year degrees received. Further, if the employee is continuing his education, his educational goals and his progress toward the completion of his education may be included. Employee attendance and completion of in-house training programs, special programs, courses, or seminars, and correspondence courses should also be included in an educational record.

Skills data comprises the third input data stream. A skills

inventory is a most valuable tool for management to use to locate employees with special abilities, talents, interests, and other qualifications. A portion of this data may be collected at the time of employment, but a significant portion of it will be accumulated over time. Provisions must be made to collect such data periodically to keep this portion of the personnel data base up to date. Since this data is very personal, the best source is an annual update of the skills profile prepared by each employee. The structure and operation of a skills locator information system will be discussed in the next section of this chapter.

For business firms that have formal employee appraisal programs, appraisal data can be included as a separate input data stream. Most often included are appraisal data, the overall appraisal rating, and whether the employee is ready for promotion now, one year hence, or at a later date. Personnel test data may also be included in this information area when it relates to the employee's potential for promotion or reassignment.

The final input data stream is employee work history. Sometimes this data stream will include previous employers and positions held, both of which would be listed on the personnel application form. The most important part of the record, however, is based on an employee's work history during his employment by the organization. Most likely to be included are job classification changes, promotions, departmental assignment changes, beginning and ending position dates, reporting location (supervisor), and salary data.

The foregoing input data streams as shown in the personnel information systems model (see figure 11-4) are keypunched into cards for entry into the system. If the total number of transactions is large, it may be advisable to transcribe the punched cards to magnetic tape, followed by a sorting operation using the employee number as the record key. This input method permits the file updating program to access the personnel data base records in their storage sequence and thereby reduces the updating program operating time. On the other hand, if the volume of input transactions is relatively low, then the updating program time savings will be offset by the increased data preparation time.

A remote input terminal is also shown on the input side of the personnel information system. This terminal, which is located in the personnel department, is used to access specific personnel records on an *ad hoc* basis. Conceivably, remote input terminals could also be used to update individual employee records within the personnel data base. This method of input entry, however, warrants very special security measures. When the input data transactions are handled as batches, input data errors discovered by the editing portion of the update program are listed on the input error report and the accepted transaction activity appears on the activity listing. Unless special precautions are taken with remote terminal transaction data, there is no audit trail to determine whether a transaction has actually been entered into the data base or what the specific content of the data that was actually entered into it is.

The main processing run is primarily a file updating process and an input error and activity listing operation. Each of the different types of input must, of course, have a transaction or activity code to identify the appropriate action for the processor to take with each transaction. For medium- to large-scale organizations, there will be sufficient activity to warrant processing the personnel transactions on a weekly basis. Since most of the other reports do not need to be prepared this frequently, separate programs or processing runs are usually used to prepare them on an as-needed basis.

The records in a personnel data base may be structured in many different ways. Some organizations use several record files, each of which stores a particular type of information, and use employee number (sometimes social security number) as the record access key for all of the data files within the entire data base. A single variable-length record has been used in our personnel information systems model to store all of the available personnel data. The principle advantage of this method of file structure over a multiple file structure is that it eliminates duplicate data and makes possible ready update and access of complete individual records. An example of a single personnel record layout is shown in figure 11-6. Record length factor is shown in the first record field to indicate the total number of characters in each personnel record. The balance of the personnel record is used to record specific data about each employee as indicated by the field identification.

The personnel information system can generate a number of different output reports that are commonly used for personnel record keeping and decision making. The following output reports are among those often prepared for the personnel function.

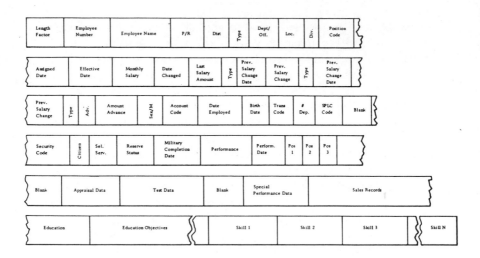

Fig. 11-6   Single personnel record layout

Input Error and Activity Listings (weekly) These reports, as we have noted in other information systems, are required to audit the transactions that have been entered into the information system. Without them there is no feasible way to determine the source of errors and omissions that will enter the system from time to time.

Personnel Activity Report (weekly) The purpose of this report is to provide the personnel department with a record of the activity that has taken place in the personnel system during the preceding week. Depending on the personnel department's wishes, the report may be listed in several different sequences using three record fields—employee number, department number, and transaction code. Since the activity sequence used during the weekly file updating run is employee number–major, and transaction code–minor, any other reporting sequence will require a sorting operation prior to printing the report.

The most usable reporting sequence for general personnel information will probably be transaction code–major, department code–intermediate, and employee number–minor. In effect, this reporting sequence will group employee activity of similar types together. The resulting report will be a combined accession listing (new hires, rehires, and reinstated employees);

a basic personnel record change of status listing (changes in address, telephone number, number of dependents, military status, and so forth); a reassignment, transfer, and promotion listing; an educational achievement and change of skill listing; and a termination listing (layoffs, voluntary resignations, retirements, and leaves of absence.)

The personnel activity report listed in the above way may be used for a variety of followup personnel activities, such as planning orientation and training sessions for the newly hired, preparing letters of commendation for the completion of educational activity and other professional recognitions, and preparing letters of appreciation together with retirement program information for new retirees.

Personnel Status Report (monthly) This report is simply a complete listing of all the employee records within the personnel data base. Since the records are filed sequentially by employee number, a sorting operation is required if the report is to be listed alphabetically by employee name. The main purpose of this report is to give the personnel department a hard copy listing of all employees in the active work force and on leaves of absence.

In some instances it might be advisable to prepare the magnetic personnel data base history tape in conjunction with the preparation of this report. The history file tape could then be used offline for the personnel status report as well as other personnel reports to be subsequently discussed. The magnetic tape history file will, of course, be stored for one or more months and may be used to reconstruct the employee data base in the event there is any difficulty during the succeeding period. If the employee records are not erased from the data base during the weekly activity updating runs, the magnetic tape history file may be used to generate certain additional information for the personnel status report. Labor turnover by department, for example, may be readily computed and printed at the end of the personnel status report.

Departmental Personnel Status Report (monthly)   This report is similar in content to the previous report and is for the use of individual department managers. The magnetic tape history file may be sorted into department code—major and employee name–minor sequence and selected information from the data base output may be placed in the report. An example of this type of report is shown in figure 11-7. As in the personnel status report above, the departmental report may also contain summarized information on certain types of activity. (See the bottom of figure 11-7.) The individual department managers should find this report useful as an historical record and as a valuable personnel data reference for their employees.

Wage and Salary Analysis Report (as required)   This report may be prepared as needed to assist the personnel department in the analysis of the wage and salary program of the organization. All of the data for its preparation is contained in the personnel data base. Ordinarily this report is prepared by sorting the data base file according to employee job classification or title. In this way all similar jobs are grouped together and the average salary or wage together with the range for each job classification may be computed. The results may then be compared to similar jobs in other business firms in the area or with similar jobs for other firms in the industry.

Other Special Reports (as required)   The wealth of data contained in the data base may be used to prepare many other special reports. Manpower planning, for example, may be examined by superimposing the available personnel on the manpower requirements projected for the future. The shortcomings and deficiencies that appear may be used as guides for future recruiting activity. Similarly, computer programs may be prepared to assign hourly employees on the basis of seniority and work experience to available positions when a reduction in manpower is necessary. The simulation of long-range managerial availability from the present personnel pool can highlight the need for management training programs and spot particular areas within the organization where either shortages or surpluses of potential managers are present.

   Another area where the data available in the personnel data base may find ready use is in the preparation of special government reports. The distribution of minority-group employees with regard to department, job classification, and salary level may be easily prepared from the data base. In the same way,

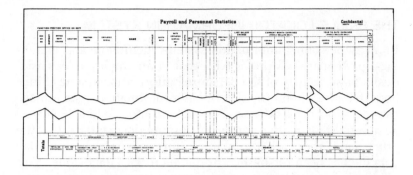

Fig. 11-7   Departmental personnel status report

reports may be prepared of the employees' military status. This information could be quite useful in the event of a national emergency. Retirement lists may be made by sorting the data base records by employee age. Many other reports may also be provided on request simply by sorting the personnel data base records according to one or more specific data fields.

In addition to the formal reports that the personnel information system may generate, the personnel department, through the use of its remote input terminal and data display screen, may access current data about any employee in a matter of seconds. All that is required to access a particular employee record is employee number, the access security code, and any relevant instructions. The employee record will then be flashed on the display screen for the personnel department to use as needed.

From our foregoing discussion of personnel information systems, it is evident that such a system can supply both the personnel department and the organization's managers with a tremendous amount of information. It is also evident that the volume of employee data in most organizations is so large and unwieldy that care must be taken to ask for only the information that is truly needed for managerial decision making. Since managers can get almost any kind of information from the personnel data base, they must be careful to request the information in the form that will be most useful to them. The responsibility for using the personnel data base to its fullest potential lies clearly with the personnel department and the organization's managers.

THE SKILLS LOCATOR INFORMATION SYSTEM

In many personnel information systems identifying and matching a particular skills profile with that of an employee is considered a basic activity of the personnel information system. Since both that system and the skills locator information system make use of the same data base, the skills locator system is viewed as a subsystem of the personnel information system. On the other hand, there are also many examples in which a separate data file has been established to maintain skills data alone. This approach is feasible because the two information systems use different data-processing techniques, sometimes have different record construction, and may be implemented at different times. In our subsequent discussion we shall use the former approach in which the data skill record fields are included in the personnel data base.

The usual purpose of a skills locator information system is to match a certain set of skill requirements against the skills of all employees in order to select employees for reassignment, transfer, or promotion. This mission differs significantly from that used in the personnel information system. The reports prepared by that system were built largely around the different sequences in which the data base could be sorted. This method of using the data base, as we have seen, can yield many insights for managerial decision making. Skills locator information systems, in contrast, are primarily concerned with the selection of specific employee records from the data base on the basis of certain pre-established criteria. As a result, the personnel information system and the skills locator system differ significantly in the manner in which they use the data base.

The principal data-processing method used by skills locator information systems is known as a file scan. In this method of data processing, each record in the entire data file is examined in turn for the presence or absence of one or more skill identifiers. When a match is found between the desired skill identification keys and the employee's skills profile, the selected employee personnel data is output on a report or flashed on a data display screen. The resulting report lists all of the employees in the organization who have certain combinations of skills, abilities, and/or qualifications.

The effectiveness of such a system depends largely on the extent and degree of skill discrimination the structure of the skill record fields permits. In turn, this structure depends on the information system's objectives. The design, therefore, of a skills locator information system should begin with a study of the desired uses of its output. When the system is to be used almost exclusively with relatively basic skill definitions, the structure of its record fields is rather simple. When, however, the system is expected to differentiate among complex skills as are found in technically-oriented organizations, the structure of the fields requires a special skills classification system.

The provided vocabulary method is the simplest means for identifying and storing skills data. In this method each employee skill or work experience is assigned a unique code number. This number, along with the number of years experience and the last year the skill was used, can be stored in a single skill field within the personnel data base. The vocabulary, in this case, is the comprehensive list of particular employee skills and work experiences. An example of a provided vocabulary work sheet with open-end provision is shown in figure 11-8.

Ordinarily, the vocabulary is based on terms used in existing personnel records, employee requisitions, and job specifications. In this way it reflects the level of detail that is presently used in job placement and classification. Care must be taken in building the vocabulary to define each skill with sufficient precision to be able to distinguish among closely related skills in the same work area. For example, computer programming, rather than being listed as a single skill, should be further broken down by specific computer language (FORTRAN, COBOL, PL/1, RPG, and so forth) or type of computer (IBM 360/50, CDC 6600, and so forth). Moreover, the vocabulary should contain provisions for adding or further defining particular skills that may be used in the future (open-end provision).

Employee skills and work experiences may also be defined for use in skills locator information systems using combinations of keywords. The keyword combination may then be stored in a single skill data field within the data base for future comparative purposes. The keyword concept is based on the implicit assumption that all individuals engaged in a particular type of work or professional field will use similar terminology to describe their skills and activities. The primary words, or keywords, used by these professional groups may consequently be defined in a master dictionary and then used to describe these individuals' activities and skills.

NAME _____

LAST   FIRST   MID INT.   SERIAL NUMBER   Page 7

DO NOT RECORD ANYTHING ON THIS PAGE UNLESS YOU HAVE WORKED IN THE FIELDS OF _____

PHOTOGRAPHY
REPRODUCTIONS–PRINTING
CONTRACT ADMINISTRATION
PURCHASING–PROCUREMENT
FOOD AND GUEST SERVICES

IF YOU HAVE WORK EXPERIENCE IN ANY OF THE AREAS LISTED BELOW, INDICATE THE NUMBER OF YEARS OF EXPERIENCE, TO THE NEAREST HALF YEAR, AND LAST YEAR YOU USED THIS EXPERIENCE. (SEE INSTRUCTIONS, PAGE 1).

ITEM	CODE	NO. YEARS	LAST YEAR	ITEM	CODE	NO. YEARS	LAST YEAR
PHOTOGRAPHY				Customer Contract Negotiation–Commercial	FJ330		
Management Experience	HS001			Customer Contract Negotiation–Government	FJ340		
Film Processing–Black and White	HS310			Research & Development Contract Negotiation	FJ350		
Film Processing–Color	HS315						
Photogrammetry	HS320			Other (Please Specify)			
Micro and Macro Photography	HS325						
Motion Picture Projectionist	HS330						
High Speed Camera Operation	HS335						
Movie Photography	HS340						
Photocomposing (Step & Repeat Operation)	HS345			**PURCHASING–PROCUREMENT**			
Photographic Applications in Manufacturing	HS350			Management Experience	ID001		
Photography, Portrait or General	HS355			Capital Equipment Purchasing	ID305		
Plugging Tool Masters	HS360			Electronic-Electrical Parts Purchasing	ID310		
Printed Circuit Etching	HS365			Electro-Mechanical Parts Purchasing	ID315		
Process Camera Work	HS370			Expediting–Vendor Control	ID320		
				Mechanical (Machines) Parts Purchasing	ID325		
Other (Please Specify)				Model Parts Purchasing	ID330		
				New Products Purchase Requirements	ID335		
				Office & Maintenance Supplies Purchasing	ID340		
				Purchase Parts (General)	ID345		
				Purchase Parts (Value) Analysis	ID350		
				Purchase Planning (Estimates, etc.)	ID355		
REPRODUCTIONS–PRINTING				Purchasing Procedures Development	ID360		
Management Experience	IJ001			Raw Materials Purchasing	ID365		
Binding, Cutting, or Drilling Paper	IJ310			Real Property Purchasing	ID370		
Collating or Folding	IJ315			Service Agreements Purchasing	ID380		
Contact Printing–Diazo or Step & Repeat	IJ320			Supplies Purchasing (Misc.)	ID385		
Electrotyper–Stereotyper	IJ325						
Embossograph	IJ330			Other (Please Specify)			
Hand Composition or Typesetting	IJ335						
Letter Press	IJ340						
Linotyping	IJ345						
Micro-Film Processing	IJ350						
Offset Duplicating	IJ355			**FOOD & GUEST SERVICES**			
Offset Printing	IJ360			Management Experience	GD001		
Plate-Making–Electrostatic	IJ365			Cashiering–Cafeteria	GD310		
Plate-Making–Electrolithic	IJ370			Cooking or Baking	GD320		
Photo-Copy Equipment Operation	IJ375			Coordinating Food Service Activity	GD330		
Photo-Engraving	IJ380			Dietician	GD340		
Process Camera Operation	IJ385			Food Processing	GD350		
Stripping & Masking Negatives	IJ390			Food Purchasing	GD360		
				Food Serving	GD370		
Other (Please Specify)				General Kitchen Work	GD380		
				Hotel or Guest Services	GD390		
				Meat Cutting	GD400		
				Menu Planning	GD410		
CONTRACT ADMINISTRATION				Warehouse or Commissary Operation	GD420		
Management Experience	FJ001						
Contracting for Consultant Services	FJ310			Other (Please Specify)			
Contracting for Personnel Services	FJ320						

Fig. 11-8 Vocabulary worksheet with open-end provision

In the following example four keywords (an action verb, two modifiers, and a verb object) are used to describe each work activity or skill.

Action Verb	First Modifier	Second Modifier	Verb Object
Prepare	Manufacturing	Cost	Budgets
Analyze	Inventory	Status	Reports
Coordinate	Sales	Promotion	Programs

The resulting keyword combination is known as a keyword matrix.

The selection of keywords must be performed carefully.

The number of action verbs is usually limited to prevent unnecessary duplication. Both modifiers and verb objects may be maintained on an open-end basis to define new activities as the need arises. Occasionally, keywords may be truncated to reduce disc storage usage, provided that in doing so their meanings do not become ambiguous.

The keyword concept has been successfully applied to other data-searching applications. Library searches for technical publications use this principle by extracting the keywords from publication titles. Medical and legal library information systems that use the keyword concept have also been developed.

The operation of a skills locator information system is uncomplicated and straightforward. Figure 11-9 depicts the general design for this type of information system. The file scan program simply examines each record and compares each skill data field with the desired one. When a match is found, selected output from the record is listed on a report or flashed on a data display screen.

CASE STUDY: THE SNOW MANUFACTURING COMPANY INSURANCE SYSTEM

The Snow Manufacturing Company has recently substantially expanded their contributory group insurance coverage for both

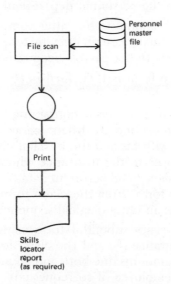

Fig. 11-9   General design of a skills locator information system

hourly and salary employees. All employees may now select one option in one or more of the following insurance catagories:

I. Hospitalization Insurance
    A. Low coverage, employee only
    B. High coverage, employee only
    C. Low coverage, employee and family
    D. High coverage, employee and family

II. Term Life Insurance
    A. Low coverage, employee only
    B. High coverage, employee only
    C. High coverage, employee and spouse
    D. High coverage, employee and family

III. Accidental Death Insurance
    A. $25,000 death benefit
    B. $50,000 death benefit
    C. $100,000 death benefit
    D. $200,000 death benefit

The present system for obtaining insurance and handling claims is as follows:

1. The employee completes an insurance form and a payroll deduction form at the time of employment, or at any time thereafter, and submits both forms to the insurance administrator in the personnel department.

2. The insurance administrator, after comparing the data on both forms to make certain they match, sends the payroll deduction form to the payroll department.

3. The insurance form is then filed in the insurance file by employee number.

4. Hospitalization claim forms containing a statement of the medical diagnosis and treatment signed by the physician and together with his and the hospital's bills are submitted by the employee to the insurance administrator. A claim number is assigned and pertinent data (name, date, department, and so forth) from the claim form is entered in the claims register in chronological sequence.

5. A three-part claim submittal form using data as needed from the insurance file and the claim form is prepared; it contains the amounts due both the physician and the hospital (or the employee, if so requested).

6. The original of the claim submittal form is grouped with the other claim submittal forms processed during the week and forwarded to the insurance company for payment.

7. The first copy of the claim sumbittal form together with all supporting documents is filed in the open claims file by claim number.

8. The second copy of the claim submittal form is sent to the employee for his information.

9. A death benefit claim form with a copy of the death certificate is submitted by the employee's family to the insurance administrator. A claim number is assigned and pertinent data from the death benefit claim form is entered into the claims register. A three-part claim submittal form is prepared and copies are distributed as in steps 6, 7, and 8. The supporting documents are then filed in the open claims file by claim number.

10. The insurance company prepares the checks for the approved and adjusted claims and mails them to the specified recipients. Copies of the disapproved and adjusted insurance claim submittal forms are returned to the insurance administrator with an explanation for the adjustment or disapproval. A list of claim payments is also sent to him.

11. For those claims that were paid in full, the insurance administrator transfers the claim record from the open claims file to the closed claims file.

12. Adjusted or disapproved claims are transferred to a claims suspense file to await investigation and final disposition. After final disposition has been determined, the records are transferred to the closed claims file.

Prepare a flowchart and analyze the manual insurance system above.

Design a computerized insurance information system to supplant the old manual system. (Assume adequate data-processing facilities are available, including a personnel master file in auxiliary storage.)

List and briefly discuss the output reports that the new insurance information system should prepare to assist the insurance administrator and personnel manager in administering the insurance system.

INVENTORY INFORMATION SYSTEMS

In the past decade materials management has come to be recognized as a separate business function that is worthy of special attention. The proper management of materials, from the time production is planned until the finished goods have been sent to the customer, is an extremely important element in determining product cost and ultimately influences corporate profits. In many manufacturing firms, materials cost may comprise fifty percent or more of the total product cost. In wholesaling and retailing business firms, materials cost usually makes up an even larger share of the total merchandise cost. For all business firms that supply goods to the market, therefore, materials management is an area of primary concern.

The materials management function has three separate areas that are especially important to management. The planning of material requirements and the subsequent procurement of these materials (material requirements and purchasing information systems) is necessary to provide an adequate, timely supply of materials for the manufacturing process at the lowest possible cost. The surveillance and control of materials from the time they are received until they are shipped to customers is most important also for safeguarding the company's assets. Analyzing both inventory composition and the essential nature of the various inventories is also an area of managerial concern. Information systems for each of these materials management areas can substantially help minimize the cost of maintaining adequate supplies of materials while they provide a satisfactory level of service for the organization.

THE INVENTORY SYSTEM

The inventory is an essential element for all types of business firms. Its principal function is to act as a buffer bridging the span between the time materials become available and the time they are needed. In this sense the role of the inventory is analogous to the role of cash assets in the business firm. Cash, in the form of bank deposits, is needed to even out fluctuations in the income and expense streams. In the same way, inventories decouple the receipt of materials from suppliers' production operations and the distribution of finished goods to customers. When sufficient inventories are on hand, production and distribution activities may be planned and performed in the most efficient way possible.

Inventories are, of course, the focal point of interest in the materials management function. Many different types of inventories may be identified. Manufacturing firms typically have the following types of physical inventories:

1. Raw materials (basic materials that are usually changed in form or shape in the manufacturing process—for example, coal, iron ore, raw sugar, cotton, basic chemicals, and wrought metal products)
2. Purchased parts (parts manufactured by other firms that are included in the final product—valves, gauges, electrical equipment, plastic products, piston rings, and zippers)
3. In-process goods (materials that have entered, but not completed, the manufacturing process)
4. Finished goods (goods awaiting sale and distribution to customers)
5. Operating supplies (materials used in the manufacturing process that do not enter into the final product—utilities, oil and grease, rags, gloves, and cleaning supplies)
6. Tools (hand and power tools, jigs and fixtures, dies, and electrical testing meters)
7. Equipment (manufacturing machinery, electric motors, pumps, conveyors, and fork-lift trucks)

8. Office equipment and supplies (typewriters, adding machines, printed forms, and pencils)

Wholesale and retail business firms are concerned with finished goods and, to a lesser extent, with operating supplies, tools and equipment, and office equipment and supplies as their basic types of inventory. The finished goods inventory difficulties faced by wholesale and retail firms, while no less important to their successful operation, are much simpler from a structural point of view because they are primarily concerned with only a single type of inventory. This advantage in systems design, however, is often offset by a much larger number of inventory items.

Although each of the inventory types listed above is very important for a firm's overall operation, our attention in the following discussion will be directed toward raw materials, in-process, and finished goods inventories. These inventories most directly and immediately influence the production and distribution of goods to the customer in manufacturing operations. Moreover, the same basic concepts of inventory planning, maintenance, and control may also be applied to the remaining inventory types when the effort is deemed appropriate.

Figure 12-1 presents a simple dynamic systems model of an inventory system in a manufacturing business firm. On the left-hand side of the diagram are the raw material inputs. The processor has been partitioned into three different areas to designate raw materials inventory, in-process inventory, and

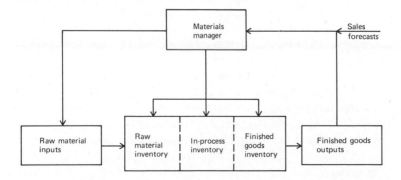

Fig. 12-1   Simple dynamic system model of an inventory system in a manufacturing firm

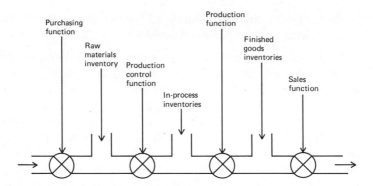

Fig. 12-2   Hydraulic analog model of the inventory system

finished goods inventory. In reality, each of these inventories are subsystems of the materials system operating in series. The system's outputs are the finished goods sent to customers.

The controller (materials manager), of course, monitors the disbursement of finished goods as well as the movement of materials into raw materials, in-process, and finished goods inventories. Using this information and production requirements information, he may then take corrective action to maintain an adequate supply of raw materials for use in the production system. The controller also utilizes separate information inputs from sales forecasts and orders for custom-made products to regulate the input flow of raw materials. In addition, he establishes policies for the maintenance of inventory levels and composition in each of the three processor areas.

Some of the difficulties involved with inventory management may be more clearly understood through the examination of a hydraulic analog model of the inventory system (figure 12-2). At the left-hand side of the diagram, the stream of raw materials enters the system. The circle with an X represents a valve that regulates the flow of raw materials into the raw materials inventory. This valve, in essence, is the procurement or purchasing function. Maintaining an adequate flow of the proper raw materials is the basic responsibility of the purchasing department. The first upright pipe represents the accumulated raw materials inventory.

The central upright section of the hydraulic analog model represents in-process inventories. The valve regulating the flow of raw materials into production operations is controlled by the production control department through the release of work or assembly orders to the production system. The release of work orders normally results in the requisition and transfer of needed materials from the raw materials inventory to in-process inventory. Through this release, the production control department determines the quantity of materials required to balance production operations for the greatest efficiency.

The valve between in-process and finished-goods inventory is controlled indirectly through the completion of scheduled manufacturing operations in the production system. To increase the flow to finished-goods inventory, a higher level of operations must be scheduled and, conversely, to reduce the flow, the level of production operations must be diminished correspondingly.

The level of the finished-goods inventory is, in turn, determined by the balance between orders received from customers and the level of production operations. For business firms that manufacture products only to customer order, the finished-goods inventory will be minimal.

As may readily be seen by examining the hydraulic analog model, the proper management of materials from the time they are ordered as raw materials until they are shipped as finished goods requires the very close coordination of purchasing, production control, production, and sales. All of these groups must interact with each other through the flow of timely, accurate information to maintain an adequate supply of materials at all stages in the production process.

Evaluating inventory system efficiency using cost as the measuring device is basically a cost minimization problem. In reality, the inventory cost minimization problem is an example of an economic tradeoff between two cost elements with conflicting characteristics. The first element, the cost of maintaining inventory, increases as the average inventory size grows larger. Counterbalancing this cost element are the procurement and stockout costs, which tend to decrease as the average inventory size increases. The relations between these cost elements is shown in figure 12-3 together with the resulting minimum total inventory cost.

The cost of maintaining inventories, also known as carrying costs, is actually an aggregate value composed of many individual cost elements. Inventories of all types cost money and immobilize a portion of the funds within the business. When the allocated funds are obtained by borrowing capital, the interest costs for the borrowed capital may be readily determined. If, as is the more common case, the source of inventory investment

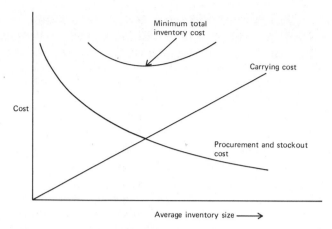

Fig. 12-3   Relations between the cost of maintaining inventory and procurement and stockout costs

funds comes from contributed capital and retained earnings, the average cost of capital for the entire business firm must be used to determine the actual inventory investment costs. Also associated with the direct inventory investment expense are the opportunity costs that result from allocating funds to inventories. The foregone income that could be generated by additional investment in plant, equipment, research and development, or sales promotion is most difficult to determine, although an approximation of the expected returns can be derived from project return evaluations in the capital budgeting process. Most firms that have such a program develop an expected rate of return value for each capital budgeting proposal. The cutoff rate of return for capital proposals, therefore, provides an indication of the rate of return that might be expected if funds were invested for uses other than inventory accumulations.

Obsolescence, deterioration, and shrinkage are other carrying costs related to inventory size. As inventory size increases, the risk of inventory obsolescence and deterioration normally increases also. Further, inventory shrinkage due to pilferage or misplacement tends to be greater as average inventory size is increased. The nature of the inventory also affects these carrying cost elements, since stable, non-perishable, and standard items are less subject to obsolescence and deterioration.

The cost of storage is an additional expense for all inventories that, generally speaking, increases with the average inventory size. This cost element is actually an aggregate of warehouse rental, utilities, materials handling, and inventory administration expenses. Taxes and insurance costs may also be included in this expense category. These costs are usually not directly proportional to inventory size, since they tend to increase with average inventory size as discrete cost increments. Within narrow average inventory size ranges, the cost of storage may actually be treated as a fixed cost.

Procurement costs, in contrast to carrying costs, tend to decrease as average inventory size increases. When the average stock levels for each inventory item are high, the frequency of reordering will be relatively low. On the other hand, if minimal inventory levels are maintained, then the frequency of reordering will be much higher. As a result the purchasing organization and the associated clerical operations must be larger, producing higher average inventory procurement costs. To minimize the procurement costs, therefore, the average inventory size should be relatively large.

Perhaps even more important than procurement costs are the costs incurred when inventory items are out of stock. In the case of raw materials inventory and in-process inventory for manufacturing firms, increased production costs are usually associated with inventory stockout situations. Production operations must be rescheduled and finished goods shipments must be delayed. For finished goods inventory, lost sales and loss of customer goodwill may result from inventory stockouts. The actual costs of these malfunctions are most difficult to ascertain. But, nevertheless, the results are very real.

The minimum total costs for maintaining inventory must recognize the peculiar performance of the cost elements discussed above. Ideally, the minimum cost for maintaining a given inventory may be determined mathematically. In practice, inventory analysts often find that inventory levels are maintained well above the sizes that would result in a minimal total inventory cost. The principal reason for this anomaly is that stockout costs resulting in production dislocations are feared more than they deserve to be. Figure 12-4 demonstrates a typical inventory situation in which inventory stock levels are maintained beyond levels needed to meet production requirements with a given level of certainty.

Inventory turnover is the chief measure of inventory efficiency using time as a measurement device. The aggregate inventory turnover value is computed by dividing the average

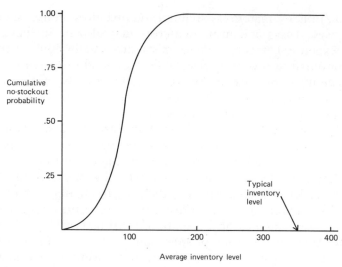

Fig. 12-4   No-stockouts probability curve

total inventory value by the daily inventory disbursements. The resulting value is the number of days for which the inventory will be sufficient. This measure may, of course, be applied to the total of all inventory items collectively or individually. Moreover, the value is usually restricted to single types of inventory, such as raw materials inventory, in-process inventory, or finished goods inventory. To determine the significance of the resulting inventory turnover values, it must be compared to a recognized standard developed empirically from historical records. Although we ordinarily assume that a low inventory value indicates greater efficiency, this is not necessarily true in all cases. Other considerations, such as inventory buildups for peak seasonal operating demands or to prepare for possible suppliers' strikes, must be evaluated before reaching a conclusion.

The quantity measurement of inventory systems efficiency is based on the materials input/output relation. The purpose of this efficiency measure is to determine the extent of material losses for the inventory system. While inventory shrinkage is often the result of pilferage by employees or in some cases theft by robbery, unplanned decreases in the number of inventory units for any reason is an erosion of the business firm's assets. Inventory shrinkage by theft is most common with finished-goods inventories since these inventory items may often be put to immediate use or sold by the thief. The amount of inventory shrinkage provides a good measure of the security effectiveness and level of care being exercised over this form of the business' assets. Pilferage may be reduced by improving security controls and by maintaining smaller inventory levels. Materials handling damage, spoilage, and obsolescence may be reduced by better administration and supervision.

The amount of inventory shrinkage is ordinarily determined by the difference in levels as computed by the inventory information control system and an actual physical count taken at periodic time intervals. The difference between the expected inventory levels and the actual ones is, of course, the amount of shrinkage that has taken place during the period. To obtain a quantitative measure of inventory system materials efficiency the following mathematical formula may be used:

$$\frac{\text{Average inventory} - \text{Inventory shrinkage}}{\text{Average inventory}} \times 100 = \frac{\text{Materials}}{\text{efficiency}}$$

A small amount of materials losses is usually considered acceptable in inventory management. The inference in this case is that security measures and administrative quality are more than adequate to prevent substantial losses while greater effort would result in only a small increase in systems efficiency.

Quality measures of systems efficiency are also applicable to inventory systems. Obsolescence, deterioration, and spoilage frequently occur. These inventory decreases are normally the result of poor inventory management. Obsolescence of inventory may occur for reasons beyond the control of the materials manager. On the other hand, the inventory manager must stay abreast of events and anticipate possible changes in inventory composition trends. Of course, when obsolescence is recognized, the best practice is usually to dispose of the obsolete inventory as quickly as possible. Not only will this practice eliminate further carrying costs but it usually provides the best opportunity for recovering the initial inventory costs.

The quality measurement of inventory systems may be computed by dividing the amount of obsolescence, deterioration, and spoilage encountered during a given period by the average total inventory value. To be useful this value must then be compared to a standard value determined from analyzing historical inventory records.

An inventory system's primary objective is to provide materials for processing or to meet customer requirements as these needs arise at minimum total cost. The measure of its effectiveness then is the degree to which it meets this objective. The evaluation of such effectiveness must be tempered by the recognition of financial constraints on inventory size. If inventory accumulation did not represent the allocation of funds, it would be possible to maintain inventory stock levels, with regard both to size and diversity, that would meet every conceivable demand. Since this is an impossible situation for most firms, expected levels of service should be established that reflect the cost or potential loss due to inventory deficiencies. Statistical analysis of the inventory records for individual items may be used to establish the demand patterns and the desired level of service. This information, in turn, may be used to establish minimum inventory levels and reorder points. An effective inventory system, therefore, should experience occasional low supply levels and even an infrequent outage to be gauged effective.

Well-designed inventory information systems should give the manager sufficient information to evaluate efficiency and effectiveness. In addition, a well-designed system should provide the inventory manager with specific information about exceptional conditions as well as insights about the behavior of the overall inventory system. In this way he may foresee difficulties before they become acute and develop management policies to achieve the highest practical inventory efficiency and effectiveness.

THE BILL OF MATERIALS INFORMATION SYSTEM

The customers of business firms order airplanes, automobiles, refrigerators, toasters, furniture, television sets, and many other finished products. While these finished products are ordered as discrete units, they are actually composed of assemblies, subassemblies, detail parts, raw materials, and purchased parts. Manufacturing firms must translate customer orders or forecast sales into the many individual parts that comprise the product in order to determine the component requirements. For finished products that are composed of many different parts, the breakdown of customer orders into the individual part requirements can be a very laborious process.

The function of the bill of materials information system (also known as the bill of materials processor or BOMP) is to perform the breakdown of customer orders into the required basic components. After the individual components have been identified, the raw materials to manufacture the parts or the purchased parts themselves may be procured and the necessary production orders released. The output of this information system may also be integrated with the prodution information system to develop other production-related information output such as production schedules and product routings.

The development of a new manufactured product ordinarily goes through a series of stages: research, feasibility studies, preliminary design, and detailed product design. The outputs of the engineering design process are engineering drawings of fabricated detail parts, subassemblies, and top-level assemblies. Included on each engineering drawing is an area known as the bill of materials block, which lists the components of the assembly and the quantity required for each. In addition, the engineering drawing may also contain blocks for the next assembly: where-used, and the end item: where-used. An example of an engineering drawing containing the bill of materials, the next assembly, and the end item blocks is shown in figure 12-5.

The first objective of a bill of materials information system is to identify all the components used to manufacture the final product. Such identification is essential to procure the necessary raw materials and purchased parts. The process of breaking down finished products into basic units is known as product explosion.

The second objective of such a system is to identify final products that use each basic component. Suppose, for example, that a particular part is redesigned to improve its performance. Determining the final products that the engineering change will affect requires that the component usage be retraced back to the finished product(s). This process, in reality, is the exact opposite of the product explosion process and is known as part or subassembly implosion.

The computer programs used in bill of materials information systems are extraordinarily complex. For this reason it is impractical in most cases to develop them from scratch. However, canned programs or processors that contain the programs necessary for operating such systems are available from computer manufacturers and other software firms. The following discussion presents the operating characteristics of a typical bill of materials processor.

A bill of materials information system requires two separate types of input (see figure 12-6). The first input data stream is the part number master record data. This record, which uses

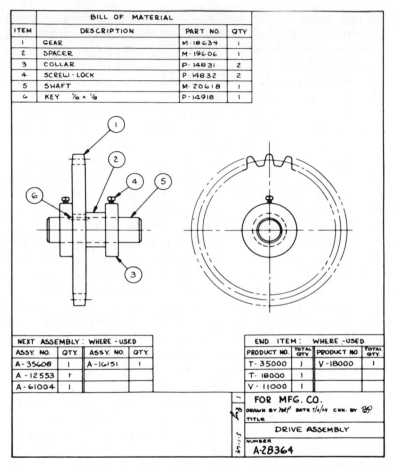

BILL OF MATERIAL			
ITEM	DESCRIPTION	PART NO.	QTY
1	GEAR	M-18634	1
2	SPACER	M-19606	1
3	COLLAR	P-14831	2
4	SCREW-LOCK	P-14832	2
5	SHAFT	M-20618	1
6	KEY ⅛ × ⅛	P-14918	1

NEXT ASSEMBLY: WHERE-USED			
ASSY. NO.	QTY.	ASSY. NO.	QTY.
A-35608	1	A-16151	1
A-12553	1		
A-61004	1		

END ITEM: WHERE-USED			
PRODUCT NO.	TOTAL QTY.	PRODUCT NO.	TOTAL QTY.
T-35000	1	V-18000	1
T-18000	1		
V-11000	1		

FOR MFG. CO.
DRAWN BY HMP DATE 7/6/41 CHK. BY BP
TITLE
DRIVE ASSEMBLY
NUMBER
A-28364

Fig. 12-5   Engineering drawing with bill-of-materials, next-assembly, and end-item blocks

part number as the record key, contains all of the details concerning each individual part, such as name, engineering drawing number, and selected procurement, inventory, and production information. This input data stream will be used to create only a single part number record for each part number in the master file. In most cases this input data stream will be a fundamental data stream and will appear in other information systems as well. Thus the part number master file will form the base file for the inventory control information system and will be used in the procurement information system and the production system also.

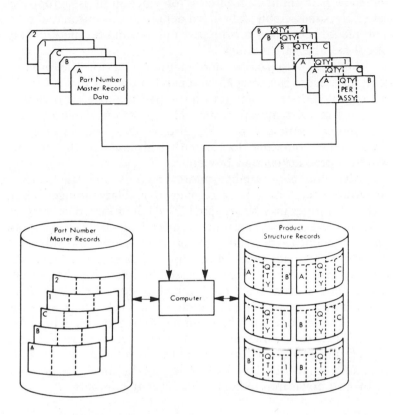

Fig. 12-6   Type of input for a bill of materials information system

The second input data stream contains the product structure record specifying the linkage between individual parts, their subassemblies, their top-level assemblies, and the final product. This data is used to create the product structure file in disc storage. The product structure input record contains one record for each subunit within the primary unit. Thus a subassembly composed of six individual parts will require six records to identify the individual parts as belonging to a particular one.

After preliminary data preparation has been completed (if required), the part number master record data stream will be processed by the P/N master record file organization and maintenance program. This program is ordinarily a separate program used only for updating the part number master record. The P/N master record file contains only one record in auxiliary storage for each part number regardless of whether it is a top-level assembly, subassembly, fabricated detail part, or purchased part. The record access key for the part number master file must be, of course, the part number.

The file organization and maintenance for the product structure record is a completely separate program that is usually not operated in conjunction with the part number file organization and maintenance program. This program, while creating the product structure records, also verifies the assembly-to-subassembly continuity to verify that all parts of the product structure tree fit together properly.

After the part number master records and the product structure records have been created in auxiliary storage, bill of materials listings may be prepared. The bill of materials retrieval program accesses the part number master record file for a given finished product to determine the product description and locate the disc storage addresses of its top-level assemblies. Next, the product structure records are accessed to determine the component assembly numbers of the finished product. From the product structure record the part number record file may again be accessed to determine pertinent information about each top-level assembly. In turn, the product structure records are accessed to determine the disc storage addresses of the subassembly components. In this back-and-forth way the final product may be broken down into individual detail part numbers.

The Product Explosion Process

The mechanics of the retrieval process may be more clearly understood through the use of an example. Product *A* is composed of three assemblies: *B, C,* and 1. Assembly *B,* in turn, is composed of three parts: *C,* 1, and 2. Figure 12-7 illustrates the component part relations for product *A.*

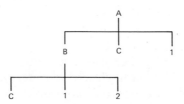

Fig. 12-7   Component part relations for product A

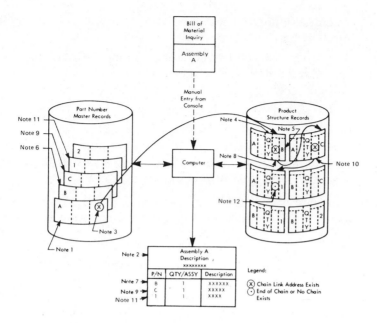

Fig. 12-8   The bill of materials retrieval program steps

The bill of materials retrieval program will trace the following steps, as shown in figure 12-8:

1. The part number master record for product *A* is accessed.

2. Basic information concerning product *A* may then be printed in the heading block of the output report.

3. The P/N master record for product *A* is checked for the address of the first assembly component.

4. The product structure record is accessed using the address found in the P/N master record.

5. The product structure record contains a field that indicates the first component of product *A* is part number *B*.

6. The master record for part number *B* is then accessed in the P/N master record file.

7. The required descriptive data for part number *B* may then be printed in the output report.

8. The original product structure record (as found in step 4 above) also contains a field with the address of the next assembly component in product *A* (P/N/C), which is accessed.

9.   The description of component C is then found in the P/N master file.

10. The product structure record of component C also contains the address of P/N 1 in the product structure file which is then accessed.

11. Descriptive data for P/N 1 may then be located in the part number master file and printed on the output report.

12. The product structure record for part number 1 under product A contains a marker that indicates that there are no more parts used in product A.

When the end of the chain marker in the product structure file has been found, the first level of product explosion has been completed.

The bill of materials retrieval program next examines each component of product A to determine whether it is an assembly or an individual unit. The program steps for breaking assembly B into its component parts follows the same pattern outlined for breaking down product A. The entire product explosion process is completed when all of the product structure records at each assembly level indicate that no additional parts are used in product A.

The output from a product explosion program may be presented in several different ways: as a single-level explosion, an indented explosion, or a summarized explosion. The uses to which the output report is to be applied will determine the most appropriate report form.

Single-level Explosion Reports

The single-level explosion process simply breaks down each assembly into its direct components and their associated quantities. The resulting output then is a bill of materials for each assembly within the final product. Let us assume, for example, that our product structure tree is given in figure 12-9. A single-level explosion for assembly A and all lower-level subassemblies (B, C, and D) will be as shown in figure 12-10.

In practice single-level explosion reports will be prepared for each assembly and will serve as a complete reference document for the assembly. Figure 12-11 depicts a bill of materials form and the types of information that may be included on it.

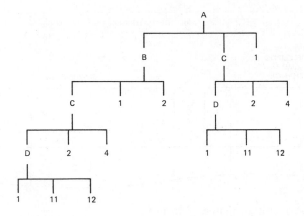

Fig. 12-9   Product structure tree

Assembly A			Assembly B			Assembly C			Assembly D	
P/N	Qty/Assy		P/N	Qty/Assy		P/N	Qty/Assy		P/N	Qty/Assy
B	1		C	1		D	1		1	1
C	1		1	1		2	1		11	1
1	1		2	1		4	1		12	1

Fig. 12-10   Single-level explosion for assembly A and lower-level subassemblies

In addition to certain standard information, the bill of materials document may contain certain special types of information as shown in figure 12-11.

The reports generated by the single-level explosion process are used by many different organizational groups in a typical manufacturing organization. Assembly material orders, or simply assembly orders, may be used as the authorization to release the necessary purchased parts and detail parts from inventory to production. Figure 12-12 depicts an assembly order containing order quantity extensions for the total quantities of each component needed to assemble a particular order. Punched card 'picking' tickets (prepunched cards authorizing inventory disburse-

BILL OF MATERIAL

ASSEMBLY NUMBER
ASSEMBLY DESCRIPTION
DRAWING NUMBER
STRUCTURE CHANGE

DRAWING SIZE

PART NO.	DESCRIPTION	TYPE	SOURCE	UNIT OF MEAS	QTY PER ASSY	STRUCTURE CHANGE	DEPT ASS'D IN	OPER ASS'D ON

Fig. 12-11   Bill of materials form

ASSEMBLY ORDER

ASSEMBLY NUMBER   20136818
ASSEMBLY DESCRIPTION   PUMP ASSY
ORDER QUANTITY   50   ORDER NUMBER   337813

PART NUMBER	DESCRIPTION	U/M	QUANTITY PER ASSY	EXTENDED QUANTITY
531674	SCREW	01	6	300
531690	WASHER	01	5	250
728419	SCREW	01	5	250
1431478	SEAL	01	2	100
3519794	MOTOR	01	1	50
3572133	SPRING	01	2	100
20136130	PUMP SHAFT ASSY	01	1	50
20136301	SET COLLAR	01	1	50
20136315	CLAMP MOUNTING	01	1	50
20136338	SHIFTER COLLAR	01	1	50
20136345	SCREW	01	4	200

Fig. 12-12   Assembly order

ments) may also be prepared concurrently for subsequent use in the inventory control system. The service and repair parts departments frequently make reference to current and out-of-production assemblies through single-level explosion documents. Engineering and production control departments often reference bill of materials reports when considering changes and revisions. The cost accounting department frequently uses single-level explosion reports in computing assembly material, labor, and overhead costs.

Indented Explosion Reports

Indented explosion reports are prepared by completely breaking a finished product or major assembly into its subassembly levels or tiers. The term *indented* refers to the method of listing assembly levels as shown in the first column of figure 12–12. The preparation of an indented explosion report breaks down the finished product vertically rather than horizontally as single-level explosions do. That is, the computer program breaks down the first assembly to its basic components before proceeding to the breakdown of the second assembly in the finished product, and so on. Note, for example, that the pump assembly listed in figure 12-13 (P/N 20136818) is composed of many parts, including a pump shaft assembly, which, in turn, is made up of two parts.

Indented explosion reports may be used by the engineering department to visualize the whole product structure tree when planning an engineering change. The production control

EXTENDED INDENTED EXPLOSION

ASSEMBLY NUMBER   144-30
ASSEMBLY DESCRIPTION   SERIES 30 SERVICE PUMP
ORDER QUANTITY   50   ORDER NUMBER   331245

LEVELS	PART NUMBER	DESCRIPTION	U/M	QUANTITY PER ASSY	EXTENDED QUANTITY
1	20136186	PUMPING ASSY	01	1	50
2	7365963	SERVICE BOX	01	1	50
2	20136812	ADAPTOR	01	2	100
2	20136813	ADAPTOR GASKET	01	2	100
2	20136818	PUMP ASSY	01	1	50
3	531674	SCREW	01	6	300
3	531690	WASHER	01	5	250
3	728419	SCREW	01	5	250
3	1431478	SEAL	01	2	100
3	3519794	MOTOR	01	1	50
3	3572133	SPRING	01	2	100
3	20136130	PUMP SHAFT ASSY	01	1	50
4	20136128	PIN	01	1	50
4	20136129	SHAFT	01	1	50
3	20136301	SET COLLAR	01	1	50
3	20136315	CLAMP MOUNTING	01	1	50
3	20136338	SHIFTER COLLAR	01	1	50
3	20136345	SCREW	01	4	200
2	20136819	DRIVING GEAR	01	1	50
2	20136878	RING LOCKING	01	1	50
2	20136899	SET RING			

Fig. 12-13   Extended indented explosion

department uses these reports in planning production routings and estimating the time needed between assembly levels. Indented explosion reports may also be used to trace the flow of detailed parts and assemblies from one shop assembly area to another.

Summarized Explosion Reports

Summarized explosion reports are prepared by completely breaking a top-level or other major assembly into all of its component parts and then summarizing the quantities of each part number found in the finished product. The summarized explosion process explodes the finished product or major assembly level by level and accumulates the required quantities of the individual components. The resulting report is then a complete summary of the material requirements for a particular product. An example of an extended summarized explosion is shown in figure 12-14.

Summarized explosion reports are especially useful for determining the material requirements for new customer orders or replenishment orders for finished-goods inventory. Summarized explosion data may be readily combined with other information for the purchasing department. A gross-to-net requirements form as shown in figure 12-15 illustrates the use of summarized explosion data in the preparation of inventory management records.

The Detailed Part Implosion Process

The part number master record file and the product structure file may also be used to determine the final product assemblies or subassemblies in which particular detail parts are used. This reverse process, known as detailed part implosion, follows a very similar programming approach to the product explosion technique already described. In this case we are simply attempting to determine where particular detail parts are used in higher-level assemblies.

Using the product structure tree shown in figure 12-9, the actual programming steps in a detailed part implosion program may be listed as follows:

1. The part number master record for P/N 1 is accessed.

GROSS REQUIREMENTS LISTING

ASSEMBLY NUMBER 144-30
ASSEMBLY DESCRIPTION SERIES 30 SERVICE PUMP
ORDER QUANTITY 50   ORDER NUMBER 331245

PART NUMBER	DESCRIPTION	U/M	TOTAL QTY REQUIRED	
231285	PIN	01	150	
356736	PIN	01	50	
481278	NUT	01	450	
496830	SCREW	01	500	
498052	BOLT	01	450	
517370	WASHER	01	450	
531674	SCREW	01	900	
531690	WASHER	01	250	
728419	SCREW	01	250	
1431478	SEAL	01	100	
3519794	MOTOR	01	50	
3572133	SPRING	01	100	
20136128	PIN	01	50	
20136129	SHAFT	01	50	
20136130	PUMP SHAFT ASSY	01	50	
20136131	VALVE			

Fig. 12-14 Extended summarized explosion

INVENTORY RECORD

PART NUMBER	DESCRIPTION	PARS TY	UNIT COST	UNIT OF MEAS	LEAD TIME	ORDERING RULES DISCRETE REORDER POINT MIN	EOQ MAX	A B C	VENDOR NO.	ON HAND
42309683	SHAFT	[X] [ ]	7.50	01	3	10	100	B	19630	40

	CURRENT	1	2	3	4	5	6	7	8	OVER 8
ON ORDER *Released Orders	100*	100*		100*		100	100			
REQUIREMENTS	110	90	20	80	30	80	90	20		
NET AVAILABLE	30	40	20	40	10	30	40	20	20	

RELEASED SHOP OR PURCHASE ORDERS	STOCK DATE	QTY	ORDER NO.	STOCK DATE	QTY	ORDER NO.	STOCK DATE	QTY	ORDER NO.	STOCK DATE	QTY	ORDER NO.
	125	100	13842	130	100	14910	140	100	15895			
	STOCK DATE	QTY	ORDER NO.	STOCK DATE	QTY	ORDER NO.	STOCK DATE	QTY	ORDER NO.	STOCK DATE	QTY	ORDER NO.

Fig. 12-15 Using summarized explosion data to prepare inventory management records

2. Basic data concerning P/N 1 is printed in the heading block of the output report.

3. The P/N master record for P/N 1 is checked for the address of the first assembly that uses this detailed part.

4. The product structure record file is accessed using the address found in the P/N master record.

5. The appropriate product structure record contains a field indicating that the first assembly using P/N 1 is part number *B*.

6. The master record for part number *B* is then accessed in the part number master record file.

7. The required descriptive data for P/N *B* is then printed on the output report.

8. The original product structure record (as found in step 4 above) also contains a field with the address of the next assembly which uses P/N 1.

9. The product structure record of the next assembly component is accessed to determine the assembly number.

10. The description of component *A* is then located through the P/N master record.

11. The product structure record of parent assembly *A* contains an end-of-chain marker, indicating there are no other components that use P/N 1.

The steps described above may be traced in figure 12-16.

Just as in the bill of materials retrieval program, the detailed part implosion program yields three different types of reports. The implosion (where used) report formats for the product structure trees of parent assemblies *A* and *K* are shown at the top of figure 12-17. The single-level implosion reports are shown at the middle of the figure and the indented implosion and summarized implosion reports are shown at the bottom.

The engineering section, when planning an engineering change in the product structure, will find single-level implosion reports very useful. Such reports may also aid manufacturing personnel in dealing with shortages of detail parts, purchased items, subassemblies, and other fabricated parts. Using single-level implosion reports, production control may readily determine the impact of shortages on released assembly orders and revise production schedules accordingly.

Indented implosion reports provide engineering with an

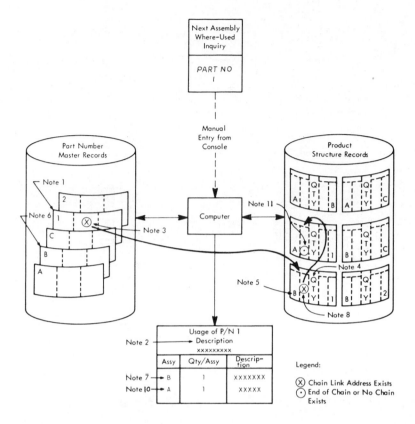

Fig. 12-16   A detailed part implosion program

overview of the direct and indirect multilevel usages for a particular part number. In this way the engineering department will
not need to make repeated requests for single-level implosion
reports to determine the magnitude of a given engineering
change.

Summarized implosion reports are invaluable tools for determining material costs. Not only may the basic material costs
for fabricated assemblies be readily determined, but proposed
cost increases or decreases for detail parts or raw materials may
be readily ascertained. This information would, of course, be
quite useful when considering price changes for the final product. Further, this information could also be used to determine
the advantages of producing particular detail parts in-house or
by purchase from outside vendors. Figure 12-18 depicts an
example of a product cost change report.

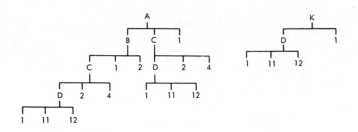

Implosion report for product structure trees A and K

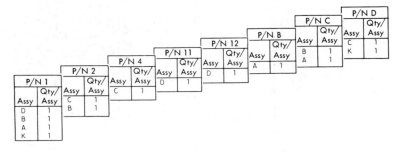

Single-level implosion reports

Part Number 1	
Assembly Indented	Qty/Assy
D	1
. C	1
. . B	1
. . . A	1
. . A	1
. K	1
B	1
. A	1
A	1
K	1

Indented implosion report

Part Number 1	
Assembly	Total Quantity
D	1
C	1
B	2
K	2
A	4

Summarized implosion report

Fig. 12-17   Implosion report formats

The concepts underlying the product structure record file and the bill of materials processor may also be applied to other areas of the firm. Consider, for example, the structure of a personnel system. The basic personnel file is analogous to the part number master file that we have just examined. A chain file

```
                    END PRODUCT COST CHANGE

PART NUMBER        143652689
PART DESCRIPTION      TAPERED ROLLER BEARING
PREVIOUS COST         1.25
NEW COST              1.45
NET CHANGE            .20 INCREASE
```

END PRODUCT	DESCRIPTION	COST CHANGE	NOTES
1346000	SERIES 60 POWER TAKE OFF	.80	
1346200	SERIES 62 POWER TAKE OFF	.60	
1346800	SERIES 68 POWER TAKE OFF	1.00	
1347000	SERIES 70 POWER TAKE OFF	.40	
1421400	SERIES 14 STD TRANSMISSION	1.80	
1451400	SERIES 14 HD TRANSMISSION	.60	
1421600	SERIES 16 STD TRANSMISSION	1.00	
1451600	SERIES 16 HD TRANSMISSION	.40	

Fig. 12-18   Product cost change report

containing departmental interrelations could be constructed
that would be analogous to the product structure record file.
Using these two files together, departmental employee lists
could be readily prepared by the implosion technique. Similarly,
in an accounts payable system, individual vouchers in voucher
number sequence would correspond to the part number file,
while a voucher date-payable structure file is akin to the product
structure record. Together these files can provide the vouchers
to be paid on a particular date. Thus the BOMP technique is
not limited solely to inventory data problems but has many applications in other information systems.

The Inventory Control Information System

Since inventory accumulation represents the allocation of a
scarce resource—money—it is imperative for the materials manager to have adequate, timely information about the use to
which this scarce resource has been put. The purpose of the
inventory control information system is to furnish operating
personnel and managers with the requisite information so that
they know what is happening to their inventories. In many respects the inventory control information system is an operating
(record keeping) information system that may also be used to

provide management with information about the nature, characteristics, and problem areas in the inventory system.

The basic function of such an information system is to maintain records of all the receipts and disbursements for each item in the entire inventory. The status of each inventory item must be current and available to both operating personnel and management at all times. Further, the activity for each inventory item must be determinable to follow the changes in inventory structure over a period of time.

A second function of nearly all inventory control information systems is to identify those items that are out of stock or in very short supply. With this information, operating personnel or managers may initiate corrective action before the inventory deficiency presents acute production or distribution problems. Also, in many cases inventory managers may wish to know which items are in oversupply so that steps may be taken to reduce their inventory levels.

Let us examine the structure of a typical inventory control information system for a single type of inventory, such as a raw materials, purchased parts, in-process, finished-goods, or operating supplies inventory. Figure 12-19 illustrates a typical inventory control information system that uses disc storage for the maintenance of the part number master file. This particular system does not use remote terminals to update inventory records, although they could be incorporated without undue difficulty.

The first input data stream is part number master record data. Before any transaction activity may be accepted and processed by the system, a part number master record must be created in disc storage. Ordinarily this record is identified by a unique part number and contains many items of information, such as part name, quantity on hand, reorder point quantity, reorder quantity, quantities on order with expected delivery dates and purchase order numbers, quantity received and disbursed week to date, month to date, and year to date, vendor identification number, item cost, price, and any other information deemed appropriate in the master record. The input data stream for the part number (P/N) master file includes, of course, both the original P/N data and P/N master file record changes and additions.

Inventory activity, as receipts or disbursements, makes up the next input data stream. Since the record key is nearly always

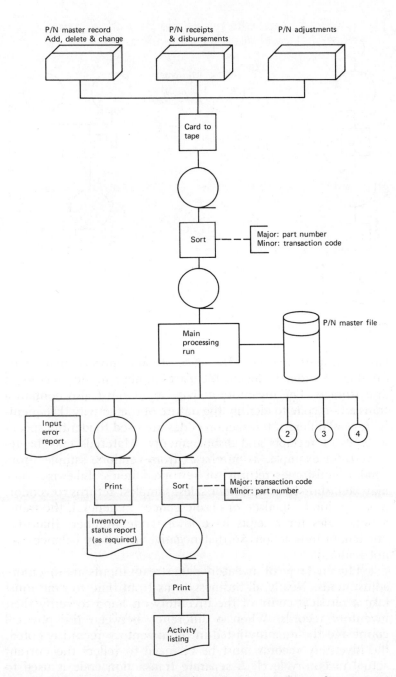

Fig. 12-19   Inventory control information system using disc storage

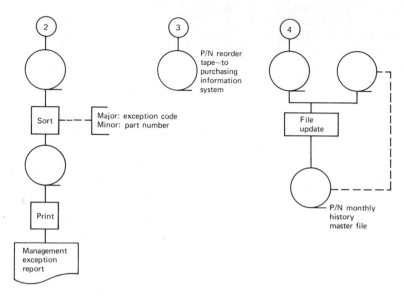

Fig. 12-19   (cont'd)

based on part number, the data stream must contain part number in order to locate the part number master record in disc storage. The inventory activity input must also contain a transaction code to identify the nature of the activity. Frequently, several different transaction codes are used to identify specific types of receipts and disbursements. Materials may be received, for example, as purchases from vendors, samples from vendors, customer returns, or reworked items. Likewise, they may be disbursed as customer sales, samples, returns to vendor, or scrap due to spoilage or obsolescence. In general, the transaction codes for receipts have lower code numbers than disbursement transactions so that negative inventory balances are not realized.

The final type of inventory data stream inputs are inventory adjustments. Nearly all business firms from time to time must take a physical count of the inventory on hand to verify their inventory records. When a difference between the physical count and the quantity listed in the inventory record is noted, the inventory records must be changed to reflect the current actual inventory level. A separate transaction code is used to identify these adjustments for management.

Selecting the best data input method depends primarily on two factors. If the transaction volume is large, it may be best to enter the activity data, sorted to P/N sequence, into the computer on magnetic tape. If up-to-the-minute records of the inventory levels for each item are needed, then remote input/output terminals will probably be required. In the latter case there is no need to perform any data preparation operations.

In our system example, the punched cards for each of the various data streams are combined for transcription to magnetic tape. Next, the individual records are sorted using the part number as the major sorting key and transaction code as the minor sorting key. The resulting sorted activity tape is then ready for the daily main processing run.

The main processing run is essentially a file maintenance operation in which several activities are performed. New part number master records must be created in the part number master record file. Inventory activity, as receipts, disbursements, or adjustments, must update the appropriate data field within the master record. Finally, the basic information for the necessary output reports must be prepared.

The output report composition follows the general pattern we have already examined for file maintenance and updating programs. The ubiquitous input error report containing those transactions that do not pass the editing tests may be output on the computer console typewriter as a separate report or as flagged items in the activity listing. An activity listing must also be prepared to provide an audit trail for the transactions that have been entered into the information system.

The inventory status report is a listing of appropriate information in part number sequence of all items maintained in the inventory. It is not essential to prepare this report daily, but it must be prepared rather frequently. Such a report is quite useful to operating personnel for determining inventory item information, especially when remote-access input/output terminals are not available. It is also quite useful for the reconstruction of inventory files should the master data file be inadvertently destroyed. This particular contingency may also be handled by preparing tapes of all the P/N master file data weekly. This tape may then be stored for an appropriate period in a safe place. By using status reports or part number file record tapes and the activity listings for the intervening periods, the part number master file may be recreated if needed.

Inventory activity reports are also a vital type of output from an inventory information system. To be most useful, these records should be sorted with the transaction code as the major sort key and part number as the minor sort key. In this way similar types of activities will be grouped together for easy identification.

Another type of very useful output report is the management exception report. During the file maintenance and update run, the computer program may check for certain error conditions that may or should be brought to the attention of management. Such conditions as negative inventory balances, unauthorized material returns, low turnover items (no inventory movement during a predetermined time period), inventory items below reorder quantity, inventory items out of stock, or late shipments may require managerial attention. Most managers do not wish to be burdened with superfluous information that requires no action on their part. To help managers use the management exception report, the various exception conditions may be assigned a special code that will enable a subsequent sorting program to group all like exceptions together. The manager, in this way, will be able to examine all of the exceptions of a particular type as a single group.

A wide variety of special reports or other outputs may also be prepared from data contained in the part number master record file. Purchase requisitions, for example, may be readily prepared when the inventory quantity falls below the reorder point. The purchasing department may then use this report to initiate purchase orders for the items that are in short supply. Material charges against work orders and/or organizational units may also be output from the inventory control information system.

A final type of output that may be very useful is the history report. Rather than maintaining historical information about usage and item turnover in the part number master file, it is often preferable to output this information on a separate form. The current history magnetic tape may subsequently be combined with the old part number master history tape to prepare a new one. We shall examine the various uses to which the master part number history tape may be applied in the next section.

The inventory control information system we have just described will provide both operating employees and inventory managers with the requisite information to manage most types of inventories. While the system we have discussed was restricted to a single type of inventory, the same concepts may be extended to cover inventory systems that operate in series—for example, raw materials to in-process to finished-goods inventories.

Inventory Analysis Information Systems

The inventory item (part number) history master file contains a wealth of information about the historical activities of individual inventory items. If we assume that history tends to repeat itself, then the analysis of historical inventory data will provide much useful information about the future activities of inventory items. By revealing these activity patterns, this information can provide a sound base for developing both efficient and effective inventory management policies.

Inventory analysis information systems are often called inventory planning, or inventory planning and control, information systems. The purpose of such systems is to extract from the accumulated historical data as much information as possible to help management exercise active control over inventory system operations. In general, managers usually wish to acquire inventory items in a timely way, to procure inventory items at the lowest total cost, and to reduce slow-moving items to a minimum.

The first general information area of management concern for finished goods is inventory item quantity control. In attempting to maintain such control, inventory managers are faced with several related difficulties: (1) sufficient average inventory stock must be maintained so that the danger of running out of an item is kept within acceptable limits, (2) the lead time for placing procurement orders must be determined to reduce stockouts from late shipments to an acceptable level and (3) order quantities must be of the proper size to minimize procurement and carrying costs. The simultaneous solution of these three problems for hundreds or thousands of inventory items can be accomplished efficiently only with a computerized information system.

The interrelated decision areas may be better understood with reference to figure 12-20, which depicts inventory quantity level for a particular item as a function of time. Assume we have an initial item supply of one hundred units. The inventory quantity will diminish, hopefully, over a period of time until

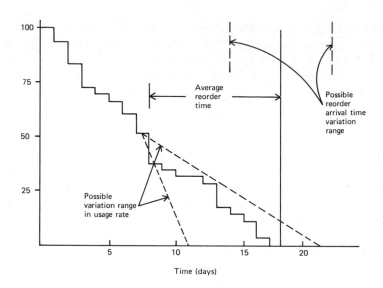

Fig. 12-20   Inventory quantity level as a function of time

the stock becomes low. At some point a reorder decision must be made. The timing of the reorder decision will be dependent upon the answers to two separate questions. First, how long will it take before we may reasonably expect the supplier to replenish the inventory? Second, how many units may we expect to be demanded during the intervening period? The analysis of historical procurement data (elapsed time between order placement and order receipt) and historical time demand data (historical usage rate) may be used to establish both the reorder time increment and the associated reorder quantity level.

Once the when-to-order question has been answered, the inventory manager is immediately faced with another. How many units should be ordered to minimize total inventory costs? The optimum order quantity may be computed with the classical economic order quantity formula,

$$\text{Economic order quantity} = \sqrt{\frac{2AS}{R}}$$

where A equals the cost per purchase order placed, S equals annual sales in dollars, and R equals the inventory carrying cost rate. If the values for the independent variables in the equation above are established, the computation of the economic order

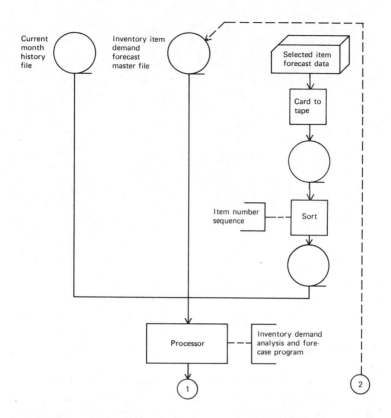

Fig. 12-21   An inventory analysis information system

quantity may be readily accomplished.

Let us turn our attention now to the design of an inventory analysis information system to cope with these difficulties. One of several possible designs is shown in figure 12-21. The first input data stream is the current month inventory item history master file. This file contains the historical data for all inventory item receipts and disbursements during the preceding month. In addition, it should include information relating to the placement and the receipt of purchased items (reorder times), item cost, economic order quantity, and other selected data.

The second input data stream is the item demand master file. The file contains the historical demand data from previous periods as well as the forecast of expected item demand computed during the preceding program cycle. Provision has also been

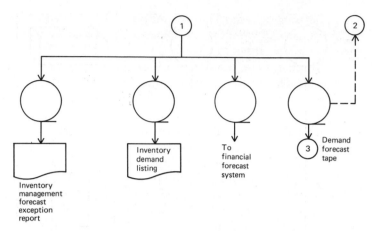

Fig. 12-21   (cont'd)

made for a data input stream of selected individual item demand forecasts. Although this particular system relies extensively on the analytical development of an item demand forecast, information concerning specific items may also be available from other sources and should be included in the development of the current demand forecast.

After the incoming data streams have been sorted to item number sequence (if required), the data may be processed by the demand analysis program. This program examines the item usage in both prior periods and the current period and selected item demand forecast data to compute and update the item demand forecast master file. In addition, it may be designed to check the forecast demand with the actual demand for the preceding month and note particular items that fall outside the forecast area tolerance range.

The first output of this program run will be an inventory management exception report that lists those items with significant deviations from forecast demand for subsequent management investigation. The second output from this program run will be an updated item demand forecast report that lists previous and expected item demand by period for each item in the inventory. The principal purpose of this report is to provide a hard copy listing of the item demand forecast. The third output report is a data tape containing pertinent financial information for future periods to be used in the financial forecasting information system. Information about future sales of finished goods inventory can be an excellent source of revenue data for a financial planning system. The last output is the inventory item demand master file, which is subsequently used in the inventory parameter update program run.

The inputs for the reorder point analysis program are similar to the inputs for the item demand analysis program. The current item history master file furnishes current data about the placement and receipt of purchased items. The reorder point analysis master file contains data on previous purchase orders for each inventory item, including the elapsed time to secure inventory replacement. The third input data stream has selected data about expected changes in the procurement process. Thus selecting a new vendor who agrees to provide better service might shorten the expected procurement time interval. Conversely, if procurement difficulties are anticipated in view of impending supplier problems (strikes, material shortages, and so forth), this information could also be entered into the program.

After sorting to item number sequence (if required), the inputs are processed by the reorder point analysis program. The purpose of this program is to compute the mean reorder time and the standard deviation for reorder time variations.

The first output information stream is a magnetic tape that contains appropriate vendor data that may be used in subsequent procurement analysis programs if desired. The second information output stream contains the reorder point analysis data for each inventory item. The magnetic tape with this data will subsequently become an input to the inventory parameter change program. The final output is the reorder point analysis master tape file. This file, as we have noted, will be one of the inputs during the next program run cycle.

The final portion of this information system involves recomputing the order point (the inventory level at which new orders are generated) and the safety stock (materials maintained to handle fluctuations in rate of demand and order time) and determining the economic order quantity. Demand data prepared by the demand analysis program must be combined with the output of the reorder point analysis program for entry into the inventory parameter change program. The inventory item master file located online in auxiliary storage will also be used for input to the inventory parameter change program, as shown in figure 12-22.

From the data available, this program recomputes the order point quantity (critical item quantity initiating purchase requisition), safety stock level (necessary reserve stock to accomodate

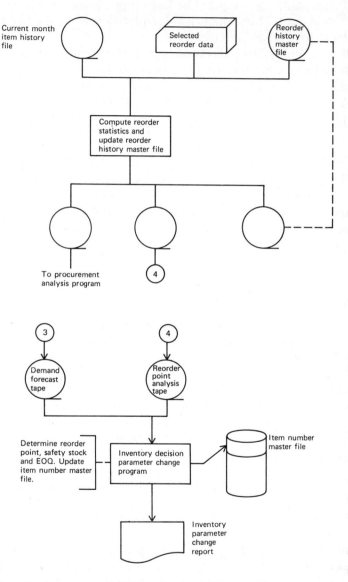

Fig. 12-22   Inventory parameter change program

usage and reorder time fluctuations), and economic order quantity. The inventory item master file located in auxiliary storage will be updated to reflect the recomputed item values. The actual computations for determining the reorder quantity and the

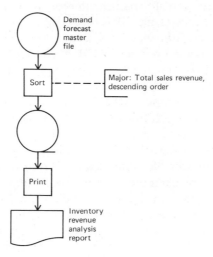

Fig. 12-23   Inventory analysis information system with demand
forecast master file report

safety stock level are based on statistical techniques in which
the degree of risk may be adjusted. The economic order quantity adjustment is performed by recalculating the economic
order quantity according to the classical formula

$$\text{Economic order quantity} = \sqrt{\frac{2AS}{R}}$$

The first output is, of course, the updated inventory item
master file. The second output information stream is the inventory parameter change report. This report furnishes a hard copy
record of the changes incorporated in the inventory item master
file. As such, it may serve both as an historical record and as
a notification to inventory management of inventory item master file changes.

The demand forecast master file may also serve as the primary input for a second type of inventory analysis information
system. The purpose of this system is to create special analytical
reports of the distribution of inventory items based on selected
criteria. Listing inventory items according to various sorting sequences provides inventory managers with substantial information regarding the nature of inventory item activity and status.
The systems flowchart for this information system is shown in
figure 12-23.

The primary input to the information system is the current demand forecast master file. This file, prepared in the preceding inventory analysis information system, covers both historical and forecast demand by inventory item number. To be significant and useful to management, this input data stream must cover an extended period of time.

The processor computes the total sales revenue over an appropriate period for each inventory item. This data is then sorted by ranking the total value of inventory sales for each item from the highest to the lowest (descending sequence). The demand forecast master file may also be sorted using other item record criteria. For example, sorting the annual sales of items from particular vendors will identify the most active item suppliers. Another processing program could sort the item inventory according to the average value of on-hand inventory. A final processor program may be prepared to sort the average item supply on hand divided by the forecast usage rate. Thus four different output reports may be prepared from the demand forecast master file by varying the sorting program.

The report prepared by the first program run is a distribution by item sales report. An example of a report containing selected items from a large inventory is shown in figure 12-24. The typical results of a distribution by item sales report, presented in graphic form, is shown in figure 12-25. This report is especially valuable in providing insights into the basic nature of inventory activity—the large versus the small revenue-generating items.

The second report that may be prepared is the distribution by vendor sales report. This report provides insights about the relations between vendor lines and sales as well as indicates the relative importance of the various suppliers. It may be of value to purchasing managers as well as inventory managers.

The third report, an average value of on-hand inventory report, may be used to identify the distribution of inventory items as a function of their respective investment of funds. Since the total funds available for investment in inventory are usually in short supply or are actually limited, identifying those items that have absorbed disproportionate amounts of funds may raise legitimate questions about the present funds/inventory allocation pattern.

This report also seeks to identify inventory items which may be over- or under-stocked as a function of forecast sales. It fo-

				Distribution by Item Sales Report		
Item Number	Item Count	Annual Units	Unit Cost	Annual Sales	Cumulative Sales	Cum. %
R3042	1	7,922	$6.06	$48,007.32	$ 48,007.32	.05
B9131	1001	1,103	5.26	5,801.78	3,840,460.17	60.41
M4001	2001	270	8.82	2,381.40	7,690,721.41	80.10
D1277	3001	63	4.16	262.08	8,602,854.40	89.62
P9044	4001	19	3.90	74.10	9,284,553.16	96.70
B6135	5008	4	7.14	28.56	9,601,400.31	100.00

Fig. 12-24   Distribution-by-item sales report

cuses on the average supply on hand relative to anticipated usage. In this way the expected high and low inventory turnover items may be identified and management may take appropriate action, if required.

The two major inventory analysis information systems thus complement each other in giving management the requisite information to make sound decisions. The first furnishes a sound

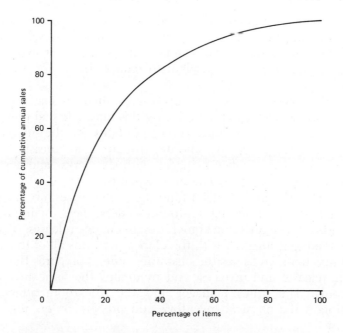

Fig. 12-25   Results of a distribution-by-item sales report

basis for operating-level decision making while the second concentrates on defining the characteristics of an item inventory. Used together, these information systems are powerful inventory planning and control tools.

CONCLUSION

Inventory management is a critical item in the operation of almost every business firm. The managerial functions of planning, organizing (operating), and control as they relate to inventories are especially important in earning and preserving profits. Inventory information systems may be devised to assist the inventory manager substantially in performing his managerial functions. Without these information systems, the inventory manager will certainly be at a disadvantage and can scarcely function effectively.

CASE STUDY: AIRSTAR SPARE PARTS INVENTORY

The Airstar Company introduced an eight-passenger executive jet airplane almost two years ago. As a part of the sales pitch, the company promised to maintain an inventory of spare parts for the aircraft at its main plant to reduce the prospective purchasers' total investment.

Mr. John Mullins had been appointed manager of the spares inventory department during this time. He had previously served in several managerial positions in the marketing branch of the company. The department now consists of five parts analysts, an office manager with six clerks, and a stores manager with eight stockroom attendants.

The parts analysts determine the proper inventory level for each part by reviewing customer orders, field maintenance reports, and engineering branch design change releases. The office manager, together with the clerks, performs all of the clerical functions—receives the customer orders, prepares the shipping releases and invoices, and maintains the basic inventory records. The stores manager and the stockroom attendants maintain the physical inventory and prepare orders for shipment.

An additional function of the stockroom attendants is the preparation of spare parts kits. When several parts are used together for minor maintenance or overhaul of field aircraft, they are combined in a kit to facilitate ordering and handling. Under these circumstances the kit number is used for identification purposes and the original part numbers are deleted. From time to time when the individual parts within a kit were temporarily out of stock as separate items, kits have been broken to fill the orders. As a result, keeping track of broken kits has been a recurring difficulty.

Parts may be added to the inventory in several different ways:

1. Orders to manufacturing
2. Overruns from manufacturing (Not infrequently more units will be started in the manufacturing process than are actually required. This is done to reduce the possibility of a rerun in case some of the parts do not pass final inspection. When all of the parts pass inspection, the excess is sent to the spares department rather than scrapping them.)
3. Reworked parts from manufacturing (Spare parts that have been changed by engineering redesign are sent back to manufacturing for rework.)
4. Customer returns (This source includes good parts that the customer no longer needs, parts that are obsolete due to engineering changes, and defective parts that must be reworked or scrapped.)

Parts may be released from the spares inventory for the following reasons:

1. Customer sales
2. Replacements for customer returns
3. Scrap due to obsolescence
4. Scrap due to damage or spoilage
5. Returns to manufacturing for rework

The present inventory information system is a mixture of manual records and punched-card data processing. The principal output reports are a weekly P/N order listing (open orders to be shipped to customers), a weekly out-of-stock listing, and a weekly shipped order summary report.

Recently the internal auditors made a spot check of the inventory to determine whether the total inventory value was below the $500,000 that has been authorized for the operation.

Their check revealed that as much as $1,500,000 worth of inventory was being maintained. A physical count of the inventory corroborated their estimate. As a result, the marketing branch manager has demoted Mr. Mullins to clerk and ordered his replacement, Mr. Jackson, to get the operation under control.

Design an information system that will provide Mr. Jackson with the information he needs to manage the operation effectively. (Assume there is a large computer with six magnetic tape drives, two printers, and sufficient random-access storage for the spare parts inventory file.)

PRODUCTION/OPERATION INFORMATION SYSTEMS

In large manufacturing firms, the production system usually receives a very large share of managerial attention. The reasons behind this are not hard to find. A large proportion of the typical manufacturing firm's assets are invested in plant, equipment, technological knowhow, and the inventories that both await processing and are in process. Further, most of the firm's personnel are usually employed in manufacturing operations. Profits are substantially influenced by variable production costs as well as fixed ones. For these and other reasons, the production system is of major importance to the manufacturing firm.

Service firms, especially large organizations such as insurance companies, government agencies, and financial institutions, also have production systems for processing documents or information. The production systems for wholesaling and retailing firms may be of lesser importance, yet they too strongly influence profitability.

In this chapter, we shall examine the production system and its associated information flows with regard to operations planning, production scheduling, and production control. The information systems in each of these areas have a great effect on the overall performance of the production system in the business firm. A knowledge of the functions these information systems perform will permit managers to obtain the most efficient and effective performance from their production system.

THE PRODUCTION SYSTEM

The production system in a manufacturing firm may be defined as the process by which raw materials and purchased parts are transformed into finished goods. While the production process is ordinarily considered to be the manufacture of specific products, we may also find many examples in our economy in which the production process results in the performance of services. In these cases the transformation process often involves performing an information-related activity for the firm's customers.

The principal objective of the production system is to transform the system's inputs into appropriate outputs in the most efficient way possible. The rudimentary system model for the production process is shown in figure 13-1. The inputs, shown on the left-hand side of the diagram, are the basic work units for the production process. These work units are composed of the essential raw materials to produce the finished goods. The processor is, of course, the plant or factory where the inputs are converted into finished goods. The processor includes the building, the equipment, the human resources (employees), the financial resources, and the technological knowhow needed for efficient manufacturing operations. The system outputs are the

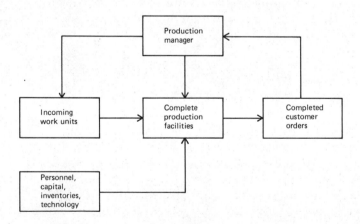

Fig. 13-1　System model for the production process

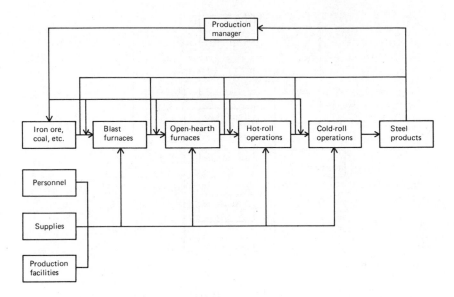

Fig. 13-2   The manufacture of rolled steel products as subsystems in series

finished goods that will be sold to customers. The production manager both controls the system by regulating the input work unit stream into the production process as well as structures the production process by implementing manufacturing policies and decisions.

In the real world, however, production systems tend to be much more complex than the simple model above. Production systems are actually composed of many separate operations, each of which may be regarded as a subsystem. The product flows between the production subsystems may be combined in parallel or in series as required. The manufacture of rolled steel products is shown in figure 13-2 as a series of major operations (subsystems) combined in series. These major operations may be further subdivided into smaller operations (sub-subsystems) functioning in parallel as shown in figure 13-3. When the production system is viewed as a complex of subsystems and sub-subsystems, exercising control seems extraordinarily difficult.

Although each production system contains much the same elements, there are many interrelated variations. For classifica-

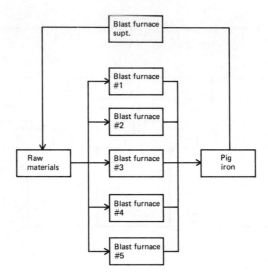

Fig. 13-3 Subsystems functioning in parallel

tion purposes we may distinguish production systems into two major categories. Some are termed *continuous* because the production process operates in a reasonably continuous fashion. The production of electric power, for example, must take place without interruption in order to furnish a constant stream of electricity. Assembly-line operations are also termed continuous because individual work operations are performed sequentially without accumulating in-process inventories.

Continuous production processes normally have the following characteristics or attributes:

1. The use of specialized machines staged in a product line layout, which reduces flexibility in product manufacture
2. High capital cost
3. High productivity per man-hour
4. The use of semi-skilled and unskilled laborers for many jobs
5. The use of fixed-path material handling equipment

Continuous production processes are therefore normally associated with large business firms with reasonably stable demands for a line of finished products. Even though the system output is continuous, the production units quite frequently are separate and distinct.

The second type of production system is termed *intermittent* or *batch* manufacturing. This type of system is especially adaptable for individual customer orders that require unique manufacturing sequences. Machine shops, furniture manufacturers, and printing operations are typical examples of intermittent manufacturing operations.

Intermittent production processes usually have the following characteristics:

1. The use of general-purpose production machinery to provide for greater flexibility in product manufacture
2. Lower capital investment costs
3. Higher unit production costs
4. The use of more high-cost skilled labor

Intermittent production processes are therefore more often found in small business firms with widely varied product demands. On-site manufacturing operations, such as building construction, may be viewed as a special type of intermittent manufacturing operation.

The two different types of production systems often use somewhat different ways for identifying the basic work units in the production system. Continuous manufacturing operations typically use serialized identification. For example, in automobile assembly operations each unit is assigned a serial number that becomes the basis for the identification of individual automobiles throughout the assembly process. This method of product identification, naturally, may be applied to continuous production processes only when the outputs are discrete units.

Intermittent manufacturing operations usually use an order number as the principal means for batch identification. The production order number may be easily related to a particular customer order and furnishes a convenient means for following individual orders through the entire production process.

Achieving the highest possible degree of systems efficiency is a paramount objective in production systems operations. Variable and fixed production costs are major determinants in the firm's ultimate profitability. Since the output composition and quantity of production systems is determined by forces outside the production system (sales), production managers tend to be very conscious of system efficiency.

The cost measure of production system efficiency is ordinarily derived from cost standards. In intermittent manufacturing operations, for example, there are usually standard costs such as direct labor and direct materials costs that may be applied to each order. Collecting and subsequently comparing the actual cost with the standard cost for each order provides an excellent index for cost efficiency. Cost efficiency may also be evaluated by using accounting responsibility information systems to show the aggregate controllable costs for a production unit over a period of time. Either or both of these cost measurement techniques may be applied to particular work operations to develop the most appropriate cost efficiency measure.

Time efficiency measures are also very important in evaluating production systems efficiency. Customers place orders with the expectation that the finished goods will be delivered on promised delivery dates. In order to meet customer schedule commitments, individual stages within the production system must be completed on time. Comparing actual order status with the expected status at a given point in time provides an excellent measure for evaluating time efficiency. The actual computation of time efficiency again may be performed on an individual order basis or aggregated on a departmental basis. Both measures may be used effectively in most production systems.

Material quantity efficiency measures may be used to evaluate the quantity efficiency of a given production system. The number of units of raw materials entering the production system relative to the number of units in the output may be used to compute the absolute quantity efficiency measure. Relative quantity measures of production systems efficiency in which the absolute quantity efficiency measure is compared to a derived standard value may also be appropriate under certain circumstances.

Quality is also a very important measure of production system efficiency. When prescribed quality levels are not achieved, production orders may be scrapped or returned for rework. In either case the production system's efficiency will be seriously reduced. Rather than wait until the entire production process has been completed before making a quality examination, most firms use in-process inspection techniques to determine quality level at critical points. In this way defective units may be found at the earliest possible times and corrective action may be taken before additional costs are incurred and the production schedule is endangered. Because of their unique character, quality measures of systems efficiency must be designed individually to fit the circumstances.

The measurement of production systems effectiveness may also be of some concern to production management. With most production systems there is a designed plant capacity range in which efficient production operations may be achieved. When the actual operations level is below or above the optimum operating range, inefficiency usually follows, as shown in figure 13-4. Production managers naturally become concerned as the upper and lower inflection points are approached. The present operating level relative to the optimum operating range may be examined to determine the system's general effectiveness. Unfortunately, there is very little production managers may do to change plant capacity in a direct way during the short run when the operating range limits are being approached or exceeded.

The information flows in production systems are exceedingly important in achieving a high degree of efficiency. Production

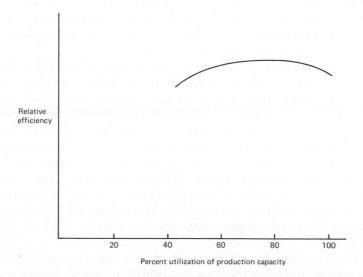

Fig. 13-4   Production systems efficiency vs. production capacity

managers need information about future order requirements.
The required production operations to be performed must be
specified as precisely as possible. Further, realistic schedules for
each step of the manufacturing process must be established.
Orders containing the necessary routing and scheduling information must be communicated to individual supervisors through
a dispatching system. Finally, production operations must be
monitored to determine impending order difficulties, production
bottlenecks, cost overruns and other systemic dysfunctions.
Fortunately, many of these information requirements may be
met through well-designed production information systems.

MANUFACTURING PLANNING INFORMATION SYSTEMS

Before production operations can be started, all of the activities
in the entire manufacturing process must be carefully planned.
Each step of the manufacturing operations must be identified,
the necessary raw materials prescribed, the manufacturing
methods specified, time standards developed, and standard costs
determined in order to minimize the total manufacturing costs.
The development of detailed plans for manufacturing operations
is known as production planning, operation planning, manufacturing engineering, process engineering, methods engineering,
and by many other names. The resulting plans that specify the
sequential operations are called production routings, operation
routings, job work sheets, and so forth.

The following information systems application will follow
the production routing preparation methods encountered in
typical job shop manufacture. Even within this general class of
manufacturing operations, there are many production system
variations found in industry today. To a great extent they reflect
peculiar differences stemming from such things as product differences, company size, market conditions, customer requirements, and production technology. On the other hand, there
are many similar information requirements in job shop manufacturing firms. To a greater or lesser extent these common
information needs may be satisfied by computerized information
systems.

Most medium- and large-scale job shop manufacturing
operations employ a group of individuals known as production

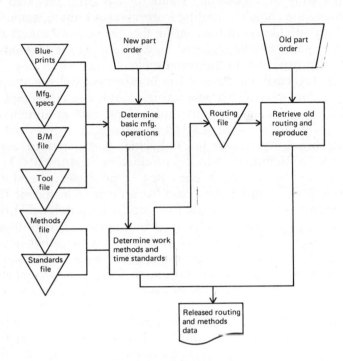

Fig. 13-5   The traditional approach to manufacturing planning

planners, process engineers, or methods engineers whose primary function is to develop the manufacturing sequences for producing component parts and subsequently assembling them into the final product. The production planners combine specific data from blueprints, manufacturing specifications, bill of materials lists, and tooling data with their knowledge of plant operations to determine the most practicable means for the production of finished goods.

The traditional approach to manufacturing planning, as shown in figure 13-5, is normally centered on a manually operated information system. The preparation of production routings for new parts or products is performed in three major steps: (1) determining the manufacturing operations and their sequence, (2) determining specific work methods, and (3) computing time and cost standards. Once the production routing together with the appropriate standards has been prepared by a planner, the complete routing instructions in mimeograph or ditto form are placed in the routing file. Subsequent orders for the same parts may be prepared by reproducing the previously prepared instructions in the routing file.

The principal objective of the information systems analyst in the automation of manufacturing planning is developing a suitable way of breaking down finished product requirements into the individual components to be assembled, to specify the manufacturing operations for individual parts, and to communicate this information to the production departments. Finished product requirements must first be processed, therefore, by the bill of materials processor to provide a listing of the component parts. Those parts that are to be purchased from outside suppliers must be identified and purchase requisitions placed for them. The manufactured parts, on the other hand, must go through a production routing preparation process for determining their production routings and the associated standards and preparing hard copy instructions for production personnel.

The first and most simple way of preparing the required manufacturing operation routing instructions for a particular manufactured part uses a product routing library. During the initial product run, the production planner determines the best manufacturing sequence to produce the part. In addition, machine allocations, special tooling and manufacturing requirements, labor standards, and cost standards are also developed at this time. The complete product routing may then be placed on magnetic tape or auxiliary storage and recalled as required to prepare production orders. The identification key in this program is part number. An example of this type of information system is shown in figure 13-6.

The principal advantage of this approach for preparing product routings is its simplicity. The new information system is simply a substitution of mechanical for human effort to prepare hard copy production routing instructions. At the time the production planners develop the initial routings for individual parts, data-processing routing master records are also prepared and filed. When orders are received, the routing instructions with their associated standards maq be quickly extracted from the file and the production routing paperwork prepared.

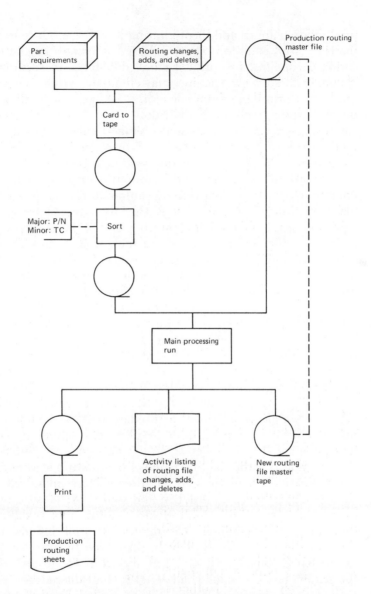

Fig. 13-6   Library-type product routing information system

This approach, however, suffers from several defects. Updating or correcting the product routings is very difficult. Over a period of time, operating personnel will often find improved manufacturing methods. Relaying this information back to the production planner and incorporating it in the product routing master record is all too often neglected. Changes in manufacturing capabilities also present many difficulties in keeping the system updated. New machines may eliminate certain operations and/or perform them more efficiently. To keep the routing files current would require an individual review of every product routing whenever an equipment change is made. Finally, this method uses a great deal of record space and would be very expensive to operate using auxiliary storage equipment.

To take full advantage of the computing capacity of modern computers, a fresh approach to automating the production planning function is required. Rather than mechanizing only a portion of the production planning process, the entire process must be automated to achieve the highest level of efficiency. If the basic manufacturing procedures may be defined for entire item or product families, then the complete regeneration of the production routing for each order should provide the most efficient means for preparing production routings. However, substituting computer logic for human decision making requires that the underlying logic or reasoning planners use to develop production routing sequences and standards first be determined.

A basic requirement for developing an automated manufacturing planning information system is the presence of identifiable part families. When a family of parts exists in which all of the parts are simply variations of a standard part, then automated manufacturing planning is quite feasible. This situation may be best understood by considering an example. A basic part for all electric motors is the shaft on which the armature is assembled. The typical electric motor manufacturer will have many different shaft configurations, some active and some obsolete, for use in his product line. While each electric motor shaft is different, there are certain common features found in all designs. Each shaft in the entire family may be identified by the definition of the parameters x_1, x_2,..., x_{19} as shown in figure 13-7. Thus the parameters of overall shaft length, shaft diameters, corner radii, keyway size, and other features will define all possible motor shaft variations.

The decision rules for determining the necessary operations and their sequence may be found by examining the product

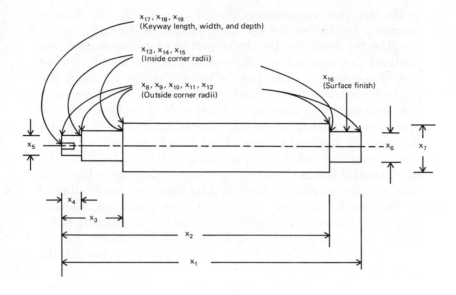

Fig. 13-7   Identifying each shaft in a family

routing variations currently in use. This study should reveal a
finite number of routing practices used to produce the family
of parts. With this information at hand, the systems analyst may
then proceed, with the assistance of the planners and manufacturing personnel, to determine the actual decision rules for
selecting one operation sequence over the others. In this way
the decision-making process that will specify the preferred manufacturing sequence may be codified and examined for inconsis-
tencies.

Operation methods analysis is the second stage in developing
an automated production planning information system. Each
operation on the routing specification must be linked to a machine or group of machines that have unique capabilities. For
example, on a lathe the machine capabilities would include the
chuck size, maximum work piece length, maximum work piece
diameter, depth of cut limitations, feed rate, and surface finish
limitations. Further, the machine capabilities must be related

to the product requirements in order to specify the detailed operating instructions for the manufacture of the part.

The third stage in the development of an automated production planning program is determining production time and/or cost standards. A setup time allowance must be made for preparing the machine to produce the part. This allowance is independent of the number of parts to be manufactured; it is ordinarily stored in standard reference tables located in auxiliary storage. The standard time per operation to produce each part may be based on calculations or found in reference tables. The time standard for the complete operation is the sum of the setup time plus the product of the standard time per part multiplied by the number of parts in the order. The result may then be output on the product routing sheet as the standard time for the operation. Standard costs for the production lot may be computed by multiplying the standard operation time by the standard machine cost rate.

An information system flowchart for an automated production planning system is shown in figure 13-8. New part orders and cost estimate requests require special part specification input data. Figure 13-9 shows a basic roller bearing engineering drawing that defines the product parameters and its input specification sheet.

The processor generates the product routings, the operation methods, time standards, and cost standards as discussed in the paragraphs above.

The first outputs of the production planning information system are the production routing instructions for production personnel. Figure 13-10 depicts the routing sheet for the production of the roller bearing shown in Figure 13-9. Order travel cards may also be prepared for each operation on the routing sheet for subsequent return to the production monitor information system.

The second output report lists the tooling requirements for the order. Tooling personnel may use this report to determine whether the proper tools are available and, if not, to take the necessary steps to obtain the proper tools. Cost estimates for new parts or customer inquiries are the next system output and may be forwarded to the interested parties.

Raw material requisition cards may also be prepared autho-

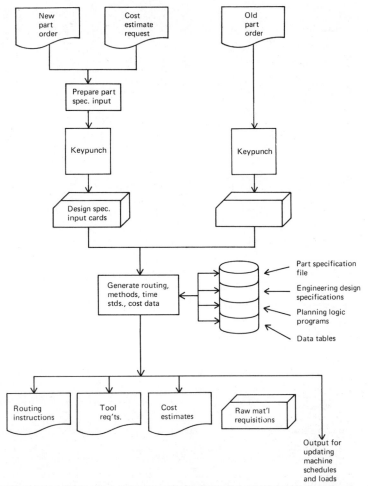

Fig. 13-8 Information system flowchart for an automated
production planning system

rizing the disbursement of the proper materials from inventory.
These cards may be used as inputs to the raw material inventory
control system and will eliminate the need to recreate the data
for that system.

The production planning information system contains data
about the production time requirements for each operation, the
assigned machine, and required delivery date. This data may

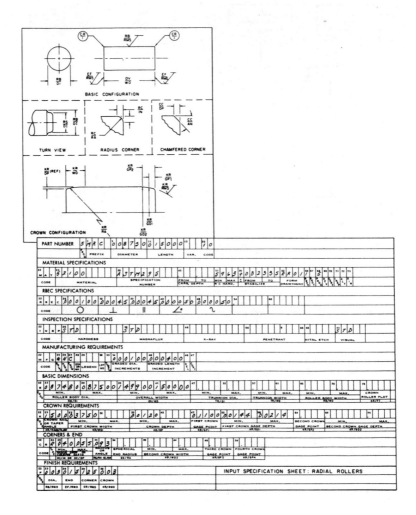

Fig. 13-9   Roller bearing input specification sheet

serve as a valuable input to the production scheduling information system. The output data stream may be collected on magnetic tape or used directly to update the machine schedule
master file located in auxiliary storage.

The automated manufacturing planning information system
outlined above overcomes the principal difficulties encountered

MFG. ORDER NUMBER	PART NUMBER	CUSTOMER AND OTHER DATA	QTY.	DATE	DUE DATE DWG.NO.	FORM NO.	LATEST ENG. REV. NO. DATE	PAGE NO.	X Y Z BEARING CO., INC. WEST END, NEW YORK
1234567	5HRC 008750015000, 10	ABC CORP.	1000	12,08,64	01,3	RR01		01	

BASIC MATERIAL	MATERIAL FORM	SPECIFICATION NO.	OUTSIDE DIA. MATL. / FINISH	INSIDE DIA. MATL. / FINISH	LENGTH MATL. / FINISH	UNIT QUANTITY	MATL. UNIT
52100	RD.BAR-C-DWN.	B&R QUALITY	00-895 / 00-875	. / .	. / .	01 500 00 3017	LBS

SEQ. NO.	WORK CTR.	OPERATION DESCRIPTION	DIM. CODE	IN PROCESS DIMEN. MINOR REF	MAX.	TOOL NAME	TOOL NUMBER	MACHINE SYMBOL	MACH. TIME	SET-UP TIME	CYCLE TIME	% ALT.
01	30 6	FORM AND CUTOFF 45 SEC. MC	RS DI / OV WD	0.883 / 1.515	0.888 / 1.520	FT-FORM-TL CAM-SET	13 1750 / 111A-801		1.900		0.266	14
02	30 0	SEPARATE CHIPS										
03	28 1	NIP PROJECTION								0.04	0.076	
04	28 2	DEBURR								0.02	0.091	
05	44 1	HARDEN PROCESS-10										
06	46 1	SANDBLAST PROCESS-1										
07	56 1	ROCKWELL HARDNESS INSPECT										
08	08 1	ROUGH GRIND OD 1 PASS	RB DI	0.8845	0.8850					0.14	0.058	
09	08 3	ROUGH GRIND END SURFACES 2 PASSES	OV WD	1.503	1.504	GARD.BUSH 37460 GARD.CARR 36323		864		0.80	0.198	
10	08 3	FINISH GRIND END SURFACES 1 PASS	OV WD	1.4998	1.5002	GARD.BUSH 37460 GARD.CARR 36323		864		1.76	0.099	
11	08 1	ROUGH GRIND OD 2 PASSES	RB DI	0.8765	0.8770					0.14	0.116	
12	56 1	MAGNAFLUX										
13	08 2	SEMI-FINISH GRIND OD 2 PASSES	RB DI	0.8751	0.8753					0.26	0.067	
14	08 9	FINISH GRIND OD 1 PASS	RB DI	0.8749	0.8750					0.15	0.075	
15	08 6	CROWN OD 3 PASSES 6 1/2DEG.	KR DP / KR WD	0.0012 / 0.375		CROWN CAM	67742				0.248	
16	56 1	FINAL INSPECTION										

Fig. 13-10   Routing sheet

in the manual MPIS. Because the entire decision-making process has been codified, the clerical portion of the production planning process may be transferred to the computer. Product routings will consistently use the best manufacturing methods. Equipment and technology improvements may be readily incorporated into the manufacturing planning process, resulting in the specification of the most current manufacturing techniques. Finally, the processing time for preparing production routings may be substantially improved through the use of automated manufacturing planning information systems. The benefits of faster processing will be improved information flows to production personnel and possibly the decrease of total manufacturing cycle time.

Although automated manufacturing information systems are not widely used in industry at the present time, the applicability of such concepts to a wide variety of manufacturing processes is unquestioned. Implementation in specific systems has been difficult and slow due to a lack of adequate hardware, software, and trained personnel. As other information systems in the production area become operational, however, the need for automated manufacturing planning information systems will become more apparent.

PRODUCTION SCHEDULING INFORMATION SYSTEMS

Once the production routing, the operation methods, and the time and cost standards have been established, production management must face the difficult task of organizing and allocating the resources to manufacture the finished product. The necessary raw materials and manpower must, of course, be available as required for the production activities. The required equipment and tooling must also be available before production can begin.

The basic objective of the production scheduling information system is to allocate the necessary resources as a function of time in order to produce the finished goods in the most efficient manner possible. Time is the critical factor in this allocation process and, in some respects, may also be considered a fragile, precious, and nonstoreable resource. Production time (manpower and equipment time) must be spent in such a way as to gain the greatest benefits for the firm.

There are several important secondary objectives that a well-designed production scheduling information system should meet. It should provide accurate and timely forecasts of expected delivery dates for finished goods. It must also permit labor force requirements in the foreseeable future to be ascertained before a labor shortage or surplus becomes acute. In some cases the production scheduling information system may even be designed to balance out work flows to provide relatively stable employment levels. It may also be used to forecast projected equipment utilization so that appropriate arrangements may be made to subcontract excess capacity or to contract for additional manufacturing capacity. Finally, it should advise production management well in advance of the expected work loads in each work center area so that they can make minor adjustments for smoother operations.

In many firms the production scheduling information system is not completely separate. Rather, its activities are performed as an adjunct to the production routing system or as an integral part of an integrated production planning and control system. In these cases the production scheduling function remains intact but the separate system identity may be lost or blurred.

There are many uncertainties to be considered in the scheduling of job shop production unit operations. The flow of customer orders and, hence, the production demands often fluctuate substantially. At times the work load may exceed the existing maximum work capacity of the production unit as determined by existing manpower levels, number of scheduled shifts, and machine capabilities. At other times the work load may not completely utilize the existing production capacity. In the short run it is usually not feasible to alter the rated maximum productive capabilities. On the other hand, changes in production demands over a period of time (several months to a year or more) require adjustments in rated production capacity.

Further complicating the production unit scheduling process are the day-to-day difficulties encountered in manufacturing operations. Machine breakdowns, rush orders, excessive scrap, employee absence, or failure to meet production standards inevitably occur in even the best-managed production organizations. These contingencies must also be considered in the production scheduling process.

The external and internal contingencies related above are usually resolved, at least partially, by adjusting the rated maximum production capacity downward to more realistic, pragmatic production capacity values. Although the exact adjustment factor will vary for each production operation, typical job shop operating capacity is about eighty percent of maximum rated capacity. Planning operations at the eighty percent level ordinarily provides the greatest operating efficiency and the most satisfactory flexibility.

The scheduling process develops the expected work loads for work centers or machines into the foreseeable future. The term *planning horizon* designates the time span over which operations are scheduled. For best results the planning horizon must be set well beyond the longest manufacturing time cycle expected. In this way schedules may always be established for new orders even when finished product delivery dates must be extended to handle production difficulties.

In connection with the planning horizon, the individual time units within the schedule must be defined. A frequently used device to define work days is the shop calendar shown in figure 13-11. Each regularly scheduled work day is assigned a number in sequence from 000 to 999. Shop calendar dates, which may be readily manipulated by computers, are very convenient means for designating particular dates in the schedule.

April						
Sunday	Monday	Tuesday	Wednesday	Thursday	Friday	Saturday
		341 1	342 2	343 3	344 4	5
6	345 7	346 8	347 9	348 10	349 11	12
13	350 14	351 15	352 16	353 17	354 18	19
20	351 21	352 22	353 23	354 24	355 25	26
27	356 28	357 29	358 30			

Fig. 13-11   Shop calendar

The remaining matter for consideration before discussing a typical production scheduling information system is the work center queue discipline. Rules for the determination of work center or machine loading sequence must be specified to provide an orderly method for allocating available production time. The simplest queue discipline to implement is first come, first served. Using this discipline, schedules through the various work centers are established as customer orders are received and their delivery dates are determined by summing the waiting time and production time for each work center.

As an example of the first-come, first-served queue discipline, let us suppose a new customer order is received that requires processing through five work centers as shown in table 13.1. The schedule for the order, as shown by the Gantt chart in figure 13-12, would then be:

Work center	Shop calendar date
WC 1	005
WC 2	008, 009, 010
WC 3	011, 012
WC 4	013
WC 5	019, 020, 021, 022

The order should be completed and ready for delivery on shop calendar date 022.

TABLE 13.1
Process Time Required for Five Work Centers

	Process Time Required (days)	Present Backlog (days)
WC 1	1	4
WC 2	3	7
WC 3	2	10
WC 4	1	8
WC 5	4	18

In actual practice, however, the scheduling process is usually a much more complicated affair. Important customers demand, and often receive, preferential consideration. Order shortages due to excessive scrap may require reruns to fill the backorders. Large customer orders must be split at times to expedite their processing through the production process. In all, many considerations must be taken into account to determine the most feasible work center loading schedule.

A frequently used solution to this dilemma is the use of order priorities. Algorithms that relate important variables such as promised delivery date, order size, customer rating, and similar items may be devised to establish an order priority rating. In turn, the priority rating is used to establish the order precedence relation.

The job shop scheduling process is normally performed immediately after the customer order is received. The hour-by-hour sequence decisions made just prior to processing an order through a production operation are known as dispatching. Depending on the circumstances, these decisions may be made by dispatchers in the production control department or by pro-

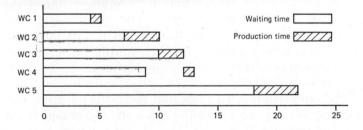

Fig. 13-12 Gantt chart

duction supervisors. Dispatching decisions are based on production conditions at the moment and thus are separate and distinct decision-making processes from scheduling. Production dispatching information systems may be designed to handle them.

The major input data stream to the production scheduling information system will be the new job orders containing the production routings. As we have seen, an automated production planning information system can prepare the routings for all new job orders automatically. The new routing list may therefore be captured as an output of the production planning information system. The second input data stream consists of jobs that have already been scheduled but must be rescheduled because of production difficulties. The input data for rescheduled job orders need contain only pertinent data, since the basic routing data is already present in the job order master file. The input data from these two data sources may be sorted to job order (major) and transaction code (minor) sequence to facilitate the first processing run.

The first processing run in the production scheduling information system performs two major tasks. First, the job order master file must be updated with the new job orders and other information on rescheduled jobs. The record access key for the job order master record file is, of course, the job order number. The job order master file is simply a collection of all open job orders in the shop. Although job order master records are created during this processing run, they will be updated and deleted upon completion by the production monitor information system.

The second task of the first processing run in the production scheduling information system is to compute an order priority rating for each job order entry. The queue discipline for allocating production time in this system is first come, first served within each priority rating. The priority rating must naturally be computed for each job order in order to establish a sequence before scheduling.

The output of the first processing run is the job order activity tape containing order priority ratings and the complete routing instructions for each order. The job order activity tape must be sorted to priority rating (major) and job order number (minor) sequence in order to schedule the high-priority orders before the low-priority ones.

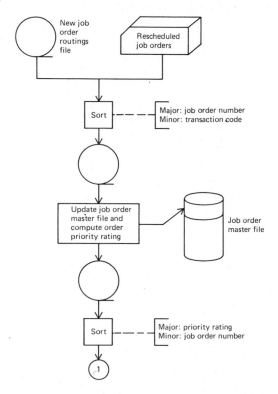

Fig. 13-13   Production scheduling information system

The second processing run in the production scheduling information system generates the schedules for each job order through each work center. The actual mechanics of the scheduling process follow the same allocation pattern discussed in the scheduling example above. The scheduled starting and completion dates are entered into the appropriate work center portions of the job order master file. In addition, the scheduled starting and completion dates for each job order are entered into the work center master file by shop calendar date. The work center master file thus contains the schedule of jobs to be processed by shop calendar date over the total planning horizon.

The only direct output from the second processing run is an activity listing of the new scheduled job orders. To locate

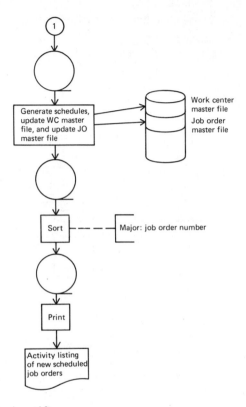

Fig. 13-13   (cont'd)

data about a particular job order, this report should be listed in job number sequence. Since the processing sequence was priority rating (major) and job order number (minor), the output data must be sorted to job order sequence. The printed activity listing will be useful primarily as an audit trail.

After updating, both the job order master file and the work center master file contain information that may be useful to management. Special report preparation runs may be performed on the job order master file and the work center master file as shown in figures 13-14 and 13-15. The principal reports generated by the report preparation runs are complete listings of all records in each master file (complete job order schedule list and complete work center load list) and reports for management use (critical schedule job order listing and work center management exception and summary report).

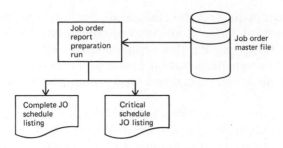

Fig. 13-14   Report preparation on the job order master file

The actual task performed by the production scheduling information system is largely clerical in nature and, considered alone, might be difficult to justify economically. However, considered as a vital link in an integrated production information system, the scheduling system assumes greater importance. The benefits gained from an integrated information system are frequently greater than the benefits gained from several independent ones.

PRODUCTION MONITOR INFORMATION SYSTEMS

Production managers at all levels of the organization are judged primarily by the efficiency of their organizational unit in processing job orders. While other factors, such as the practice of good human relations and the development of trained subordinates, are very important in the evaluation of managerial performance, they are important because they affect the productivity of the organizational unit in the long run (and often in the short run as well). Since the primary responsibility of the

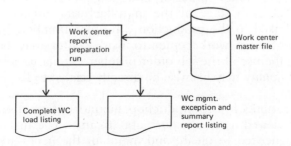

Fig. 13-15   Report preparation on the word center master file

production manager is the efficient production of goods and services, he must know at all times about the production-related activities taking place in his organizational unit. He must have sufficient current information about departmental accomplishments to plan, organize, direct, and control the production system.

The primary objective of the production monitor information system is to provide management with control over the production process from beginning to end. Once production job orders have been released to the shop floor, their progress must be followed until the orders have been completed. After job order completion, either in total or in part, the departmental performance against standards must be determined and presented to management for evaluation.

The secondary objectives of the production monitor information system are:

1. To accumulate the expenses for each job order at each work center for comparing these expenses to standard costs
2. To keep track of job order movements through the production process relative to initial or revised schedules
3. To follow the material quantities on each job order through the stages of production
4. To monitor product quality at appropriate points in the production process

Cost, time, quantity, and quality are the efficiency measures applied to the evaluation of production system performance.

The production job order number (work order number, customer order number, lot number, batch number, and so forth) is the principal means for identifying work units throughout the production process. Material, labor, and equipment charges at each stage of the manufacturing process may be readily linked to the production job order number. Job order movement from work center to work center may be traced through the use of the job order number. Similarly, job quantities and quality may likewise be directly related to the job order number.

The inputs to the production monitor information system may be viewed as two major data streams. The first contains the data needed to create and maintain the necessary master files. Job order and work center data may be generated by output from the production planning and scheduling information systems. Basic employee and departmental data must be entered as separate input data streams if required.

The second major input data stream is the record of production performance as generated by shop activity. These input transaction records list the actual performance on each job order by work center and contain such data items as work center number, performance time, quantities started and completed, and quality measures, where appropriate.

There are many different means for collecting data from the shop floor. Travel cards issued with the job order instructions may be completed by an employee for subsequent entry to the production monitor information system. However, when production data is gathered this way, there is usually a delay of a day or two before reports are available to production management. To get around this time lag, remote input terminals produced by several different manufacturers are becoming more widely used for collecting production data. The data, of course, is more current and with suitable safeguards input data accuracy may be quite good. In all likelihood, this method of production data capture will become much more widespread in the future.

Under ordinary circumstances there is a substantial time difference between creating the master files and reporting production activity. Since these two input data streams are readily separable in practice, the file creation programs are usually separate and distinct from the record updating programs. Figure 13-16 depicts the file creation program runs and figure 13-17

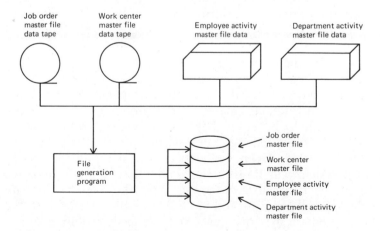

Fig. 13-16   File creation program runs

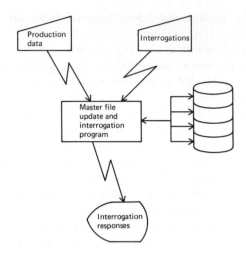

Fig. 13-17   Updating in the production monitor information system

depicts the updating operation.

The use of remote terminals for the input of production data, as shown in figure 13-17, eliminates the need for a sorting operation. The individual records update the master files immediately on entry into the system. Since production data entry into the system is sporadic, the computer operating control system must temporarily switch from the regular data-processing run, update the master files, and then return to the regular run. Switching from one program to another in rapid sequence is known as multiprogramming and is performed by the software (the computer operating control systems) supplied by computer manufacturers.

The sequential operating steps in multiprogrammed operations call for the current running program to check for input messages at regular frequent intervals. When the presence of an input message is noted, the computer operating control system issues instructions calling for the production monitor update program to be entered into core storage from auxiliary storage. The input message will then be processed and the master files updated. Upon completion, the computer operating control system will transfer the production monitor updating program back to auxiliary storage and the regular program operations will be resumed. The switch from and back to the regular program may take place only at specific points, known as the exit and entrance parameters respectively, in the regular program.

The production monitor information system normally uses several different master files for collecting data. As we have noted, the job order master file is the principal means for storing production planning data and accumulated production statistics. It contains descriptive job order data (heading data), routing data, and the operations schedule through each work center. The job order number, which must be present in all input data, is the access key for individual records.

As an adjunct of the job order master files, virtually all production monitor information systems also utilize work center master files. The purpose of these supporting files is to maintain scheduled and completed activity records on a work center basis for interrogation and subsequent analysis. The work center master file maintains the activity records as a function of shop calendar date or some other time measure. Essentially, the job order and work center master files contain the planning data (standards) against which the production performance will be compared.

Some production monitor information systems also use other master files to collect data for specific purposes. For example, employee activity master files may be used to collect employee job performance data on specific job orders. Planning and collecting data on this basis may be appropriate when incentive pay systems are being used or when employee performance must be related to product quality. Likewise, departmental activity master files may be used for collecting production data where the department contains several work centers and management deems this basis of data collection necessary.

The master files updating process in the production monitor information system is rather complex. When data from one or more input data streams is used to update two or more master files, this process is called multiple-entry record updating. The procedural aspects of multiple-entry record updating are similar to the double-entry method for maintaining accounting records. In the double-entry accounting method, a single business transaction provides both debit and credit entries to the accounting records, thus keeping the records in balance at all times.

Multiple-entry record updating in computerized information systems operates in the same fashion but serves a totally different purpose. When a single business transaction contains data relevant to several master files, the most efficient way for keeping all of the files current is to update all of them at the same time. This approach eliminates redundant processing of the same record and, at the same time, reduces the opportunity for the master files to get out of balance with each other.

The production monitor information system updating program is an example of multiple-entry record updating. The completion of a single production operation, for instance, contains the necessary data to update the job order master record, the work center master record, the employee activity master record (if used), and the department activity master record (if used). Updating all these master files is accomplished by including as an integral part of the transaction data the job order number (to access the job order master file), the work center number (to access the work center master file), the employee number (to access the employee activity master file), and the department number (to access the department activity master file). In some cases it may be feasible to update a master file indirectly with fewer input data elements. For example, if the work center master file contains the department number in the record heading, then the update program may reference this record field to find the access key for the department activity master file records.

The outputs from the production monitor information system may be prepared by stripping required information from the various master files. The most direct method of output preparation is to generate all of the reports based on each master file with a single processing operation. Since there are four separate master files in our example system, let us examine the possible outputs that may be prepared from each of them.

Figure 13-18 depicts a systems flowchart for the job order output preparation run. The weekly job order activity report lists all the activity on each job during the preceding week. The report includes information such as work centers performing the operations, incurred expenses, actual processing times versus the standard time allowance, quantities processed, and quality measurements performed. As many of the standard efficiency measures as possible should be used to define the actual job order efficiency fully. In addition, a weekly job order management exception report may be prepared listing those job orders that failed to meet one or more established criteria. A completed job order cost tape may be prepared that contains

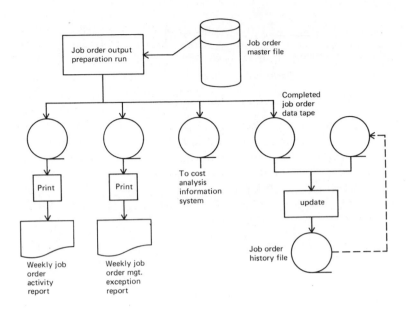

Fig. 13-18   Job order output preparation run

all of the incurred expenses for each completed job order; it is forwarded to the cost analysis information system. Finally, the selected historical data from each completed job order may be output and combined with the job order history file. As may be required from time to time, the job order history file tape may be processed to prepare special analytical reports for management.

The outputs that may be generated from the work center master file are shown in figure 13-19. The work center backlog report lists the job orders (and their standard processing times) that await processing through each work center. This report may be quite useful to management for determining overload conditions as well as determining under-utilization of productive capacity. This report may also be quite helpful in making dispatching decisions during the forthcoming periods. The weekly work center activity report simply presents all of the work center activities during the preceding week in chronological sequence. The work center history tape for the current week updates the accumulated work center history file tape.

In addition to the primary reports above, the employee activity master file may prepare an output tape that lists the activity of each employee for the payroll information system. Like-

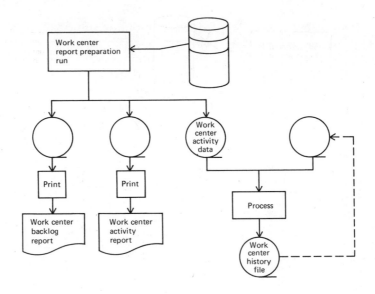

Fig. 13-19   Outputs generated from the work center master file

wise, the department activity master file contains the data necessary to prepare a department activity summary report.

As shown in figure 13-17, this particular computer system configuration has remote terminal interrogation capabilities. Simply by entering the job order number or work center number and the proper interrogation instructions, data from either file may be accessed and flashed on a cathode ray tube (CRT) screen. Instantaneous record access is quite helpful in answering customer inquiries about particular orders and for making quick dispatching decisions.

The measurement of production monitor information system efficiency is, of course, based on the standard efficiency measures: cost, time, quantity, and quality. There are economic tradeoffs among all of these efficiency measures. Shop floor remote terminals connected to a computer with auxiliary storage is a very time-efficient means for updating production records. On the other hand, the equipment cost will be relatively high. Likewise, shop floor input data accuracy may be improved (assuming adequate employee instruction) only by more complex editing programs and more expensive data input equipment. Only a thorough cost/benefit analysis can determine the proper balance among these factors to obtain the highest overall efficiency.

The effectiveness of production monitor information systems depends in part on well-functioning production routing and production scheduling information systems. Thorough, complete, and accurate production work order plans must be available to direct production personnel and provide the basic standards for measuring their performance. If then, performance is reported to production management in a timely, comprehensible form, the production/operation system may be readily controlled.

CONCLUSION

Increasing competition in our free enterprise economy is creating increased emphasis on developing efficient and effective production systems. To be successful, manufacturing firms must strive by all possible means to improve the performance of their operations. Production managers need to understand their operations better and to know what is happening at all times in their organizations.

Production information systems may be designed that will substantially assist the production manager to plan production operations, organize the needed resources, direct operations, and control performance. Moreover, such systems may increase the production manager's understanding of the important relations within the production process.

When the information that is potentially available to the production manager with a well-constructed production information system is used intelligently, the efficiency of the managerial decision-making process may be substantially improved. In like manner, the effectiveness of the resulting decisions will be enhanced when the production manager has the required information at hand. Good decisions do, indeed, depend on good information.

CASE STUDY: THE PENINSULA TELEPHONE COMPANY

The Peninsula Telephone Company maintains a fleet of about sixty automobiles for use by upper-level managers and employees on company business. At the present time approximately half of the autos have been assigned more or less permanently to executives and the remainder are used by employees.

Mr. Dyer is the auto pool department manager. The service

and repair section of the auto pool department services the cars (for gas, oil, and so forth), performs preventive maintenance, and makes minor repairs. The office section of the department performs the clerical activities in connection with assigning cars and maintaining records.

The present procedure for the allocation and control of autos is:

1. The original requestor (executive or employee) prepares a trip request (TR) listing name, department, work order or job authorization number, required dates, purpose of the trip(s), and estimated mileage. The TR is a two-part form.

2. The TR is forwarded to the appropriate manager for authorization. If approved, the TR is sent to the auto pool department. Dissapproved TRs are returned to the originator.

3. Upon receipt of the approved TRs by the auto pool department, the availability of cars on the specified date(s) is checked on a large Gantt chart.

   A. If a car is available, an entry is made in the trip ticket journal. A trip ticket number is then assigned (in chronological sequence) and entered on the Gantt chart. The original of the TR is filed in the open trip ticket file (in trip ticket number sequence), and the first copy is returned to the originator with a confirmation note.

   B. If the availability of a car is doubtful, an appropriate entry is made in the trip ticket journal. A trip ticket number is assigned and entered on the Gantt chart with a "tentative" notation. The original of the TR is filed in the open trip ticket file, and the first copy is returned to the originator with a standby notation. The originator must check on a car's availability the day before he wants it.

   C. If no auto is available, the original and first copy of the TR are returned to the originator with an "auto-unavailable" notation.

4. The original requestor presents the validated TT when he picks up the auto. The attendant prepares an auto use ticket with the initial mileage, the TT number, the auto number, and the pickup time. The AU ticket and the TT are maintained by the attendant until the car is returned.

5. When the car is returned, the mileage is again checked and

noted on the AU ticket along with the return time. After the ticket is completed, it is turned over to the auto pool department clerks and selected data from it is entered in the auto log (a file on the use of each car by auto number). The AU ticket is then combined with its copy in the open TT file; both copies are then transferred to the closed TT file.

6. Monthly, an auto usage transmittal form containing selected data from each TT set in the closed TT file is prepared and sent to accounting for expense distribution. This data includes user name, department, work order number, and computed charges (mileage × standard mileage expense).

7. Quarterly, the auto pool clerks compute and review the accumulated expenses and the total mileage for each auto. New standard mileage charges are prepared using the formula

$$\frac{\text{Total accumulated expenses for all autos}}{\text{Total mileage for all autos}} = \frac{\text{Standard mileage}}{\text{charge}}$$

The new standard mileage charge, if in line with previous values, is then used to compute mileage charges during the following quarter. If not, send it to the auto pool manager for disposition.

Prepare a flowchart for the manual trip ticket information system.

Design a computerized TT information system. (Assume the project is economically feasible and adequate computer facilities are available.)

List and briefly discuss the system outputs (purpose, frequency, and general content) that should be helpful in administering the auto pool department.

Briefly discuss the necessary data files (structure, record key, and general content) and their functional roles in the operation of the TT information system.

14

MARKETING INFORMATION SYSTEMS

The marketing function plays a vital role in determining relative success for all business firms. The marketing branch for the typical business firm is charged with the responsibility for generating sales to customers at prices that will give the business firm an adequate profit margin. To meet this responsibility, marketing management typically exercises a substantial degree of control over the price of the finished goods, the types of product promotion that will be used, the channels of distribution through which the products will move, and the composition of the product line that the business firm will offer. The term *marketing mix* designates the marketing policies applied in each of these responsibility areas. The total impact of the marketing mix is reflected in the sales revenue generated by the marketing system.

THE MARKETING SYSTEM

The marketing system is a dynamic system that bridges the interface between the business firm and its customers. Finished goods and services must be transformed into the fulfilled requirements of customers. The principal purpose of this system is to facilitate the flow of goods and services from the producer to the consumer. A dynamic system model of the marketing system is shown in figure 14-1.

The finished goods and/or the available services are shown as inputs on the left-hand side of the diagram. In retail and wholesale merchandising firms, the finished goods are normally in the firm's possession at the time of sale. Manufacturing firms

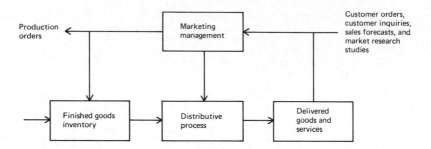

Fig. 14-1   Dynamic system model of the marketing system

more typically produce finished goods per individual customer order or maintain limited stocks of standard products.

The processor may be described as an amorphous interface between the marketing branch of the firm and the prospective purchasers. The processor includes the promotional means by which potential customers are made aware of the firm's goods and services; thus it also consists of actual contact with sales representatives and the channels of distribution through which the goods and services move.

The outputs of the marketing system are the goods to which the customer has taken legal title or services for which he has assumed a financial liability. To thrive, the business firm must both satisfy its present customers and continue to find new ones with unsatisfied needs.

The controller in the marketing system is both a very critical and a very complex system element. One of the major informational streams to the controller is, of course, the data records of customer sales. However, the marketing manager also has other information input streams that may be as important as sales data. Customer inquiries about products and services not currently offered as standard products may reveal future product trends. Forecasts developed by sales personnel will also provide valuable input information about sales trends in various product lines as well as estimates of future sales revenues. Background data on the expected future condition of the economy is also a valuable input to the marketing manager. Finally, the activities of marketing research and/or operations research organizational units may provide valuable studies with regard to potential sales in specific marketing areas.

The marketing manager must assimilate these input information streams and determine the marketing policies (marketing mix) that appear most likely to be successful in the foreseeable future. The marketing manager will also direct the flow of finished goods into the channels of distribution. The control of inputs may be direct, as by releasing shipping orders for finished goods inventory, or indirect, as by issuing sales orders to the production system.

Compared to the other subsystems within the firm, the marketing subsystem (system) behaves much more as an open system than any of the others. Forces or trends in the business environment quite often are more important in the marketing manager's decision making than is current product sales activity. In addition, the marketing manager may not be able to exercise reasonable control over the quantity and quality of the finished-goods inputs to the marketing system. Thus external forces and internal conditions have a great influence on the behavior of the marketing system, creating a more open system than is found in other portions of the firm.

The standard measures of efficiency applied to the firm's other subsystems are equally applicable to the marketing system. The measure of cost efficiency is of major importance. Marketing costs include not only the direct sales expenses (sales commissions, sales expense accounts, sales office overhead, and similar costs) but also such items as promotion (advertising) expenses, discounts, price adjustments for merchandise of substandard quality, customer returns, and the expenses of the market research group. Individual expense items or the sum of all marketing expense items may be compared to the total sales revenue to develop measures of relative cost efficiency.

In recent years the time efficiency of the market system has become an important factor. In some instances, such as airline ticket sales, time is the critical element for customer inquiries, order receipts, and acknowledgements. In other cases, such as catalog sales, the time span between the customer order receipt (by telephone or mail) and the shipping order release is critical. Increasing organization size, all other things being equal, has a tendency to reduce time efficiency in market system operation. The maintenance of satisfactory time efficiency levels is, therefore, also a major concern in large business firms.

Quantity measures of marketing system efficiency are ordinarily determined by such measures as number of units sold, number of customer orders processed, or sales revenue generated. Other aspects of marketing system quantity efficiency are also important to marketing management. The level and magnitude of customer returns for various reasons as well as price adjustments to accomodate customer dissatisfaction is very important. There is usually an economic trade-off between the total quantity of merchandise sold and the quantities returned by customers. When there are no customer returns or complaints, one or several of the following conditions may be present: product quality is too high, product packaging is too good, product price is set too low, or the customers' actual product requirements are not properly understood. Under normal business conditions, maximum profitability is usually achieved when some customer returns or adjustments must be made but the total amount is relatively small.

The quality measure of marketing systems efficiency is more nebulous and difficult to define. One important aspect of quality efficiency is the generation of company reputation and product image. The character of a business firm is, to a certain extent, reflected by the quality of its promotional effort and the loyalty of its customers. Although these aspects of quality efficiency are very difficult to quantify in a meaningful way, they are nevertheless very important in marketing system operation.

The effectiveness of the marketing system may be evaluated by noting the degree to which it is generating sales relative to the total demand of the product market. Share of the market is perhaps the best single indicator of marketing system effectiveness. Product leadership is also an important, although less tangible, measure of effectiveness. In the final analysis, marketing system effectiveness is most often evaluated by noting sales revenue trends over an extended time.

The operating information system portion of the market information system is most concerned with customer order receipt and acknowledgement, the maintenance of credit data, the transmission of customer order requirements to production or preparation of shipping order releases, the preparation of shipping papers (bills of lading, packing slips, and so forth), and the maintenance of shipping records. Invoice preparation may be handled by the marketing information system or, alternatively, by the accounts receivable section of the finance system. When the transaction volume becomes large, computerized data-processing systems offer significant efficiency advantages.

The management information system portion of the marketing information system must extract meaningful information from the data within the files for presentation to management. Activity reports, in either complete or summary form, of customer order receipts and shipments made are usually required. Status reports of open customer orders, orders in production, backorders, or orders awaiting shipment are usually quite useful to marketing management. Management exception reports are very important in calling unusual conditions to the attention of marketing managers before crises arise. Analytical reports derived from historical data may be invaluable to management by pointing out important but otherwise unknowable relations and trends within the marketing system. The planning, operation, and control of the marketing system demands well-conceived, well-designed, and well-implemented information systems for efficient and effective operation.

ORDER COLLECTION AND TRANSMISSION INFORMATION SYSTEMS

Passenger Airline Reservation System—PARS

One of the most important functions marketing information systems perform is collecting and transmitting customer orders from their point of origin to the central office of the firm. Historically, the customer order process has been performed by sales representatives who have relayed customer orders to company headquarters, by receipt of customer orders through the mail, and by telephone orders. These methods are still commonly used for collecting and transmitting many types of customer orders and adequately serve the needs of many business firms.

There are, however, a large number of situations today for which the conventional order collection and transmission process is totally inadequate. Many customers have grown accustomed to prompt service and become irritated when they must wait for an extended period of time for confirmation of their orders. Moreover, the conventional methods of order collection and transmission may well result in under-utilization of plant and equipment through ineffective communication. For these reasons computer-based order collection and transmission information systems have become a necessity for certain firms that operate in dynamic environments.

The major airlines are an excellent example of the need for rapid, accurate communications between the firm and the customer. Prospective passengers need to know flight schedule information, air fares, and the availability of seats on particular flights without an inconvenient wait. The airlines, in turn, must have this information immediately available lest they miss the opportunity for ticket sales or overbook a flight. In this respect the airlines have a very real problem. The difference between operating losses and significant profits is usually a few percentage points in the seat occupancy rate or "load factor." Even a small overall improvement in load factor will increase profits substantially.

The need for a real-time passenger airline reservation system became critical for the major airlines early in the 1960s. The SABRE system (an acronym developed from the original title of the project, Semi-Automatic Business Environment Research) was developed by IBM for American Airlines at that time. The original SABRE system has since been modified and developed extensively. Today the system is known as PARS (Passenger Airline Reservation System) and is used by most of the major airlines.

The simplified systems flowchart for PARS, shown in figures 14-2 and 14-3, has two primary data input streams. The first is the primary data base records for collecting and maintaining passenger reservations. It is composed of the basic records for all of the scheduled flights, identified by flight number and date, during the coming year. Within the record heading are such data items as flight origin, intermediate stops, and destination with their corresponding arrival and departure times, air fare schedules, number of first-class and tourist seats available, and other pertinent data. These major input data records create

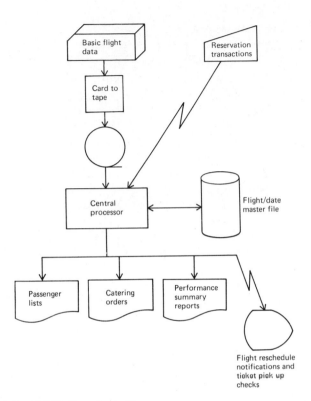

Fig. 14-2   PARS flowchart (1)

corresponding major records in direct-access storage for each scheduled flight between two points for the coming year. In addition to the record heading data, each of these major records located in auxiliary storage has record space reserved for the names of all passengers as well as for special passenger data.

The second major data input stream is the passenger reservation transactions that originate in the airline's sales offices. Each sales office has one or more remote input/output terminals connected online through a data transmission network to the computers at reservation headquarters. Reservation inquiries, air fare quotations, new reservations, reservation changes or cancellations, and confirmations may all be entered through the remote I/O terminal. The daily PARS transaction volume for a major airline may be as high as 90,000 telephone calls, 35,000 requests for fare quotations, 45,000 passenger reservations, 35,000 queries to and from other airlines, and 25,000 ticket sales.

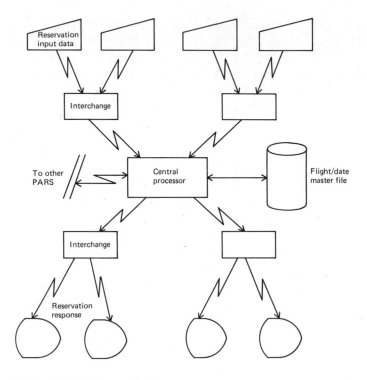

Fig. 14-3   PARS flowchart (2)

The typical input activity transaction sequence is initiated when passengers contact sales agents and ask for space on a particular flight on a certain date. The sales agent keys the proper data into the special remote I/O terminal. If space is available on the requested flight, there will be an immediate response from the computer to the remote I/O terminal indicating that such space is available and is temporarily being held pending completion of the sales transaction. If the flight has been sold out, this condition will also be flashed back to the remote I/O terminal. The sales agent, after discussion with the customer, may reserve the seat(s) by pressing the reservation key on the I/O terminal. The transaction is not completed, however, until the sales agent enters certain required data about the passenger: name, number of seats, accomodation class (first-class or tourist), who made the reservation, where the passenger can be reached, when the reservations will be picked up, and any special passenger requests such as wheelchairs or rental cars. All of this data is entered into the passenger list section of the flight/day master record located in auxiliary storage. The complex PARS operating programs have been designed to conduct rather extensive dialogue with the customer to make certain the input messages are complete and all transaction options have been examined.

Input messages from the remote I/O terminals are sent to a local data interchange system, which concentrates the input messages and holds them for a split second before they are relayed over leased telephone lines to the central data-processing facility. Upon receipt at the central computer facilities, the input messages are processed on a large-scale computer system. Response messages are relayed back to the remote I/O terminal in a reverse manner.

Because the operation of the order collection and transmission system is so important to the airlines, two computers are available for processing the input messages. Only one computer at a time is actually required for processing, however. A second computer is on standby to pick up data-processing operations in the event that the first malfunctions. The second computer, in the meantime, automatically monitors the first computer's operations while processing data for the other information systems in the airline. In this way, a malfunction in the airline reservation system may be noted immediately and the switchover in operations may be accomplished without any time loss. Both central computers may, of course, locate and update all master file records in the large-scale direct access storage devices.

The passenger airline reservation system is much more than a giant bookkeeping operation. The data contained in the direct-access files has many other important uses. The following system outputs are among the most important produced by PARS:

Passenger Reservation Requests to Other Airlines

Since many passenger itineraries involve flights on other airlines, an important requirement for all passenger airline reservation systems is the ability to interface with the PARS of other carriers. In this way a passenger request that involves other scheduled airlines may be handled with a single inquiry. This feat is accomplished by entering the inquiry message to a data interchange for the second passenger airline reservation system. Responses are relayed back to the original PARS and thence to the customer. In effect, all of the passenger airline reservation systems for the major scheduled airlines make up one huge airline reservation system.

Customer Notification of Schedule Changes   From time to time flight schedule adjustments must be made to accommodate unusual conditions. When this occurs, the passenger records within each flight/date record may be accessed to provide the necessary information for contacting the customer. Customer contact must, of course, be conducted by reservation clerks using the telephone.

Ticket Pick-Up Check   At the time airline reservations are made, the customer will be asked to state the time and place for ticket pick-up. When that time has passed, the customer will be called to verify his flight plans. In this way, the airlines can identify many of the "no-shows" that would reduce the load factor on the flight. This followup procedure does not eliminate the no-show problem, but does reduce it substantially.

Passenger Lists   Shortly before departure, the flight/date master records may be accessed to prepare passenger boarding lists. These lists may then be used at the boarding gate to determine precisely which passengers have boarded the flight. Similarly, passenger arrival lists may be prepared to identify the deplaning passengers at each scheduled stop. The flight crew also usually has a copy of the passenger list to verify passengers' travel plans during the flight.

Catering Orders   Food and beverages are served on many flights. The flight/date master record contains the number of passengers by accommodation class and, hence, the number of meals that must be prepared and an indication of the beverages that will be needed. This information is submitted to the caterers in time for adequate quantities of food and beverages to be delivered to the flight.

Operating Performance Reports   Summary operating reports are most important to airline managers for determining the airline system's operating efficiency. The flight/date master file contains basic data about the actual seat utilization and total air fares earned. When this data is combined with actual versus planned departure and arrival times, it is possible to determine the quantity, time, and cost efficiencies of the airline system for each leg in every scheduled flight. Airline management may then be advised very quickly of the overall system efficiency by flight leg, flight number, type of aircraft, flight crew, and date. These reports may also be forwarded to central flight operations to maintain the current status of all aircraft within the airline system. Central flight operations must have this information to maintain control over the aircraft in the airline system as well as for background data when emergency rescheduling must be done.

Load Factor Trend Analysis   These analytical reports are valuable management information inputs for planning future flight operations. Analyzing load factor data enables airline management to identify unprofitable routes as well as those routes for which additional airline service may be advisable. Actually this information is only one of many possible flight analysis reports that may be generated to assist managerial planning efforts.

As we have seen, the passenger airline reservation system is vital for the operation of modern scheduled airlines. Not only does PARS expedite the reservations process and increase the load factor by reducing the number of no-shows, but it also provides important information for many associated activities the airlines perform. The passenger airline reservation system has so successfully met its basic objectives that few of the major airlines could function today without it.

CREDIT AUTHORIZATION INFORMATION SYSTEMS

BankAmericard Service Exchange—BASE

Consumer credit sales, through the use of the ubiquitous credit card, have increased at an enormous rate during the past decade. The major oil companies introduced the credit card concept and were quickly followed by American Express, Diners Club, and Carte Blanche. In the past several years banks have entered the credit card field and have provided instant credit for the purchase of many consumer goods and services. National BankAmericard,

Inc. and Mastercharge, Inc. pioneered this area and are the most widely known bank-associated credit card firms. The credit authorization system discussed in the following pages is the Bank-Americard Service Exchange—BASE.

The use of credit cards to purchase consumer goods and services continues to increase each year. Retailers have embraced credit card purchasing because it increases total sales volume (or at least maintains sales volume in the face of increasing competition) and increases their cash flow by eliminating the need to carry customer charge accounts. Consumers like credit card purchasing because it gives them wider access to credit and permits better financial management. Needless to say, the banks have encouraged credit card use to use their financial resources more profitably. In all, credit card usage provides a very desirable service for a very nominal cost.

This change in consumer purchasing habits has been made possible by the introduction of computerized data-processing systems. Computers are, of course, admirably suited for processing huge quantities of transactions at a very low cost per transaction and with a high degree of accuracy. A major oil company, for example, may have several million active credit card accounts in a particular geographic region. If we assume an average of five sales transactions per month per credit card, the computer system must be able to process over ten million separate sales transactions each month. In addition, customer statements must be prepared monthly and payments must be credited to each account as received. All in all, the vast amount of data processing required to sustain a major credit card operation is feasible only with computerized operations.

The principal objective of a credit authorization information system is to control the use of credit by credit card holders. Credit control is administered by a pre-action control process. Whenever a credit card customer wishes to make a purchase exceeding the floor limit, credit approval must be obtained from the issuing bank that has the customer's account. Ordinarily BankAmericard member banks will not authorize credit purchases when any of the following conditions exist:

1. The credit card has been reported as lost or stolen
2. The purchase would exceed the customer's established credit limit
3. The customer's account is delinquent beyond a certain period

4. The customer's account has become strangely active (an inordinate amount of charges within a predetermined period, for example)

Credit approval is automatically granted when no negative conditions exist.

The development of a sound data base is a prime requirement for all associated credit card information systems. The credit authorization information system is dependent on a well-developed, readily accessible data base to determine the condition of the customers' accounts. So also are the account posting, billing, and payment information systems. Adequate and readily available data for input to management information systems also depends on a sound data base.

The development of the data base for each customer account is usually begun by submitting a rather detailed customer background data sheet to the member bank. The completed credit application form is carefully screened by credit investigators to determine the potential customer's quality. Credit approval and the establishment of the credit limit are based on factors such as family income, number of dependents, degree of indebtedness, and previous credit history. If there is evidence that the applicant will be unable or unwilling to assume the inherent obligations of increased credit availability, then the application will be denied. The member bank maintains records of previous and present credit applications.

Selected data from the credit application form is the first input data stream for the creation of the data base. Each new input record creates a record in the active account master file that includes such data as name, address, social security number, credit limit, and other items of interest. The record key is a nine-digit account number assigned by the issuing bank to each credit card holder. It is preceded by a four-digit member bank identification number, which is assigned by National Bank-Americard, Inc.

The second major input data stream is the charges and payments (debits and credits) made by the credit card customer. This data stream is, of course, essential for maintaining the current status of each customer account. A systems flowchart depicting the creation and maintenance of the data base is shown in figure 14-4.

The credit authorization information system for BASE recognizes three separate credit approval situations:

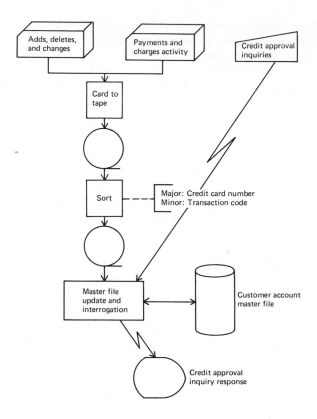

Fig. 14-4   Creating and maintaining the data base

1. Requests for credit approval from merchants within the member bank geographic territory during regular operating hours

2. Requests for credit approval from merchants in other parts of the country during regular operating hours

3. Requests for credit approval when the issuing bank is closed

The credit interrogation procedures and their associated systems are different for each of the situations listed above. Let us examine the actual systems in each case.

In the first situation above, the local merchant simply telephones the authorization clerk at the issuing bank for approval of the sales transaction. While the local merchant holds the line, the credit clerk at the issuing bank keys the customer identification number into a remote input/output terminal connected online to the bank's computer that contains the customer account master file. In turn, selected data from the customer's master account record is flashed on the CRT screen of the remote I/O terminal. The authorization clerk, using a programmed authorization code provided by the computer, relays credit approval or disapproval to the merchant. The entire process is totally contained within the issuing bank and is usually completed in just a few seconds.

When authorization inquiries must be made from outside the issuing bank area during operating hours, the process becomes more complex. The authorization process is begun by the merchant placing a telephone call to the authorization clerk at the nearest BankAmericard authorizing member. The clerk enters a predetermined prefix code, the issuing bank identification number, the nine-digit account number, the card expiration date, and the amount of charge in dollars and cents into a remote I/O terminal connected online to a computer at the regional BankAmericard concentrator (data collection center). BankAmericard has four regional concentrators covering the south, east coast, midwest, and west coast. In all cases the interrogatory message is forwarded to BASE Central on the west coast through the regional concentrator. The interrogatory message is then switched automatically to the appropriate regional concentrator and thence to the issuing member bank with the customer's account.

After the interrogatory message is received at the local member bank, the credit approval process is performed by the authorization clerk in the same way as outlined in the first case above. The response message is keyed into the BASE remote I/O terminal and relayed through the same communication channels back to the requesting member bank. The authorization clerk at the requesting bank may then advise the merchant whether credit approval has been granted or not. The credit approval process, even when performed in this way, is usually completed in about one minute.

The final credit approval situation (when the member bank is not open) employs a somewhat different approach for granting credit approvals. BASE Central maintains a data base consisting of three files: (1) an exception file listing lost, stolen, or other

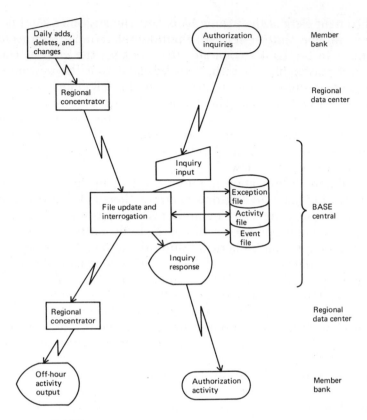

Fig. 14-5   BASE system

special credit card numbers together with a preprogrammed response that the card-issuing bank wants given whenever that card number is used, (2) an activity file listing predetermined parameters as supplied by member banks, and (3) an event file containing approved or disapproved sales transactions made during the off-operating hours of the member bank. The member banks have the capability, via terminal, to supply BASE Central with the adds, deletes, and changes to the exception file daily. They receive transactions at the beginning of daily operations from the event file for updating their customer account master files.

The actual credit authorization procedure during off-duty hours is begun by the merchant placing a call to the member bank. The call is automatically redirected to BASE Central on the west coast. An authorization operator at BASE Central responds to the diverted call that was placed by the merchant. The exception and activity files are checked to determine whether credit approval should be granted. If no negative conditions exist, approval is usually granted. Pertinent data about the sales transaction is then entered in the event file for transmission to the member bank on the following day. The authorization clerk at BASE Central relays the authorization approval or disapproval message back to the merchant. Total transaction time for off-hour credit approvals is ordinarily well under one minute.

In spite of the reasonably good inquiry response time, BASE still offers opportunities for further improvement. The interface between BASE Central and the member bank computers requires manual input of data from one system to the other. A direct linkage would permit data from one system to be input directly to the other. Point-of-sale credit card readers linked directly to the member bank computer would drastically reduce the quantity of authorization clerks now required and would automatically update the customer's account. Perhaps some day the ubiquitous credit card will become the means for complete personal financial management.

SALES ANALYSIS INFORMATION SYSTEMS

For the sales manager the analysis of sales data offers many intriguing possibilities for improving sales revenue, product mix, and market penetration as well as for increasing the overall profitability of the business firm. To the extent that sales managers understand who their customers are, the types of products their customers are seeking and purchasing, and the distribution of their customers within sales units or geographic territories, they will be able to appreciate more fully the actual market potential for their goods and services. This information, in turn, may be of immense value in determining market strategies and in developing promotion programs to improve sales performance. It is incumbent, therefore, on sales managers to make the best possible use of the sales data within the organization to improve the effectiveness of their marketing efforts and thereby improve the effectiveness of the business firm as a whole.

There are, of course, many sources of information to help the sales manager in planning marketing operations. Market research studies for new and improved products may yield valuable insights for improving the marketing system's operation. Published reports of economic forecasts and purchasing plans may also offer significant insights into the market's future behavior. Individual sales forecasts of the anticipated purchases for each potential customer, as prepared by the sales force, is still another means for determining future market performance. All of these sources may be of considerable value to the sales manager for planning future sales operations.

Marketing management also has an additional information source that may be used in combination with the approaches above to yield further information about future as well as present and past marketing performance. This information source is the accumulated data from past customer sales. As customers have placed their orders over an extended period, sales records have been created. These accumulated customer sales records offer the opportunity for analysis through the determination of customer importance (sales revenue), purchasing habits, type of products purchased, and their geographic distribution. For marketing management to make inadequate use of this information source is to overlook a powerful tool for improving marketing performance.

The basic data for a sales analysis information system may usually be found in two different data files within the marketing information system. The first of these data files is the customer order history file. As customer orders are received and filled (closed out), the record of the customer order may be transferred to the customer order history file. This file thus contains the basic data on all completed customer orders. Because its size will become quite large over a period of time, it is often advisable to create separate customer order history files for each major time period, such as three months, six months, or one year. This input data stream to the sales analysis information system is shown in figure 14-6.

The second major input data stream is the open customer order master file. The data in this file is, of course, created by the receipt of customer orders from the field. As each incoming customer order is received, basic data such as customer name, address, order receipt date, required delivery date, salesman, quantity of each product ordered, unit price, extended price, total price, terms, and destination, is entered into the corresponding customer order record in the open customer order

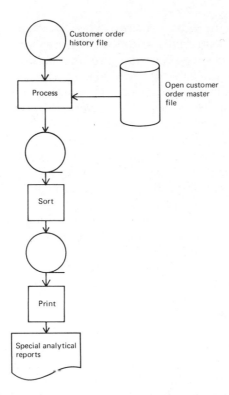

Fig. 14-6 Input data stream to the sales analysis information system

master file. The purpose of this data stream in the sales analysis information system is, naturally, to supply current marketing data for sales analysis.

The basic processing techniques for developing analytical sales reports are data extraction, sorting, and summarizing. First, the proper data items must be read from the two files. Next, sorting is required to prepare analytical reports in sequences other than customer order number. Finally, customer order data is often summarized to make the resulting reports more understandable and meaningful to marketing management. The usual processing sequence, therefore, is extraction of the required data from the two information streams, followed by sorting to arrange the data in the proper sequence, and completed by summarizing the data as illustrated in figure 14-6.

The individual programs to perform these processing operations may be prepared without undue difficulty by programmers employed by the business firm. This, incidentally, is the approach we have implicitly assumed to be used for the preparation of all data-processing programs presented up to this point in the book. However, this particular application, as well as many previously discussed applications, are also well suited for the use of certain proprietary programs furnished by specialized computer software firms.

Software is a generic term that may be defined as consisting of proprietary computer programs designed to improve computer operating efficiency, to improve program preparation efficiency, and to increase information systems effectiveness. Many software packages are produced by the computer manufacturers to assist users of their computers. Computer operating control systems are used to monitor computer operations and maximize throughput and are available for all commercial computer systems. Among the functions performed by such systems are the maintenance of processing run records, the effective integration of peripheral equipment (card readers, magnetic tape drives, direct-access storage devices, printers, and so forth), and the sequencing of program runs to minimize the transition time from one program to the next. Computer manufacturers also provide program compilers for various programming languages, such as FORTRAN, COBOL, PL/1 and RPG, to improve program preparation efficiency. The use of program compilers eliminates the need to write the program in object code and enables programmers to write programs much more quickly. Computer manufacturers also provide utility programs, such as general-purpose sorting programs, to extend the usefulnes of their products. The availability of manufacturer-produced software is usually a vital consideration in the selection of specific computer configurations.

There are also many independent software firms and program libraries from which programs are available. The software firms, for the most part, are engaged in the preparation and sale of general-purpose operating programs and special-purpose application programs. Program libraries primarily provide specialized application programs.

An excellent example of a general-purpose software package is the MARK IV file management system produced and marketed by Informatics, Inc., of Canoga Park, California. The MARK IV file management system was designed to make the computer directly available to the user by reducing program writing requirements to an absolute minimum. Rather than being a special-purpose application system, MARK IV is applications-independent and may be used for many different business data-processing applications.

The MARK IV file management system is composed of preprogrammed subroutine modules that perform all of the basic file maintenance tasks. The most important functions performed by MARK IV are:

1. Read data from punched cards, magnetic tapes, and auxiliary storage devices

2. Create files on punched cards, magnetic tapes, and auxiliary storage devices using either fixed- or variable-length record formats

3. Maintain files by performing record additions, changes, and deletions

4. Select records from magnetic tape and direct-access storage devices to meet specific information requirements

5. Extract prescribed data from selected records

6. Perform arithmetic computations for updating master files and preparing various output reports

7. Arrange output by sorting, sequencing, and grouping

8. Summarize data to as many levels as required for report preparation

9. Produce new files, parts of files, combinations of files, and audit files on magnetic tape, punched cards, and auxiliary storage devices

10. Print reports in attractive, understandable formats

Requests for special analytical reports are communicated to MARK IV through the use of an information request form. This form requires certain data to be entered in appropriate places in order to initiate report preparation. Once the information request data is input to the computer, the MARK IV system performs the remaining programming activities automatically. All programming effort to prepare special analytical reports is completely eliminated.

As is true for most proprietary software, the MARK IV file management system may be leased for periods of three months, six months, and one year, and is also available for direct purchase. The lease cost ranges from approximately $500 to $1500 per month depending on the computer system configuration and other factors. The MARK IV system, like many other proprietary software systems, is supported by field systems engineers who make regular visits to the software users. The lease agreement also provides for the MARK IV system to be updated as computer hardware and manufacturer software is augmented and improved. In addition, Informatics, Inc., sponsors an association of MARK IV users called the "IV League" to exchange system information among the users. Thus the MARK IV file management system, in common with many other proprietary systems, is not only produced but is also completely serviced by the software firm.

The number of different data combinations and sequences in which sales analysis reports may be prepared are quite numerous. However, there are several broad information areas for which analytical reports may be especially valuable. Analytical reports that emphasize customer data are among the most interesting to sales management. The basic purpose of customer data analytical reports is to gain a better understanding of the customer's relative importance to the business firm and his purchasing habits. Customer activity may be examined from several different perspectives simply by changing the sort sequence for the customer files. For example, the customer list may be sorted in descending sequence according to such criteria as total sales revenue during a preceding period, mean sales revenue per customer order, and mean order frequency. These reports may be made still more meaningful by categorizing data within the major sorting sequence. While sorting the customer lists by total sales revenue over the preceding year, for instance, the sales revenue by month for the preceding year may also be included in the report. The resulting report not only provides sales management with an indication of the customer's relative importance with regard to total sales revenue but also provides insights about recent trends in customer purchasing activity.

Product line analysis offers another valuable perspective for evaluating sales activity. The principal classification means for these reports is product line classification data. Examining sales data by items within product line readily distinguishes the slow-moving or low-revenue-producing items from the fast-moving or high-revenue-producing items in each product line. Further, the total contributions of the various product lines may be compared to each other to evaluate their relative importance to the firm. Using product line data, the sales manager may consider product items or product lines for increased sales emphasis, or, conversely, product items or lines for possible deletion.

A final area of particular interest to sales management is the performance of sales units within the organization. If sales forecast data is included in the customer order file records or entered as a separate data input to the sales analysis information system, the relative performance of individual salesmen, sales offices, or geographic regions may be easily determined. This type of analysis is especially important in evaluating individual and group sales performance.

There are, of course, many other classification means by which sales activity may be examined. Sales management, if they are truly aware of the potential information available through the analysis of sales activity, can raise many penetrating questions about the efficiency and effectiveness of the marketing system. The answers to these questions can provide important guidelines for improving sales performance.

CONCLUSION

Marketing information systems do not have as many separate functions to perform as financial information systems do; neither do they have as much systems design complexity as inventory information systems. Their outstanding characteristic is the great emphasis placed on response time and processing speed as opposed to the other information systems we have examined previously. The hardware and software difficulties encountered in large-scale communication networks has further complicated the design and installation of marketing information systems.

The rewards gained from efficient, functional marketing information systems, however, have justified and amply rewarded the effort and expense in most instances. The increase in organization size and geographic dispersion is a modern reality. Through the development and implementation of computerized marketing information systems, organizational size and dispersion problems may be overcome to the ultimate benefit of all consumers.

MOTEL RESERVATION SYSTEM PROJECT

There are several national motel chains (Holiday Inn, Ramada, Quality Courts, Howard Johnson, Sheraton, and so forth) that provide central reservation service for the entire motel chain. Visit a local unit and obtain the answers to the following questions:

1. How are requests for reservations at other locations usually obtained?
2. What reservation data is required for input to the reservation system?
3. What happens if pertinent input data is omitted?
4. How are reservation requests transmitted to the central reservation computer facility?
5. Where is the central reservation computer facility located?
6. How does the central facility handle reservation inquiries and requests?
7. How and when does the local motel unit receive and process the reservation request?
8. How are "no-shows," both guaranteed and unguaranteed, handled by the local motel unit?
9. Is special reservation input data ever needed to update the central facility direct access files? If so, what are the data transaction types and when are they input?
10. Are daily or weekly occupancy reports required by the central computer facility?
11. Is the communication system used for other purposes such as ordering supplies? If so, what are they?
12. How are the system operating expenses prorated?
13. What are the major difficulties encountered in the operation of the reservation system?
14. What improvements in the design and operation of the reservation system would the manager like to have?
15. What is the local manager's personal evaluation of the present system's overall efficiency and effectiveness?

Prepare a flowchart of the existing reservation information system.

What are the principal input messages?

What are the principal output messages?

In what respects is this information system a management information system?

Give your personal evaluation of the cost, time, quantity, and quality efficiencies of the present system.

Give your personal evaluation of the effectiveness of the present system.

What changes and improvements in system design and operation would you recommend?

15

INTEGRATED INFORMATION SYSTEMS APPLICATIONS

INTEGRATED INFORMATION SYSTEMS

When business-oriented computer systems were first introduced during the 1950s, their data-processing prowess was held in great awe. Such reverence was due in large measure to the magical aura that surrounded computer technology. Great accomplishments were expected from these new intellectual monsters. If computers were, indeed, giant brains, then obviously they could be made to assimilate and retain all of an entire company's business data and use it on command to make decisions. However, this dream of a total information system faced many unseen obstacles.

The image of super-intelligence attributed to the computer began to disappear early in the 1960s. Computer designers, systems analysts, and data-processing managers quickly came to appreciate the magnitude of the total information systems task. Creating one huge information system that could take all business data inputs and rearrange them to provide any type of managerial information was recognized as a *theoretically* attainable ideal, subject to overcoming many practical difficulties.

First of all, there was the difficulty of obtaining adequate computer hardware to perform the total information systems task. Larger, more powerful, and faster computers would be needed to process the greatly expanded quantity of data. Vast quantities of direct-access storage capacity would have to be readily available to store the mass of raw data. Increased core storage would also be required to store the computer operating system programs as well as the regular operating programs. Further, remote terminal hardware and communication networks sufficient to service a total information system would have to be developed.

Software difficulties were just as numerous as hardware obstacles. Computer operating systems with multiprogramming capabilities were still not truly operational. Software to support manifold remote terminal system entry was under development. The program operating efficiency of the higher-level language compilers (FORTRAN, COBOL, and so forth) was still below user expectations. Each intervening hardware and software obstacle posed a separate problem to be met and overcome before the total information system could be anything more than a dream.

Simply because the ultimate in information systems design was unobtainable at the present, however, did not lead information systems designers to despair. Small, individual, compartmentalized information systems had become relatively common by the mid-1960s. Also by that time, many firms had implemented payroll, accounts receivable, purchasing, and inventory information systems. Professionals in data processing began to see the opportunity to begin linking different information systems together into organized networks. Although this objective was still short of the total information system ideal, the technology was rapidly becoming available to create operational integrated information systems.

An integrated information system consists of two or more information systems in which the outputs of one system become a portion of the inputs to the other. In the simplest case, the two information systems may be viewed as two subsystems connected in series. For example, one of the outputs from an accounts payable information system is the basic data for preparing checks (voucher data). This data is also needed, of course, as a primary input to the check-writing and reconciliation information system. If the data from the accounts receivable information system is placed in the proper format to be input to the check-writing system and the operation of the two systems is coordinated, the combined information systems become an integrated information system.

The complexity of an integrated information system may be increased by linking other information systems in series and/or in parallel to the existing integrated system. As the growth

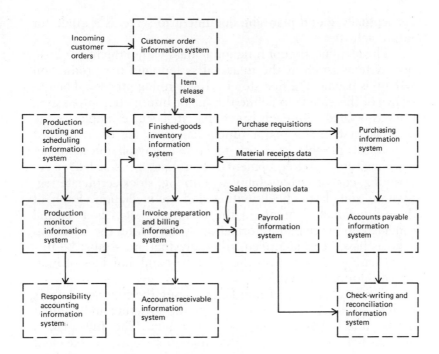

Fig. 15-1   An integrated information system

process continues, the integrated system takes on the appearance of a network with many data transfer cross-linkages between the individual subsystems. An example of an integrated information system network containing only the primary intersystem data flows is shown in figure 15-1.

The size and scope of integrated information systems require well-conceived, soundly planned development programs. In the early days, middle-level operating managers in the business firm often initiated information system projects to satisfy their particular needs with little regard for the information requirements of other parts of the organization. Naturally, this myopic approach resulted in poor use of information system resources and efforts. Integrated information systems simply cannot be developed by piecemeal efforts conducted by different individuals for diverse objectives. Substantial planning effort by operating managers and systems personnel is therefore an essential prerequisite for developing a successful integrated information system. Moreover, such planning effort should result in a conceptually sound planning document to serve as a guide for future activities.

The identification of functional areas within the major business systems (such as the financial system and the production system) is usually the first step in the planning process. The objective of this step is to define the major information processing tasks associated with each functional area. For example, in the financial system the major functional areas are often defined as accounts payable, accounts receivable, payroll and labor accounting, asset and equipment accounting, general ledger accounting, cost or responsibility accounting, stock certificate registration and, last, check writing and reconciliation. Each of these functional elements in the financial system is a natural candidate for a separate information system. After the functional areas have been identified, the individual areas must be further examined to establish the objectives and activities of individual information systems.

The boundaries and interfaces among the functional areas need to be closely examined to define the structure and content of the intersystemic information transfers. The information linkages between contiguous information systems are excellent checkpoints for determining data availability and compatibility. Certain data requirements for a particular information system may strongly influence the content of the original business transaction input and sometimes will even influence the mode of data input. Studying the information flows sometimes provides insights into the uses (as well as the sources) of managerial information.

One particularly important portion of the planning effort for an integrated information system is the design of the data base. Information systems designed for specific application areas often utilize only one or two specially structured data files (files with a single record access key containing only the data immediately required for the system's operation). The data base for an integrated information system cannot be designed with such a narrow perspective. Within the limits imposed by security regulations, the individual records in such a data base must be accessible by all parts of the integrated information system for updating, interrogation, and report preparation. The data base is an integral part of the entire integrated system, not simply one particular information system.

The universal nature of the data base in an integrated information system poses two separate system design difficulties: record accessibility and record completeness. The most straight-forward solution to the record accessibility problem is to require that all business transaction data inputs contain the record key(s) for all accessed files in the data base. This was the approach used in the production monitor information system (chapter 13) to update the production system-related data base files.

Indirect means may also be used to access various files within an integrated information system's data base. Abbreviated reference tables located in direct-access storage devices may be very appropriate for locating record access keys (table lookup) when the level of activity is significant. For example, a firm might maintain the accounts payable information system's open customer account file in customer number sequence. A cross-reference table of customer names with their corresponding numbers would provide a means for locating customer activity data without the customer number.

A variation of the table lookup approach—file chaining—may also be used to locate particular information in the data base without the appropriate record key. In this case a known record key for a certain file could be used to access a specified record. In turn, another data field within the specified record would become the record access key to a second file in the data base. The process may be repeated until the proper record has been accessed. Ordinarily this method of record access is only used for special file interrogations since it is inefficient.

The final means for locating information when incomplete data has been input into the information system is the item-structure file. This particular application was discussed at length in the bill of materials information system in chapter 12. The item-structure file method is very useful for establishing separate structural patterns in a single data file. The item-structure file approach has been used to define organizational relations (assignments) in personnel information systems and due dates for accounts payable vouchers. When properly used, item-structure files can add new dimensions to the data base.

The record completeness problem may only be solved by having each file in the data base contain all of the data items needed both now and in the future. However, the requirement that each record contain all of the data associated with it may easily lead to rather lengthy records. A common technique for handling this difficulty is to segment records, separating certain broad classes of data within particular records and storing them in other locations. Another commonly used technique when total record length varies is to use variable-length records in the data file. Regardless of the record-length solution used, data in integrated information systems must be carefully examined to make certain all necessary present and future data is included in the record layout design.

Hardware considerations figure prominently in the design of integrated information systems. Since the implementation program is normally accomplished in a series of steps as individual information systems are added to the integrated information system, the hardware requirements also increase stepwise. However, data-processing capacity increases must precede the implementation of each additional information system. Thus hardware specifications and equipment orders must be prepared well in advance of the planned DP increases.

The implementation of integrated information systems should follow the old adage—plan big; implement small. The most frequent development and implementation pattern is to design, install, and thoroughly debug each information system before proceeding to the next one. By gradually working through the entire integrated information system network and introducing changes to only one system at a time, the integrated system may be implemented with minimum difficulty and, in all probability, in the shortest possible time. Further, a policy of implementing only contiguous information systems provides an early opportunity to check intersystemic data transfer for possible transmission difficulties.

Both efficiency and effectiveness benefits normally follow the implementation of fully integrated information systems. Total operating cost is usually reduced by eliminating the preparation and entry of redundant data, consolidating data files, and eliminating marginal value reports. Since remote input/output terminals are often incorporated into integrated information systems design and data bases must be established for ready access, the overall time efficiency of integrated information system operation is usually good. Data accuracy and reliability also tend to be better because more attention has been devoted to the analysis and design of the data collection process. With regard to systems effectiveness, the integrated information system is usually far superior to disjointed individual systems.

Such integrated systems can supply management with more complete and more reliable information for determining the past, present, and future conditions of their operating systems. The efficiency and effectiveness of managerial decision-making thus becomes a more direct function of the manager's personal competence.

POINT-OF-SALE INFORMATION SYSTEMS (SEARS, ROEBUCK AND COMPANY)

Sears, Roebuck and Company is the world's largest retailer with annual sales in 1972 of about eleven billion dollars. It is almost five times as large as its nearest competitor, the J. C. Penney Company. Sears offers consumers over 150,000 different items through some 30,500 stores and other outlets. To support their vast retail effort, Sears relies on more than 16,000 suppliers for merchandise. In addition to their preeminence in retail merchandising, Sears, through its Allstate group of companies, is the second largest insurer of automobiles and homes in the world. The magnitude of Sears' operations may be emphasized further by recognizing that Sears, Roebuck and Company supplies well over one percent of the gross national product.

Sears has traditionally relied on decentralized managerial decision making to provide the effective customer service necessary for continued growth and development. Individual managers down to the lowest levels in the organization are given authority to make many decisions and are then held accountable for their results. Each department, retail store, group, zone, and territory is considered a profit center. Profit performance was, and still is, a key element in the evaluation of managerial performance. Sales turnover, payroll/sales ratio, and old merchandise reduction are also important criteria for the evaluation of managerial activity.

On the other hand, Sears also makes many decisions centrally. Product line and general pricing guideline decisions are made by corporate buyers at central headquarters in Chicago, Illinois. Products are evaluated, suppliers are selected, and merchandise contracts are negotiated centrally also. However, individual purchase orders for replacement merchandise are placed locally.

The physical separation of field and headquarters decision

makers has led to tremendous information problems in the past. Many years ago, one of the most practicable ways for headquarters personnel to determine the sales activity level for a product line was to ask their suppliers to furnish this information! Until the introduction of a computerized data-processing system over a decade ago, field reports of sales activity were slow, incomplete, and inadequate. By necessity, headquarters personnel were forced to make many decisions without adequate background information.

If the statement "As the size of an organization increases arithmetically, the intraorganizational information requirements for successful operation increase geometrically" is assumed to be correct, then the magnitude of Sears' information difficulties may be more fully appreciated. Small decisions for Sears often involve millions of dollars. Poor decisions due to information deficiencies and data inaccuracies can produce very consequential results for a company as large as Sears. Moreover, our fast-moving, dynamic economy demands a high degree of marketing flexibility and adaptability at the national as well as the local level, lest the organization fail to stay abreast of current trends. In effect, Sears' management in the early 1960s faced the dilemma of reconciling the efficiency of the ponderous super-corporation with the quickly changing market demands of a large-scale economy. The only viable solution to this dilemma was to provide more accurate, more timely, more reliable, and more complete information for decision makers throughout the entire company.

To remedy these information difficulties, in 1963 Sears began establishing their twenty-two regional computer centers covering the entire United States. Initially, the regional computer systems processed customer credit accounts and general accounting data. Later, merchandising and inventory information systems were established for retail and catalog branches.

In 1966 Sears' management initiated the research and development of an integrated merchandising information system to collect and maintain many kinds of operating information and also to provide management with information for decision making. A point-of-sale information system was to be the basic means for gathering sales activity data for the integrated information system. One of the first priorities in the program was obtaining the point-of-sale data-entry hardware. Fortunately, the Business Machines Division (formerly the Friden Calculator Company) of the Singer Company had been experimenting for several years on the design of point-of-sale equipment. Through cooperative effort extending over a period of several years, Singer successfully developed a point-of-sale register that met Sears' exacting specifications. Other problems, such as specifications for the minicomputers to be located at each retail store and data transmission difficulties, were largely resolved during the late 1960s and early 1970s. Concurrently, operating programs were also prepared to make the integrated merchandising information system functional. The great transition to the integrated merchandising information system began in 1971 and is scheduled to be completed by 1976.

A generalized system flowchart for the point-of-sale portion of Sears' integrated merchandising information system is shown in figure 15-2. Sales transaction data entered through the point-of-sale registers supplies the bulk of the input activity data to the integrated merchandising information system. Point-of-sale transaction data is input to the system by depressing selected

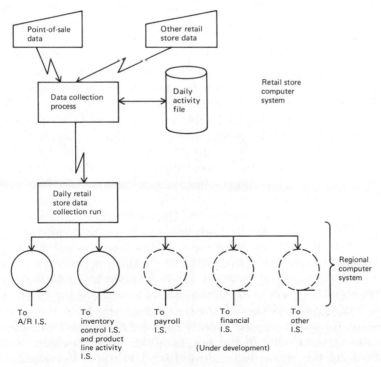

Fig. 15-2   Point-of-sale portion of Sears' merchandising information system

keys on a register according to a specified sequence. Ordinarily the following descriptors are required for each sales transaction: employee identification number, merchandise division, item identification number, quantity, unit price, type of transaction (cash sale, credit sale, C.O.D., layaway, or return), and customer account number from the credit card (credit sale only). After all of the transaction data has been input, the point-of-sale register automatically computes the extended price for each line item, sums the extended prices for all line items, determines the applicable state and local sales tax, and computes the total price for the merchandise. The register also prints out a sales receipt for the customer.

All of the point-of-sale registers in each retail store are connected online to a minicomputer located in the store. One of the principal functions of the minicomputer is to collect and temporarily store all point-of-sale transaction data accumulated during the store's operating hours each day. In this way all stored data may be forwarded each night as a single batch to the regional computer center. In addition to the data storage function, the minicomputer also performs certain other data-processing tasks such as credit checks.

After the batches of data from each retail store are received at each regional computer center, they are processed to create separate activity files for the integrated merchandising information system.

The first output stream from the daily retail data collection run is the accounts receivable activity file. This combined activity file contains all of the credit sales transactions from the preceding day for all retail stores in the entire region. After the file is sorted to customer account number sequence, it becomes one of the inputs to the daily A/R master file updating run. The data-processing operations from this point onward follow the typical pattern for an accounts receivable information system.

The second output stream is a data file listing of all items sold and received at each retail store on the preceding day. The item activity data file will become a primary input to a major information system producing both inventory control information for each retail store and product line activity-reporting information. Both of these reports use essentially the same input data but for vastly different purposes. The primary objective of the retail store inventory control information system is to maintain the status of inventories at each retail store. The product line activity-reporting information system, on the other hand, presents summarized item sales activity.

The item activity data file is used to prepare item sales activity reports for territorial management and corporate buyers. These reports are essential to the buyers for evaluating existing product lines and determining future product line components.

The third output stream from the daily retail data collection run is sales commission data for the payroll information system. Development is progressing to allow time card data for personnel on both hourly and salary schedules to be forwarded through the data collection run to the payroll information system at regional headquarters. The payroll information system, of course, prepares the payroll checks and maintains the necessary payroll records.

The last major output stream to the integrated merchandising information system is the financial data from the preceding day's operations. This stream not only supplies the accounting departments with financial data for maintaining the basic accounting and financial records but in the future will furnish the basic data for determining the profitability of each retail department, retail store, group, zone, territory, and region. The output to the financial information systems, after suitable manipulation and transformation, will become a principal means for evaluating managerial performance.

The daily retail data collection run also processes certain data that is not directly associated with the integrated merchandising information system. For example, when catalog sales data is entered in the POS system (a project still in development) the orders will be forwarded to the catalog merchandise distribution centers for subsequent use.

The magnitude of the systems implementation task for the integrated merchandising information system is exceedingly large. When fully implemented, the point-of-sale information system will have between thirty and forty thousand registers in operation across the nation. The 640 minicomputers located at the retail stores will be linked to large-scale IBM 370 computers. The cost for implementing the complete program will be about 150 million dollars—a gigantic sum for a firm to spend for improved information. On the other hand, only through such an integrated merchandising information system can the information support be provided for Sears to continue as the outstanding retailer in the world.

INTEGRATED PRODUCTION INFORMATION SYSTEMS

The various production-related information systems are a natural application area for developing an integrated information system network. In such systems the necessary data is usually convenient; such systems share a substantial body of data; they have many specialized, yet related, activities that occur continuously; their users are concentrated; and their managers usually have clearly defined areas of authority and responsibility. When these conditions exist concurrently, the opportunities as well as the need for building an integrated information system become quite apparent.

To examine the interlocking structure of such integrated production information systems, let us consider an integrated information system in a relatively simple production operation. The Worcester Valve Company, located in West Boylston, Massachusetts, produces a full line of ball and butterfly valves and valve actuators that are sold by distributors throughout the United States and the world. The company has grown from a sales level of slightly more than one million dollars in 1955 to almost eighteen million dollars in 1972. In addition to domestic operations, the parent company, Worcester Controls Corporation, also has extensive manufacturing and distribution operations overseas.

The production process for the manufacture of valves and actuators may be divided into three functional areas:

1. Purchasing, receiving, inspecting, and storing raw materials and finished parts
2. Manufacturing finished parts
3. Assembling finished parts into valves and actuators and shipping

In order to meet customer demands for speedy delivery, the activities in each of these areas must be very closely coordinated.

The purchasing department orders raw materials and finished parts produced by outside suppliers well in advance of anticipated production requirements. The suppliers maintain basic inventories of many items for the Worcester Valve Company. Delivery is taken as needed to meet forthcoming production schedules established by the production control department. The purchasing department selects the supplier, determines the economic order quantity, and expedites the delivery of out-of-stock raw materials and finished parts. Upon receipt, materials and parts are inspected and placed, respectively, in raw materials and finished-parts inventory.

Worcester Valve manufactures many different finished parts from raw materials at their main plant. The manufacturing process is composed primarily of metalworking operations performed on several different types of machines. The production routings, time standards, and cost standards for manufactured parts are maintained in a mechanized production-routing file that is prepared and updated by the manufacturing planners. Manufacturing schedules are prepared several weeks in advance to meet current customer orders and replenish the finished-parts inventory. To provide control over manufacturing operations, remote-entry input terminals located in the manufacturing area update the manufacturing order records.

In the assembly process, the component finished parts are put together to produce valves and actuators. Although the process is essentially a manual operation, jigs and fixtures are sometimes used to improve efficiency. After assembly, most orders are sent directly to the shipping department for immediate delivery to the customer. A small finished-product inventory of standard, widely used valves and actuators is maintained to provide a limited stock of finished parts for immediate shipment.

The flow of materials from suppliers through manufacturing, assembly, and shipping to the customer is shown in the bottom portion of figure 15-3. The top half of the diagram depicts the primary information flows among the departments of the organization. A careful inspection of this figure will reveal the basic dynamic systems model outline. The material flows through the production departments is the transformation process. The information flows together with the staff departments are the control loop for the dynamic system.

The integrated production information system occupies a central dominating position in the information flow pattern. Its operation is, in some respects, analogous to the operation of the central switchboard of a telephone system. Both the IPIS and the central telephone switchboard link various organizational units together by performing centralized, coordinating information-processing activities. The IPIS processes formal, structured information while the central switchboard processes informal information flows.

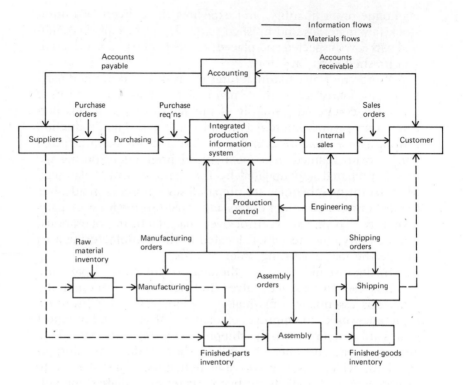

Fig. 15-3   Major intraorganizational information and material flows

The individual information systems that comprise the integrated production information system at Worcester Valve are:

1. Product order information system
2. Assembly order information system
3. Accounts receivable information system
4. Parts inventory forecast information system
5. Manufacturing order information system
6. Purchase order information system
7. Accounts payable information system

These systems are linked; the output of one becomes the input to another, as shown in figure 15-4. Each of the information systems above performs a unique function in the processing of

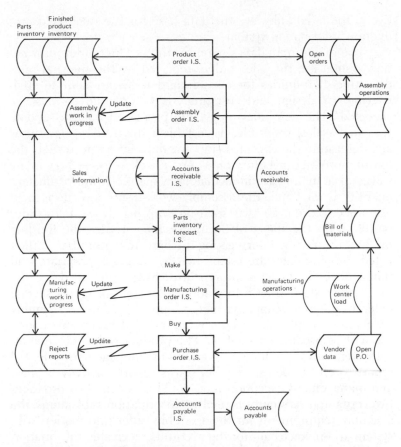

Fig. 15-4 Linked information systems at Worcester Valve Company

data used for planning, organizing, and controlling the entire production process and its associated activities. Except for the output/input data links, the input data streams and the output reports of individual information subsystems are not shown in figure 15-4.

In addition to the information subsystem linkage function, the integrated production information system also makes use of a common data depository for the entire organization. The data base is organized into fifteen separate direct-access data files, as shown in figure 15-4. The files that each subsystem accesses and/or updates are designated by information flow lines. Collectively, these data files are the data base for the integrated production information system.

The major input data stream for the product order information system are the sales orders received by the internal sales department. Inquiries for nonstandard items are sent to engineering for design and cost analysis before sales orders are accepted. The new sales orders are processed daily to update the open (sales) order file. To establish the initial order status and determine the expected shipping date for a sales order, the finished-product inventory file is first checked to see how many valves or actuators are immediately available. If an insufficient quantity is on hand, the assembly work-in-process file is next examined to see if any will soon be available. If the sales order is still short, the status of the necessary parts for the finished product is noted by interrogating the parts inventory file. Anticipated shipping dates are established by adding appropriate lead times, depending on inventory status, to the present date.

The product order information subsystem produces several different outputs. Shipping papers are prepared daily as assembly orders are completed. Inventory control and exception reports are sent to production control. The product order information subsystem also produces a variety of management-oriented reports such as open sales order status reports, activity listings, and management exception reports. This system also produces two very important outputs to other information subsystems: the assembly requirements for the assembly order information subsystem and invoice data for the accounts receivable information subsystem.

The principal functions of the assembly order information subsystem are to prepare and monitor assembly orders. Since the valves and actuators are assembled largely by hand, the assembly order specifies only the components and any required tools, jigs, or fixtures. Components are listed in the bill-of-materials file. A listing of required tools, jigs, and fixtures, as well as the assembly time standards, is in the assembly operations file. Assembly order activity (order releases, starts, and completions) is monitored with a remote-terminal shop-floor communication network. The current status of open assembly orders is maintained in the assembly work-in-process file. Parts inventory disbursements and finished product receipts are entered into their respective files as activity occurs.

As shipping orders are prepared by the product order information subsystem, invoice data is also output to the accounts receivable subsystem. There, the file of current customer accounts is maintained by conventional A/R operation. Historical sales data is collected in the sales information file for periodic analysis.

One of the key information subsystems in the entire integrated system is the parts inventory forecast information subsystem. Orders that cannot be filled with the necessary finished parts cannot be released to the assembly order information subsystem directly. Any finished-part shortages must be either manufactured or purchased. The principal function of the parts inventory forecast subsystem is to monitor the present parts inventory levels (raw materials and finished parts), the quantity of finished parts on order from purchasing and manufacturing, and the incoming parts requirements from sales orders. Through a complex decision-making process, the PIFIS directs both purchasing and manufacturing departments to restock the finished-parts inventory to predetermined levels.

The manufacturing order information subsystem prepares production orders for the manufacturing department from data stored in two files. The manufacturing operations file contains the routings for each part, together with its time and cost standards. The work center load file lists the open manufacturing time by work (machine) center. After production orders have been released, their progress is reported and recorded in the manufacturing work-in-process file. In addition to outputting production orders, the manufacturing order subsystem outputs both status and activity reports for management.

The purchase order subsystem receives purchase requisition output from the parts inventory forecast subsystem. Purchase orders or purchase order releases are prepared and forwarded to the suppliers. The purchase order subsystem also receives inputs from the receiving and quality control departments to close out purchase orders and releases. The reject report file is the quality record of suppliers' products and is used to prepare vendor-analysis reports periodically.

The completed purchase order or release data is input to the accounts receivable information subsystem; appropriate data is stored in the A/P file. As payments for individual orders come due, checks are prepared and forwarded to the suppliers.

One way to evaluate the effectiveness of an integrated information system is to note the efficiency improvement of the associated production/operations system over a period of time. Table 15.1 compares certain efficiency attributes of the Worcester Valve Company's domestic operations for 1961 and 1972.

The integrated information system, of course, is not responsible by itself for the improvement in operating results shown in the table. However, good managers who receive well-designed, accurate, reliable, timely reports can make sound decisions to produce results similar to those in the table.

INFORMATION SYSTEMS IN NONPROFIT ORGANIZATIONS

The information systems applications presented up to this point have all been taken from business operations. This does not mean that only business firms may use computer-based information systems to good advantage. There are, of course, many other types of organizations that can and do put information systems technology to excellent use. Let us examine several areas in nonbusiness organizations to which computerized information systems have been successfully applied.

Many nonprofit organizations face the same information difficulties as business firms. Although the profit motive may not be present, the desires for operating cost reduction and service improvement usually are. Nonprofit organizations also employ people, purchase and pay for supplies, maintain inventories (at times), provide some sort of service to society, and (often) collect money. The performance of these activities on a significant scale requires personnel and payroll information systems, an accounts payable information system, a purchasing information system, an inventory control information system, a production or marketing-type information system to follow the authorization and delivery of the service, and an A/R information system. Counterparts of most of these business information systems are therefore also usually found in nonprofit organizations. Moreover, the structure and operation of these systems are virtually identical to those of the corresponding business information systems.

In addition to having similar information systems, several areas at the city and county level of government are readily adaptable to special forms of computerized data processing. For example, property tax information systems have been established in many communities to mechanize property tax computation, prepare tax notices, and follow up on delinquent tax accounts

TABLE 15.1
Worcester Valve Company Domestic Operations

Operations Data	Year	
	1961	1972
Sales	$2,600,000	$9,000,000
Number of employees	145	180
Average value, inventory	$900,000	$1,100,000
Average delivery time	6 weeks	3 weeks

promptly. Local income or occupational tax information systems can often pay for themselves by picking up new residents more quickly, by checking taxpayer computations to find errors and ommissions, and by providing quick follow-up for late-paying taxpayers. Business licenses and city vehicle registration records may also be computerized for more efficient record-keeping and billing purposes. For large local government units, police and court information systems provide further opportunities for utilizing electronic data processing.

State governments and many state agencies also provide application opportunities for computerized information systems. Personal and business income tax as well as sales tax collections are well adapted to becoming computerized to maintain voluminous records and monitor the tax collection process. Several states are now using legislative information systems to follow the progress of bills through the legislature. Various state agencies, such as penal and correctional institutions, mental hospitals, and state-operated educational institutions also make generous use of electronic data-processing facilities to maintain their records and provide their directors with managerial information. Some states are even investigating the feasibility of establishing a direct-access master file of all licensed drivers within the state and keeping a central record of all traffic-related law violations.

At the federal level, there are a host of large-scale information system applications. The Internal Revenue Service operates a vast information system to maintain income tax records of all taxpayers. The Social Security Administration makes extensive use of computerized information systems for preparing and reconciling social security checks. Even the Library of Congress has a rather sophisticated information system for filing and retrieving documents of all types.

Military information systems have many application areas with much diversity and great breadth. In addition to the conventional information systems, military organizations make, perhaps, the greatest use of all organizations of decision-making information systems. The SAGE system for monitoring aircraft entering the United States is an excellent example of a complex decision-making information system. Military organizations also use computers extensively in combat simulation exercises, and many other military operations rely on scientific computer applications.

Also, many hospitals now use computers to process patient-related data. Maintaining medical records and collecting charges for each patient is remarkably similar to functions performed by production monitor and control information systems, except in this case the patient is the work unit that receives services. Scientific, diagnostic, and library (information retrieval) information systems are now frequently found in hospitals and clinics. In addition to the specialized information systems, hospitals also make extensive use of the standard business information systems.

Schools, colleges, and universities now maintain many of their student records on computerized equipment. Programming instruction and computer-assisted instruction (CAI) are flourishing at many educational institutions. Universities in particular employ many sophisticated research-oriented special-purpose information systems.

The preceding discussion of information system applications in nonprofit organizations is not meant to be exhaustive, but rather to illustrate that such organizations can make substantial use of both standard and special-purpose information systems adapted to satisfy their peculiar information needs. The study, analysis, design, and implementation of information systems is essentially the same for both nonprofit organizations and business firms.

CONCLUSION

In most firms, integrated information systems are the result of the evolution of a sound systems development program. To take full advantage of electronic data-processing opportunities, the systems development program must incorporate joint data collecting, preparing, processing, and reporting activities whenever possible. Jointly used data files (the data base) eliminate needless duplication of data-processing effort. The various information systems must be mutually supportive to gain the full efficiency and effectiveness benefits that integrated information systems offer.

The first major difficulty encountered in integrated information systems is data collection. It often happens that data sources are widespread and that input data transactions are sporadic. Moreover, the volume of input transactions frequently tends to be rather large. Under these conditions, the design and operation of data collection activities require a great deal of attention. Point-of-sale information systems, such as the Sears system, offer a most expedient way to solve data collection difficulties under certain conditions. Remote-terminal online data collection, as found in the passenger airline reservation system, is another very satisfactory solution to the data collection problem. Finding a solution to this problem is critical to the overall success of integrated information system operation.

Another critical area of integrated information systems application is the establishment and maintenance of the data base. As we noted in the Worcester Valve application, the data base may be comprised of a dozen or more direct-access files. Not only are we concerned with identifying these files and specifying their contents, but also file interrogation and updating through the various information subsystems often gets quite involved. To the greatest extent possible, these difficulties must be anticipated and resolved during the planning stages of the integrated information system.

16

INFORMATION SYSTEMS TRENDS

Information systems analysis has been recognized as an occupational specialty and a skills area only during the past few years. Prior to this time, systems and procedures technicians established data-processing procedures that clerks performed on unit-record equipment. Ordinarily, the technicians did not need to specify each clerical task's individual operations in detail, since human beings can think and learn complex tasks rather quickly. Rather, their efforts tended to focus on the procedures for processing paper work.

The introduction of business computer applications about twenty years ago changed the old systems and procedures approach to systems design. Computers demand precise, detailed instructions (programs) to function. In addition, business computer applications also require individuals with the ability to conceptualize computer applications and devise detailed plans for their implementation —systems analysts. Thus information systems analysis has come to be a separate and distinct activity because of changes in data-processing technology.

Information systems analysis, in turn, has also been an agent of change. For example, during a systems investigation, business practices and procedures are thoroughly examined. As a result many operating and managerial inefficiencies become quite evident. Eliminating these operational inefficiencies through improved information handling has increased the tempo of business activity, increased productivity, reduced costs, and provided better service to virtually all the consumers in our economy.

Information systems analysis has therefore emerged as a result of developments in data-processing technology and, in turn, has produced profound changes in the business environment. Now let us consider both how new developments in such technology are changing future information systems design and applications and how information systems will continue to change the business firm.

TRENDS IN INFORMATION SYSTEMS DESIGN AND APPLICATION

As we have already pointed out, the largest single step in introducing detailed, logical, analytical thinking into the processing of information was the development of the computer. From 1953 to the present, developments and refinements in computer technology have continued to influence information systems design in several ways.

With regard to computer hardware, the prospect of ever-larger fast memory (core storage) promises to become a reality. In turn, the availability of larger fast memories will make online information systems more practical and economically competitive. Online information systems require a large amount of fast memory to store the computer operating system control programs, the programs that are in use at the moment, and the data being processed by the active programs. Therefore the availability of more fast memory will provide the opportunity to operate many different computer programs simultaneously and to manipulate more different kinds of data concurrently. The result of this capability will be to make online information systems much more practical and applicable to current batch-processing information systems. The improved timeliness of operating and managerial information derived from such systems will thereby improve the efficiency of the managerial decision-making process.

A second trend in computer hardware developments that will influence information systems design and application is larger direct-access storage capacity. Increased direct-access storage capacity not only permits the storage of more records, but also much longer and more complete records. With more direct-access storage capacity, data files with many thousands of full records can be constructed and accessed as required. The ready accessibility of data from many different data files is necessary for the successful implementation of full-scale integrated information systems. Thus fully integrated information systems for many medium- and large-scale organizations will become more feasible in the future.

Ready accessibility to many detailed records poses some difficult security problems. How can data within data banks be restricted to those and only those individuals with a demonstrated need to have the information? Another important question is: how can record accuracy be maintained if the data files can be updated from several different sources? At the present time, security precautions are usually based on file security checks that are a part of the file interrogation and updating programs. In addition to these questions, there are also unresolved legal questions about record tampering and the acquisition of data by unauthorized persons.

The increased availability and improved quality of computer software will also exert a significant influence on information systems design in future years. Raw computer power serves little purpose without the program packages to apply it in specific areas. According to a recent study, the market for packaged computer software and services will rise from $770 million in 1972 to $1.5 billion in 1975 and thence to over $2 billion by 1982.[1] The net effect of this market growth will be to broaden the feasible computer applications in business and industry.

The increasing use of software packages and services should not appreciably reduce the demand for information systems analysts. While there are many standard computer applications, a great many firms have special data-processing or information requirements that must be handled on an individual basis by systems analysts. As software packages continue to improve, a further requirement for systems analysts in the future will be a knowledge of the outlines and characteristics of the major software packages available in each application area. In this role the systems analyst will become the technical intermediary between the software producer and the user business firm. Thus the analyst's background knowledge and activities will probably change somewhat in the future, but his basic function of developing new information systems will remain the same.

---

1. *Datamation,* July 1973, p. 106.

ORGANIZATIONAL CHANGES

Almost from the moment computers are introduced into a business firm, its organizational structure begins to change also. The evolution process that responds to this new force usually takes a general direction toward the centralization of data-processing activities. The tempo of the evolutionary process will, of course, be determined by many factors such as organization size, available resources, managerial leadership, and the level of technical expertise. Let us trace the typical evolution pattern in organization structure and operation that computer technology introduces to the business firm.

Historically, the first user of the computer in most business firms has been the accounting department. Many of their operations are strictly clerical and highly repetitive. Customer billing, accounts-receivable record maintenance, payroll preparation, the payment of accounts, and check writing and reconciliation are all activities that most businesses perform. These activities are also admirably suited to computerized data processing. Hence, accounting departments have usually been in the best position to justify the initial acquisition of a computer.

The typical organization structure for an embryonic data-processing organization is shown in figure 16-1. In such a small unit, the manager usually doubles as a systems analyst and may even occasionally perform some programming.

The second stage of the evolutionary process occurs after the accounting department gets the computer and develops operating programs for their principal clerical tasks. Other parts of the firm then begin to take an interest in data-processing

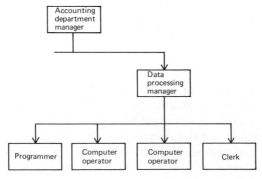

Fig. 16-1   Typical structure for a beginning DP organization

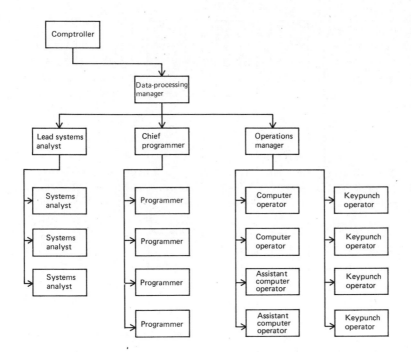

Fig. 16-2   Organization chart for a department in the second stage
of development

operations. Inventory, production, marketing, and personnel
management note opportunities in their respective areas for
computer applications. However, since the management of the
computer has been vested in the accounting department, organizational stresses quite often accompany such interest. The
questions of computer use and systems development priorities
are usually the most immediate and difficult points to resolve.

The solution to this conflict has most often been to move
the data-processing unit out of the accounting department and
establish it as a separate department. An organizational chart
for a typical department in the second stage of development is
shown in figure 16-2. At this development stage, the new department reports to top management through the office manager,
the comptroller, or the treasurer. The ties with the finance
branch are not completely severed: the data-processing unit has
simply been promoted out of the accounting department.

The third stage in the evolution process begins with the
recognition of the importance of the data and information pro-

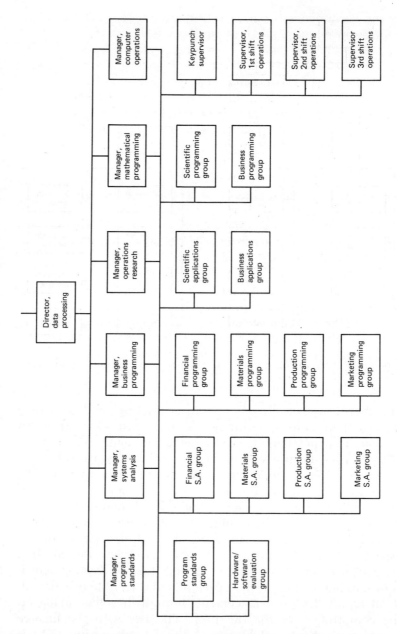

Fig. 16-3 Organization structure for a fully developed DP department

cessing function at the highest corporate levels. At this stage the data-processing branch of the organization is elevated to a full corporate-level position. The organizational structure of a completely developed data-processing branch is shown in figure 16-3. The data-processing manager, who will report to the president or chief executive officer of the firm, will often have a title such as vice president of administrative services. When this level has been reached, top management has fully demonstrated their appreciation of information processing as a major integrating and coordinating activity in the business firm.

The growth and centralization of the data-processing function has several implications for organization behavior. First, certain organizations, such as accounting, will have a significant portion of their present activities usurped by the DP organization. In time, accountants may well become technical specialists, as engineers have become, working with and through the computer.

Another result of increased computerization is likely to be greater accountability of managers to their superiors. This follows from the fact that managers will have much more information available to them for their decisions. If they are unable to use this information to make better decisions consistently, then their superiors may wish to take appropriate action.

Finally, the continued implementation of better information systems should ultimately provide richer, more rewarding be efits to the customers of business enterprises and the ultimate consumer. Increased productive capacity is not only derived from increased capital investment but also from the better use of our available resources. If we know what our resources are and how they may be used most effectively, then we may certainly improve the lot of mankind.

INDEX